THE

CENSUS OF IOWA

AS RETURNED IN THE YEAR 1869:

SHOWING, IN DETAIL, THE POPULATION, AGRICULTURAL STATISTICS, DOMESTIC AND GENERAL MANUFACTURES, AND OTHER ITEMS OF INTEREST.

Published under direction of the Census Board.

CENSUS BOARD:

SAMUEL MERRILL, GOVERNOR,
ED WRIGHT, SECRETARY OF STATE,
JOHN A. ELLIOTT, AUDITOR OF STATE,
SAMUEL E. RANKIN, TREASURER OF STATE

DES MOINES:
F. M. MILLS, STATE PRINTER.
1869.

ERRATA.

Page 11.—For "6 Insane not in Hospital, January 1, 1869," read "6 Deaf and Dumb not in Asylum, January 1, 1869."

Page 15.—In second column, Clinton county, the Range should be East.

Page 30.—In second column, Jackson county, the Range should be East.

Page 44.—Muscatine county, in column of "No. of Dwelling-Houses," in the total footing of county, read "4214," instead of "4207;" and in total county, exclusive of city, "read "2558", instead of "2551."

Page 54—Tama county, in column "No. of Militia," read "2374," instead of "3374."

Page 69.—For "Milton," Muscatine county, read "Wilton,"

Page 81—In footing of totals of fifth column, read "1,735,293," instead of "1,950,307."

page 169.—For "Allamakee" and "French Creek" Post-Offices, in Adair county, read "Allamakee" and "French Creek," Allamakee county.

Page 204.—For "Lewis J. Coulter," in list of State officers and Deputies, read "Lewis I. Coulter."

Page 206.—In blank opposite Second Circuit, Sixth Judicial District, insert Stephen N. Lindley, Jasper county, appointed December 9th, 1869, *vice* H. S. Winslow, resigned.

Page 215.—For "Isaac T. Gibson," Trustee Iowa Reform School, read "Thomas E. Corkhill appointed December 8, 1869, *vice* Isaac T. Gibson, resigned

Page 216.—For "Elijah Odell," Commissioner of Legal Inquiry, read "James O. Crosby, Garnavillo, appointed December 9th, 1869."

Page 229.—For "fourth Monday in January and July," opposite Pottawattamie county, read "first Tuesday of June and December."

TABLE OF CONTENTS.

CENSUS RETURNS

SHOWING THE POPULATION OF THE SEVERAL COUNTIES OF IOWA FOR THE YEAR 1869, BY TOWNSHIPS, TOWNS, AND CITIES.

ADAIR COUNTY.

No. of Township.	Range.	Names of Townships, Towns, and Cities.	No. of Dwelling Houses	No. of Families.	No. of White Males.	No. of White Females.	Total White Population	No. of Colored Males.	No. of Colored Females	Total Colored Population.	Total Population.	No. entitled to Vote.	No. of Foreigners not Naturalized.	No. of Militia.	No. of Blind not in Asylum Jan. 1, 1869.	No. of Deaf and Dumb not in Asy. Jan. 1, '69	No. of Insane not in Hospital, Jan. 1, '69	No. of Colleges, Academies and Universities	No. of Teachers in Colleges, Universities, etc.	No. of Students in Colleges, Universities, etc.
..74 75	30	Grand River..........	52	53	144	120	264	....	....	....	264	65	....	50	....	....	....	....	....	....
..74 75	31	Greenfield...........	40	40	112	101	213	....	....	....	213	59	....	54	....	....	....	....	....	....
......76	...*31	Grove.......	11	14	36	32	68	....	....	....	68	20	1	16	....	....	....	....	....	....
......76	30	Harrison.............	68	63	169	150	319	....	....	....	319	72	1	56	....	....	....	....	....	....
..75 76	33	Jackson..............	41	41	123	91	214	....	....	....	214	54	....	42	....	....	....	....	....	....
......77	.. †31	Jefferson............	25	25	99	91	190	1	....	1	191	42	1	32	....	....	....	....	....	....
......77	30	Lincoln	36	36	109	88	197	....	....	....	197	41	....	42	....	....	....	....	....	....
......74	... 32	Richland.............	26	26	77	69	146	....	....	....	146	32	....	26	....	....	....	....	....	....
..75 76	32	Summerset............	41	49	115	111	226	....	....	....	226	77	3	52	....	....	2	....	....	....
......77	.32 33	Walnut...............	12	13	48	42	90	....	....	....	90	20	3	16	....	....	....	....	....	....
......74	33	Washington	58	67	209	175	384	....	....	....	384	75	1	58	....	....	4	....	....	....
....	......	Total...	410	427	1241	1070	2311	1	....	1	2312	557	10	444	....	....	6	....	....	....

* And sections 31, 32, and 33, of township 77, range 31, west. † Except sections 31, 32, and 33.

ADAMS COUNTY.

No. of Township.	Range.	Names of Townships, Towns, and Cities.	No. of Dwelling Houses	No. of Families.	No. of White Males.	No. of White Females	Total White Population	No. of Colored Males.	No. of Colored Females	Total Colored Population.	Total Population.	No. entitled to Vote.	No. of Foreigners not Naturalized.	No. of Militia.	No. of Blind not in Asylum, Jan. 1, 1869.	No. of Deaf and Dumb not in Asy. Jan. 1, '69	No. of Insane not in Hospital, Jan. 1, '69.	No. of Colleges, Academies and Universities	No. of Teachers in Colleges, Universities, etc.	No. of Students in Colleges, Universities, etc.
......73	33	Carl................	43	43	122	107	229	...	...	...	229	50	...	38	...	...	...	...	...	...
......73	32	Colony..............	21	25	61	51	112	...	...	...	112	26	...	26	...	...	...	...	...	...
......72	35	Douglas	44	44	145	114	259	...	...	...	259	68	2	46	...	...	...	...	...	...
......71	34	Jasper..............	66	66	174	161	335	...	...	...	335	71	...	58	...	...	...	...	...	...
......73	35	Lincoln.............	17	17	46	35	81	...	...	...	81	18	...	17	...	...	...	...	...	...
......71	33	Mercer..............	12	14	40	30	70	...	...	...	70	20	2	15	...	...	...	...	...	...
......71	35	Nodaway.............	77	77	244	217	461	...	...	...	461	96	...	76	...	...	...	...	...	...
...pt 72	...34	Quincy..............	137	137	361	318	679	2	4	6	685	169	2	99	...	...	...	...	...	...
......72	33 pt 34	Queen City..........	51	57	207	156	363	...	...	...	363	94	...	71	...	...	...	...	...	...
...71 72	...32	Union...............	43	47	142	108	250	...	...	...	250	57	...	59	...	...	...	...	...	...
......73	34	Washington..........	78	84	239	218	457	...	...	...	457	91	2	78	...	1	...	...	...	...
....	......	Total............	589	611	1781	1515	3296	2	4	6	3302	760	8	583	...	1	...	...	...	...

ALLAMAKEE COUNTY.

No. of Township.	Range.	Names of Townships, Towns, and Cities.	No. of Dwelling Houses	No. of Families.	No. of White Males.	No. of White Females	Total White Population	No. of Colored Males.	No. of Colored Females	Total Colored Population.	Total Population.	No. entitled to Vote.	No. of Foreigners not Naturalized.	No. of Militia.	No. of Blind not in Asylum, Jan. 1, 1869.	No. of Deaf and Dumb not in Asy. Jan. 1, '69	No. of Insane not in Hospital, Jan. 1, '69.	No. of Colleges, Academies and Universities	No. of Teachers in Colleges, Universities, etc.	No. of Students in Colleges, Universities, etc.
......98	4	Center..............	132	132	429	375	804	...	...	...	804	123	53	87	1	...	1	...	...	...
...pt 96	...3 4	Fairview............	*	*	300	245	545	...	...	...	545	100	3	52	...	...	...	...	...	...
......96	5	Franklin............	152	147	387	396	783	...	...	...	783	146	7	113	...	1	1	...	...	...
......99	5	French Creek........	117	117	382	331	713	...	...	...	713	121	14	64	...	...	...	...	...	...
..... 99	6	Hanover.............	80	80	242	217	459	...	...	...	459	73	19	46	2	...	...	...	...	...
.....100	4 pt 3	Iowa................	66	67	190	167	357	...	...	...	357	75	13	44	1	1	...	...	...	...
......97	5	Jefferson...........	190	210	583	519	1102	...	...	...	1102	233	18	153	1	1	...	...	...	...
...pt 98	...2 3	LaFayette...........	187	188	528	524	1052	...	...	...	1052	195	8	119	3	1	...	...	...	...
......99	4 pt 3	Lansing, excl. of city..	118	118	382	305	687	...	...	...	687	123	32	67	...	...	...	...	...	...

...pt 96	4	Linton	125	125	339	316	655	....	....	....	655	125	10	87	....	1	1	....	....	....
......97	6	Ludlow	141	144	362	375	737	....	....	....	737	132	10	110	....	....	....	....	....	....
......98	5	Makee	301	324	922	862	1784	1	....	1	1785	374	33	209	1	....	....	....	....	....
......97	4	Paint Creek	194	202	594	535	1129	....	....	....	1129	189	47	172	2	....	....	....	....	....
......96	6	Post	253	262	634	632	1266	....	....	....	1266	281	5	186	1	....	1	....	....	....
...pt 97	...2 3	Taylor	120	120	396	385	781	....	....	....	781	159	6	92	....	....	....	....	....	....
.....100	5	Union City	78	78	220	215	435	....	....	....	435	75	11	53	....	....	....	....	....	....
......98	6	Union Prairie	170	170	413	424	837	....	....	....	837	164	10	68	....	....	....	....	....	....
.....100	6	Waterloo	146	145	342	317	659	5	9	14	673	94	45	97	....	....	....	....	....	....
...in 99	3	Lansing, town of	280	280	989	972	1961	3	2	5	1966	363	30	293	....	....	....	1	....	381
....	......	Total	2850	2908	8634	8112	16746	9	11	20	16766	3145	374	2112	12	5	4	1	....	381

* Not reported.

APPANOOSE COUNTY.

pt 68 69	18	Bellair	114	114	347	189	536	....	....	....	536	129	....	96	....	....	....	....	....	....
pt 68 69	.17 18	Center	302	302	833	766	1599	5	11	16	1615	365	2	268	1	2	2	....	....	....
...pt 70	18	Chariton	148	146	405	418	823	....	....	....	823	168	....	139	....	....	2	....	....	....
......67	17	Caldwell																		
...pt 68	17	Caldwell	212	212	514	474	988	....	1	1	989	197	....	108	....	....	2	....	....	....
...pt 67	16	Caldwell																		
...69 70	...17	Douglas	91	91	270	294	564	....	....	....	564	111	....	77	....	....	....	....	....	....
67 pt 68	19	Franklin	130	139	384	371	755	....	....	....	755	157	....	116	....	....	....	....	....	....
......70	19	Independence	117	118	463	426	889	....	....	....	889	179	....	131	....	....	....	....	....	....
......69	19	Johns	142	142	466	425	891	....	....	....	891	172	....	148	....	1	1	....	....	....
...pt 68	19	Lincoln	99	101	292	274	566	....	....	....	566	107	1	87	....	....	....	....	....	....
67 pt 68	18	Pleasant	199	226	576	525	1101	3	3	6	1107	240	3	190	....	3	....	....	....	1
...68 69	17	Sharon	100	100	314	271	585	....	....	....	585	105	1	84	....	....	....	....	....	....
......70	17	Taylor	187	193	538	490	1028	....	....	....	1028	209	1	167	2	....	....	....	....	....
......70	16	Union	126	129	341	334	675	....	....	....	675	136	....	106	....	1	2	....	....	....
...69 70	...16	Udell	140	159	420	400	820	....	....	....	820	166	....	127	....	....	....	....	....	....
...68 69	16	Washington	208	208	582	570	1152	....	....	....	1152	237	....	155	....	....	....	....	....	....
...67 68	16	Wells	156	156	478	435	913	2	4	6	919	192	....	146	3	....	....	....	....	....
...69 70	18	Walnut	126	126	342	369	711	....	....	....	711	140	....	104	....	....	....	....	....	....
......	......	Total	2597	2662	7565	7031	14596	10	19	29	14625	3010	8	2249	6	7	9	....	....	1

AUDUBON COUNTY.

No. of Township.	Range.	Names of Townships, Towns and Cities.	No. of Dwelling Houses	No. of Families.	No. of White Males.	No. of White Females	Total White Population	No. of Colored Males.	No. of Colored Females	Total Colored Population.	Total Population.	No. entitled to Vote.	No. of Foreigners not Naturalized.	No. of Militia.	No. of Blind not in Asylum, Jan. 1, 1869.	No. of Deaf and Dumb not in Asy. Jan. 1, '69	No. of Insane not in Hospital, Jan. 1, 1869	No. of Colleges, Academies and Universities	No. of Teachers in Colleges, Universities, etc.	No. of Students in Colleges, Universities, etc.
..78 79	... 34	Audubon...........																		
..80 81	34	Audubon...........	58	59	158	152	310	....	....	....	310	72	....	52	....	....	....	....	....	....
..pt 78	35	Audubon.........																		
..79 80	35	Exira..............																		
.....81	35	Exira..............	57	56	190	175	365	....	....	....	365	91	....	75	1	...	....	....	....	....
..pt 78	35	Exira..............																		
..80 81	36	Oakfield...........																		
..78 79	36	Oakfield...........	68	68	191	163	354	2	1	3	357	85	3	77	....	....	....	....	....	1
..pt 78	35	Oakfield...........																		
....	......	Total...........	183	183	539	490	1029	2	1	3	1032	248	3	204	1	....	....	....	....	1

BENTON COUNTY.

No. of Township.	Range.	Names of Townships, Towns and Cities.	No. of Dwelling Houses	No. of Families.	No. of White Males.	No. of White Females	Total White Population	No. of Colored Males.	No. of Colored Females	Total Colored Population.	Total Population.	No. entitled to Vote.	No. of Foreigners not Naturalized.	No. of Militia.	No. of Blind not in Asylum, Jan. 1, 1869.	No. of Deaf and Dumb not in Asy. Jan. 1, '69	No. of Insane not in Hospital, Jan. 1, 1869	No. of Colleges, Academies and Universities	No. of Teachers in Colleges, Universities, etc.	No. of Students in Colleges, Universities, etc.
..pt 85	..9 10	Benton	145	149	421	407	828	....	....	....	828	149	....	115	....	....	....	....	....	....
......84	11	Big Grove.........	139	139	399	319	718	....	....	....	718	172	3	137	....	....	....	....	....	3
......86	12	Bruce.............	75	82	223	194	417	....	....	....	417	87	11	76	....	....	....	....	....	....
......84	9	Canton............	270	274	742	677	1419	....	....	....	1419	319	5	266	....	....	....	....	....	....
..pt 86	.10 11	Cedar.............	171	172	464	430	894	....	....	....	894	197	5	165	....	....	....	....	....	....
......84	10	Eden..............	132	132	402	342	744	....	....	....	744	168	10	147	....	....	....	....	....	....
......83	10	Eldorado..........	85	85	248	204	452	....	....	....	452	80	33	68	....	....	....	....	....	....
......82	9	Florence..........	174	176	519	491	1010	2	....	2	1012	158	72	187	....	....	....	....	....	....
......83	9	Fremont...........	131	131	398	324	722	....	....	....	722	115	56	140	....	....	....	....	....	....
..pt 86	10	Harrison..........	100	103	309	265	574	....	....	....	574	123	5	104	....	....	....	....	....	....
......84	12	Homer.............	64	64	182	173	355	....	....	....	355	84	6	69	....	....	....	....	....	....

......82	...12	Iowa..................	328	328	1223	1006	2239	10	4	14	2253	388	13	223	....	....	....	....	....	....
......85	11	Jackson............	140	144	445	374	819	....	....	....	819	177	4	135	....	....	....	....	....	3
......83	12	Kane................	107	104	290	243	533	....	....	....	533	87	....	59	....	....	....	....	....	....
......83	11	Leroy	329	335	863	813	1676	....	....	....	1676	335	20	270	....	....	2	....	....	....
......85	12	Monroe.............	*	*	427	376	803	....	....	....	803	147	4	105	....	....	....	....	....	....
pt 85 86	9	Polk................	240	251	657	598	1255	....	....	....	1255	247	8	173	....	....	....	....	....	....
......82	10	St. Clair............	110	110	330	275	605	....	....	....	605	127	1	83	....	....	....	....	....	....
...pt 85	10	Taylor...............	420	14	1371	1429	2800	....	....	....	2800	607	61	361	....	....	....	....	....	1
......83	11	Union...............	96	98	309	232	541	....	....	....	541	102	25	103	....	1	....	....	....	....
....	.....	Total...............	3256	2891	10232	9172	19404	12	4	16	19420	3869	342	2986		1	2	....		7

*Not reported.

BLACK HAWK COUNTY.

......89	...11	Barclay..............	147	154	410	386	796	....	....	....	796	162	23	120	....	....	....	....	....	....
......90	12	Bennington..........	91	91	279	228	507	....	....	....	507	99	13	75	....	....	....	....	....	....
...pt 87	11 12	Big Creek............	213	218	630	528	1158	4	6	10	1168	192	11	146	....	1	....	....	....	....
......88	...14	Black Hawk.........	101	101	305	252	557	....	....	....	557	113	15	86	....	....	....	....	....	....
pt 87 88	12	Cedar................	107	107	353	297	650	....	....	....	650	121	21	109	....	....	....	....	....	....
......89	14pt13	Cedar Falls—exc. city	166	167	432	422	854	....	....	....	854	174	18	130	....	....	....	....	....	....
......87	13	Eagle................	71	71	220	177	397	....	....	....	397	79	12	70	....	....	....	....	....	....
pt 88 89	12	East Waterloo........	150	150	434	391	825	....	....	....	825	172	13	107	....	1	....	....	....	....
......88	11	Fox..................	127	127	341	338	679	....	....	....	679	135	26	102	....	....	....	....	....	....
......90	11	Lester................	147	163	426	377	803	....	....	....	803	171	14	127	....	3	....	....	....	....
......87	14	Lincoln..............	55	55	157	135	292	2	....	2	294	69	10	64	....	....	....	....	....	....
......90	... 13	Mount Vernon......	175	175	505	429	934	....	....	....	934	211	....	168	....	....	....	....	....	....
......88	13	Orange..............	121	135	422	337	759	....	....	....	759	186	7	135	....	....	....	....	....	....
pt 87–89	12	Poyner...............	181	181	417	427	844	....	....	....	844	185	5	121	....	....	....	....	....	....
...pt 87	11	Spring Creek........	120	118	381	329	710	....	....	....	710	139	5	106	....	....	....	....	....	....
...pt 90	14	Union................	64	64	163	160	323	....	....	....	323	69	5	47	....	....	....	....	....	....
......90	14	Washington..........	99	105	283	279	562	1	....	1	563	112	3	83	....	1	2	....	....	....
...pt 89	13 14	Waterloo exc. city....	80	80	210	220	430	....	....	....	430	89	8	57	....	1	....	....	....	....
....	.....	Total...............	2215	2262	6368	5712	12080	7	6	13	12093	2478	209	1863	....	7	2	....	....	....
....	.....	Waterloo, city of—																		
....	.....	1st ward.........	187	189	522	499	1021	1	....	1	1022	236	13	105	....	....	....	....	....	....
....	.....	2d ward	170	172	389	406	795	5	2	...7	802	185	12	33	....	....	....	....	....	....
....	.....	3d ward	183	182	446	448	894	....	....	....	894	204	8	98	....	....	....	....	....	....

BLACK HAWK COUNTY—Continued.

No. of Township.	Range.	Names of Townships, Towns, and Cities.	No. of Dwelling Houses	No. of Families.	No. of White Males.	No. of White Females.	Total White Population	No. of Colored Males.	No. of Colored Females.	Total Colored Population.	Total population.	No. entitled to Vote.	No. of Foreigners not Naturalized.	No. of Militia.	No. of Blind not in Asylum, Jan. 1, 1869.	No. of Deaf and Dumb not in Asy. Jan. 1. '69	No. of Insane not in Hospital, Jan. 1, 1869	No. of Colleges, Academies and Universities	No. of Teachers in Colleges, Universities, etc.	No. of Students in Colleges, Universities, etc.
		4th ward	192	193	479	465	944				944	218	3	127						
		Total	732	736	1836	1818	3654	6	2	8	3662	843	36	363						
		Cedar Falls, city of.																		
		1st ward	106	111	467	432	899	1		1	900	150	25	121						
		2d ward	124	139	389	351	740				740	141	22	152						
		3d ward	142	145	375	370	745				745	161	12	126						
		4th ward	156	172	408	412	820	1		1	821	164	7	109						
		Total	528	567	1639	1565	3204	2		2	3206	616	66	508						
		Total of county	3475	3565	9843	9095	18938	15	8	23	18961	3937	311	2734						

BOONE COUNTY.

No. of Township.	Range.	Names of Townships, Towns, and Cities.	No. of Dwelling Houses	No. of Families.	No. of White Males.	No. of White Females.	Total White Population	No. of Colored Males.	No. of Colored Females.	Total Colored Population.	Total population.	No. entitled to Vote.	No. of Foreigners not Naturalized.	No. of Militia.	No. of Blind not in Asylum, Jan. 1, 1869.	No. of Deaf and Dumb not in Asy. Jan. 1. '69	No. of Insane not in Hospital, Jan. 1, 1869	No. of Colleges, Academies and Universities	No. of Teachers in Colleges, Universities, etc.	No. of Students in Colleges, Universities, etc.
pt 82	26 27	Cass	128	229	361	333	694				694	135	17	102						
84 pt 84 pt 83	26 25 27 25 26	Des Moines, exc. of Boonsboro and Montana.	371	371	1084	938	2022				2022	362	106	247	2	1				
85	26pt27	Dodge	181	198	626	524	1150				1150	222	29	187						
82	25pt26	Douglas	218	229	657	592	1249				1249	225	46	222						
85 pt 84	25	Jackson	80	81	247	234	481				481	102	5	71	1					
83 pt 83 pt 83	27 26 28	Marcy Marcy Marcy	325	325	927	778	1705	1	1	2	1707	270	956	258						
85	28pt27	Pilot Mound	84	87	269	226	495				495	65	47	50						

......82	28	Union............																		
...pt 82	27	Union............	48	48	147	112	259	....	....	....	259	63	...	47	....	....	....	...	....	....
...pt 83	28	Union																		
...pt 83	25	Worth............																		
...pt 82	26	Worth............	129	148	382	338	720	....	....	....	720	134	5	110	....	1	..	....	....	....
...pt 83	26	Worth............																		
......84	28pt27	Yell..............	180	182	683	588	1271	...	....	....	1271	234	17	183	1	....	1	...	...	....
...In 84	26	Boonsboro, town of...	345	345	886	859	1745	2	....	2	1747	398	68	302	....	....	1	....	....	....
....	.....	Total............	2089	2243	6269	5522	11791	3	1	4	11795	2210	1296	1779	4	2	2	....	....	....
...In 84	26	Montana, city of—																		
....	......	1st ward	47	50	136	122	258	3	3	6	264	44	9	35	....	...	....	....	....	...
....	......	2d ward..........	111	111	291	304	595	....	....	....	595	133	5	114	....	....	....	....	....	....
....	......	3d ward..........	120	122	337	345	682	2	2	4	686	123	....	103	....	...	....	....	....	....
....	......	4th ward	68	68	339	228	567	....	5	5	572	75	5	49	....	....	....	....	....	....
....	......	Total city of Montana	346	351	1103	999	2102	5	10	15	2117	375	19	302	....	....	....	...	....	...
		Total of county...	2435	2594	7372	6521	13893	8	11	19	13912	2585	1315	2081	4	2	2	....	....	....

BREMER COUNTY.

......92	11	Dayton..	61	61	171	161	332	....	....	....	332	60	8	38	....	....	....	....	....	....
......93	13	Douglas	72	75	203	177	380	....	....	....	380	78	12	70	....	....	....	....	....	....
......91	11	Franklin...........	90	94	229	173	402	....	.. .	....	402	100	1	80	....	....	....	....	....	....
..w½ 93	12	Frederika..........	52	58	167	146	313	....	...	....	313	70	2	36	....	....	1	....	...	....
w½ §34 "	12	Frederika..........																		
... ..92	12	Fremont............	96	96	261	230	491	....	...	....	491	78	28	46	1	....	....	....	....	...
...s½ 91	...14	Jackson............	216	209	582	559	1141	3	5	8	1149	253	11	167	....	....	...	....	....	....
s½ w⅓ 91	13	Jackson............																		
...e⅔ 91	13	Jefferson..........	138	141	400	358	758	....	...	....	758	157	22	119	....	....	....	....	....	....
n 5-6 92	14	Lafayette..........	148	145	442	357	799	....	....	....	799	198	...	106	....	....	....	....	....	....
...e½ 93	12	Leroy..............	54	57	157	139	296	....	....	....	296	59	7	30	....	....	...	....	....	....
w 1-6 93	11	Leroy..............																		
......91	12	Maxfield...........	89	89	261	214	475	....	....	....	475	67	7	50	....	...	....	....	....	....
......93	14	Polk...............	203	208	579	536	1115	2	....	2	1117	252	12	165	...	...	....	....	....	....
e 5-6 93	... 11	Sumner.............	80	82	244	194	438	2	....	2	440	94	5	69	....	...	....	...	....	....
......92	13	Warren.............	138	142	421	364	785	....	....	....	785	148	13	111	....	....	....	....	...	...

BREMER COUNTY—Continued.

No. of Township.	Range.	Names of Townships, Towns, and Cities.	No. of Dwelling Houses	No. of Families.	No. of White Males.	No. of White Females.	Total White Population	No. of Colored Males.	No. of Colored Females	Total Colored Population.	Total Population.	No. entitled to Vote.	No. of Foreigners not Naturalized.	No. of Militia.	No. of Blind not in Asylum, Jan. 1, 1869.	No. of Deaf and Dumb not in Asy. Jan. 1, '69	No. of Insane not in Hospital, Jan. 1, 1869	No. of Colleges, Academies and Universities	No. of Teachers in Colleges, Universities, etc	No. of Students in Colleges, Universities, etc
n ½ 91	14	Washington }																		
s ⅙ 92	14	Washington }	172	172	487	451	938	....	....	....	938	189	5	126	....	....	....	....	....	....
n ½ w⅜91	13	Washington }																		
....	......	Waverly, city of *	483	517	1372	1309	2681	2	....	2	2683	568	...	320	...	...	....	....	....	...
....	......	Total	2092	2146	5976	5368	11344	9	5	14	11358	2571	133	1533	1	..	1	....	....	...

*Part of Washington township, embracing S. ½ sections 34 and 35, T. 92 R. 14, and sections 2 and 3, and N. ½ of sections 10 and 11, T. 91, R 14.

BUCHANAN COUNTY.

No. of Township.	Range.	Names of Townships, Towns, and Cities.	No. of Dwelling Houses	No. of Families.	No. of White Males.	No. of White Females.	Total White Population	No. of Colored Males.	No. of Colored Females	Total Colored Population.	Total Population.	No. entitled to Vote.	No. of Foreigners not Naturalized.	No. of Militia.	No. of Blind not in Asylum, Jan. 1, 1869.	No. of Deaf and Dumb not in Asy. Jan. 1, '69	No. of Insane not in Hospital, Jan. 1, 1869	No. of Colleges, Academies and Universities	No. of Teachers in Colleges, Universities, etc	No. of Students in Colleges, Universities, etc
90	8	Buffalo	90	90	244	224	468	....	....	....	468	114	4	80	....	....	....	....	....	...
89	8	Byron	191	191	592	493	1085	1	....	1	1086	267	5	237	...	...	2	....	....	...
87	8	Cono	72	75	220	194	414	....	....	....	414	88	4	67	....	...	....	....	....	....
90	10	Fairbank	208	216	604	539	1143	....	....	....	1143	240	25	163	....	2	....	....	....	....
89	7	Fremont	96	96	265	235	500	....	....	....	500	97	9	70	....	....	....	....	....	....
90	9	Hazelton	152	152	404	365	769	....	....	....	769	182	15	151	1	2	....	....	....	....
87	9	Homer	74	75	211	204	415	....	....	....	415	86	....	68	....	1	....	....	....	....
87	10	Jefferson	122	122	447	404	851	....	....	....	851	185	6	165	....	....	2	....	....	4
88	8	Liberty	244	258	672	656	1328	....	....	....	1328	302	10	211	....	1	1	....	....	....
88	7	Middlefield	77	87	269	246	515	....	....	....	515	97	2	65	....	....	....	....	....	...
90	7	Madison	99	100	281	260	541	..	....	....	541	117	5	74	...	....	....	....	....	...
87	7	Newton	132	169	473	482	955	....	....	....	955	169	8	129	....	....	....	....	..	....
89	10	Perry	284	284	773	711	1484	....	...	..	1484	345	22	255	....	....	1	....	1	1
pt 88	9	Sumner	72	73	189	174	363	....	....	....	363	90	....	56	....	....	....	....	....	....

......88	10	Westburg............	74	74	199	189	388	....	....	....	388	83	....	65	....	....	....	....	....	....
89 pt 88	9	Washington, exc. of Independence....	191	190	526	509	1035	1	...	1	1036	206	14	144	....	....	....	....	....	1
....	......	Independence, city of	476	505	1364	1353	2717	....	....	....	2717	591	5	440	...	...	....	....	....	....
....	......	Total............	2654	2757	7733	7238	14971	2	....	2	14973	3259	134	2440	1	6	6	....	1	6

2

BUENA VISTA COUNTY.

...90–93	.35–38	Barnes....	54	54	132	110	242	....	....	...	242	64	8	49	....	....	....	....	....	....

BUTLER COUNTY.

......90	16	Albion...............	151	151	407	362	769	....	....	....	769	185	....	102	....	....	....	....	....	....
......90	15	Beaver	199	186	494	440	934	....	....	....	934	235	....	165	....	....	....	....	....	....
......93	18	Bennezett............	26	26	86	70	156	....	....	....	156	30	2	23	....	....	....	....	....	....
......92	15	Butler....	210	263	663	604	1267	4	3	7	1274	288	11	206	....	....	....	....	....	....
......93	17	Coldwater.....	64	64	194	182	376	....	....	....	376	71	1	53	....	....	....	....	....	....
......93	16	Dayton...............	63	61	168	171	339	....	....	....	339	74	3	60	....	....	....	....	....	....
......93	15	Fremont....	67	72	201	178	379	....	....	....	379	89	5	66	....	....	2	....	....	....
......92	16	Jackson	77	80	226	209	435	....	....	....	435	94	1	66	....	....	....	....	....	....
......91	16	Jefferson	96	100	259	257	516	....	....	....	516	114	1	73	....	....	....	....	....	....
......91	18	Madison..............	39	39	114	97	211	....	....	....	211	52	....	45	....	....	....	....	....	....
......90	17	Monroe...............	98	98	280	236	516	....	....	....	516	105	13	103	1	....	....	....	....	....
......92	18	Pittsford............	72	85	199	186	385	....	....	....	385	90	1	61	....	....	....	....	....	....
......91	17	Ripley	46	46	137	118	255	....	....	....	255	55	1	32	....	....	....	....	....	....
......91	15	Shellrock............	211	211	552	511	1063	....	....	....	1063	281	....	219	....	....	....	....	....	....
......90	18	Washington..........	48	48	157	139	296	....	....	....	296	57	8	43	1	....	....	....	....	....
......92	17	West Point..........	42	42	126	109	235	....	....	....	235	42	19	27	....	....	....	....	....	....
....	......	Total............	1509	1572	4263	3869	8132	4	3	7	8139	1862	66	1344	2	....	2	....	....	....

CALHOUN COUNTY.

...86 87	.31–33	Calhoun....	33	34	91	99	190	....	....	....	190	38	....	32	....	....	....	....	....	....
...86–89	34	Jackson....	69	68	206	155	361	....	....	....	361	77	1	66	1	....	....	....	....	....
......88	31	Lincoln............ }																		
......88	32	Lincoln............ }	76	76	186	129	315	....	....	....	315	76	2	56	....	....	....	....	....	....
......89	31	Lincoln............ }																		

CALHOUN COUNTY—Continued.

No. of Township.	Range.	Names of Townships, Towns, and Cities.	No. of Dwelling Houses	No. of Families.	No. of White Males.	No. of White Females	Total White Population	No. of Colored Males.	No. of Colored Females	Total Colored Population.	Total Population.	No. entitled to Vote.	No. of Foreigners not Naturalized.	No. of Militia.	No. of Blind not in Asylum, Jan. 1, 1869.	No. of Deaf and Dumb not in Asy. Jan. 1, '69	No. of Insane not in Hospital, Jan. 1, 1869	No. of Colleges, Academies and Universities	No. of Teachers in Colleges, Universities, etc.	No. of Students in Colleges, Universities, etc.
......88	33	Sherman..........																		
......89	32	Sherman..........	14	15	43	35	78	....	....	....	78	14	....	9	....	....	....	....	....	....
......89	33	Sherman..........																		
....	.....	Total..........	192	193	526	418	944	....	....	....	944	205	3	163	1	....	....	....	....	....

CARROLL COUNTY.

No. of Township.	Range.	Names of Townships, Towns, and Cities.	No. of Dwelling Houses	No. of Families.	No. of White Males.	No. of White Females	Total White Population	No. of Colored Males.	No. of Colored Females	Total Colored Population.	Total Population.	No. entitled to Vote.	No. of Foreigners not Naturalized.	No. of Militia.	No. of Blind not in Asylum, Jan. 1, 1869.	No. of Deaf and Dumb not in Asy. Jan. 1, '69	No. of Insane not in Hospital, Jan. 1, 1869	No. of Colleges, Academies and Universities	No. of Teachers in Colleges, Universities, etc.	No. of Students in Colleges, Universities, etc.
pt 83 84	34 '5 '6	Carroll..........	42	42	106	96	202	....	....	....	202	51	15	51	....	....	....	....	....	1
......84	33	Glidden..........	53	53	146	132	278	....	....	....	278	60	8	57	....	....	..	....	....	...
......85	33	Jasper..........	29	29	104	72	176	....	....	....	176	34	...	27	....	....	....	....	....	...
pt 82 83	34 '5 '6	Newton..........	45	42	134	189	323	....	....	....	323	53	...	48	....	....	....	....	....	...
..... 85	34 '5 '6	Sheridan..........	14	14	31	39	70	....	....	....	70	13	....	10	...	....	....	....	....	...
...82 83	33	Union..........	58	58	151	250	401	....	....	....	401	45	....	41	....	....	....	....	....	...
....	......	Total..........	241	238	672	778	1450	....	....	....	1450	256	23	234	....	....	....	....	....	1

CASS COUNTY.

No. of Township.	Range.	Names of Townships, Towns, and Cities.	No. of Dwelling Houses	No. of Families.	No. of White Males.	No. of White Females	Total White Population	No. of Colored Males.	No. of Colored Females	Total Colored Population.	Total Population.	No. entitled to Vote.	No. of Foreigners not Naturalized.	No. of Militia.	No. of Blind not in Asylum, Jan. 1, 1869.	No. of Deaf and Dumb not in Asy. Jan. 1, '69	No. of Insane not in Hospital, Jan. 1, 1869	No. of Colleges, Academies and Universities	No. of Teachers in Colleges, Universities, etc.	No. of Students in Colleges, Universities, etc.
pt 76 77	37	Brighton..........	40	40	212	96	308	....	....	....	308	54	9	48	....	....	...	....	....	....
.....75	36	Cass..........	185	191	582	551	1133	1	....	1	1134	265	7	213	....	....	....	....	....	1
74 '5pt76	37	Cass..........																		
......74	.34–36	Edna..........	52	55	158	139	297	1	....	1	298	58	4	53	....	....	1	....	....	....
...76 77	34	Grant..........	42	42	118	111	229	....	....	....	229	46	5	39	..	....	1	....	....	....
pt 76 77	35	Grant..........																		

......77	36	Pymosa............ }	142	142	455	377	832	2	....	2	834	220	5	215	1	....	....	....	....	2
pt 76 77	35 37	Pymosa........ ... }																		
...pt 76	35 36	Turkey Grove...... }	186	186	385	328	713	....	....	....	713	156	3	128	....	....	....	....	....	1
...pt 77	35	Turkey Grove...... }																		
..... 75	34 35	Union................	15	15	46	42	88	....	....	....	88	21	1	17	....	....	....	....	....	....
....	......	Total	662	671	1956	1644	3600	4	....	4	3604	820	34	713	1	....	2	....	....	4

CEDAR COUNTY.

pt. 80 81	...2 3	Center, exc. of Tipton.	271	290	857	754	1611	1	1	2	1613	360	13	198	....	4	....	....	....	8
pt. 80 81	...3 4	Cass....	98	106	311	275	586	1	....	1	587	134	4	95	....	....	3	....	....	....
......82	2	Dayton. exc. Clarence..	115	115	341	279	620	....	....	....	620	123	18	113	....	....	....	....	....	....
...pt 81	2	Fairfield	98	98	291	248	539	....	....	....	539	120	6	94	....	....	....	....	....	....
......79	 1	Farmington exc Durant	156	160	471	422	893	1	....	1	894	173	45	118	....	1	....	....	....	12
......82	3	Fremont	140	151	423	372	795	....	....	....	795	187	4	158	....	....	1	....	....	....
...pt 80	..3 4	Gower................	126	126	400	335	735	4	5	9	744	165	7	122	....	....	....	....	....	....
......80	1	Inland	170	182	480	506	986	2	....	2	987	214	20	130	1	....	....	....	....	....
pt 79 80	3	Iowa...........	209	223	595	565	1160	3	2	5	1165	271	13	193	....	....	....	....	....	....
...pt 81	...3 4	Linn	75	79	250	277	527	....	....	....	527	119	1	91	....	....	....	....	....	....
......82	1	Massillon............	181	185	537	450	987	....	....	....	987	199	35	106	....	....	....	....	....	....
......82	4	Pioneer, exc. Mechanicsville............	162	162	488	435	923	....	....	....	923	210	1	152	....	....	....	....	....	....
...pt 81	...2 3	Red Oak............	88	88	284	286	570	....	....	....	570	113	4	72	....	....	....	....	....	....
pt 79 80	...2 3	Rochester............	151	151	435	428	863	....	....	....	863	172	....	127	....	....	....	....	....	8
......79	4	Springdale	277	277	694	650	1344	5	2	7	1351	314	16	220	1	2	....	....	....	....
......81	1	Springfield...........	246	259	733	646	1379	....	....	....	1379	257	58	177	2	....	3	....	....	....
...pt 79	2	Sugar Creek..........	128	128	389	350	739	1	1	2	741	160	13	110	....	....	1	....	....	....
...in 82	2	Clarence, town of....	127	127	393	341	734	....	....	....	734	185	21	157	....	....	....	....	....	....
......79	1	Durant, town of......	67	70	196	150	346	....	....	....	346	91	10	67	....	....	....	....	....	....
......82	4	Mechanicsville, town of	131	138	293	287	580	....	1	1	581	156	1	116	....	....	....	....	....	....
....	.....	Tipton, town of.......	280	290	614	665	1279	6	7	13	1292	307	....	185	2	....	....	....	....	1
....	.....	Total.........	3296	3405	9475	8721	18196	24	19	43	18239	4030	290	2801	6	7	8	....	....	29

CERRO GORDO COUNTY.

No. of Township.	Range.	Names of Townships, Towns, and Cities.	No. of Dwelling Houses	No. of Families.	No. of White Males.	No. of White Females.	Total White Population	No. of Colored Males.	No. of Colored Females	Total Colored Population.	Total Population.	No. entitled to Vote.	No. of Foreigners not Naturalized.	No. of Militia.	No. of Blind not in Asylum, Jan. 1, 1869.	No. of Deaf and Dumb not in Asy. Jan. 1 '69	No. of Insane not in Hospital, Jan. 1, 1869	No. of Colleges, Academies and Universities	No. of Teachers in Colleges, Universities, etc.	No. of Students in Colleges, Universities, etc.
...pt 94	22	Clear Lake.........	28	32	77	81	158	....	....	....	158	38	2	28	...	1	....	....	....	....
......95	22	Clear Lake.........																		
pt 95 96	.21 22	Clear Lake.........	82	90	251	246	497	....	....	....	497	94	14	82	....	..	....	....	....	....
......97	19pt20	Falls...............																		
......94	20	Geneseo..............	31	34	73	73	146	....	....	....	146	32	1	21	....	....	....	....	....	....
...pt 94	.19 21	Geneseo..............	19	20	52	49	101	....	....	....	101	23	....	20	...	1	....	....	....	....
......97	22	Grant................																		
...pt 96	.21 22	Lake	41	43	121	116	237	....	....	...	237	57	....	32	...	1	....	....	....	....
...pt 95	21	Lake	35	39	104	110	214	....	....	....	214	48	....	35	....	....	....	....	....	....
pt 96 97	21	Lincoln.............																		
pt 94 95	.21 22	Mason...............	143	162	428	367	795	....	....	....	795	224	6	134	....	....	....	....	....	....
...pt 97	.20 21	Mason...............																		
pt 94 96	19	Owens...............	28	28	79	71	150	....	....	....	150	27	....	17	....	....	....	....	....	....
......95	19	Owens...............	35	35	96	72	168	....	....	....	168	38	2	29	....	....	....	....	....	....
...pt 96	19	Portland............																		
....	.....	Total............	442	483	1281	1185	2466	....	....	....	2466	581	25	398	....	3	....	....	....	....

CHEROKEE COUNTY.

No. of Township.	Range.	Names of Townships, Towns, and Cities.	No. of Dwelling Houses	No. of Families.	No. of White Males.	No. of White Females.	Total White Population	No. of Colored Males.	No. of Colored Females	Total Colored Population.	Total Population.	No. entitled to Vote.	No. of Foreigners not Naturalized.	No. of Militia.	No. of Blind not in Asylum, Jan. 1, 1869.	No. of Deaf and Dumb not in Asy. Jan. 1 '69	No. of Insane not in Hospital, Jan. 1, 1869	No. of Colleges, Academies and Universities	No. of Teachers in Colleges, Universities, etc.	No. of Students in Colleges, Universities, etc.
......92	.39–42	Cherokee............	35	39	75	73	148	....	....	....	148	39	....	32	....	..	....	....	....	...
......93	.39–42	Spring..............	14	14	41	23	64	...	....	....	64	19	....	18	....	....	....	....	....	...
......91	.39–42	Pilot........	30	30	79	61	140	....	....	....	140	33	1	30	....	....	....	....	....	...
......90	.39–42	Willow...............	13	14	58	49	107	....	...	....	107	26	....	21	....	....	....	....	....	...
....	......	Total............	92	97	253	206	459	....	....	....	459	117	1	101	....	....	....	....	....	....

CHICKASAW COUNTY.

94	14	Bradford	318	346	872	841	1713				1713	440	3	279		2	2	1	3	125
95	14	Chickasaw	174	177	538	452	990	1		1	991	210	17	133						
95	13	Dayton	86	86	307	227	534				534	96	26	102						
96 pt 97	14	Deerfield	87	94	263	242	505				505	107	5	71						
94	12	Dresden	73	74	195	183	378				378	87	2	67						
94	11	Fredericksburg	78	103	263	233	496		1	1	497	118		69						
96 pt 97	12	Jacksonville	132	137	421	376	797				797	151		112						
95	12	New Hampton	145	156	465	388	853				853	203	10	159						
94	13	Richland	73	83	219	212	431	1		1	432	91	4	70						
95	11	Stapleton	83	83	280	240	520				520	101	15	76						
96 pt 97	11	Utica	135	135	408	379	787				787	123	28	74	1		1			
96 pt 97	13	Washington	91	91	264	242	506				506	94	4	67						
		Total	1475	1565	4495	4015	8510	2	1	3	8513	1821	114	1279	1	2	3	1	3	125

CLARKE COUNTY.

71	27	Doyle	175	184	473	447	920				920	202		145						
71	24	Franklin	106	106	289	265	554				554	120		85						2
73	25	Fremont	89	89	225	218	443				443	92		75						
71	25	Green Bay	89	89	265	259	524				524	109	1	78						
72	24	Jackson	143	142	399	373	772				772	153	29	127						2
71	26	Knox	124	126	387	354	741				741	140		110						
73	24	Liberty	132	145	382	354	736				736	165		115						
73	27	Madison	72	72	174	173	347				347	72		53			2			
72	25	Osceola	414	414	939	852	1791	18	13	31	1822	463	16	365						
72	27	Troy	43	47	128	120	248				248	57	3	43						
73	26	Washington	104	105	279	290	569	1		1	570	113	1	87						
72	26	Ward	63	63	176	174	350				350	62		56						
		Total	1454	1583	4116	3879	7995	19	13	32	8027	1748	50	1339			2			4

CLAY COUNTY.

		Total	90	100	255	185	450				450	109		91		1				

CLAYTON COUNTY.

No. of Township.	Range.	Names of Townships, Towns, and Cities.	No. of Dwelling Houses	No. of Families.	No. of White Males.	No. of White Females.	Total White Population	No. of Colored Males.	No. of Colored Females	Total Colored Population.	Total Population.	No. entitled to Vote.	No. of Foreigners not Naturalized.	No. of Militia.	No. of Blind not in Asylum, Jan. 1, 1869.	No. of Deaf and Dumb not in Asy. Jan. 1 '69	No. of Insane not in Hospital, Jan. 1, 1869	No. of Colleges, Academies, and Universities	No. of Teachers in Colleges, Universities, etc	No. of Students in Colleges, Universities, etc
93	5	Boardman	301	301	862	805	1667	1	1	2	1669	360	25	275	...	...	...	...	...	...
91	1	Buena Vista	60	60	169	145	314	...	...	...	314	59	14	25	...	...	...	...	...	...
pt 93 94	3	Clayton*	136	...	423	381	804	1	...	1	805	154	13	100	...	...	...	...	...	...
92	5	Cox Creek	167	170	492	440	932	...	...	...	932	171	24	108	...	1	...	...	...	...
91	6	Cass	217	217	566	529	1095	...	...	...	1095	234	23	131	...	...	...	1	3	18
91	4	Elk	149	149	434	389	823	...	...	...	823	140	16	100	...	...	...	...	...	...
94	4	Farmersburg	...*	...*	606	555	1161	...	...	...	1161	228	13	180	...	1	...	...	...	...
pt 93	3 4	Garnavillo	204	204	597	551	1148	...	...	...	1148	224	38	141	...	1	...	...	...	...
95	4	Giard	225	225	620	567	1187	...	...	...	1187	200	32	125	...	...	...	...	...	...
95	6	Grand Meadow	143	143	408	373	781	...	...	...	781	138	39	106	...	...	...	...	...	...
93	6	Highland	133	133	392	330	722	...	...	...	722	127	20	80	...	...	...	...	...	...
pt 92	2 3	Jefferson, exclusive of town of Guttenberg.	208	208	634	577	1211	...	...	...	1211	198	41	118	...	...	...	...	...	...
91	5	Lodomillo	191	191	500	452	952	...	...	...	952	224	1	157	...	...	...	...	...	...
91	3	Mallory	189	189	525	515	1037	...	...	...	1037	233	...	170	...	...	...	...	...	...
94	6	Marion	125	139	406	405	811	...	...	...	811	99	90	119	...	...	...	...	...	...
94 95	3	Mendon	319	328	886	842	1728	...	...	...	1728	239	25	157	...	...	...	...	...	...
91	2	Millville	152	152	424	413	837	1	...	1	838	169	21	107	...	...	...	...	...	...
95	5	Monona	283	283	744	702	1446	...	...	...	1446	389	17	288	1	...	...	...	...	...
pt 93	4	Read	160	165	526	411	937	1	...	1	938	160	66	112	1	3	1	...	...	...
92	6	Sperry	157	162	444	412	859	...	...	...	859	185	4	114	7	...	1	...	...	...
92	pt 3	Volga	232	232	611	553	1164	...	...	...	1164	244	51	127	...	...	...	...	...	...
94	5	Wagner	169	169	467	443	910	...	...	...	910	143	68	134	3	1	2	...	1	...

....	......	Guttenberg, town of*	208	208	525	482	1007	...	...	...	1007	222	21	111	...	1	...	...	...	...
....	......	Total..........	4128	4028	12261	11272	23533	4	1	5	23538	4540	653	3085	12	8	4	1	4	18
....	......	McGregor, city of.....																		
....	......	1st ward.........	127	131	356	362	718	2	5	7	725	141	...	137	...	...	...	...	...	...
....	......	2d ward..........	116	147	375	434	809	...	...	...	809	208	7	173	...	...	...	...	...	...
....	......	3d ward..........	73	78	226	196	422	2	2	4	426	98	5	85	...	...	...	...	...	...
....	......	4th ward.........	65	65	173	161	334	...	...	...	334	59	3	40	...	...	...	...	...	...
....	......	Total, city.....	381	421	1130	1153	2283	4	7	11	2294	506	15	435	...	...	...	...	...	...
		Total of County.......	4509	4449	13391	12425	25816	8	8	16	25832	5046	678	6510	12	8	4	1	4	18

* Census of 1867, no returns of 1869 having been received.

CLINTON COUNTY.

......82	2	Berlin...............	99	106	324	247	571	...	...	...	571	103	34	69	...	1	1	...	...	...
.....83	3	Bloomfield...........	not	rep.	550	503	1053	...	...	...	1053	223	10	165	...	1	...	...	...	...
......83	2	Brookfield...........	162	163	501	390	891	...	...	...	891	171	42	127	...	...	...	...	...	...
..pt80 81	.5, 6, 7	Camanche, exc. town..	94	94	266	251	517	2	...	2	519	123	5	79	...	...	...	...	...	...
......82	5	Center...............	188	239	607	517	1124	...	...	...	1124	165	107	99	...	...	...	...	...	...
..pt81 82	..6. .7	Clinton, exc. Clinton..	249	259	723	676	1399	2	...	2	1401	276	69	128	...	1	1	..	2	6
......81	4	De Witt, exc. De Witt	257	257	746	643	1389	1	1	2	1391	271	15	141	...	...	...	...	...	1
......83	5	Deep Creek..........	no	rep.	537	475	1012	...	...	...	1012	159	107	201	1	...	...	...	...	...
..pt80 81	.. 4, .5	Eden.	no	rep.	425	368	793	...	...	...	793	165	38	128	...	...	...	...	...	...
......83	..6, .7	Elk River........	215	215	656	528	1184	...	...	...	1184	197	77	226	2	1	...	...	...	...
....pt 82	6	Hampshire...........	159	159	494	410	904	...	...	...	904	146	82	78	...	...	...	...	...	...
......82	1	Liberty..............	151	151	440	366	806	...	...	...	806	166	22	82	...	...	...	...	9	1
....pt 82	7	Lyons, exc. Lyons....	74	77	216	194	410	...	...	...	410	81	39	26	...	...	1	...	...	...
..pt80 81	...2, .3	Orange	167	170	463	434	897	...	...	...	897	179	30	100	...	...	1	...	...	...
..pt80 81	2	Olive................	243	243	708	640	1348	...	...	...	1348	242	91	158	...	1	...	...	...	3
......83	1	Sharon..............	294	212	609	532	1141	...	...	...	1141	224	36	134	1	1	...	...	...	...
......81	1	Spring Rock.........	no	rep.	653	623	1276	2	1	3	1279	254	36	204	...	...	...	...	...	...
......82	4	Washington..........	no	rep.	491	400	891	...	...	...	891	169	32	124	...	...	...	...	...	...
......83	4	Waterford...........	175	175	506	471	977	...	...	...	977	188	15	141	...	...	1	...	...	...
......82	3	Welton..............	154	156	458	402	860	1	...	1	861	150	28	102	...	...	...	...	...	...
....	.....	Clinton, city of.......	1051	1138	3315	2921	6236	42	29	71	6307	1247	109	761	...	...	1	...	...	...
...In 82	7	Lyons, city of........	n. r	635	1804	1815	3619	4	9	13	3632	727	74	223	...	...	...	1	6	36
....	......	Camanche, town of...	161	177	344	371	715	4	2	6	721	115	15	109	...	...	...	...	...	...

CLINTON COUNTY—CONTINUED.

No. of Township.	Range.	Names of Townships, Towns, and Cities.	No. of Dwelling Houses	No. of Families.	No. of White Males.	No. of White Females	Total White Population	No. of Colored Males.	No. of Colored Females	Total Colored Population.	Total Population.	No. entitled to Vote.	No. of Foreigners not Naturalized.	No. of Militia.	No. of Blind not in Asylum, Jan. 1, 1869.	No. of Deaf and Dumb not in Asy. Jan. 1, '69	No. of Insane not in Hospital, Jan. 1, 1869	No. of Colleges, Academies and Universities	No. of Teachers in Colleges, Universities, etc	No. of Students in Colleges, Universities, etc
...in 81	4	De Witt.............	No	rept	887	934	1821	10	8	18	1839	399	38	319	....	3	....	...	....	....
....	......	Total............	3803	4626	16723	15111	31834	68	50	118	31952	6140	1151	3924	4	9	6	1	17	47

CRAWFORD COUNTY.

No. of Township.	Range.	Names of Townships, Towns, and Cities.	No. of Dwelling Houses	No. of Families.	No. of White Males.	No. of White Females	Total White Population	No. of Colored Males.	No. of Colored Females	Total Colored Population.	Total Population.	No. entitled to Vote.	No. of Foreigners not Naturalized.	No. of Militia.	No. of Blind not in Asylum, Jan. 1, 1869.	No. of Deaf and Dumb not in Asy. Jan. 1, '69	No. of Insane not in Hospital, Jan. 1, 1869	No. of Colleges, Academies and Universities	No. of Teachers in Colleges, Universities, etc	No. of Students in Colleges, Universities, etc
.. 82–85	...41	Boyer...............	25	25	71	70	141	....	....	....	141	37	4	30	...	....	....	....	....	....
pt 83 84	37–40	Denison.	114	114	321	293	614	....	....	..	614	132	14	123	....	....	....	....	....	....
... ..85	37–40	Jackson...........	31	31	88	83	171	....	....	....	171	16	26	10	....	....	....	....	....	....
pt 84 85	37–40	Milford..	79	79	248	110	358	....	....	....	358	98	....	85	...	....	....	....	....	....
......82 ......82 pt... .83	37 38 39 40 . ..40	Union..... .... Union... ... . Union...........	67	67	201	152	353	.. 2	1	3	356	65	6	56	....	....	....	....	....	....
....	......	Total....	316	316	929	708	1637	2	1	3	1640	348	50	304	....	....	....	....	....	....

DALLAS COUNTY.

No. of Township.	Range.	Names of Townships, Towns, and Cities.	No. of Dwelling Houses	No. of Families.	No. of White Males.	No. of White Females	Total White Population	No. of Colored Males.	No. of Colored Females	Total Colored Population.	Total Population.	No. entitled to Vote.	No. of Foreigners not Naturalized.	No. of Militia.	No. of Blind not in Asylum, Jan. 1, 1869.	No. of Deaf and Dumb not in Asy. Jan. 1, '69	No. of Insane not in Hospital, Jan. 1, 1869	No. of Colleges, Academies and Universities	No. of Teachers in Colleges, Universities, etc	No. of Students in Colleges, Universities, etc
......79 ......78 ... pt 78	27pt28 ....28 27	Adel, exc. of town.. Adel, exc. of town.. Adel, exc. of town..	537	544	1582	1404	2986	1	1	2	2988	676	50	601	1	....	....	....	....	...
......81	27	Beaver..............	41	42	116	98	214	....	....	....	214	56	6	34	....	....	....	....	....	....
......78	26pt27	Boone...............	143	143	489	429	918	5	3	8	926	196	15	143	....	5	....	....	....	....
......81	29	Dallas..............	55	55	160	131	291	....	....	...	291	67	...	51	....	....	....	....	....	3
......81	26	Des Moines...........	129	129	411	362	773	...	1	1	774	151	10	123	...	....	....	....	....	....

80	26	Grant	43	49	141	136	277				277	56	2	41						
80	29	Lincoln	20	20	61	51	112				112	23		23						
79	29	Linn	123	124	345	319	664	1		1	665	143	1	110						
81	28	Spring Valley	107	108	365	271	636	2	3	5	641	156		139						
80	27	Sugar Grove	97	97	275	224	499				499	97	11	84						
78 pt 79	29 28	Union Union	302	323	919	812	1731				1731	420	7	322						
79	26	Walnut	55	65	138	143	281				281	69		59						
80	28	Washington	40	45	139	119	258				258	52	1	43						
		Adel, town of	112	112	367	332	699	3	2	5	704	180	3	136						
		Total	1804	1856	5508	4831	10339	12	10	22	10361	2342	106	1909	1	5				3

DAVIS COUNTY.

pt 68–69	13 14	Bloomfield, exc of town	218	226	629	606	1235	7	10	17	1252	281		214			1			
pt 69	14	Drakeville, exc of town	63	63	157	166	323				323	64		38						
69 pt 68	15	Fox River	212	212	612	604	1216				1216	242	1	192	1	1	1			
67 pt 68	15	Fabius	271	268	760	743	1503				1503	293		226			2			
67 pt 68	13	Grove	198	198	566	582	1148	1		1	1149	224	15	164						
70	13	Lick Creek	233	232	629	641	1270				1270	270		207						
70	15	Marion	125	125	370	386	756				756	188		146						
pt 69	13	Perry	135	135	373	362	735	3	4	7	742	165		122		3				3
pt 68	12	Prairie	105	105	299	293	592				592	124	7	91						
67 pt 68	12	Roscoe	83	87	238	228	466	3	1	4	470	89	9	74			1			
70	14	Soap Creek	148	147	445	395	840				840	187	2	134			2			
70	12	Salt Creek	192	192	515	509	1024	2	4	6	1030	219		152		1				
69	12	Union	217	217	614	631	1245				1245	272		205		1		1	1	22
67 pt 68	14	Wycondah	266	275	786	773	1559	1		1	1560	303		218			2			
In 69	14	Bloomfield, town of	141	141	400	349	749	3	3	6	755	207		178			1			
In 69	14	Drakeville, town of	44	45	99	119	218				218	42		26			1			
		Total	2651	2668	7492	7387	14879	20	22	42	14921	3170	34	2387	1	6	11	1	1	25

DECATUR COUNTY.

68	27	Bloomington	40	40	113	103	216				216	39		38	1		1			
68	26	Burrell	138	138	386	370	756				756	144		109						
69	25	Center	287	287	804	778	1582	1	2	3	1585	325		231						

DECATUR COUNTY—Continued.

No. of Township.	Range.	Names of Townships, Towns, and Cities.	No. of Dwelling Houses	No. of Families.	No. of White Males.	No. of White Females.	Total White Population	No. of Colored Males.	No. of Colored Females	Total Colored Population.	Total Population.	No. entitled to Vote.	No. of Foreigners not Naturalized.	No. of Militia.	No. of Blind not in Asylum, Jan. 1, 1869.	No. of Deaf and Dumb not in Asy. Jan. 1, '69	No. of Insane not in Hospital, Jan. 1, 1869	No. of Colleges, Academies and Universities	No. of Teachers in Colleges, Universities, etc	No. of Students in Colleges, Universities, etc
......69	26	Decatur..............	117	117	330	318	648	1	....	1	649	140	1	106	....	....	....	....	....	....
......68	25	Eden...............	169	169	553	482	1035	2	1	3	1038	203	2	153	1	....	2	....	....	....
......67	27	Fayette..............	42	42	123	112	235	....	....	....	235	51	1	39	....	....	....	....	....	....
......70	25	Franklin............	86	94	239	198	437	....	....	....	437	93	3	65	2	....	....	....	....	....
......70	24	Garden Grove.......	140	140	406	327	733	7	6	13	746	133	3	132	1	....	1	....	1	1
......69	27	Grand River.........	44	46	120	110	230	5	2	7	237	59	....	37	....	....	1	....	....	....
......67	25	Hamilton...........	163	173	328	298	626	1	1	2	628	138	....	121	....	....	....	....	....	....
......69	24	High Point...........	123	125	330	335	665	3	4	7	672	132	4	93	....	....	....	....	....	....
......70	26	Long Creek..........	124	124	334	302	636	7	8	15	651	135	....	108	....	....	....	....	....	....
......67	24	Morgan..............	90	90	255	271	526	....	....	....	526	....	....	84	1	....	1	....	....	....
......67	26	New Buda..........	84	84	226	199	425	13	....	13	438	83	....	67	1	....	....	....	....	....
......70	27	Richland............	144	150	395	368	763	....	....	....	763	165	....	130	....	....	....	....	....	....
......68	24	Woodland...........	113	113	322	440	762	....	....	....	762	129	30	62	....	....	....	....	....	....
....	......	Total...........	1904	1932	5264	5011	10275	40	24	64	10339	1969	44	1575	7	....	6	....	1	1

DELAWARE COUNTY.

No. of Township.	Range.	Names of Townships, Towns, and Cities.	No. of Dwelling Houses	No. of Families.	No. of White Males.	No. of White Females.	Total White Population	No. of Colored Males.	No. of Colored Females	Total Colored Population.	Total Population.	No. entitled to Vote.	No. of Foreigners not Naturalized.	No. of Militia.	No. of Blind not in Asylum, Jan. 1, 1869.	No. of Deaf and Dumb not in Asy. Jan. 1, '69	No. of Insane not in Hospital, Jan. 1, 1869	No. of Colleges, Academies and Universities	No. of Teachers in Colleges, Universities, etc	No. of Students in Colleges, Universities, etc
......87	6	Adams...............	99	99	341	281	622	1	...	1	623	114	3	73	....	....	....	....	....	....
......89	3	Breman..............	111	113	364	328	692	....	....	....	692	122	31	118	....	....	....	....	....	....
......89	6	Coffin's Grove........	199	199	439	398	837	1	....	1	838	179	9	111	....	....	....	....	1	2
......90	3	Colony...............	237	237	649	610	1259	....	....	....	1259	270	31	194	....	....	....	....	....	....
......89	5	Delaware, excl. city of Manchester........	235	235	530	522	1052	1	....	1	1053	232	6	157	....	....	....	....	....	....
......88	4	Delhi................	214	214	611	588	1199	1	...	1	1200	252	21	176	....	....	....	....	....	3

90	4	Elk	165	165	460	419	879				879	192	11	144						
87	5	Hazel Green	109	114	317	281	598				598	124	7	99						1
90	5	Honey Creek	205	205	506	511	1017				1017	276	4	184						2
88	5	Milo	140	140	391	341	733				733	166	1	119			1			
88	3	North Fork	141	146	429	418	847				847	145	20	90	2					
89	4	Oneida	237	237	637	582	1219	1		1	1220	281	28	188						6
88	6	Prairie	61	61	177	169	346	3		3	349	60	6	45						
90	6	Richland	149	154	417	384	801				801	153	20	90	2	1				
87	3	South Fork	260	260	693	671	1364	3	2	5	1369	268	17	183				1	4	90
87	4	Union	134	139	359	345	704				704	138	15	104			1			2
in 89	5	Manchester, town of	282	282	686	689	1375				1375	360	13	285	1					5
		Total	2978	3000	8606	7538	15544	11	2	13	15557	3332	243	2360	5	1	2	1	5	111

DES MOINES COUNTY.

pts 69	4 5	Augusta	102	102	299	265	564				564	118	5	81	1					
71	2	Benton	218	219	613	596	1209				1209	244	15	180	1					
pt68-9 70	2	Burlington, exl. of city	386	386	1137	992	2129	20	18	38	2167	426	20	266		1	1			
70	4	Danville	258	264	756	703	1459				1459	312	4	215			1			4
70	3	Flint River	223	233	661	616	1277	6	1	7	1284	257	21	190	1	1	1			
71	3	Franklin	255	268	786	773	1559				1559	326	15	226			2			
pt 72	1 2	Huron	134	134	382	342	724				724	155	15	100						
pt 71	1	Jackson	27	27	77	69	146				146	28		22						
71	4	Pleasant Grove	149	149	526	485	1011				1011	219	24	190	3	2	1			
pts 68 69	3	Union	220	220	649	595	1244	7	12	19	1263	253	26	165		1				2
72	4	Washington	164	164	459	453	912				912	192		142						
72	3 pt 2	Yellow Springs	318	318	860	794	1654				1654	340	41	246		1				
in 69 70	2	Burlington, city of	1810	2144	6325	5535	11860	91	83	174	12034	2111	499	1286	1	2	2	1	6	108
		Total	4264	4628	13530	12218	25748	124	114	238	25986	4981	685	3309	7	8	8	1	6	114

DICKINSON COUNTY.

		Centre Grove	39	45	115	88	203				203	44		37						
		Fair Grove	16	17	57	45	102				102	25		15						
		Okoboji	32	32	86	83	169				169	41		29						
		Tusculum	24	24	52	36	88				88	24								
		Total	111	118	310	252	562				562	134		81						

DUBUQUE COUNTY.

No. of Township.	Range.	Names of Townships, Towns, and Cities.	No. of Dwelling Houses	No. of Families.	No. of White Males.	No. of White Females.	Total White Population	No. of Colored Males.	No. of Colored Females	Total Colored Population.	Total Population.	No. entitled to Vote.	No. of Foreigners not Naturalized.	No. of Militia.	No. of Blind not in Asylum Jan. 1, 1869.	No. of Deaf and Dumb not in Asy. Jan. 1, '69	No. of Insane not in Hospital, Jan. 1, '69	No. of Colleges, Academies and Universities	No. of Teachers in Colleges, Universities, etc.	No. of Students in Colleges, Universities, etc.
87	2 w	Cascade	214	216	610	603	1213	....	....	....	1213	212	31	155	....	....	....	....	....	....
89	1e	Center	221	222	630	604	1234	...	....	....	1234	2 3	45	171	....	....	1	....	....	....
90	1 w	Concord	175	175	552	533	1085	....	....	....	1085	221	7	124	....	....	....	....	....	....
88	2 w	Dodge	128	128	404	353	757	1	....	1	758	151	17	136	....	....	1	....	....	....
89	1 w	Iowa	137	137	468	393	861	....	....	....	861	154	2	81	...	...	....	....	....	...
90	1e	Jefferson	246	248	734	657	1391	....	....	....	1391	294	23	174	....	....	....	....	....	..
89	2e	Julian, exc'e of city of Dubuque	228	228	700	662	1362	1	....	1	1363	261	41	152	1	17	....	....	....	....
90	2 w	Liberty	151	151	510	443	953	....	....	....	953	135	28	84	....	....	....	....	....	....
88	3e	Mosalem	113	113	375	357	732	....	....	....	732	143	10	100	....	....	....	....	....	....
89	2 w	New Wine	275	275	991	836	1827	....	....	....	1827	350	80	312	....	....	....	....	....	1
90	2e	Peru	171	177	517	434	951	....	....	....	951	189	23	131	....	....	....	....	....	....
87	1e	Prairie Creek	135	135	484	386	870	....	....	....	870	178	12	105	....	....	....	....	....	....
88	2e	Table Mound	164	164	488	534	1022	....	....	....	1022	152	13	119	....	....	....	....	....	....
88	1 w	Taylor	251	251	793	680	1473	....	....	....	1473	330	11	224	1	....	....	....	....	....
88	1e	Vernon	183	184	599	509	1108	1	....	1	1109	264	29	131	...	2	....	....	....	....
87	2e	Washington	153	164	483	456	939	....	....	....	939	175	15	103	....	....	3	....	....	....
87	1 w	White Water	199	199	554	526	1080	....	1	1	1081	203	32	118	....	....	....	....	....	6
		Total	3144	3167	9892	8966	18858	3	1	4	18862	3645	419	2424	2	19	5	....	...	7
In 89	2e	Dubuque, city of—																		
		1st ward	652	655	1733	1672	3405	3	4	7	3412	642	41	337	...	....	....	....	1	76
		2d ward	312	324	1024	798	1822	12	9	21	1843	416	43	305	....	....	...	....	1	....
		3d ward	870	892	2114	2160	4274	21	22	43	4317	785	123	470	1	....	....	....	2	23

....	.....	4th ward.........	950	980	2251	2508	4759	18	21	39	4798	932	42	588	....	....	....	1	10	120
....	.....	5th ward.........	758	761	1866	1833	3699	6	9	15	3714	673	115	402	..	....	3	....	7	47
....	.....	Total of city..	3542	3612	8988	8971	17959	60	65	125	18084	3448	364	2102	1	....	4	1	21	266
....	......	Total of county...	6686	6779	18880	17937	36817	63	66	129	36946	7093	783	4526	3	19	9	....	21	273

EMMET COUNTY.

...98 99	.. 31	Armstrong Grove. ..	14	14	30	22	52	....	....	....	52	19	....	9	....	....	....	....	....	...
......99	33 32	Center	26	26	64	57	121	....	....	....	121	12	....	16	....	....	....	....	....	....
.....100	33	Ellsworth..........	17	17	19	21	40	...	....	...	40	9	2	4	....	....	....	....	....	....
.....100	34	Emmet..........	31	33	90	75	165	...	....	...	165	39	3	34	....	....	....	....	....	....
......99	34	Estherville..........	67	67	187	153	340	1	....	1	341	75	....	52	....	....	....	....	....	....
.....100	31 32	Fairview	8	8	30	18	48	....	...	....	48	11	...	....	....	....	....	....	....	....
......98	32 pt33	High Lake..........	37	37	75	58	133	....	...	....	133	21	15	21	....	....	....	....	....	....
......98	33 pt34	Peterson...........	17	17	56	34	90	....	....	....	90	17	2	10	....	....	....	....	....	....
......	......	Total	217	219	551	438	989	1	....	1	990	203	22	146	....	..	...	....	....	....

FAYETTE COUNTY.

......95	9	Auburn..............	187	187	514	502	1016	....	....	....	1016	219	7	142	1	....	....	....	....	....
......93	...10	Banks..............	29	29	87	70	157	....	....	....	157	37	17	29	....	....	....	....	....	....
......93	9	Center	87	88	223	194	417	....	....	....	417	104	3	76	....	....	....	....	....	....
......95	7	Clermont............	233	233	652	624	1276	....	....	....	1276	266	26	187	2	...	....	....	....	....
......95	8	Dover..............	190	190	560	514	1074	....	....	....	1074	183	34	129	....	...	....	....	....	....
......95	10	Eden..............	164	163	488	438	926	....	....	....	926	209	10	132	....	....	....	....	....	....
......92	7	Fairfield............	219	219	604	551	1155	....	....	....	1155	248	29	192	....	....	....	....	....	....
......92	10	Fremont............	83	83	220	216	436	....	....	....	436	86	7	60	....	....	....	....	....	....
......92	9	Harlan.............	54	57	150	133	283	....	....	....	283	68	....	54	....	....	....	....	....	....
......93	7	Illyria	179	179	527	501	1028	7	4	11	1039	201	15	138	....	1	....	....	....	....
......91	9	Jefferson............	94	97	276	263	539	....	....	....	539	117	16	85	....	....	....	....	....	....
......91	...10	Oran	121	131	347	323	670	....	....	....	670	141	....	97	....	....	....	....	....	....
......94	7	Pleasant Valley......	213	221	622	567	1189	....	....	....	1189	214	40	157	....	....	....	....	....	....
......91	7	Putnam..........	135	135	381	339	720	....	....	....	720	151	46	109	....	....	....	....	....	....
......94	10	Richland............	58	58	162	159	321	....	....	....	321	67	4	37	....	....	....	....	....	....
......91	8	Scott...............	40	40	109	107	216	....	....	....	216	42	2	33	....	....	....	....	....	....
......92	8	Smithfield...........	119	120	324	298	622	....	....	....	622	143	1	92	....	....	....	....	....	1
......93	8	Westfield...........	295	315	724	645	1369	64	69	133	1502	326	...	211	....	....	..	1	6	....
......94	9	Windsor............	133	133	392	355	747	....	....	....	747	171	....	127	....	....	....	....	....	....

FAYETTE COUNTY—CONTINUED.

No. of Township.	Range.	Names of Townships, Towns, and Cities.	No. of Dwelling Houses	No. of Families.	No. of White Males.	No. of White Females.	Total White Population	No. of Colored Males.	No. of Colored Females	Total Colored Population.	Total Population.	No. entitled to Vote.	No. of Foreigners not Naturalized.	No. of Militia.	No. of Blind not in Asylum, Jan. 1, 1869.	No. of Deaf and Dumb not in Asy. Jan. 1, '69	No. of Insane not in Hospital, Jan. 1, 1869	No. of Colleges, Academies and Universities	No. of Teachers in Colleges, Universities, etc	No. of Students in Colleges, Universities, etc
...In 94	8	West Union, exclusive of town..........	187	190	524	513	1037	....	....	....	1037	171	2	103	....	....	....	....	....	....
....	......	West Union, town of..	203	211	516	529	1045	2	2	4	1049	250	7	179	....	....	....	....	....	....
....	......	Total..........	3023	3079	8402	7841	16243	73	75	148	16391	3414	266	2369	3	1	....	1	6	1

FLOYD COUNTY.

No. of Township.	Range.	Names of Townships, Towns, and Cities.	No. of Dwelling Houses	No. of Families.	No. of White Males.	No. of White Females.	Total White Population	No. of Colored Males.	No. of Colored Females	Total Colored Population.	Total Population.	No. entitled to Vote.	No. of Foreigners not Naturalized.	No. of Militia.	No. of Blind not in Asylum, Jan. 1, 1869.	No. of Deaf and Dumb not in Asy. Jan. 1, '69	No. of Insane not in Hospital, Jan. 1, 1869	No. of Colleges, Academies and Universities	No. of Teachers in Colleges, Universities, etc	No. of Students in Colleges, Universities, etc
......97	.15 16	Cedar................	60	61	154	148	302	....	....	...	302	73	4	53	....	....	...	....	...	....
......96	.16 17	Floyd...............	221	255	662	605	1267	....	....	....	1267	299	1	182	....	2	1	....	....	1
......96	15	Niles..............	79	80	193	208	401	....	....	....	401	97	6	83	....	....	....	....	....	....
. 94	16	Pleasant Grove	47	51	122	130	252	....	....	...	252	55	6	44	....	....	....	....	....	....
......94	15	Riverton	127	134	385	391	776	....	....	...	776	164	4	84	....	....	....	....	....	....
pt 95 96	18	Rockford....	118	133	313	286	599	....	....	....	599	166	2	122	....	....	....	....	....	....
pt 96 97	.17 18	Rock Grove.	161	180	500	414	914	....	....	...	914	199	37	132	....	....	....	....	....	....
94 pt 95	...18	Scott..............	21	21	76	62	138	....	....	....	138	29	1	19	....	....	....	....	....	....
......95	.15 16	St. Charles........ ..	434	497	1379	1292	2671	....	....	....	2671	608	79	495	1	....	2	....	....	....
pt 95 96	...17	Ulster..............	71	71	172	142	314	....	....	....	314	67	11	53	....	....	....	....	....	....
94 pt 95	17	Union..	147	148	429	402	831	....	....	....	831	184	5	134	....	1	....	....	....	....
....	......	Total...........	1486	1631	4385	4080	8465	....	...	...	8465	1941	156	1401	1	3	3	....	....	1

FRANKLIN COUNTY.

......93	.20 21	Clinton																		
...pt 92	.20 21	Clinton	40	40	122	108	230	....	....	....	230	52	....	38	....	....	....	....	....	....
......93	22	Clinton																		
......91	19	Geneva	64	65	186	170	356	....	....	....	356	83	..	70	....	....	....	....	....	....
......92	... 19	Ingham	42	42	141	96	237	....	....	....	237	58	....	41	....	....	....	....	....	....
...91 92	22	Morgan	30	30	99	74	173	4	3	7	180	31	3	19	....	....	....	....	....	....
......90	22pt21	Oakland	55	55	160	158	318	....	....	....	318	61	4	45	....	1	....	....	....	....
......90	19pt20	Osceola	76	82	245	215	460	1	....	1	461	96	6	75	....	....	....	....	....	....
pt 90 91	.20 21	Reeve	133	134	362	349	711	1	....	1	712	146	2	92	....	....	....	....	....	....
pt 91 92	.20 21	Washington	85	85	186	199	385	1	....	1	386	91	....	78	....	....	....	....	....	....
......93	19	West Fork	42	42	96	99	195	....	....	....	195	48	....	37	....	....	....	....	....	....
....	......	Total	567	575	1597	1468	3065	7	3	10	3075	666	15	495	....	1	....	....	....	....

FREMONT COUNTY.

pt 68 69	.43 44	Benton	117	117	351	288	639	....	....	....	639	182	3	136	....	....	....	....	....	....
pt67'8'9	40	Fisher	69	69	180	146	326	..	....	....	326	74	....	50	....	....	....	....	....	....
pt 67 68	.42 43	Franklin	230	230	555	566	1121	1	....	1	1122	258	....	151	1	1	1	....	....	....
pt 67 68	.41 42	Madison	159	159	487	393	880	4	4	8	888	199	....	142	....	4	....	....	....	....
...pt 69	.40 41	Monroe																		
......70	40	Monroe	85	85	286	258	544	....	....	....	544	118	....	92	....	....	....	....	....	....
...pt 70	...41	Monroe																		
......70	41pt42	Ross, exc. of Tabor	146	162	468	414	882	2	....	2	884	183	6	150	....	....	....	....	....	23
......70	43	Scott	261	261	661	632	1293	....	....	...	1293	286	....	222	....	....	....	....	....	..
......69	42	Sidney																		
...pt 69	.41 43	Sidney	389	439	1086	1011	2097	2	5	7	2104	457	3	330	...	....	....	...	....	....
......68	41'2'3	Sidney																		
...In 20	42	Tabor, town of	45	45	120	129	249	2	....	2	251	64	...	44	....	....	....	....	9	40
....	......	Total	1501	1567	4194	3837	8031	11	9	20	8051	1821	12	1317	1	5	1	....	9	63

GREENE COUNTY.

83 84 85	30	Jefferson, exc of town																		
pt 83 84	.30 31	Jefferson, exc of town	202	201	539	495	1034	....	....	....	1034	231	10	187	1	1	....	....	....	1
...pt 82	.30 31	Jefferson, exc of town																		

GREENE COUNTY—Continued.

No. of Township.	Range.	Names of Townships, Towns, and Cities.	No. of Dwelling Houses	No. of Families.	No. of White Males.	No. of White Females.	Total White Population	No. of Colored Males.	No. of Colored Females	Total Colored Population.	Total Population.	No. entitled to Vote.	No. of Foreigners not Naturalized.	No. of Militia.	No. of Blind not in Asylum, Jan. 1, 1869.	No. of Deaf and Dumb not in Asy. Jan. 1 '69	No. of Insane not in Hospital, Jan. 1, 1869	No. of Colleges, Academies, and Universities	No. of Teachers in Colleges, Universities, etc	No. of Students in Colleges, Universities, etc
82 83 84	32	Kendrick																		
pt 81 83	31	Kendrick	128	128	349	327	676	....	....	....	676	145	4	127	....	....	....	....	..	....
...pt 84	...31	Kendrick																		
...82 83	29	Washington........																		
...84 85	29	Washington	151	202	434	468	902	....	....	....	902	172	8	144	....	....	....	....	....	....
...E½ 82	...30	Washington																		
......85	.31 32	Cedar	38	38	91	88	179	....	....	...	179	46	...	26	....	....	....	....	....	....
....	......	Jefferson, town of.....	159	159	371	332	703	....	....	...	703	189	5	154	....	....	....	....	....	....
....	......	Total	678	728	1784	1710	3494	....	....	....	3494	783	27	638	1	1	....	....	....	1

GRUNDY COUNTY.

No. of Township.	Range.	Names of Townships, Towns, and Cities.	No. of Dwelling Houses	No. of Families.	No. of White Males.	No. of White Females.	Total White Population	No. of Colored Males.	No. of Colored Females	Total Colored Population.	Total Population.	No. entitled to Vote.	No. of Foreigners not Naturalized.	No. of Militia.	No. of Blind not in Asylum, Jan. 1, 1869.	No. of Deaf and Dumb not in Asy. Jan. 1 '69	No. of Insane not in Hospital, Jan. 1, 1869	No. of Colleges, Academies, and Universities	No. of Teachers in Colleges, Universities, etc	No. of Students in Colleges, Universities, etc
......89	16	Beaver	48	51	132	126	258	....	....	...	258	53	22	44	...	....	....	....	....	....
......87	15	Black Hawk	45	45	127	101	228	1	....	1	229	56	6	45	....	...	....	....	....	....
......86	17	Clay	36	36	84	82	166	....	....	....	166	46	....	43	....	....	....	....	....	....
......89	15	Fairfield	108	126	322	290	612	....	....	....	612	129	6	108	....	....	....	....	....	....
......86	18	Felix	86	89	232	242	474	....	....	....	474	96	....	86	....	...	....	....	....	....
......89	... 18	German.............	78	80	228	189	417	....	....	....	417	51	..	37	....	....	....	...	....	....
......88	...15	Grant...............	29	29	92	74	166	..	....	....	166	28	10	23	....	....	....	....	....	....
......88	.16 17	Lincoln.............	35	35	100	103	203	1	....	1	204	37	12	30	....	....	....	....	....	....
......87	78	Melrose.............	60	60	193	153	346	....	....	....	346	83	3	75	...	....	....	....	....	...
......87	.16 17	Palermo	93	93	261	223	484	....	....	....	484	124	7	109	....	....	....	....	....	....
... ..89	17	Pleasant Valley.......	41	42	112	88	200	....	....	....	200	49	5	42	....	....	....	....	....	....

88	18	Shilo	59	59	166	128	294	...	...	...	294	46	28	46	...	...	...	...	...	...
		Total	718	745	2049	1799	3848	2	...	2	3850	798	99	688	...	...	...	...	...	...

GUTHRIE COUNTY.

79	33pt32	Bear Grove	53	53	172	132	304	...	...	...	304	71	...	53	...	...	...	...	...	...
78 pt 79	31	Beaver	44	44	135	142	277	...	...	...	277	61	3	50	...	...	...	...	...	...
80	30	Cass																		
pt 79	30 31	Cass	286	286	745	714	1459	1	...	1	1460	327	4	228	...	...	...	...	...	...
pt 80	31	Cass																		
pt 79 80	31 32	Center	124	124	372	328	700	...	...	...	700	168	6	130	...	...	...	...	...	...
81 pt 80	31	Dodge	43	43	102	106	208	2	2	4	212	44	1	44	...	...	...	...	...	...
81	32	Highland	27	27	75	72	147	...	...	...	147	34	...	28	...	...	...	...	...	...
pt 78	30	Jackson																		
pt 78	31	Jackson	154	157	457	404	861	...	...	...	861	183	6	147	...	...	...	...	...	...
pt 79	30	Jackson																		
81	33	Orange	42	42	103	90	193	...	...	...	193	52	.	38	...	...	...	...	...	...
78	30	Penn	77	77	226	201	427	...	...	...	427	98	4	78	...	...	...	...	...	...
81	30	Richland	10	10	24	23	47	...	...	...	47	12	...	9	...	...	...	...	...	...
78	32 33	Thompson	78	78	223	215	438	...	...	...	438	88	...	93	...	...	...	...	...	...
80	33pt32	Union	26	26	83	70	153	...	...	...	153	27	1	24	...	...	...	...	...	...
		Total	964	967	2717	2497	5214	3	2	5	5219	1164	25	922	...	...	...	...	...	...

HAMILTON COUNTY.

89	23	Blairsburg																		
pt 88	23 24	Blairsburg	39	39	92	69	161	...	...	...	161	39	...	36	...	...	...	...	...	...
pt 89	24	Blairsburg																		
pt 88	24'5'6	Boone	214	241	654	612	1266	...	1	1	1267	302	5	250	...	...	...	...	...	2
89	25pt24	Cass	58	60	174	143	317	...	...	...	317	63	2	...	...	...	...	...	...	...
86	25	Clear Lake	10	9	24	29	53	...	...	...	53	8	1	10	...	...	...	...	...	...
86	24	Ellsworth	29	29	81	78	159	...	...	...	159	22	15	21	...	...	...	...	...	...
89	26	Fremont	54	57	148	148	296	1	...	1	297	70	...	61	...	1	...	...	...	...
87	25pt24	Hamilton	79	80	235	217	452	...	...	...	452	103	...	85	...	...	...	...	...	...
87	23pt24	Lyon	23	23	71	50	121	...	...	...	121	23	...	15	...	...	...	...	...	...
86	26pt87	Marion	91	91	267	224	491	...	...	...	491	98	21	80	...	...	...	...	...	...
pt 88	23 24	Rose Grove	14	14	32	33	65	...	...	...	65	15	1	10	...	...	...	...	...	...

HAMILTON COUNTY—Continued.

No. of Township.	Range.	Names of Townships, Towns, and Cities.	No. of Dwelling Houses	No. of Families.	No. of White Males.	No. of White Females.	Total White Population	No. of Colored Males.	No. of Colored Females	Total Colored Population.	Total Population.	No. entitled to Vote.	No. of Foreigners not Naturalized.	No. of Militia.	No. of Blind not in Asylum, Jan. 1, 1869.	No. of Deaf and Dumb not in Asy. Jan. 1, '69	No. of Insane not in Hospital, Jan. 1, 1869	No. of Colleges, Academies and Universities	No. of Teachers in Colleges, Universities, etc.	No. of Students in Colleges, Universities, etc.
......86	23	Scott..............	35	35	92	98	190	....	....	....	190	28	19	18	....	....	....	....	....	....
pts 87 88	26	Webster............	120	122	363	332	695	....	....	....	695	145	2	91	1	....	....	....	....	....
....	......	Total	766	800	2233	2033	4266	1	1	2	4268	916	66	677	1	1	....	....	....	2

HANCOCK COUNTY.

No. of Township.	Range.	Names of Townships, Towns, and Cities.	No. of Dwelling Houses	No. of Families.	No. of White Males.	No. of White Females.	Total White Population	No. of Colored Males.	No. of Colored Females	Total Colored Population.	Total Population.	No. entitled to Vote.	No. of Foreigners not Naturalized.	No. of Militia.	No. of Blind not in Asylum, Jan. 1, 1869.	No. of Deaf and Dumb not in Asy. Jan. 1, '69	No. of Insane not in Hospital, Jan. 1, 1869	No. of Colleges, Academies and Universities	No. of Teachers in Colleges, Universities, etc.	No. of Students in Colleges, Universities, etc.
.....94	24, '5'6	Amsterdam																		
...pt 94	23	Amsterdam	32	33	83	86	169	....	....	....	169	42	....	30	....	....	....	....	....	....
...pt 95	26	Amsterdam........																		
...pt 94	23	Avery............																		
...pt 96	26	Avery............	16	16	38	27	65	....	....	....	65	19	...	11	....	....	....	...	....	....
......95	23, '4'5	Avery																		
...pt 97	23	Ellington..........																		
...pt 96	26	Ellington	40	40	122	106	228	....	....	....	228	49	....	42	....	....	....	....	....	....
......96	23, '4'5	Ellington																		
...pt 97	23	Madison..........																		
...pt 96	26	Madison	22	22	52	58	110	....	....	....	110	22	....	20	...	....	....	....	....	....
......96	24, '5'6	Madison																		
....	......	Total..........	110	111	295	277	572	...	....	....	572	132	....	103	..	....	....	....	....	....

HARDIN COUNTY.

No. of Township.	Range.	Names of Townships, Towns, and Cities.	No. of Dwelling Houses	No. of Families.	No. of White Males.	No. of White Females.	Total White Population	No. of Colored Males.	No. of Colored Females	Total Colored Population.	Total Population.	No. entitled to Vote.	No. of Foreigners not Naturalized.	No. of Militia.	No. of Blind not in Asylum, Jan. 1, 1869.	No. of Deaf and Dumb not in Asy. Jan. 1, '69	No. of Insane not in Hospital, Jan. 1, 1869	No. of Colleges, Academies and Universities	No. of Teachers in Colleges, Universities, etc.	No. of Students in Colleges, Universities, etc.
......89	22pt 21	Alden.......	126	128	352	297	649	....	....	....	649	137	15	109	....	....	....	....	....	....
......88	22	Buckeye............	23	23	56	51	107	....	....	....	107	31	....	26	....	....	....	....	.. .	....

88	19	Clay	189	191	488	489	977				977	217	8	139						
87	19	Eldora	320	357	986	829	1815	4	2	6	1821	436	24	347	1					
88	21	Ellis	78	84	238	229	467				467	94		62						
89	19	Etna	220	225	540	545	1085				1085	250	25	195						
86	21 22	Grant	*	*	27	24	51				51	*		15						
pt. 89 89	21 20	Hardin	400	400	971	922	1893	7	8	15	1908	440	33	304	1		1			1
88	20	Jackson	125	129	360	334	694				694	138	18	109						
87	20	Pleasant	145	140	372	315	687				687	150	25	85						
86	20	Providence	208	240	577	575	1152				1152	261	1	209						
87	21 22	Tipton	79	85	237	201	438				438	104	9	83						
86	19	Union	164	175	489	481	970	1		1	971	200		165						
		Total	2077	2177	5693	5292	10985	12	10	22	11007	2458	153	1848	2		1			1

*Not reported.

HARRISON COUNTY.

80	42	Boyer	88	88	264	226	490				490	105	2	81						
79	41	Cass }	33	33	95	87	182				182	35	6	26						
pt 78	42	Cass }																		
pt 79	43	Calhoun	62	62	192	174	366				366	87		69	3					
79	45	Clay	129	129	242	213	455				455	103	6	50						1
78	45	Cincinnati	48	48	165	116	281				281	55		26						
80	41	Douglas	32	32	92	89	181				181	32	11	144						
81	41	Harrison	134	134	364	320	684				684	186	71	34						
pt 80 81	44	Jackson	37	37	79	81	160				160	46		108						
79	42	Jefferson	116	116	361	268	629				629	156	11	14						
81	42	Lincoln	15	15	52	32	84				84	17	11	105						
81	45	Little Sioux }																		
pt 80 81	44	Little Sioux }	174	185	305	261	566				566	120		51						
pt80	45	Little Sioux }																		
pt78	42 43	Lagrange	50	50	154	131	285				285	61	5	110						
pt79 80-1	43	Magnolia	118	120	230	207	437				437	195	3	64			1			
pt 80	45	Morgan	65	65	213	180	393				393	81	4	50						
pt 80	44	Raglan	55	55	159	155	314				314	60	1	250						
78	44pt43	St. John	241	241	712	566	1278	2		2	1280	310	37	72	2					
79	44	Taylor	76	76	238	183	421				421	95	4	93						
78	41pt42	Union	40	37	108	95	203				203	42	4	42						
		Total	1513	1523	4025	3384	7409	2		2	7411	1736	176	1389	5		1			1

HENRY COUNTY.

No. of Township.	Range.	Names of Townships, Towns and Cities.	No. of Dwelling Houses	No. of Families.	No. of White Males.	No. of White Females.	Total White Population	No. of Colored Males.	No. of Colored Females	Total Colored Population.	Total Population.	No. entitled to Vote.	No. of Foreigners not Naturalized.	No. of Militia.	No. of Blind not in Asylum, Jan. 1, 1869.	No. of Deaf and Dumb not in Asy. Jan. 1, '69	No. of Insane not in Hospital, Jan. 1, 1869	No. of Colleges, Academies and Universities	No. of Teachers in Colleges, Universities, etc.	No. of Students in Colleges, Universities, etc.
......70	5	Baltimore..................	185	185	483	505	988	9	9	18	1006	206	8	143	....	....	....	1	2	1
......72	5	Canaan..............	40	40	334	308	642	...	....	...	642	139	6	115	....	1	....	....	....	1
......71	6	Center,exc Mt Pleasant	*	*	1007	991	1998	10	7	17	2015	345	41	220	....	3	....	....	....	....
......70	6	Jackson............	226	227	619	546	1165	11	6	17	1182	256	4	170	....	....	...	1	....	....
......73	7	Jefferson..........	278	279	751	712	1463	..	....	....	1463	306	39	206	....	....	....	....	....	....
......72	6	Marion...............	243	246	666	666	1332	8	7	15	1347	284	10	231	1	1	....	....	....	....
......71	5	New London,exc town	245	..	629	607	1236	11	8	19	1255	314	5	239	....	1	1	....	....	2
......70	... 7	Salem, exc of town. ..	249	261	749	672	1421	4	3	7	1428	315	....	229	....	2	...	1	4	102
......73	5	Scott.................	187	188	522	499	1021	1	....	1	1022	236	4	193	2	....	....	....	....	...
......71	7	Tippecanoe....... .. .	300	308	795	799	1594	11	7	18	1612	315	6	236	....	4	1	....	....	....
......72	7	Trenton........	265	265	732	672	1404	13	17	30	1434	263	20	185	....	....	....	....	....	....
......73	6	Wayne	246	246	621	542	1163	1	1	2	1165	237	18	178	....	....	....	....	....	....
.. in 71	6	Mt. Pleasant, city of..	819	840	2035	2148	4183	129	113	242	4425	968	21	676	....	....	....	3	17	448
.. in 71	5	New London, town of	104	104	223	240	463	1	1	2	465	94	2	61	1	....	....	....	....	....
.. in 70	7	Salem, town of.......	108	108	249	261	510	....	....	....	510	128	....	94	....	....	....	....	....	....
... .	......	Total............	3495	3297	10415	10168	20583	209	179	388	20971	4406	184	3176	4	12	2	6	23	554

* No report.

HOWARD COUNTY.

No. of Township.	Range.	Names of Townships, Towns and Cities.	No. of Dwelling Houses	No. of Families.	No. of White Males.	No. of White Females.	Total White Population	No. of Colored Males.	No. of Colored Females	Total Colored Population.	Total Population.	No. entitled to Vote.	No. of Foreigners not Naturalized.	No. of Militia.	No. of Blind not in Asylum, Jan. 1, 1869.	No. of Deaf and Dumb not in Asy. Jan. 1, '69	No. of Insane not in Hospital, Jan. 1, 1869	No. of Colleges, Academies and Universities	No. of Teachers in Colleges, Universities, etc.	No. of Students in Colleges, Universities, etc.
pt 97 98	14	Afton..............	94	99	189	235	424	....	....	....	424	109	....	72	...	....	....	....	....	....
.... 100	11	Albion..............	109	109	277	249	526	....	....	...	526	119	2	91	...	....	....	....	....	....
.....100	13	Chester..............	50	50	130	116	246	...	....	...	246	52	2	39	1	....	..	...	....	....
.... 100	12	Forest City....	147	154	426	354	780	1	....	1	781	203	11	155	1	....	....	....	...	....
pt 97 88	13	Howard..............	31	31	89	76	165	....	....	....	165	37	3	23	....	....	....	1	2	59

......99	... 12	Howard Centre.......	38	38	107	85	192	...	...	...	192	45	3	39	...	...	...	...	...	...
......99	14	Jamestown..........	51	56	147	125	272	...	...	...	272	52	1	42	...	...	...	...	...	2
pt 97 98	11	New Oregon........	183	183	524	451	975	...	...	...	975	182	38	127	...	...	...	...	...	...
......100	14	Oakdale	20	20	59	50	109	...	...	...	109	27	...	15	...	...	...	...	...	...
pt 97 98	12	Paris.............	40	44	136	105	241	...	...	...	241	50	6	38	...	...	...	...	...	...
......99	13	Saratoga	16	16	46	37	83	...	...	...	83	20	...	15	...	...	...	...	...	...
......99	11	Vernon Springs.......	792	792	602	530	1132	3	...	3	1135	272	19	227	...	...	...	...	...	...
....	.....	Total...........	1571	1592	2732	2413	5145	4	...	4	5149	1173	85	883	2	...	...	1	2	61

HUMBOLDT COUNTY.

......92	 28	Dakota............ }																		
......91	 27	Dakota .... }	89	89	227	227	454	...	...	...	454	94	...	81	...	...	...	...	...	...
......91	 28	Dakota............ }																		
......93	.28 29	Humboldt..........	73	73	204	184	388	...	...	...	388	89	...	68	...	...	...	...	...	...
......92	.29 30	Rutland	44	44	108	93	201	...	...	...	201	53	...	51	...	...	...	...	...	...
......91	.29 30	Spring Vale.........	65	65	186	162	348	...	...	...	348	84	2	64	...	...	...	...	...	...
...92 93	 27	Vernon	67	67	188	169	357	...	...	...	357	75	...	62	...	...	...	...	...	...
......93	 30	Wacousta...........	14	14	32	30	62	...	...	...	62	15	...	14	...	...	...	...	...	...
....	.....	Total...	352	352	945	865	1810	...	...	...	1810	410	2	340	...	...	...	...	...	...

IDA COUNTY.

....	......	Corwin.............	23	23	64	50	114	...	...	...	114	39	...	28	...	...	...	...	...	...
....	......	Douglas	6	6	13	17	30	...	...	...	30	6	...	7	...	...	...	...	...	...
....	.....	Total...	29	29	77	67	144	...	...	...	144	45	...	35	...	...	...	...	...	...

IOWA COUNTY.

...pt 80	10	Amana........... }																		
...pt 81	9	Amana........... }	160	206	636	642	1278	...	...	...	1278	306	104	162	...	...	...	...	...	...
...pt 81	10	Amana........... }																		
pt 81 80	.10 11	Como..............	45	44	115	97	212	...	...	...	212	50	2	28	...	...	...	...	...	2
......78	12	Dayton............	141	143	433	373	806	...	...	...	806	170	9	134	2	...	2	...	...	...
......78	11	English............	295	298	769	772	1541	...	...	...	1541	366	6	229	...	...	...	...	...	...
......78	10	Fillmore..........	176	182	525	495	1020	...	...	...	1020	206	9	165	1	...	...	...	...	...
......78	9	Greene............	172	167	531	445	976	...	...	...	976	178	5	127	...	...	...	...	...	...

IOWA COUNTY--CONTINUED.

No. of Township.	Range.	Names of Townships, Towns, and Cities.	No. of Dwelling Houses	No. of Families.	No. of White Males.	No. of White Females.	Total White Population	No. of Colored Males.	No. of Colored Females	Total Colored Population.	Total Population.	No. entitled to Vote.	No. of Foreigners not Naturalized.	No. of Militia.	No. of Blind not in Asylum, Jan. 1, 1869.	No. of Deaf and Dumb not in Asy. Jan. 1 '69	No. of Insane not in Hospital, Jan. 1, 1869	No. of Colleges, Academies and Universities	No. of Teachers in Colleges, Universities, etc.	No. of Students in Colleges, Universities, etc.
80	12	Hartford	157	154	501	480	981	2		2	983	245	15	191						
pt 80	10	Hilton	73	75	209	171	380				380	77	9	58						
pt 81	11 12	Honey Creek	191	191	545	478	1023				1023	228	...	167						
pt 80	10	Iowa }	137	159	418	387	805				805	160	34	105						
80	9	Iowa }																		
pt 80 81	9 10	Lenox	76	76	237	207	444				444	94	9	69						
79	12	Lincoln	50	59	162	148	310				310	70	7	52			1			
pt 80 81	10 11	Marengo, exc. of town	170	170	488	430	918				918	202	14	153		1				2
79	11	Pilot	84	94	259	223	482				482	98	11	69						
pt 80	11	Sumner	106	106	270	269	539				539	128	8	101						
79	10	Troy	133	132	415	377	792				792	150	14	112						
pt 81	10 11	Washington	104	104	315	259	574				574	124	14	58						
79	9	York	92	92	221	219	440				440	90	8	68						
in 81	10 11	Marengo, town of	329	344	598	613	1211	1	3	4	1215	280	16	200						
		Total	2691	2796	7647	7085	14732	3	3	6	14738	3162	294	2248	3	1	3			4

JACKSON COUNTY.

No. of Township.	Range.	Names of Townships, Towns, and Cities.	No. of Dwelling Houses	No. of Families.	No. of White Males.	No. of White Females.	Total White Population	No. of Colored Males.	No. of Colored Females	Total Colored Population.	Total Population.	No. entitled to Vote.	No. of Foreigners not Naturalized.	No. of Militia.	No. of Blind not in Asylum, Jan. 1, 1869.	No. of Deaf and Dumb not in Asy. Jan. 1 '69	No. of Insane not in Hospital, Jan. 1, 1869	No. of Colleges, Academies and Universities	No. of Teachers in Colleges, Universities, etc.	No. of Students in Colleges, Universities, etc.
86	5 pt 4	Bellevue, exc of town	152	152	492	450	942	2		2	944	160	17	111			1			
85	1	Brandon	208	207	576	500	1076	1		1	1077	230	4	153			1			
86	1	Butler	129	129	381	359	740				740	163	11	89						
84	4	Fairfield	136	136	406	376	782	1	2	3	785	149	12	108						
85	2	Farmers' Creek	290	309	818	800	1618	1		1	1619	331	11	185	2		1			1
pt 84 85	6	Iowa	215	215	533	516	1049				1049	192	44	131						

......85	4	Jackson............	161	161	429	415	844	....	....	....	844	167	21	132	1	....	1	....	....	....
......84	3	Maquoketa, exclusive of town...........	146	147	453	424	877	....	....	....	877	185	6	106	1	....	....	....	....	....
......84	1	Monmouth	180	180	486	455	941	....	....	....	941	203	28	172	....	1	....	....	....	....
......86	2	Otter Creek	158	158	461	427	888	....	....	....	888	181	22	96	....	....	....	....	....	2
......85	3	Perry, exc. of Andrew	131	131	392	345	737	....	....	....	737	168	1	99	....	....	....	....	....	....
......87	3	Prairie Springs.......	182	186	544	499	1043	....	1	1	1044	199	27	121	....	....	....	....	....	....
......86	3	Richland..........	171	180	523	543	1066	1	....	1	1067	196	20	90	....	....	....	....	....	3
......84	2	South Fork	144	144	397	397	794	....	....	....	794	180	8	104	....	....	....	....	....	....
...pt 87	...4 5	Tete Des Morts.......	161	163	492	441	933	....	....	....	933	141	81	98	....	....	....	1	2	7
......84	...6 7	Union, ex. of Sabula..	37	40	123	102	225	....	....	....	225	44	15	26	....	....	....	....	....	....
...pt 84	5	Van Buren..........	191	191	519	495	1014	....	....	....	1014	209	41	153	....	....	....	....	....	....
pts 84 85	...5 6	Washington..........	183	188	477	460	937	....	....	....	937	168	25	134	....	....	....	....	....	....
.. In 85	3	Andrew, town of.....	75	75	182	174	356	1	....	1	357	78	5	69	....	....	....	....	....	....
.. In 84	7	Sabula, town of......	189	189	429	388	817	....	....	....	817	177	....	132	....	....	....	....	....	....
.. In 86	4	Bellevue, town of.....	294	294	749	790	1539	2	1	3	1542	338	29	255	....	....	....	....	....	....
.. In 84	3	Maquoketa, town of..	278	278	659	685	1344	1	3	4	1348	287	9	168	....	....	1	....	....	....
....	......	Total........ ...	3812	3853	10521	10041	20562	10	7	17	20579	4146	437	2732	4	1	5	1	2	13

JASPER COUNTY.

......79	18	Buena Vista..........	184	192	520	445	965	..	....	....	965	211	3	174	2	1	5	....	....	....
......81	21	Clear Creek..........	176	176	550	527	1077	1	....	1	1078	207	4	159	1	....	....	....	....	....
.......78	21pt20	Des Moines	378	386	1102	986	2088	2	1	3	2091	485	7	382	....	6	2	....	....	11
...pt 78	.18 19	Elk Creek...........	190	205	560	535	1095	2	....	2	1097	240	8	170	....	....	....	....	....	....
...pt 78	.19 20	Fairview....	439	433	1187	1104	2291	2	....	2	2293	522	15	398	....	....	....	....	....	....
......81	17	Hickory Grove.......	53	55	171	143	314	....	....	....	314	64	....	49	....	1	....	....	....	....
......81	20	Independence........	159	163	438	393	831	....	....	....	831	184	7	147	....	....	1	....	....	....
......80	18	Kellogg.............	217	220	643	585	1228	5	7	12	1240	257	30	201	....	....	....	....	....	18
......78	17	Lynn Grove..........	835	835	677	561	1238	....	....	....	1238	293	4	236	....	....	....	....	....	....
......81	19	Malaka............. Malaka............ }	149	149	449	374	823	....	....	....	823	172	12	135	....	....	....	....	....	....
...pt 80	19																			
......81	18	Mariposa.......	54	54	150	135	285	....	....	....	285	57	8	45	....	....	....	....	....	....
...pt 79	.20 21	Mound Prairie	175	175	493	436	929	1	1	2	931	202	1	168	....	....	....	....	....	....
pt 79 80	19 20	Newton, exc of town..	244	246	706	622	1328	6	3	9	1337	290	9	247	1	1	....	....	....	....
......80	21	Poweshiek	214	214	605	515	1120	....	....	....	1120	252	4	191	....	....	....	....	....	....
pt 78 79	19	Palo Alto	146	149	407	346	753	....	....	....	753	133	7	104	....	....	....	....	....	....
......79	17	Richland...........	125	126	359	304	663	....	....	....	663	148	4	98	....	....	....	....	....	....

JASPER COUNTY—Continued.

No. of Township.	Range.	Names of Townships, Towns, and Cities.	No. of Dwelling Houses	No. of Families.	No. of White Males.	No. of White Females.	Total White Population	No. of Colored Males.	No. of Colored Females	Total Colored Population.	Total population.	No. entitled to Vote.	No. of Foreigners not Naturalized.	No. of Militia.	No. of Blind not in Asylum, Jan. 1, 1869.	No. of Deaf and Dumb not in Asy. Jan. 1, '69	No. of Insane not in Hospital, Jan. 1, 1869	No. of Colleges, Academies and Universities	No. of Teachers in Colleges, Universities, etc	No. of Students in Colleges, Universities, etc.
......80	17	Rock Creek..........	72	78	204	185	389	...	...	...	389	83	...	46	...	...	...	...	...	...
......80	20	Sherman.......... ..	129	129	373	310	683	...	...	...	683	165	4	110	...	...	...	...	...	...
......79	21	Washington..........	75	75	192	146	338	...	...	...	338	80	27	70	...	1	...	...	...	...
....	......	Newton, town of.....	345	345	807	841	1648	15	16	31	1679	382	...	245	...	...	...	...	...	...
....	......	Total	4359	4405	10593	9493	20086	34	28	62	20148	4427	154	3375	4	10	8	...	...	29

JEFFERSON COUNTY.

No. of Township.	Range.	Names of Townships, Towns, and Cities.	No. of Dwelling Houses	No. of Families.	No. of White Males.	No. of White Females.	Total White Population	No. of Colored Males.	No. of Colored Females	Total Colored Population.	Total population.	No. entitled to Vote.	No. of Foreigners not Naturalized.	No. of Militia.	No. of Blind not in Asylum, Jan. 1, 1869.	No. of Deaf and Dumb not in Asy. Jan. 1, '69	No. of Insane not in Hospital, Jan. 1, 1869	No. of Colleges, Academies and Universities	No. of Teachers in Colleges, Universities, etc	No. of Students in Colleges, Universities, etc.
......73	10	Black Hawk..... ..	163	162	509	468	977	...	...	...	977	211	2	164	...	...	2	...	...	...
......72	9	Buchanan............	242	251	700	670	1370	1	...	1	1371	297	7	198	...	1	1	...	...	1
......71	9	Cedar	142	152	347	357	704	10	9	19	723	204	18	78	...	...	...	...	...	...
......71	11	Des Moines..........	199	198	556	589	1145	1	1	2	1147	242	2	158	1	...	...	...	...	...
72 pt 71	10	Fairfield	268	298	807	805	1612	...	...	...	1612	334	...	197	...	...	...	1	2	90
...pt 71	10	Liberty	193	196	560	502	1062	...	...	...	1062	244	3	177	...	...	...	...	...	...
......72	8	Lockridge	290	305	857	791	1648	4	2	6	1654	277	68	197	1	1	...	...	...	...
......72	11	Locust Grove........	252	266	715	697	1412	1	...	1	1413	310	3	229	...	1	2	...	1	3
......73	9	Penn	276	276	822	745	1567	3	3	6	1573	340	4	244	1	1	2	...	...	...
......73	11	Polk.................	231	234	643	604	1247	...	...	...	1247	264	4	209	...	...	...	...	...	...
......71	8	Round Prairie........	196	196	541	505	1046	3	2	5	1051	243	6	186	1	...	...	...	...	1
......73	 8	Walnut.........	201	201	587	566	1153	...	...	...	1153	235	18	172	...	...	...	...	...	...
...In 72	10	Fairfield, city of.....	354	361	853	922	1775	6	8	14	1789	411	11	274	...	...	...	...	...	...
....	......	Total	3007	3096	8497	8221	16718	29	25	54	16772	3612	146	2483	4	4	7	1	3	95

JOHNSON COUNTY.

pt 81	6	Big Grove	211	221	671	590	1261	1	1	2	1263	235	21	114					
81	5	Cedar	175	192	495	497	992				992	176	31	119					
5pt 79, 80	7	Clear Creek	120	122	375	336	711				711	134	17	104					7
77	5pt 6	Fremont	163	164	430	399	829				829	172	3	98					
pt 80	5	Graham	156	160	452	462	914	1		1	915	164	12	132			1		6
pt 79	8	Hardin	100	100	267	316	583				583	114	5	98					
79 pt80	6	Iowa City exclusive of city	368	402	1033	1029	2062	21	16	37	2099	348	88	279	1				
pt 81	7	Jefferson	138	145	415	392	807				807	112	57	117					
pt 78	6	Liberty	108	108	351	300	651				651	123	13	85	1				
pt 80 81	7	Madison	128	128	401	387	788				788	156	45	124			1		
pt 81	80	Monroe	140	140	437	432	869				869	128	44	103		3			
pt 80	5	Newport	133	133	345	343	688				688	126	17	90					
80 pt81	8	Oxford	153	156	458	424	882	5	4	9	891	180	15	104					
pt80 81	6 7	Penn	120	120	341	320	661				661	132	2	87	1			1	1	6
78	5pt 6	Pleasant Valley	208	208	584	543	1127	2		2	1129	235	34	180					
79	5	Scott	151	150	430	415	845	3	6	9	854	207	8	138					9
78	7	Sharon	174	174	569	515	1084				1084	200	24	145				1	
pt 79	7 8	Union	107	110	350	310	660				660	136	11	103					
78	8	Washington	156	156	481	409	890	1		1	891	197	13	154		1			
In 79	6	Iowa City, city of	1051	1051	3255	3293	6548	13	22	35	6583	1152	98	743				2	28	658
		Total	4060	4140	12140	11712	23852	47	49	96	23948	4427	558	3117	3	4	2	4	29	686

JONES COUNTY.

85	4	Cass	152	157	439	389	828	4		4	832	190	6	149	1	2			
86	4	Castle Grove	158	158	456	375	831				831	173	42	115					
85	1	Clay	177	177	485	466	951				951	200	2	91					1
84	4	Fairview, exclusive town of Anamosa	210	210	581	566	1147				1147	244	2	161					
83	4	Greenfield	177	177	507	502	1009				1009	200	2	174					
83	2	Hale	157	157	427	417	844				844	145	11	115					
84	3	Jackson	146	146	427	375	802				802	188	2	138					
84	2	Madison	149	151	428	408	836				836	175	5	120					
86	3	Monticello, exc. of town	143	148	445	387	832				832	176	12	101					
83	1	Oxford	186	186	536	425	961	1		1	962	186	28	150					4

JONES COUNTY—Continued.

No. of Township.	Range.	Names of Townships, Towns, and Cities.	No. of Dwelling Houses	No. of Families.	No. of White Males.	No. of White Females.	Total White Population	No. of Colored Males.	No. of Colored Females	Total Colored Population.	Total Population.	No. Entitled to Vote.	No. of Foreigners not Naturalized.	No. of Militia.	No. of Blind not in Asylum, Jan. 1, 1869.	No. of Deaf and Dumb not in Asy. Jan. 1, '69	No. of Insane not in Hospital, Jan. 1, 1869	No. of Colleges, Academies, and Universities	No. of Teachers in Colleges, Universities, etc	No. of Students in Colleges, Universities, etc
86	2	Richland	143	148	435	396	831		1	1	832	180	11	103	1	1				
83	3	Rome	180	192	550	515	1065	4	2	6	1071	233	2	167						
85	2	Scotch Grove	138	138	405	375	780				780	176	2	103		1				
85	3	Wayne	184	148	556	533	1089				1089	222	36	160			5			
86	1	Washington	160	160	509	419	928				928	184	37	88						
84	1	Wyoming	218	219	610	590	1200				1200	285	5			2				
		Anamosa, town of	341	390	928	937	1865	13	15	28	1893	421	7	320						
		Monticello, town of	236	270	612	661	1273	1		1	1274	329	4	177		2				
		Total	3255	3362	9336	8736	18072	23	18	41	18113	3907	216	2432	2	8	5			5

KEOKUK COUNTY.

No. of Township.	Range.	Names of Townships, Towns, and Cities.	No. of Dwelling Houses	No. of Families.	No. of White Males.	No. of White Females.	Total White Population	No. of Colored Males.	No. of Colored Females	Total Colored Population.	Total Population.	No. Entitled to Vote.	No. of Foreigners not Naturalized.	No. of Militia.	No. of Blind not in Asylum, Jan. 1, 1869.	No. of Deaf and Dumb not in Asy. Jan. 1, '69	No. of Insane not in Hospital, Jan. 1, 1869	No. of Colleges, Academies, and Universities	No. of Teachers in Colleges, Universities, etc	No. of Students in Colleges, Universities, etc
77	12	Adams	118	137	405	360	765				765	167	7	135	1	2				
74 pt 75	13	Benton	178	194	574	533	1107				1107	324		193						
75	10	Clear Creek	185	186	496	505	1001				1001	192	23	131						
77	11	English River	217	227	624	606	1230				1230	232	3	198			1			
76 pt 75	11	German	237	238	739	669	1408				1408	260	44	174	2					
74	11	Jackson	232	232	680	645	1325				1325	280	2	219		1	1			
76	10	La Fayette	144	146	413	375	788				788	166	25	117	1					
pt 74 75	11 12	Lancaster	259	272	783	727	1510				1510	301	6	227	2	3	2			
77	10	Liberty	164	166	506	463	969				969	209		155		1				
77	13	Prairie	102	107	303	272	575	1		1	576	135	7	118		1				
74	10	Richland	280	275	765	713	1478				1478	334		253						

...pt 75	.11 12	Sigourney, exclusive of																	
...pt 76	12	town..............	101	100	280	260	540	....	....	....	540	109	....	83	....	....	....	....	....	....
......74	12	Steady Run............	189	207	512	507	1019	....	....	....	1019	210	....	170	....	1	1	....	....	1
......76	12	Van Buren............	164	166	503	473	976	....	....	....	976	180	8	150	1	....	1	....	....	....
......75	13	Warren............	130	132	375	371	746	....	....	....	746	158	1	125	....	....	....	....	....	....
......76	13	Washington............	174	175	483	441	924	....	....	....	924	194	8	104	....	....	....	....	....	....
....	......	Sigourney, town of......	180	190	453	464	917	1	....	1	918	225	4	180	....	....	....	....	....	....
....	......	Total..............	3054	3150	8894	8384	17278	2	....	2	17280	3676	138	2732	7	9	6	....	....	1

KOSSUTH COUNTY.

...96 97	.27 28	Algona..............																	
...98 99	.29 30	Algona..............																	
100 pt 95	.29 30	Algona..............	273	277	718	632	1350	....	....	....	1350	335	....	256	....	....	....	....	....	....
pt 94 95	28'9 30	Cresco..............	52	52	121	123	244	....	....	....	244	53	3	38	....	....	....	....	....	....
......94	.27 28	Irvington..............																	
pt 94 95	27'8'9	Irvington..............	58	58	182	172	354	1	....	1	355	73	12	65	....	....	....	....	....	....
....	......	Total..............	383	387	1021	927	1948	1	....	1	1949	461	15	359	....	....	....	....	....	....

LEE COUNTY.

......69	7	Cedar..............	206	208	622	536	1158	14	10	24	1182	246	3	183	....	....	....	....	....	13
......67	6	Charleston..............	170	170	574	541	1115	....	....	....	1115	234	10	168	....	....	....	....	....	....
......69	4	Denmark..............	180	180	451	459	910	22	22	44	954	218	1	159	1	....	....	1	6	124
......66	6	Des Moines..............																	
...pt 66	...5 7	Des Moines..............	203	203	528	457	985	44	43	87	1072	230	13	176	1	2	....	....	....	....
......68	6	Franklin..............	312	315	924	907	1831	....	1	1	1832	326	37	273	....	....	2	....	....	....
pt 68 69	...2 3	Green Bay..............	111	111	369	305	674	....	....	....	674	135	9	101	1	....	1	....	....	....
......68	7	Harrison..............	183	183	497	462	959	15	9	24	983	279	7	153	1	....	....	....	....	1
......65	5 pt 6	Jackson, excl. of Keokuk	211	211	551	510	1061	67	46	113	1174	242	24	154	....	....	....	....	....	....
......67	5	Jefferson..............	*	206	507	439	946	30	17	47	993	210	....	157	....	....	....	....	....	....
......67	4	Madison..............	*	*	2403	1786	4189	30	23	53	4242	670	34	432	....	....	....	....	....	....
......69	6	Marion..............	253	253	708	629	1337	2	4	6	1343	312	30	205	....	....	....	....	....	....
......66	5	Montrose, exc. of town..	156	156	570	479	1049	13	21	34	1083	295	....	37	....	....	....	....	....	....
......69	5	Pleasant Ridge..........	147	*	450	438	888	4	1	5	893	191	....	131	....	....	....	....	....	....
67 pt 66	7	Van Buren..............	164	164	549	511	1060	....	1	1	1061	184	3	138	1	....	....	....	....	....
......68	4	Washington..............	194	196	571	512	1083	7	5	12	1095	236	11	154	....	....	....	....	....	6
......68	5	West Point, exc. of town	196	193	578	525	1103	4	3	7	1110	235	19	107	1	3	2	....	....	....

LEE COUNTY—CONTINUED.

No. of Township.	Range.	Names of Townships, Towns, and Cities.	No. of Dwelling Houses	No. of Families.	No. of White Males.	No. of White Females.	Total White Population	No. of Colored Males.	No. of Colored Females	Total Colored Population.	Total Population.	No. entitled to Vote.	No. of Foreigners not naturalized.	No. of Militia.	No. of Blind not in Asylum, Jan. 1, 1869.	No. of Deaf and Dumb not in Asy. Jan. 1, '69	No. of Insane not in Hospital.	No. of Colleges, Academies and Universities.	No. of Teachers in Colleges, Universities, etc.	No. of Students in Colleges, Universities, etc.
...In 66	5	Montrose, town of	150	142	392	342	734	....	....	....	734	163	3	5	....	....	....	....	....	....
...In 68	5	West Point, town of	164	164	420	413	833	....	....	....	833	160	9	102	1	1	....	....	....	....
....	......	Total..............	3000	3055	11664	10251	21915	252	206	458	22373	4566	213	2635	7	6	5	1	6	144
...In 65	5	Keokuk city—																		
....	......	First ward..........	184	189	500	577	1077	35	21	56	1133	266	20	222	....	....	1	....	....	....
....	......	Second ward........	306	334	848	783	1631	73	89	162	1793	469	37	383	....	....	1	....	....	....
....	......	Third ward.........	630	654	1900	1803	3703	174	198	372	4075	757	123	571	....	....	....	....	....	....
....	......	Fourth ward........	854	908	2107	2215	4322	218	213	431	4753	870	58	723	....	....	....	....	....	....
....	......	Total city.........	1974	2085	5355	5378	10733	500	521	1021	11754	2362	238	2099	....	....	2	....	....	....
....	......	Total county	4974	5140	17019	15629	32648	752	727	1479	34127	6928	451	4734	7	6	7	1	6	144

* Not reported.

LINN COUNTY.

No. of Township.	Range.	Names of Townships, Towns, and Cities.	No. of Dwelling Houses	No. of Families.	No. of White Males.	No. of White Females.	Total White Population	No. of Colored Males.	No. of Colored Females	Total Colored Population.	Total Population.	No. entitled to Vote.	No. of Foreigners not naturalized.	No. of Militia.	No. of Blind not in Asylum, Jan. 1, 1869.	No. of Deaf and Dumb not in Asy. Jan. 1, '69	No. of Insane not in Hospital.	No. of Colleges, Academies and Universities.	No. of Teachers in Colleges, Universities, etc.	No. of Students in Colleges, Universities, etc.
pt 82 83	6	Bertram..............	158	158	496	401	897	....	....	....	897	209	7	162	....	....	....	....	....	1
......86	5	Bowlder..............	160	160	415	375	790	....	....	....	790	177	11	115	2	....	....	....	....	....
......84	5	Brown................	270	249	757	688	1445	....	....	....	1445	326	3	246	....	....	....	....	....	....
...pt 85	5	Buffalo..............	82	82	269	230	499	....	....	....	499	104	41	72	....	....	....	....	....	....
......83	8	Clinton..............	204	227	593	556	1149	1	....	1	1150	253	25	225	1	....	....	....	....	....
......82	7	College..............	246	250	720	626	1346	....	....	....	1346	235	27	199	....	....	....	1	6	130
......82	8	Fairfax..............	173	173	477	441	918	....	....	....	918	182	44	114	....	....	....	1	1	11
pt 84 85	8	Fayette..............	165	165	445	401	846	....	....	....	846	194	....	155	....	....	....	....	....	....
......82	5	Franklin.............	368	368	1166	1207	2373	10	9	19	2392	508	9	148	....	....	....	1	10	385
... ..86	6	Jackson..............	166	168	459	443	902	....	....	....	902	209	6	161	1	....	....	....	....	....

83	5	Linn	200	200	547	510	1057	....	....	....	1057	239	3	184	....	1	4	....	....	....
85	5 pt 6	Maine	155	155	464	430	894	....	....	....	894	212	11	171	1	....	....	....	....	2
84	6	Marion, exc town of...																		
pt 83	6 7	Marion, exc town of...	347	373	1098	1019	2117	....	....	....	2117	484	361	....	....	....	2	....	....	....
pt 84	7	Marion, exc town of...																		
pt 84	7 8	Monroe	153	153	424	408	832	....	....	....	832	183	....	131	....	....	....	....	....	....
pt 84 85	7 8	Otter Creek	275	279	832	752	1584	....	....	....	1584	302	10	235	1	1	....	....	....	....
pt 82 83	6	Putnam	122	122	380	332	712	1	1	2	714	118	35	92	....	2	....	....	....	....
83	7	Rapids, exc city of Cedar Rapids	307	307	921	865	1786	23	22	45	1831	294	45	14	....	....	....	....	....	....
86	7	Spring Grove	113	121	346	287	633	....	....	....	633	126	3	82	....	2	2	....	....	....
86 pt 85	8	Washington	265	266	713	647	1360	....	....	....	1360	303	7	238	....	....	....	....	....	....
....	....	Marion, town of	327	377	932	952	1884	8	1	9	1893	428	7	337	....	....	....	....	....	....
....	....	Cedar Rapids, city of	593	625	1656	1686	3342	12	13	25	3367	738	108	561	....	....	....	....	....	....
....	....	Total	4849	4978	14110	13256	27366	55	46	101	27467	5824	402	4003	6	6	8	3	17	529

LOUISA COUNTY.

pt 74 75	4 5	Columbus City	395	413	1126	1033	2159	4	2	6	2165	488	12	364	....	....	....	1	....	....
75	4	Concord	145	146	437	415	852	....	....	....	852	182	2	146	1	....	1	....	....	....
pt 73	1 2	Eliot	56	56	175	145	320	....	....	....	320	66	2	52	....	....	....	....	....	....
pt 74	4 5	Elm Grove	116	116	356	301	657	4	2	6	663	148	1	113	....	....	....	....	....	....
pt 74 75	3	Grand View	271	271	699	674	1373	8	7	15	1388	328	13	217	....	....	....	1	3	35
pt 73 74	1 2 3	Jefferson	160	166	438	383	821	12	6	18	839	187	3	130	1	....	....	....	....	6
pt 73 74	4	Marshall	168	175	486	463	949	....	....	....	949	203	3	149	....	....	....	....	....	3
pt 73	3 4	Morning Sun, exc. of town	155	155	467	434	901	....	....	....	901	207	....	172	....	....	....	....	....	....
pt 76	5	Oakland																		
pt 75	4	Oakland	94	94	303	274	577	....	....	....	577	132	2	110	....	....	....	....	....	....
pt 75	5	Oakland																		
pt 74 75	2 3	Port Louisa	147	147	438	397	835	....	....	....	835	188	1	131	....	....	....	....	....	....
pt 75 76	5	Union	97	97	282	269	551	....	....	....	551	128	....	102	....	....	....	....	....	....
pt 73 74	3 4	Wapello, exc. of city of	179	194	538	504	1042	5	2	7	1049	247	....	175	1	....	....	....	....	....
in 74	3	Wapello, city of	156	162	433	412	845	4	2	6	851	180	8	111	....	....	....	....	....	....
in 73	4	Morning Sun, town of	53	54	139	140	279	....	....	....	279	60	....	48	....	....	....	....	....	....
....	....	Total	2192	2246	6317	5844	12161	37	21	58	12219	2744	47	2020	3	....	1	2	3	44

LUCAS COUNTY.

No. of Township.	Range.	Names of Townships, Towns, and Cities.	No. of Dwelling Houses	No. of Families.	No. of White Males.	No. of White Females.	Total White Population	No. of Colored Males.	No. of Colored Females	Total Colored Population.	Total Population.	No. entitled to Vote.	No. of Foreigners not Naturalized.	No. of Militia.	No. of Blind not in Asylum, Jan. 1, 1869.	No. of Deaf and Dumb not in Asy. Jan. 1, '69	No. of Insane not in Hospital, Jan. 1, 1869	No. of Colleges, Academies and Universities	No. of Teachers in Colleges and Universities	No. of Students in Colleges and Universities
71	21	Benton	103	103	309	294	603	....	....	....	603	120	....	79	....	....	....	....	....	....
72	20	Cedar	150	150	383	374	757	....	....	....	757	162	2	127	1	1	....	....	....	....
72	21	Chariton, exc of town	253	257	506	499	1005	7	2	9	1014	205	12	134	....	1	1	....	....	1
73	21	English	149	156	478	420	898	....	....	....	898	165	....	130	....	....	....	....	....	....
72	23	Jackson	76	79	201	200	401	....	....	....	401	80	4	65	....	....	2	....	....	....
73	22	Liberty	93	93	289	261	550	1	....	1	551	105	2	78	....	....	....	....	....	....
73	23	Otter Creek	105	114	328	319	647	....	....	....	647	126	2	107	....	....	....	....	....	....
73	20	Pleasant	97	97	276	280	556	....	....	....	556	107	....	85	....	2	....	....	....	....
71	23	Union	147	123	355	344	699	....	....	....	699	133	....	112	....	....	....	....	....	....
71	22	Warren	134	146	434	385	819	1	....	1	820	169	17	100	....	....	....	....	....	....
71	20	Washington	104	104	316	250	566	....	....	....	566	123	....	101	....	....	....	....	....	....
72	22	Whitebreast	102	102	256	224	480	....	....	....	480	96	3	64	....	....	....	....	....	....
In 72	21	Chariton, town of	220	220	580	573	1153	21	19	40	1193	310	6	236	....	....	....	....	....	....
....	....	Total	1733	1744	4711	4423	9134	30	21	51	9185	1901	48	1418	1	4	3	....	....	1

LYON COUNTY—NOT ORGANIZED.

MADISON COUNTY.

No. of Township.	Range.	Names of Townships, Towns, and Cities.	No. of Dwelling Houses	No. of Families.	No. of White Males.	No. of White Females.	Total White Population	No. of Colored Males.	No. of Colored Females	Total Colored Population.	Total Population.	No. entitled to Vote.	No. of Foreigners not Naturalized.	No. of Militia.	No. of Blind not in Asylum, Jan. 1, 1869.	No. of Deaf and Dumb not in Asy. Jan. 1, '69	No. of Insane not in Hospital, Jan. 1, 1869	No. of Colleges, Academies and Universities	No. of Teachers in Colleges and Universities	No. of Students in Colleges and Universities
76	26	Crawford	116	115	337	316	653	....	....	....	653	130	2	86	2	1	1	....	....	....
76	28	Douglas	169	150	484	435	919	....	....	....	919	207	....	163	....	....	....	....	....	....
74	29	Grand River	96	96	272	260	532	....	....	....	532	98	....	82	1	....	....	....	....	....
76	29	Jackson	87	87	263	239	502	....	....	....	502	115	2	99	....	....	....	....	....	....

......77	27	Jefferson.............	109	113	313	285	598	....	....	....	598	114	....	128	....	....	....	....	....	....
......75	28	Lincoln...............	152	157	446	412	858	....	....	....	858	182	3	113	....	....	....	....	....	....
......77	26	Lee..................	54	55	179	139	318	....	....	....	318	62	....	44	....	....	....	....	....	....
......77	28	Madison...............	134	143	405	383	788	....	....	....	788	170	8	125	....	....	....	....	....	....
......74	28	Monroe................	73	73	217	186	403	....	....	....	403	84	....	68	....	....	....	....	....	....
......74	26	Ohio..................	102	102	293	281	574	....	....	....	574	148	....	95	....	....	....	....	....	....
......77	29	Penn..................	89	92	239	215	454	....	....	....	454	110	....	112	....	....	....	....	....	....
......75	27	Scott.................	183	183	502	488	990	....	....	....	990	214	1	183	1	1	....	....	....	....
......75	26	South.................	150	150	410	373	783	1	....	1	784	166	....	125	....	....	....	....	....	....
......76	27	Union.................	118	118	364	353	717	....	....	....	717	141	....	107	....	....	....	....	1	....
......74	27	Walnut................	125	125	423	367	790	....	....	....	790	165	....	129	1	....	....	....	....	....
......75	29	Webster...............	72	73	194	183	377	....	....	....	377	79	1	67	....	....	....	....	....	....
......76	28	Winterset, city of.....	288	326	807	751	1558	1	1	2	1560	400	....	330	....	....	1	....	....	....
....	......	Total.............	2117	2158	6148	5666	11814	2	1	3	11817	2585	17	2055	5	2	2	....	1	....

MAHASKA COUNTY.

...pt 76	15	Adams.................	121	130	411	368	779	....	....	....	779	172	1	148	1	....	....	....	....	....
......76	17	Black Oak.............	128	127	369	347	716	1	....	1	717	152	9	127	....	....	....	....	....	....
......74	14	Cedar.................	200	200	553	580	1133	7	2	9	1142	246	....	180	....	....	....	....	....	....
......74	16	Des Moines............	191	191	540	515	1055	1	....	1	1056	218	1	164	....	....	2	....	....	....
......74	15	Harrison..............	215	219	596	568	1164	4	3	7	1171	255	8	213	....	....	2	....	....	....
74 pt 75	17	Jefferson.............	191	191	572	495	1067	....	....	....	1067	226	6	186	....	....	....	....	....	....
......76	14	Monroe................	228	227	576	564	1140	....	....	....	1140	257	1	198	....	....	....	....	....	....
......76	16	Madison...............	119	119	392	323	715	2	2	4	719	153	....	98	....	....	....	....	1	....
......75 ...pt 76	.15 16 15	Oskaloosa, exclusive of city.............	468	508	1318	1298	2616	8	2	10	2626	577	1	437	1	....	1	1	....	3
......77	14	Pleasant Grove.........	161	162	496	439	935	....	....	....	935	192	4	120	1	....	1	....	....	13
......77	16	Prairie...............	236	243	658	558	1216	6	5	11	1227	274	46	213	....	....	....	....	....	....
......77	17	Richland..............	271	272	777	665	1442	....	....	....	1442	320	18	268	....	....	....	....	....	4
...pt 75	17	Scott.................	184	193	532	525	1057	....	....	....	1057	212	....	168	....	....	1	....	....	....
......77	15	Union.................	183	183	539	524	1063	6	3	9	1072	220	21	140	....	....	1	....	....	....
......75	14	White Oak.............	173	173	486	498	984	....	....	....	984	202	....	158	....	....	....	....	....	....
...In 75	16	Oskaloosa, city of......	631	631	1374	1490	2864	42	36	78	2942	684	....	572	....	....	....	....	....	....
....	......	Total.............	3700	3769	10189	9757	19946	77	53	130	20076	4360	116	3390	3	....	8	1	1	20

MARION COUNTY.

No. of Township.	Range.	Names of Townships, Towns, and Cities.	No. of Dwelling Houses	No. of Families.	No. of White Males.	No. of White Females.	Total White Population	No. of Colored Males.	No. of Colored Females	No. of Colored Population.	Total Population.	No. entitled to Vote.	No. of Foreigners not Naturalized.	No. of Militia.	No. of Blind not in Asylum, Jan. 1, 1869.	No. of Deaf and Dumb not in Asy. Jan. 1, '69	No. of Insane not in Hospital, Jan. 1, 1869	No. of Colleges, Academies and Universities	No. of Teachers in Colleges, Universities, etc	No. of Students in Colleges, Universities, etc
75 pt 76	18	Clay	230	230	698	626	1324				1324	281		215						
74	21	Dallas	179	179	510	505	1015				1015	220	6	174	1					
75	21	Franklin	105	105	291	271	562				562	125		104						
74	19	Indiana	228	228	593	611	1204	18	13	31	1235	262	3	205	2	3	1			
75 pt 76	19 20	Knoxville. exc. of town	645	647	1897	1808	3705	5	3	8	3713	756	14	572	1	2	1			
77 pt 75 76	18 18	Lake Prairie. exclusive of town of Pella	525	545	1583	1419	3002				3002	545	120	539	1		2	1	5	140
74	18	Liberty	265	273	768	732	1500				1500	322	2	253						
pt 77	21	Perry	89	89	244	232	476				476	104	1	76						6
pt 76	21	Pleasant Grove	231	235	716	638	1354				1354	288	3	219						
pt 76	19	Polk	144	144	449	392	841				841	178	14	142	1					
pt 76 77	20	Red Rock	248	248	692	668	1360				1360	262		194	2		1			
77	19	Summit	232	232	717	663	1380				1380	272	42	212						
pt 76 77	21	Swan	192	192	560	478	1038				1038	224		154		1				
pt 76 77	20	Union	119	119	365	339	704				704	157		121		2				
74	20	Washington	224	229	619	597	1216				1216	271		199			3			
In 75	19	Knoxville, town of	177	177	426	447	873				873	215		144						
In 76	18	Pella, town of	373	398	933	914	1847				1847	350	90	220	1					
		Total	4206	4270	12061	11340	23401	23	16	39	23440	4832	295	3743	9	8	8	1	5	146

MARSHALL COUNTY.

No. of Township.	Range.	Names of Townships, Towns, and Cities.	No. of Dwelling Houses	No. of Families.	No. of White Males.	No. of White Females.	Total White Population	No. of Colored Males.	No. of Colored Females	No. of Colored Population.	Total Population.	No. entitled to Vote.	No. of Foreigners not Naturalized.	No. of Militia.	No. of Blind not in Asylum, Jan. 1, 1869.	No. of Deaf and Dumb not in Asy. Jan. 1, '69	No. of Insane not in Hospital, Jan. 1, 1869	No. of Colleges, Academies and Universities	No. of Teachers in Colleges, Universities, etc	No. of Students in Colleges, Universities, etc
pt 85	19	Bangor	150	150	438	382	820	3	3	6	826	186		143						
83	20	Eden	105	117	319	273	592				592	146		112						

......82	17	Green Castle	110	110	310	267	577	....	....	....	577	141	....	120	1	1	....	....	....	....
85 pt 84	18	Iowa }	270	297	814	766	1580	1	....	1	1581	367	2	239	1	....	1	....	....	....
...pt 85	19	Iowa }																		
......82	18	Jefferson	95	97	303	258	561	....	....	....	561	111	14	83	....	....	....	....	....	....
......83	17	Le Grand	299	303	824	716	1540	....	....	....	1540	335	57	291	....	....	....	1	3	80
......85	20	Liberty	114	124	326	320	646	....	....	....	646	143	3	125	1	1	....	....	....	....
...pt 84	17	Marion	164	154	491	421	912	....	....	....	912	210	5	156	....	....	....	....	....	....
......84	19	Marietta	190	*	510	421	931	1	....	1	932	194	3	140	....	....	....	....	....	....
...pt 84	.17 18	Marshall, exc. of city	161	173	448	436	884	15	10	25	909	197	8	163	1	....	3	....	....	....
......84	20	Minerva	97	97	252	234	486	....	....	....	486	79	....	76	....	....	....	....	....	....
......83	20	State Center, exc. of town	59	59	183	144	327	1	....	1	328	76	3	68	....	....	....	....	....	....
......83	18	Timber Creek	143	144	405	372	777	....	....	....	777	166	4	115	....	....	....	....	....	....
......85	17	Vienna	132	134	357	293	650	....	....	....	650	159	2	134	....	....	....	....	....	....
...82 83	19	Washington	103	112	309	246	555	1	....	1	556	136	22	116	....	....	....	....	....	....
...In 84	18	Marshalltown, city of	508	606	1618	1535	3153	10	9	19	3172	820	57	557	1	1	1	....	....	....
...In 83	20	State Center, town of	74	97	254	215	469	....	....	....	469	115	1	108	....	....	....	....	....	....
....	.....	Total	2774	2774	8161	7299	15460	32	22	54	15514	3581	181	2746	5	3	5	1	3	80

* Not reported.

MILLS COUNTY.

......73	40pt41	Anderson	74	74	206	195	401	....	....	....	401	98	10	163	....	....	....	....	....	....
...pt 72	.42 43	Glenwood	307	280	882	776	1658	1	....	1	1659	320	....	226	1	....	....	....	....	....
......72	40pt41	Indian Creek	68	68	210	188	398	....	....	....	398	88	....	69	....	1	....	....	....	....
...pt 73	.41 42	Ingraham	48	48	135	125	260	....	....	....	260	58	....	44	....	....	....	....	....	....
......71	43	Lyons	167	168	495	441	936	1	....	1	937	205	7	174	....	....	....	....	....	....
...pt 73	.42 43	Oak	104	104	316	269	585	....	....	....	585	111	29	98	....	....	1	....	....	....
...pt 72	.43 44	Platteville	115	115	308	336	644	....	....	....	644	129	....	78	....	....	....	....	....	....
......71	42	Rawles	111	121	321	280	601	....	....	....	601	135	4	91	1	....	....	....	....	....
...pt 72	.41 42	Silver Creek	128	128	421	336	757	....	....	....	757	196	24	168	....	....	....	....	....	....
...pt 73	.43 44	St. Mary	46	46	111	88	199	....	....	....	199	43	1	24	....	....	....	....	....	....
......71	.40 41	White Cloud	80	80	270	224	494	....	....	....	494	123	1	113	....	....	....	....	....	....
....	.....	Total	1248	1232	3675	3258	6933	2	....	2	6935	1506	76	1248	2	1	1	....	....	....

MITCHELL COUNTY.

pt 98 99	16	Burr Oak	75	75	211	173	384	....	....	....	384	91	....	51	....	....	....	....	....	....
pt 97 98	.17 18	Cedar	119	121	331	289	620	....	....	....	620	119	24	81	....	....	....	....	....	1
......98	15	Douglas	49	49	120	118	238	....	....	....	238	48	3	37	....	....	....	....	....	....

MITCHELL COUNTY—Continued.

No. of Township.	Range.	Names of Townships, Towns, and Cities.	No. of Dwelling Houses	No. of Families.	No. of White Males.	No. of White Females.	Total White Population	No. of Colored Males.	No. of Colored Females	Total Colored Population.	Total Population.	No. entitled to Vote.	No. of Foreigners not Naturalized.	No. of Militia.	No. of Blind not in Asylum, Jan. 1, 1869.	No. of Deaf and Dumb not in Asy. Jan. 1, '69	No. of Insane not in Hospital, Jan. 1, 1869	No. of Colleges, Academies and Universities	No. of Teachers in Colleges and Universities	No. of Students in Colleges and Universities
......99	15	Jenkins	91	93	253	220	473				473	105		76						
pt 97 98	.15 16	Lincoln	59	63	164	172	336				336	68	2	51						
pt 98 99	17	Mitchell	166	213	529	504	1033				1033	254	9	192						
.. pt 99	18	Newburg	68	68	204	185	389	1		1	390	46	2	70						
pt 97 98	.16 17	Osage	286	305	842	798	1640	4		4	1644	387	30	298						
.....100	18	Otranto	85	85	253	230	483				483	73	41	36						
......98	18	Rock	51	59	185	128	313				313	66	7	48	1	2				
...pt 99	.17 18	St. Ansgar	91	95	285	236	521				521	108	13	67						
100 pt 99	16	Stacyville	63	65	165	181	346				346	247		53						
.....100	17	Union	41	46	129	117	246				246	52	5	37						
.....100	15	Wayne	47	47	135	126	261				261	60		41						
		Total	1291	1384	3806	3477	7283	5		5	7288	1724	136	1138	1	2				1

MONONA COUNTY.

No. of Township.	Range.	Names of Townships, Towns, and Cities.	No. of Dwelling Houses	No. of Families.	No. of White Males.	No. of White Females.	Total White Population	No. of Colored Males.	No. of Colored Females	Total Colored Population.	Total Population.	No. entitled to Vote.	No. of Foreigners not Naturalized.	No. of Militia.	No. of Blind not in Asylum, Jan. 1, 1869.	No. of Deaf and Dumb not in Asy. Jan. 1, '69	No. of Insane not in Hospital, Jan. 1, 1869	No. of Colleges, Academies and Universities	No. of Teachers in Colleges and Universities	No. of Students in Colleges and Universities
......84	45pt46	Ashton	19	20	36	35	71				71	17	1	8						
...pt 83	.43 44	Belvidere	*	*	87	74	161	9	10	19	180	33	6	16		1				
......84	43	Center	19	20	57	58	115				115	20		15			1			
...pt 85	47	Fairview	21	21	62	47	109				109	17	15	10						
......83	pt44'5'6	Franklin	64	80	186	161	347	1		1	348	91	7	79						
......85	44pt43	Grant	37	37	107	91	198				198	45		32						
pt 83 84	.43 44	Kennebeck	54	55	151	130	281				281	65	3	50						
...pt 85	46	Lake	21	22	71	45	116				116	30	2	25						
...pt 84	46pt47	Lincoln	46	49	113	102	215				215	58	5	41						

......85	42pt43	Maple	48	48	137	119	256	....	....	....	256	60	....	31	....	....	....	....	....	....
......82	.44-45	Sherman	38	38	114	79	193	....	....	....	193	45	9	37	....	....	....	....	....	....
...83 84	42	Soldier	20	20	42	38	80	....	....	....	80	25	....	20	....	....	....	....	....	....
......82	.42-43	Spring Valley	16	16	44	29	73	....	....	....	73	23	2	19	....	....	....	....	....	....
......85	45pt46	West Fork	6	7	19	21	40	....	....	....	40	8	1	6	....	....	....	....	....	....
....	......	Onawa, town of	69	71	206	197	403	1	....	1	404	94	11	67	....	....	1	....	....	....
....	......	Total	478	504	1432	1226	2658	11	10	21	2679	631	62	456	....	1	2	....	....	....

* Not reported.

MONROE COUNTY.

......73	17	Bluff Creek	178	178	513	472	985	....	....	....	985	194	....	137	....	....	1	....	....	2
......73	19	Cedar	130	134	407	379	786	....	....	....	786	146	....	108	....	1	....	....	....	....
......71	18	Franklin	111	111	323	297	620	1	....	1	621	125	8	90	....	....	....	....	....	1
......72	18	Guilford	142	142	453	353	806	....	....	....	806	155	5	85	1	....	1	....	....	....
......71	19	Jackson	140	150	413	392	805	1	....	1	806	134	....	140	....	....	....	....	....	....
......72	16	Mantua	191	191	578	554	1132	1	....	1	1133	194	11	133	....	1	....	....	....	....
......71	17	Monroe	139	147	399	350	749	....	....	....	749	163	3	111	1	1	....	....	....	....
......73	16	Pleasant	186	186	571	498	1069	3	1	4	1073	203	21	147	1	1	....	....	....	5
......72	17	Troy, exc. of Albia	216	216	529	504	1033	15	15	30	1063	242	8	163	1	2	....	....	....	....
......73	18	Union	213	213	592	591	1183	....	....	....	1183	235	....	164	....	....	....	....	....	....
......71	16	Urbana	151	151	440	409	849	....	....	....	849	174	....	135	....	1	....	....	....	....
......72	16	Wayne	118	118	329	323	652	....	....	....	652	123	30	91	....	....	....	....	....	....
...In 72	17	Albia, town of	256	271	639	616	1255	15	14	29	1284	328	....	280	....	....	....	....	....	5
....	......	Total	2171	2208	6186	5738	11924	36	30	66	11990	2416	86	1784	4	7	2	....	....	13

MONTGOMERY COUNTY.

......73	36	Douglas	67	67	192	183	375	....	....	....	375	74	9	69	....	1	....	....	....	....
73 pt 72	37	Frankfort	47	47	119	118	237	....	....	....	237	51	1	37	....	....	....	....	....	....
...pt 71	.37 38	Grant	40	40	103	88	191	....	....	....	191	51	....	38	....	....	....	....	....	....
...pt 71	.36 37	Jackson	78	78	226	198	424	....	....	....	424	92	....	75	....	....	....	....	....	....
73 pt 72	39	Lincoln	13	13	48	41	89	....	....	....	89	16	....	13	....	....	....	....	....	....
......72	38	Red Oak }																		
...pt 71	.37 38	Red Oak }	157	157	442	378	820	....	....	....	820	210	....	154	....	....	....	....	....	....
...pt 72	.37 38	Red Oak }																		
......73	38	Sherman	34	34	100	84	184	....	....	....	184	42	....	37	....	....	1	....	....	....

MONTGOMERY COUNTY.--Continued

No. of Township.	Range.	Names of Townships, Towns and Cities.	No. of Dwelling Houses	No. of Families.	No. of White Males.	No. of White Females.	Total White Population	No. of Colored Males.	No. of Colored Females	Total Colored Population.	Total Population.	No. entitled to Vote.	No. of Foreigners not Naturalized.	No. of Militia.	No. of Blind not in Asylum, Jan. 1, 1869.	No. of Deaf and Dumb not in Asy. Jan. 1. '69	No. of Insane not in Hospital, Jan. 1, 1869	No. of Colleges, Academies and Universities	No. of Teachers in Colleges, Universities, etc	No. of Students in Colleges, Universities, etc
......72	36	Washington																		
...pt 71	.36 37	Washington..........	52	58	178	156	334	....	....	....	334	70	....	59	....	....	....	....	....	....
...pt 72	.36 37	Washington																		
71 pt 72	39	West	45	45	133	105	238	....	....	....	238	55	....	45	....	....	....	....	....	....
....	......	Total............	533	539	1541	1351	2892	....	....	....	2892	661	10	527	....	1	1	....	....	....

MUSCATINE COUNTY.

No. of Township.	Range.	Names of Townships, Towns and Cities.	No. of Dwelling Houses	No. of Families.	No. of White Males.	No. of White Females.	Total White Population	No. of Colored Males.	No. of Colored Females	Total Colored Population.	Total Population.	No. entitled to Vote.	No. of Foreigners not Naturalized.	No. of Militia.	No. of Blind not in Asylum, Jan. 1, 1869.	No. of Deaf and Dumb not in Asy. Jan. 1. '69	No. of Insane not in Hospital, Jan. 1, 1869	No. of Colleges, Academies and Universities	No. of Teachers in Colleges, Universities, etc	No. of Students in Colleges, Universities, etc
...pt 76	...3w	Bloomington } exc. of																		
......76	...2w	Bloomington } Musca-	276	264	737	685	1422	4	4	8	1430	328	8	207	2	....	....	....	....	....
......77	...2w	Bloomington } tine																		
...pt 76	...4w	Cedar..................	79	80	230	224	454	....	....	...	454	106	1	77	....	....	....	....	....	....
......78	....1e	Fulton	206	202	682	533	1215	1	....	1	1216	191	71	203	....	1	....	....	....	7
......78	...3w	Goshen	238	240	700	654	1354	....	....	....	1354	316	9	236	1	1	1	....	....	....
...pt 77	...3w	Lake..................	145	146	449	385	834	7	2	9	843	150	14	94	....	....	....	....	....	3
...pt 78	...2w	Moscow, exc. of town....	123	131	373	322	695	....	....	....	695	148	12	111	....	....	....	....	....	....
...pt 77	....1e	Montpelier	122	122	405	334	739	....	....	....	739	146	19	112	....	....	....	....	....	....
...pt 76	...4w	Orono..................	51	53	164	141	305	....	....	....	305	54	....	58	....	....	....	....	....	....
...pt 77	. 3 4w	Pike	114	113	323	287	610	....	....	....	610	136	5	100	....	....	....	3	1	....
...pt 76	...3w	Seventy-Six............	162	165	434	458	892	....	....	....	892	192	....	148	....	1	1	....	....	....
pt 77 78	...1w	Sweetland..............	265	271	735	690	1425	1	....	1	1426	294	27	192	....	....	....	....	....	....
......78	...4w	Wapsinonoc exc. W. Lib.	152	152	490	439	929	8	5	13	942	204	17	154	....	1	....	....	....	....
...pt 78	. 1 2w	Wilton, exc. of town....	199	201	604	533	1137	4	3	7	1144	216	38	201	....	1	....	1	6	140
...In 78	...1w	Wilton, town of.........	187	198	507	502	1009	....	....	....	1009	257	11	187	....	....	....	....	....	....

...In 78	4	West Liberty, town of...	169	158	388	379	767	1	....	1	768	209	3	155	....	....	....	....	....	....
...In 78	2	Moscow, town of........	70	77	165	166	331	....	....	....	331	66	7	36	....	1	1	....	....	....
....	......	Total...............	2551	2573	7386	6732	14118	26	14	40	14158	3013	242	2271	3	6	3	4	7	150
...In 77	...2 w	Muscatine, city of—																		
....	......	1st ward............	702	674	2112	2076	4188	38	33	76	4264	765	139	442	2	1	....	....	....	....
....	......	2d ward............	397	381	1239	1154	2393	25	22	47	2440	508	78	376	2	1	1	1	4	54
....	......	3d ward............	557	505	1705	1716	3421	28	25	53	3474	582	35	425	....	....	....	....	....	....
....	......	Total city.........	1656	1560	5056	4946	10002	91	85	176	10178	1855	252	1243	4	2	1	1	4	54
....	......	Total county........	4207	4133	12442	11678	24120	117	99	216	24336	4868	494	3514	7	8	4	5	11	204

O'BRIEN COUNTY.

...94-97	.39-42	Waterman.............	7	12	30	21	51	....	....	....	51	15	1	13	....	....	....	....	....	....

OSCEOLA COUNTY—NOT ORGANIZED.

PAGE COUNTY.

......67	37	Amity.................	160	160	438	381	819	15	20	35	854	134	6	131	....	....	....	1	3	75
......67	36	Buchanan..............	135	135	456	434	890	....	....	....	890	161	....	140	....	....	....	....	....	....
......70	37	Douglas...............	50	55	187	154	341	....	....	....	341	63	....	54	....	....	....	....	....	....
......68	36	East River............	157	157	442	435	877	....	....	....	877	162	1	143	....	....	....	....	....	....
......70	38	Fremont...............	31	31	86	80	166	....	....	....	166	31	....	25	....	....	....	....	....	....
......68	37	Harlan................	120	120	304	270	574	5	8	13	587	130	13	119	....	....	....	....	....	....
......68	.38 39	Lincoln...............	71	77	228	221	449	3	....	3	452	93	8	73	....	....	....	....	....	....
...pt 69	36	Nebraska..............	124	124	341	327	668	15	6	21	689	155	....	132	....	....	....	....	....	....
......69	37pt36	Nodaway...............	289	300	789	731	1520	33	43	76	1596	359	6	266	1	....	1	....	....	....
......70	39	Pierce................	37	47	104	107	211	....	....	....	211	46	....	37	....	....	....	....	....	....
......69	.38 39	Tarkio................	47	47	145	125	270	1	....	1	271	60	....	48	....	....	....	....	....	....
......70	36	Valley................	91	91	282	251	533	....	....	....	533	113	....	88	....	....	....	....	....	....
......67	.38 39	Washington............	66	67	209	166	375	1	....	1	376	72	6	46	....	....	1	....	....	....
....	......	Total.................	1378	1411	4011	3682	7693	73	77	150	7843	1579	40	1302	1	....	2	1	3	75

PALO ALTO COUNTY.

No. of Township.	Range.	Names of Townships, Town, and Cities.	No. of Dwelling Houses	No. of Families.	No. of White Males.	No. of White Females.	Total White Population	No. of Colored Males.	No. of Colored Females.	Total Colored Population.	Total Population.	No. entitled to Vote.	No. of Foreigners not Naturalized.	No. of Militia.	No. of Blind not in Asylum, Jan. 1, 1869.	No. of Deaf and Dumb not in Asy. Jan. 1, '69	No. of Insane not in Hospital, Jan. 1, 1869	No. of Colleges, Academies and Universities	No. of Teachers in Colleges, Universities, etc.	No. of Students in Colleges, Universities, etc.
......97	.31–34	Emmetsburg..........																		
......96	.31 32	Emmetsburg..........	36	36	104	92	196	....	....	....	196	42	2	23	....	....	....	....	....	....
...pt 96	.33 34	Emmetsburg..........																		
......95	.33 34	Great Oak............																		
...pt 96	33	Great Oak............	13	13	44	41	85	....	....	....	85	15	....	15	....	....	....	....	....	....
...pt 96	34	Great Oak............																		
......95	32	Nevada..............																		
...pt 94	34	Nevada..............	11	11	27	26	53	....	....	....	53	10	2	8	....	....	....	....	....	....
......94	.32 33	Rush Lake............																		
...pt 94	31	Rush Lake............	16	16	33	28	61	....	....	....	61	18	....	16	....	....	....	....	....	....
...pt 94	34	Rush Lake............																		
.95 pt 94	31	West Bend..............	35	35	83	57	140	....	....	....	140	33	1	23	....	....	....	....	....	....
....	......	Total................	111	111	291	244	535	....	....	....	535	118	5	85	....	....	....	....	....	....

PLYMOUTH COUNTY.

No. of Township.	Range.	Names of Townships, Town, and Cities.	No. of Dwelling Houses	No. of Families.	No. of White Males.	No. of White Females.	Total White Population	No. of Colored Males.	No. of Colored Females.	Total Colored Population.	Total Population.	No. entitled to Vote.	No. of Foreigners not Naturalized.	No. of Militia.	No. of Blind not in Asylum, Jan. 1, 1869.	No. of Deaf and Dumb not in Asy. Jan. 1, '69	No. of Insane not in Hospital, Jan. 1, 1869	No. of Colleges, Academies and Universities	No. of Teachers in Colleges, Universities, etc.	No. of Students in Colleges, Universities, etc.
....	......	Lincoln.................	32	32	94	85	179	....	....	....	179	45	....	37	....	....	....	....	....	....

POCAHONTAS COUNTY.

No. of Township.	Range.	Names of Townships, Town, and Cities.	No. of Dwelling Houses	No. of Families.	No. of White Males.	No. of White Females.	Total White Population	No. of Colored Males.	No. of Colored Females.	Total Colored Population.	Total Population.	No. entitled to Vote.	No. of Foreigners not Naturalized.	No. of Militia.	No. of Blind not in Asylum, Jan. 1, 1869.	No. of Deaf and Dumb not in Asy. Jan. 1, '69	No. of Insane not in Hospital, Jan. 1, 1869	No. of Colleges, Academies and Universities	No. of Teachers in Colleges, Universities, etc.	No. of Students in Colleges, Universities, etc.
......92	31	Clinton..............																		
...pt 91	31	Clinton..............	9	10	21	17	38	....	....	....	38	13	....	13	....	....	....	....	....	....
...pt 91	32	Clinton..............																		

......91	.33 34	Des Moines.........																		
......92	.32-34	Des Moines.........	39	42	92	84	176				176	42		37						
......93	31	Des Moines.........																		
.90 pt91	.31-34	Lizard..............	56	61	178	156	334				334	65	4	57						
......93	.32-34	Powhattan..........	22	24	50	39	89				89	16	6	16						
....	......	Total...............	126	137	341	296	637				637	136	10	123						

POLK COUNTY.

...pt 78	23	Allen...............	159	159	452	426	878	3	3	6	884	174	1	131						
...pt 78	.24 25	Bloomfield...........	155	157	440	414	854	3	3	6	860	171	2	122						
......79	22	Beaver..............	157	157	454	358	812	1		1	813	185		169						2
pt 77 78	2	Camp...............	253	256	706	710	1416				1416	304	1	249						
......79	23	Deleware............	375	373	435	378	813	3	2	5	818	170	11	226						
...pt 78	24	Des Moines, (see city of)																		
......80	23	Douglass............	83	91	250	209	459				459	100	3	85						
......81	23	Elkhart.............	128	128	340	314	654				654	128	15	102	1	1				
......80	22	Franklin............	91	94	271	270	541				541	112	7	74	1	1	1			1
...pt 78	.22 23	Four Mile...........	115	115	297	259	556				556	110		83						
pt 79 80 81	.24 25	Jefferson...........	128	131	385	353	738	6	3	9	747	169	5	150						
pt 78 79	.23 24	Lee, exc. three wards in city of Des Moines....	135	135	397	359	756	5	5	10	766	178	7	134						
......81	24	Madison............																		
...pt 81	25	Madison............	399	418	1221	1113	2334	1		1	2335	438	49	390	2	1				
...pt 80	.24 25	Madison............																		
pt 79 80	24	Saylor..............	184	184	533	465	998	5	5	10	1008	230	7	171						
...pt 79	24	Valley..............	98	98	309	247	556	1		1	557	114	1	107	1					
...pt 81	22	Washington..........	74	74	208	181	389				389	87		69						
pt 78 79	.24 25	Walnut..............	210	210	661	553	1214	6	6	12	1226	241	21	200						
....	......	Total..............	2744	2780	7359	6609	13968	34	27	61	14029	2911	130	2462	5	3	1			3
..In 78	24	Des Moines, city of, in Des Moines Township																		
....	......	1st ward...........	198	213	637	674	1311	18	23	41	1352	321		279						
....	......	2d ward............	285	285	1293	1117	2410	11	8	19	2429	630	7	588						
....	......	3d ward............	413	415	1107	1203	2310	19	18	37	2347	519		462						
....	......	4th ward...........	268	272	800	807	1607	2	2	4	1611	210	1	55						
....	......	Total west side......	1164	1185	3837	3801	7638	50	51	101	7739	1680	8	1384						

POLK COUNTY—CONTINUED.

No. of Township.	Range.	Names of Townships, Towns, and Cities.	No. of Dwelling Houses	No. of Families.	No. of White Males.	No. of White Females.	Total White Population	No. of Colored Males.	No. of Colored Females.	Total Colored Population.	Total Population.	No. entitled to Vote.	No. of Foreigners not Naturalized.	No. of Militia.	No. of Blind not in Asylum, Jan. 1, 1869.	No of Deaf and Dumb not in Asy. Jan. 1, '69	No. of Insane not in Hospital, Jan. 1, 1869	No. of Colleges, Academies and Universities	No. of Teachers in Colleges, Universities, etc	No. of Students in Colleges, Universities, etc
...in 78	24	Des Moines, city of, in Lee township—																		
....	......	5th ward	231	263	667	717	1384	12	14	26	1410	272	10	213	....	2	....	....	....	....
....	......	6th ward	203	207	949	850	1799	....	....	....	1799	289	7	229	....	....	....	....	....	....
....	......	7th ward	223	261	769	590	1359	37	35	72	1431	202	72	148	....	....	....	....	....	....
....	......	Total east side......	657	731	2385	2157	4542	49	49	98	4640	763	89	590	....	2	....	....	....	....
....	......	Total county	4565	4696	13581	12567	26148	133	127	260	26408	5354	227	4436	5	5	1	....	....	3

POTTAWATTAMIE COUNTY.

No. of Township.	Range.	Names of Townships, Towns, and Cities.	No. of Dwelling Houses	No. of Families.	No. of White Males.	No. of White Females.	Total White Population	No. of Colored Males.	No. of Colored Females.	Total Colored Population.	Total Population.	No. entitled to Vote.	No. of Foreigners not Naturalized.	No. of Militia.	No. of Blind not in Asylum, Jan. 1, 1869.	No of Deaf and Dumb not in Asy. Jan. 1, '69	No. of Insane not in Hospital, Jan. 1, 1869	No. of Colleges, Academies and Universities	No. of Teachers in Colleges, Universities, etc	No. of Students in Colleges, Universities, etc
.....77	.42 43	Bloomer...............	69	75	197	197	394	....	....	....	394	67	12	49	....	....	....	....	....	....
......75	39	Center...............																		
...pt 76	39	Center...............	77	77	229	181	410	....	....	....	410	81	....	65	....	1	1	....	....	1
pt 75 76	40	Center...............																		
......76	43	Crescent.............																		
...pt 76	42	Crescent.............	184	184	483	435	918	....	....	....	918	170	42	125	....	....	....	....	....	....
...pt 76	44	Crescent.............																		
......74	39	Grove	48	61	147	140	287	3	2	5	292	58	1	40	....	....	....	....	....	....
......75	41	James................																		
...pt 75	40	James................	33	33	116	90	206	....	....	....	206	47	1	39	....	....	....	....	....	....
...pt 76	40	James................																		
...76 77	38	Knox.................																		
......77	38	Knox.................	92	92	305	255	560	....	....	....	560	131	2	113	....	1	....	....	....	....
...pt 76	.39 40	Knox.................																		

......75 74 pt 74 75	.42 43 ....43 44	Kane, exc city of Council Bluffs	181	185	553	484	1037	....	1	1	1038	235	24	52	....	....	....	....	....	....
......74	40	Macedonia	38	40	112	111	223	....	....	....	223	36	2	26	....	....	....	....	....	....
......77	44	Rockford	107	107	324	272	596	....	....	....	596	152	....	113	....	....	....	....	2	....
......74	.41 42	Silver Creek	27	27	78	66	144	....	....	....	144	30	....	23	....	....	....	....	1	1
...74 75	38	Walnut Creek	48	49	126	126	252	....	....	....	252	52	....	34	....	....	....	....	....	....
......76 ......77 ...pt 76	....41 ....41 42	York York York	26	26	76	72	148	....	....	....	148	28	5	22	....	....	....	....	....	....
......	......	Total	930	956	2746	2429	5175	3	3	6	5181	1087	89	701	....	2	1	....	3	2
.. In 75	.43 44	Council Bluffs, city of—																		
......	......	1st ward	194	200	478	430	908	....	....	....	908	189	45	155	....	....	....	....	....	....
......	......	2d ward	341	350	895	688	1583	11	11	22	1605	398	86	383	....	....	....	....	....	....
......	......	3d ward	167	171	496	430	926	3	....	3	929	236	21	229	....	....	....	....	....	....
......	......	4th ward	317	320	998	796	1794	6	4	10	1804	442	31	395	....	....	....	....	....	....
......	......	5th ward	134	137	277	268	545	1	1	2	547	127	14	142	....	1	....	....	5	110
......	......	Total city	1153	1178	3144	2612	5756	21	16	37	5793	1392	197	1304	....	1	....	....	5	110
......	......	Total county	2083	2134	5890	5041	10931	24	19	43	10974	2479	286	2005	....	3	1	....	8	112

POWESHIEK COUNTY.

......80	14	Bear Creek	230	230	719	689	1408	2	....	2	1410	288	4	223	....	....	1	....	....	....
......81	16	Chester	69	69	199	165	364	2	....	2	366	100	....	64	....	....	....	....	....	....
......78	13	Deep River	134	134	416	340	756	2	....	2	758	156	9	136	1	....	....	....	....	....
......80	16	Grinnell, exc. town	120	120	340	274	614	2	....	2	616	142	4	115	....	....	....	....	1	7
......78	14pt15	Jackson, exclusive town of Montezuma	183	183	547	511	1058	2	2	4	1062	217	....	187	....	....	....	....	....	....
......81	13	Jefferson	124	124	442	358	800	....	....	....	800	155	5	142	1	3	1	....	....	....
......79	13	Lincoln	100	100	298	274	572	....	....	....	572	132	13	89	....	....	....	....	....	....
......81	14	Madison	111	111	349	288	637	....	....	....	637	145	16	122	....	....	....	....	....	....
......80	15	Malcom	110	110	310	254	564	2	....	2	566	130	18	114	....	....	....	....	....	....
......79	15	Pleasant	100	100	286	265	551	6	3	9	560	127	1	102	....	3	....	....	....	....
......79	14	Scott	78	78	235	212	447	....	....	....	447	89	13	66	....	....	....	....	....	....
......78	16	Sugar Creek	106	106	433	358	791	....	....	....	791	152	....	57	....	....	....	....	....	....
......81	15	Sheridan	58	58	196	161	357	1	....	1	358	81	1	69	....	....	....	....	....	....
...pt 78	15	Union	144	144	506	475	981	1	....	1	982	157	3	94	....	....	....	....	....	....

POWESHIEK COUNTY—CONTINUED.

No. of Township.	Range.	Names of Townships, Towns, and Cities.	No. of Dwelling Houses	No. of Families.	No. of White Males.	No. of White Females.	Total White Population	No. of Colored Males.	No. of Colored Females	Total Colored Population.	Total Population.	No. entitled to Vote.	No. of Foreigners not Naturalized.	No. of Militia.	No. of Blind not in Asylum, Jan. 1, 1869.	No. of Deaf and Dumb not in Asy. Jan. 1, '69	No. of Insane not in Hospital, Jan. 1, 1869.	No. of Colleges, Academies and Universities.	No. of Teachers in Colleges, Universities, etc.	No. of Students in Colleges, Universities, etc.
......79	16	Washington............	94	94	312	284	596	2	1	3	599	122	7	80	....	1	1	....	....	....
......80	13	Warren................	122	122	364	288	652	1	....	1	653	126	4	102	....	....	1	....	....	1
...In 80	16	Grinnell, town of........	220	220	604	641	1245	18	14	32	1277	270	21	212	....	....	....	1	8	290
...In 78	14	Montezuma, town of	98	98	240	241	481	....	1	1	482	115	2	90	....	....	....	....	....	....
....	......	Total...............	2201	2201	6796	6078	12874	41	21	62	12936	2704	121	2064	2	7	4	1	9	298

RINGGOLD COUNTY.

No. of Township.	Range.	Names of Townships, Towns, and Cities.	No. of Dwelling Houses	No. of Families.	No. of White Males.	No. of White Females.	Total White Population	No. of Colored Males.	No. of Colored Females	Total Colored Population.	Total Population.	No. entitled to Vote.	No. of Foreigners not Naturalized.	No. of Militia.	No. of Blind not in Asylum, Jan. 1, 1869.	No. of Deaf and Dumb not in Asy. Jan. 1, '69	No. of Insane not in Hospital, Jan. 1, 1869.	No. of Colleges, Academies and Universities.	No. of Teachers in Colleges, Universities, etc.	No. of Students in Colleges, Universities, etc.
...67 68	28	Athens................	72	72	197	174	371	....	....	....	371	78	....	50	....	1	....	....	....	....
......68	31	Benton................	48	52	146	141	287	....	....	....	287	62	2	51	....	....	....	....	....	....
......67	31	Clinton...............	59	58	160	166	326	....	....	....	326	66	....	48	....	....	....	....	....	....
......70	30	Jefferson	76	76	219	220	439	....	....	....	439	87	2	74	1	....	....	....	....	....
67 pt 68	29	Lott's Creek...........	99	104	325	285	610	....	....	....	610	111	....	96	....	....	1	....	....	....
......69	29	Liberty...............	39	39	113	109	222	....	....	....	222	42	....	34	....	....	....	....	....	....
67 pt 68	30	Middle Fork...........	60	60	193	195	388	....	....	....	388	68	3	59	....	....	....	....	....	....
......69	28	Monroe................	34	34	83	117	200	....	....	....	200	41	1	38	....	....	....	....	....	....
...pt 68	.29 30	Mount Ayr............	118	125	331	336	667	3	2	5	672	146	2	114	....	....	1	....	....	....
...69 70	31	Platt..................	72	71	206	206	412	....	....	....	412	84	....	71	....	....	....	....	....	....
......70	.28 29	Sand Creek............	102	158	318	305	623	....	....	....	623	131	....	89	....	....	....	....	....	....
......69	30	Washington	74	80	243	236	479	....	....	....	479	80	9	68	....	....	....	....	....	....
....	......	Total...............	853	929	2534	2490	5024	3	2	5	5029	996	19	792	1	1	2	....	....	....

SAC COUNTY.

89 pt 88	.35 38	Douglas	30	29	77	75	152				152	39		27						
pt 87 88	.35 38	Jackson	55	53	148	159	307				307	77		61						
86 pt 87	.35 38	Sac	61	61	187	194	381				381	82		67						
		Total	146	143	412	428	840				840	198		155						

SCOTT COUNTY.

80	2	Allen's Grove	98	102	330	271	601	1		1	602	101	40	112						
78	2	Blue Grass	226	234	710	611	1321				1321	204	164	248		1				
n ⅔ 77	2	Buffalo, exc. of town	176	181	553	479	1032	2		2	1034	212	40	196	1					
80	4	Butler	157	157	464	419	883				883	159	48	105						
79	1	Cleona	133	138	435	319	754				754	117	105	186						
78	.3 pt 4	Davenport, excl of city	514	514	1683	1513	3196	8	5	13	3209	495	137	364	1	5	3			5
79	2	Hickory Grove	197	197	645	566	1211				1211	183	142	250						
s ⅜ 79	5	Leclaire, exc of town																		
s ⅜ e ⅙ 79	4	Leclaire, exc of town	153	153	452	389	841	3	2	5	846	201	13	136						
e ¾ 78	5	Leclaire, exc of town																		
80	1	Liberty	194	205	612	509	1121				1121	198	76	144			1			
w 5-6 79	4	Lincoln	156	156	462	406	868				868	189	21	113						
pt 78	4 5	Pleasant Valley	138	138	391	376	767	5	3	8	775	174	30	100						
n ⅓ 79	5	Princeton, exc of town																		
n⅓ e⅙ 79	4	Princeton, exc of town	125	135	369	346	715				715	156	16	131						
80	5	Princeton, exc of town																		
77 pt 78	3	Rockingham	50	50	163	149	312	1		1	313	51	30	37			1			
79	3	Sheridan	185	185	558	485	1043	1		1	1044	164	111	106	1					
80	3	Winfield	183	185	498	467	965				965	154	42	103						
In 77	2	Buffalo, town of	73	75	179	187	366		1	1	367	73	14	54						
In 79	5	Leclaire, town of	205	205	508	487	995	1	1	2	997	245	8	190			1			
In 79	5	Princeton, town of	119	112	276	249	525				525	126	4	95				1	2	35
		Total, exc Davenport	3082	3122	9288	8228	17516	22	12	34	17550	3202	1041	2670	3	6	6	1	2	40
In 78	3	Davenport, City of																		
		1st ward	825	1014	2640	2488	5128	15	10	25	5153	713	437	283			1			
		2d ward	408	559	1501	1307	2808	10	13	23	2831	421	250	144			1			
		3d ward	397	480	1604	1305	2909	1	3	4	2913	517	153	143						
		4th ward	528	578	1601	1830	3431	19	14	33	3464	650	53	300						

SCOTT COUNTY—Continued.

No. of Township.	Range.	Names of Townships, Towns, and Cities.	No. of Dwelling Houses	No. of Families.	No. of White Males.	No. of White Females.	Total White Population	No. of Colored Males.	No. of Colored Females	Total Colored Population.	Total Population.	No. Entitled to Vote.	No. of Foreigners not Naturalized.	No. of Militia.	No. of Blind not in Asylum, Jan. 1, 1869.	No. of Deaf and Dumb not in Asy. Jan. 1, '69	No. of Insane not in Hospital, Jan. 1, 1869	No. of Colleges, Academies, and Universities	No. of Teachers in Colleges, Universities, etc	No. of Students in Colleges, Universities, etc
....	......	5th ward...........	518	602	1889	1786	3675	43	44	87	3762	725	52	191	....	....	....	....	....	....
....	......	6th ward...........	336	356	1016	915	1931	6	5	11	1942	335	66	84	....	....	....	....	....	....
....	......	Total City of Davenport.	3012	3589	10251	9631	19882	94	89	183	20065	3361	1011	1145	....	....	2	....	....	....
....	......	Total County.......	6094	6711	19539	17859	37398	116	101	217	37615	6563	2052	3815	3	6	8	1	2	40

SHELBY COUNTY.

No. of Township.	Range.	Names of Townships, Towns, and Cities.	No. of Dwelling Houses	No. of Families.	No. of White Males.	No. of White Females.	Total White Population	No. of Colored Males.	No. of Colored Females	Total Colored Population.	Total Population.	No. Entitled to Vote.	No. of Foreigners not Naturalized.	No. of Militia.	No. of Blind not in Asylum, Jan. 1, 1869.	No. of Deaf and Dumb not in Asy. Jan. 1, '69	No. of Insane not in Hospital, Jan. 1, 1869	No. of Colleges, Academies, and Universities	No. of Teachers in Colleges, Universities, etc	No. of Students in Colleges, Universities, etc
......78	39	Fairview............																		
......78	40	Fairview............	68	68	184	162	346	....	....	....	346	58	20	63	1	....	....	....	....	....
...pt 79	38	Fairview............																		
......81	38 39 40	Gallands Grove.......																		
...pt 80	39	Gallands Grove.......	104	104	304	288	592	3	8	11	603	120	7	99	....	....	....	....	....	....
...pt 80	40	Gallands Grove.......																		
......79	.39 40	Harlan..............																		
...pt 79	.38 40	Harlan..............	65	69	162	175	337	....	....	....	337	81	2	61	....	....	....	....	....	....
...pt 80	.38 40	Harlan..............																		
......78	37	Indian Creek.........																		
...pt 78	.37 38	Indian Creek.........	20	21	42	38	80	....	....	....	80	18	2	16	1	....	....	....	....	....
......79	.37 38	Indian Creek.........																		
...80 81	37	Jackson.............																		
...pt 79	.37 38	Jackson.............	60	60	196	182	378	....	....	....	378	72	....	66	....	....	....	....	....	....
...pt 80	.37 80	Jackson.............																		
....	......	Total..............	317	322	888	845	1733	3	8	11	1744	349	31	305	2	....	....	....	....	....

SIOUX COUNTY—NOT REPORTED.

STORY COUNTY.

......82	21	Collins	87	87	274	232	506	....	....	....	506	94	....	77	....	....	....	....	....	....
......84	24	Franklin	129	129	376	347	723	2	....	2	725	160	3	137	....	....	1	....	....	....
......83	23	Grant	62	62	162	174	336	....	....	....	336	65	....	42	....	....	....	....	....	....
......85	23 w½22	Howard	124	125	386	353	739	....	....	....	739	92	77	71	....	....	....	....	....	....
......82	22	Indian Creek	180	199	485	515	1000	....	....	....	1000	210	4	155	....	....	....	....	....	....
......85	24	La Fayette	31	31	152	134	286	....	....	....	286	25	27	20	....	....	....	....	....	....
......85	21 ε qr 22	Lincoln	27	28	69	69	138	....	....	....	138	30	4	20	....	....	....	....	....	....
......84	23	Milford	67	72	241	192	433	....	....	....	433	87	7	79	....	....	....	....	....	....
w¾83w¼84	22	Nevada	249	261	650	659	1309	....	....	....	1309	271	14	214	....	1	1	....	....	....
......83	21 eqr22	New Albany	135	145	415	407	822	....	....	....	822	160	2	130	....	....	....	....	....	....
......82	24	Palestine	103	111	361	297	658	....	....	....	658	80	44	92	....	....	....	....	....	....
......84	31 ehf22	Sherman	60	62	175	165	340	....	....	....	340	62	2	53	....	....	....	....	....	....
......82	33	Union	173	173	486	464	950	....	....	....	950	184	7	146	....	....	....	....	....	....
......83	24	Washington	244	254	557	545	1102	2	1	3	1105	285	8	223	....	....	....	1	4	75
....	......	Total	1671	1739	4789	4553	9342	4	1	5	9347	1805	199	1459	....	1	2	1	4	75

TAMA COUNTY.

......86	14	Buckingham	81	81	257	194	451	....	....	....	451	92	20	63	....	....	....	....	....	....
......85	15	Crystal	70	70	221	192	413	....	....	....	413	78	21	93	....	....	....	....	....	....
......85	13	Clark	31	34	89	85	174	....	....	....	174	36	....	29	....	....	....	....	....	....
......84	14	Carroll	93	93	168	134	302	....	....	....	302	60	6	41	....	....	....	....	....	....
......84	16	Carlton	141	141	298	380	678	....	....	....	678	165	....	111	....	....	....	....	....	....
......82	15	Columbia	103	109	282	273	555	....	....	....	555	128	1	97	....	....	....	....	....	....
......86	15	Grant	23	23	72	68	140	....	....	....	140	19	12	19	....	....	....	....	....	....
......86	13	Geneseo	92	98	261	223	484	....	....	....	484	96	8	79	....	....	....	....	....	....
......84	15	Howard	167	167	486	457	943	....	....	....	943	204	5	175	....	....	....	....	....	....
......82	16	Highland	71	71	215	173	388	....	....	....	388	72	4	79	....	....	....	....	....	....
......83	16	Indian Village	227	229	749	782	1531	1	....	1	1532	366	11	288	4	....	....	....	....	....
......86	16	Lincoln	19	19	48	33	81	....	....	....	81	16	23	11	....	....	....	....	....	....
......83	14	Otter Creek	150	155	446	369	815	....	....	....	815	147	36	102	....	4	....	....	....	....
......84	13	Oneida	90	90	266	224	490	....	....	....	490	92	14	84	....	....	....	....	....	....
......85	14	Perry	108	112	356	281	637	1	....	1	638	123	16	106	....	....	....	....	....	....

TAMA COUNTY - CONTINUED.

No. of Township.	Range.	Names of Townships, Towns, and Cities.	No. of Dwelling Houses	No. of Families.	No. of White Males.	No. of White Females.	Total White Population	No. of Colored Males.	No. of Colored Females	Total Colored Population.	Total Population.	No. entitled to Vote.	No. of Foreigners not Naturalized.	No. of Militia.	No. of Blind not in Asylum, Jan. 1, 1869.	No. of Deaf and Dumb not in Asy. Jan. 1, '69	No. of Insane not in Hospital, Jan. 1, 1869.	No. of Colleges, Academies and Universities	No. of Teachers in Colleges and Universities	No. of Students in Colleges and Universities
82	14	Richland	149	149	413	382	795				795	180	1	117						
82	13	Salt Creek	203	203	554	510	1064				1064	203	30	146					1	
85	16	Spring Creek	74	74	193	207	400				400	104	2	79						
83	13	York	139	139	487	415	902				902	121	84	147						
pt 83	15	Toledo, exc. of town	110	111	324	301	625				625	130	1	99						
pt 83	15	Tama	118	118	744	697	1441				1441	303	12	254						
In 83	5	Toledo, city of	198	197	462	440	902	17	24	41	943	224	20	155						
		Total	2457	2483	7391	6820	14211	19	24	43	14254	2959	327	3374	4	4			1	

TAYLOR COUNTY.

No. of Township.	Range.	Names of Townships, Towns, and Cities.	No. of Dwelling Houses	No. of Families.	No. of White Males.	No. of White Females.	Total White Population	No. of Colored Males.	No. of Colored Females	Total Colored Population.	Total Population.	No. entitled to Vote.	No. of Foreigners not Naturalized.	No. of Militia.	No. of Blind not in Asylum, Jan. 1, 1869.	No. of Deaf and Dumb not in Asy. Jan. 1, '69	No. of Insane not in Hospital, Jan. 1, 1869.	No. of Colleges, Academies and Universities	No. of Teachers in Colleges and Universities	No. of Students in Colleges and Universities
68	34	Benton	Not reported.	Not reported.	352	344	696	8	13	21	717	146		118				1	3	
68	33	Clayton			211	224	435	1	1	2	437	85		69	1					
69	35	Dallas			284	259	543	5	7	12	555	123		98						
70	34	Holt			138	109	247	6	4	10	257	55	1	43						
67 68	32	Jefferson			370	335	705	3	4	7	712	151		108		2				
67	33	Jackson			169	148	317	4	3	7	324	56	1	42	1					
69 70	33	Marshall			101	99	200	3	4	7	207	46		32						
68	35	Mason			285	239	524				524	100	2	85						2
70	35	Nodaway			128	110	238	2		2	240	56		40						
67	35	Polk			360	327	687	1		1	688	123		100						
69 70	32	Platte			74	67	141				141	32		29						
67	34	Ross			224	233	457				457	104		86		1				

69	34	Washington	*	*	171	161	332				332	70	1	60						
		Total			2867	2655	5522	33	36	69	5591	1147	5	910	2	3		1	3	2

* Not reported.

UNION COUNTY.

73	29	Dodge	28	30	92	90	182				182	32	2	23						
22 73	31	Douglas	30	35	120	105	225				225	45	2	40						
71 pt 72	30	Highland	27	27	65	75	140				140	25		24						
72	28	Jones	36	41	121	114	235				235	49	2	38						
73 pt 72	30	Lincoln	69	69	220	196	416				416	88		62						
73	28	New Hope	39	40	140	117	257				257	61		50						
71	31	Platte	72	72	237	200	437	1		1	438	91	1	76		1				
71	28	Pleasant	98	101	264	270	534				534	106	4	69						
71	29	Sand Creek	38	38	114	105	219	3	2	5	224	48		32						
72	29	Union	265	243	571	595	1166	2	2	4	1170	296	5	241						
		Total	702	696	1944	1867	3811	6	4	10	3821	841	16	655		1				

VAN BUREN COUNTY.

pt 68	8	Bonaparte	239	260	662	675	1337	8	3	11	1348	291	13	207	1					36
70	8	Cedar	200	206	558	515	1073				1073	234	3	179						
69	11	Chequest	151	164	497	442	939				939	196	7	159			7			
68 pt 67	10	Des Moines	218	218	512	473	985				985	229	1	153						
pt 67 68	8	Farmington	150	150	391	401	792	6	11	17	809	181	4	115		1	2			
69	8	Harrisburg	199	199	545	501	1046				1046	246	4	172	1					9
pt 67 68	11	Jackson	237	237	660	635	1295		1	1	1296	318		241						
70	10	Lick Creek	204	205	543	544	1087	5	7	12	1099	229		193			2			
70	9	Union	197	197	378	482	860	5	3	8	868	242	1	148						
68 pt 67	9	Vernon	263	263	709	643	1352				1352	326		233						
69	10 pt 9	Van Buren	265	265	740	692	1432	15	11	26	1458	314		197						
70	11	Village	282	282	732	712	1444				1444	291	3	218						
pt 69	9	Washington	102	102	264	264	528	3	3	6	534	125	2	85						
In 70	9	Birmingham, town of	105	105	300	295	595	13	11	24	619	131		101						
In 68	9	Bentonsport, town of	88	92	219	235	454				454	105	1	62	1					
In 68	8	Farmington, town of	133	143	336	321	657				657	141	2	82						
In 69	10	Keosauqua, town of	185	185	364	400	764	45	49	94	858	184	1	114		1				
		Total	3218	3273	8410	8230	16640	100	99	199	16839	3783	42	2659	3	2	11			45

WAPELLO COUNTY.

No. of Township.	Range.	Names of Townships, Towns, and Cities.	No. of Dwelling Houses	No. of Families.	No. of White Males.	No. of White Females.	Total White Population	No. of Colored Males.	No. of Colored Females	Total Colored Population	Total Population.	No. entitled to Vote.	No. of Foreigners not Naturalized.	No. of Militia.	No. of Blind not in Asylum, Jan. 1, 1869.	No. of Deaf and Dumb not in Asy. Jan. 1, '69	No. of Insane not in Hospital, Jan. 1, 1869.	No. of Colleges, Academies and Universities	No. of Teachers in Colleges, Universities, etc.	No. of Students in Colleges, Universities, etc.
......71	15	Adams	249	249	751	679	1430	....	....	....	1430	310	1	210	2	....	....	....	....	....
...pt 71	13	Agency, exc. of city....																		
pt 71 72	13	Agency, exc. of city....	106	106	276	269	545	2	1	3	548	112	....	95	....	....	....	....	....	....
...pt 72	12	Agency, exc. of city....																		
pt 72 73	.14 15	Cass	154	156	405	369	774	....	....		774	178	10	147	....	....	....	....	....	2
...pt 72	.13 14	Center, exc. city Ottumwa	301	301	803	777	1580	9	8	17	1597	334	6	254	2	1	4	....	....	....
...pt 73	15	Columbia, exc. town of Eddyville	145	145	447	383	830	2	4	6	836	172	....	122	....	....	....	....	....	....
......73	12	Competine	164	166	465	424	889	....	....	....	889	179	141	....	....	....	....	....	....	....
...pt 72	13	Dahlonega	154	154	326	296	622	....	1	1	623	135	3	100	....	....	2	....	....	....
......71	14	Green	226	233	664	627	1291	....	....	....	1291	252	....	167	1	4	....	....	....	....
......73	13	Highland	154	154	426	412	838	....	....	....	838	196	3	140	....	1	....	....	....	....
...pt 71	13	Keokuk	126	126	339	317	656	1	1	2	658	138	1	94	....	....	2	....	....	....
...pt 72	12	Pleasant	208	208	597	587	1184	....	....	....	1184	262	....	188	....	....	....	....	....	....
...pt 71	13	Polk	181	181	531	521	1052	....	....	....	1052	182	41	128	1	....	....	....	....	....
......73	14	Richland	239	239	645	623	1268	7	10	17	1285	289	3	185	....	....	2	....	....	....
......71	12	Washington	262	262	683	653	1336	....	....	....	1336	285	2	226	....	....	....	....	....	....
...In 73	15	Eddyville, town of	339	339	566	565	1131	5	6	11	1142	242	45	166	....	2	....	....	....	....
...In 72	13	Agency City, town of	149	149	312	320	632	....	....	....	632	139	4	91	....	1	....	....	....	....
....	......	Total	3157	3168	8236	7822	16058	26	31	57	16115	3405	260	2313	6	9	10	....	....	2
...In 72	14	Ottumwa—																		
....	......	1st ward	309	313	1112	881	1993	21	17	38	2031	479	70	494	....	....	1	....	....	....
....	......	2d ward	134	134	339	324	663	18	16	34	697	156	6	123	....	....	....	....	....	....

		3d ward	126	126	362	343	705	2	2	4	709	190	2	177			1			
		4th ward	212	212	542	568	1110	4	6	10	1120	214	9	178		1				
		Total city	781	785	2355	2116	4471	45	41	86	4557	1039	87	972		1	2			
8		Total County	3936	3953	10591	9938	20529	71	72	143	20672	4444	347	3285	6	10	12			2

WARREN COUNTY.

pt 77	23	Allen	128	128	376	366	742				742	144	2	112						
75	22	Belmont	147	166	439	395	834				834	184	1	127			2			
pt 77 76	24	Greenfield	247	247	714	705	1419	3	4	7	1426	290	5	228						
77	25	Jackson	82	82	250	235	485				485	95		74						
76	25	Jefferson	158	158	463	423	886				886	185		155						
74	23	Liberty	129	132	388	356	744				744	148		111						
77	25	Lynn	139	139	426	393	819				819	171		128						
77	23	Otter	138	136	401	382	783	5	2	7	790	151	8	119						
pt 76 77	22 23	Palmyra	237	253	683	672	1355	1		1	1356	262	1	212	1	1	2			
pt 77	22	Richland	250	255	711	717	1428				1428	291	3	202		1				
74	24	Squaw	106	106	340	313	653				653	129	2	100		2				
pt 76	22	Union	162	162	508	483	991				991	189		146						
74	25	Virginia	90	94	200	184	384	1		1	385	82		68		1				
pt 76 77	23 24	Washington, exclusive of Indianola	284	286	825	800	1625	5	2	7	1632	328		274	1					
77	22	Whitebreast	136	136	359	412	771				771	149	1	117	2		2			
75	24	White Oak	94	94	254	236	490				490	113	4	90						1
In 76	24	Indianola, city of	330	330	678	662	1340	20	18	38	1378	333	3	294			2	1	7	200
		Total	2857	2904	8015	7734	15749	35	26	61	15810	3244	30	2557	4	5	8	1	7	201

WASHINGTON COUNTY.

pt 74	8	Brighton	241	242	636	575	1211				1211	285		195						
pt 76	8	Cedar	177	177	487	528	1015				1015	202		150						
74	9	Clay	128	133	385	350	735				735	167	3	120						
pt 74	6	Crawford	249	260	695	632	1327				1327	319	4	227			1			
75 pt 74	9	Dutch Creek	229	234	724	647	1371	1		1	1372	272	7	226						
pt 77	7 8	English River	201	220	725	697	1422	3	1	4	1426	242	40	161						
pt 75 76	8	Franklin	171	171	380	345	725				725	164	2	176						
76	6	Highland	116	116	351	312	663				663	177	7	162						

WASHINGTON COUNTY—Continued.

No. of Township.	Range.	Names of Townships, Town, and Cities.	No. of Dwelling Houses	No. of Families.	No. of White Males.	No. of White Females.	Total White Population	No. of Colored Males.	No. of Colored Females.	Total Colored Population.	Total Population.	No. entitled to Vote.	No. of Foreigners not Naturalized.	No. of Militia.	No. of Blind not in Asylum, Jan. 1, 1869.	No. of Deaf and Dumb not in Asy. Jan. 1, '69	No. of Insane not in Hospital, Jan. 1, 1869	No. of Colleges, Academies and Universities	No. of Teachers in Colleges, Universities, etc.	No. of Students in Colleges, Universities, etc.
...pt 77	...6 7	Iowa	145	145	495	435	930	....	....	....	930	186	24	118	....	1	1	....	....	....
......76	7	Jackson	176	180	529	506	1035	3	....	3	1038	200	30	159	....	5	....	....	....	....
......77	9 pt 8	Lime Creek	287	287	686	695	1381	....	....	....	1381	284	15	213	....	....	1	....	....	....
...pt 74	...7 8	Marion	177	177	558	487	1045	1	....	1	1046	199	10	143	....	....	....	....	....	....
75 pt 74	6	Oregon	231	231	566	640	1206	....	....	....	1206	294	10	225	1	....	....	....	....	....
......76	9	Seventy-Six	125	127	354	346	700	....	....	....	700	141	4	125	....	....	....	....	....	....
pt 74 75	...7 8	Washington, exc. of town	282	177	635	631	1266	2	....	2	1268	345	....	255	....	....	....	....	....	....
...In 75	7	Washington, town of	412	422	1251	1320	2571	16	18	34	2605	533	12	370	....	....	....	1	2	60
....	......	Total	3347	3399	9457	9146	18603	26	19	45	18648	4010	168	3025	1	6	3	1	2	60

WAYNE COUNTY.

No. of Township.	Range.	Names of Townships, Town, and Cities.	No. of Dwelling Houses	No. of Families.	No. of White Males.	No. of White Females.	Total White Population	No. of Colored Males.	No. of Colored Females.	Total Colored Population.	Total Population.	No. entitled to Vote.	No. of Foreigners not Naturalized.	No. of Militia.	No. of Blind not in Asylum, Jan. 1, 1869.	No. of Deaf and Dumb not in Asy. Jan. 1, '69	No. of Insane not in Hospital, Jan. 1, 1869	No. of Colleges, Academies and Universities	No. of Teachers in Colleges, Universities, etc.	No. of Students in Colleges, Universities, etc.
......69	22	Benton	130	130	419	394	813	....	....	....	813	149	....	111	....	....	....	....	....	....
......69	23	Clay	56	56	154	170	324	....	....	....	324	64	....	44	....	....	....	....	....	....
......67	22	Clinton	106	106	289	286	575	....	....	....	575	109	....	76	....	1	....	....	....	....
......69	21	Corydon	189	189	542	512	1054	....	....	....	1054	234	1	200	....	....	....	....	....	....
......67	23	Grand River	129	129	331	340	671	....	....	....	671	137	....	105	1	....	2	....	....	....
......67	21	Howard	121	135	220	229	449	....	....	....	449	102	....	61	....	....	....	....	....	....
......68	21	Jackson	45	50	131	110	241	....	....	....	241	51	....	43	....	....	1	....	....	....
......68	23	Jefferson	118	118	329	314	643	....	....	....	643	137	....	90	....	....	....	....	....	....
......67	20	Monroe	83	96	259	287	546	....	....	....	546	101	....	77	....	1	....	....	....	....
......70	23	Richman	57	57	160	141	301	....	....	....	301	73	....	53	....	....	....	....	....	....
......69	20	South Fork	124	128	355	386	741	....	....	....	741	143	....	109	....	....	....	....	....	....
......70	21	Union	143	151	446	403	849	1	....	1	850	171	1	135	1	2	....	....	....	....

68	20	Walnut	104	104	268	287	555				555	111		93						
68	22	Warren	59	59	192	151	343				343	59		44						
70	22	Washington	108	108	310	323	633				633	126		88						
70	20	Wright	152	153	428	399	827				827	167		132	1		3			
		Total	1724	1769	4833	4732	9565				9566	1934	2	1461	3	4	6			

WEBSTER COUNTY.

90	.27 28	Badger	21	21	83	68	151				151	34		19						
86	28pt27	Dayton	146	162	453	384	837				837	122	57	121						
89	29	Douglas	67	67	183	151	334				334	86	6	52						
90	29	Deer Creek	29	29	87	78	165				165	37	1	21			1	1		
88	30	Fulton	15	16	50	37	87				87	15	39	9						
86	29pt27	Hardin	67	83	196	174	370				370	46	42	19			3			
90	30	Jackson	45	46	149	132	281				281	55		38						
89	30	Johnson	53	53	162	136	298				298	64	4	40						
88	29pt28	Otho	80	99	245	251	496	1		1	497	107	10	70						
87	.28 29	Sumner	97	97	261	246	507				507	110		96		2	1			
89	27	Wahkonsa																		
89	28	Wahkonsa	438	*	1404	1256	2660	5	3	8	2668	639	22	496						2
pt 88	28	Wahkonsa																		
88	27pt28	Washington	113	113	362	307	669				669	143	1	102						
87	30pt27	Webster	88	95	266	250	516				516	105		73						
86	30	Yell	73	73	224	208	432				432	83		60						
pt 87	27	Yell																		
		Total	1332	954	4125	3678	7803	6	3	9	7812	1666	182	1216		2	5	1		2

WINNEBAGO COUNTY.

Not reported	Not reported	Center	40	40	130	114	244				244	46		37						
		Forest	24	24	73	69	142				142	37		23						
		Iowa	*	70	175	154	329				329	55	15							
		Norway	25	25	60	67	127				127	20		13						
		Pleasant	50	51	125	105	230				230	45	9	21						
		Total	139	210	563	509	1072				1072	203	24	94						

* Not reported,

WINNESHIEK COUNTY.

No. of Township.	Range.	Names of Townships, Towns, and Cities.	No. of Dwelling Houses	No. of Families.	No. of White Males.	No. of White Females.	Total White Population	No. of Colored Males.	No. of Colored Females	Total Colored Population.	Total Population.	No. Entitled to Vote.	No. of Foreigners not Naturalized.	No. of Militia.	No. of Blind not in Asylum, Jan. 1, 1869.	No. of Deaf and Dumb not in Asy. Jan. 1, '69	No. of Insane not in Hospital, Jan. 1, 1869	No. of Colleges, Academies, and Universities	No. of Teachers in Colleges, Universities, etc	No. of Students in Colleges, Universities, etc
96	7	Bloomfield	210	220	604	543	1147	1	....	1	1148	251	22	162	....	....	....	....	....	....
99	9	Bluffton	131	138	386	332	718	....	....	....	718	136	13	80	....	....	....	....	....	....
100	9	Burr Oak	178	178	494	420	914	....	....	....	914	200	15	144	....	....	....	....	....	....
97	9	Calmar	285	309	834	782	1616	4	1	5	1621	258	105	222	....	....	....	....	....	....
99	8	Canoe	154	154	429	399	828	....	....	....	828	152	44	99	4	1	1	....	....	....
98	8	Decorah, exc. of town	220	222	743	574	1317	....	....	....	1317	206	35	131	....	....	1	1	6	93
97	7	Franklin	165	164	510	435	945	....	....	....	945	201	38	147	....	....	....	....	....	....
100	10	Fremont	111	113	323	312	635	....	....	....	635	134	9	110	1	....	....	....	....	....
98	7	Glenwood	185	173	600	599	1199	....	....	....	1199	170	102	100	....	2	....	....	....	....
100	8	Hesper	174	187	529	479	1008	2	....	2	1010	192	27	173	....	....	4	....	....	....
100	7	Highland	128	128	461	419	880	....	....	....	880	111	90	77	1	2	1	....	....	....
96	10	Jackson	91	95	276	257	533	....	....	....	533	92	34	60	....	....	....	....	....	....
98	10	Lincoln	109	109	367	337	704	....	....	....	704	96	59	80	....	2	....	....	....	....
98	9	Madison	111	125	413	326	739	....	....	....	739	103	78	89	....	1	1	....	....	....
96	8	Military	251	251	763	693	1456	....	....	....	1456	237	73	156	....	....	....	....	....	....
99	10	Orleans	108	108	302	282	584	....	....	....	584	124	....	99	....	....	....	....	....	....
99	7	Pleasant	145	176	511	489	1000	....	....	....	1000	128	76	82	....	4	4	....	....	....
97	8	Springfield	155	150	558	526	1084	....	....	....	1084	136	109	179	....	1	....	....	....	....
97	10	Sumner	133	138	414	355	769	....	....	....	769	108	54	115	....	....	....	....	....	....
96	9	Washington	182	202	535	469	1004	....	....	....	1004	174	101	124	....	....	....	....	....	....
In 98	8	Decorah, town of	337	358	950	984	1934	13	12	25	1959	372	55	231	1	....	....	....	....	....
....	....	Total	3563	3698	11002	10012	21014	20	13	33	21047	3581	1139	2660	7	13	12	1	6	93

WOODBURY COUNTY—NOT REPORTED.

WORTH COUNTY.

......92	22	Bristol	84	84	212	204	416	1	....	1	417	76	15	70	....	....	....	....	....	....
pt 98 99	.20 21	Brookfield	24	24	80	82	162	....	....	....	162	29	7	21	....	....	....	....	....	....
......98	22pt21	Fertile	16	17	37	42	79	....	....	....	79	18	....	16	....	....	....	....	....	....
100 pt 99	21	Hartland	92	105	291	268	559	....	....	....	559	71	42	53	....	....	....	....	....	....
100 pt 99	.19 20	Northwood	84	84	236	204	440	....	....	....	440	88	12	51	1	....	1	....	....	....
.....100	22	Silver Lake	62	70	171	149	320	....	....	....	320	42	26	29	....	....	....	....	....	....
......98	19	Union }																		
...pt 98	20	Union }	27	27	79	79	158	....	....	....	158	22	6	17	....	....	....	....	....	....
...pt 99	.19 20	Union }																		
....	......	Total	389	411	1106	1028	2134	1	....	1	2135	346	108	257	1	....	1	....	....	....

WRIGHT COUNTY.

93 pt 92	24	Belmont	40	46	132	108	240	1	....	1	241	54	2	39	....	....	....	....	....	....
......93	.25 26	Boone	26	26	63	68	131	1	1	2	133	26	....	27	....	....	....	....	....	....
pt 91 92	.24 25	Clarion	16	16	46	40	86	....	....	....	86	20	....	13	....	....	....	....	....	....
......91	26pt25	Eagle Grove	26	26	83	64	147	....	....	....	147	28	4	25	....	....	....	....	....	....
pt 91 92	.23 24	Iowa	27	27	83	68	151	....	....	....	151	41	2	32	....	....	....	....	....	....
......92	26pt25	Liberty	49	50	127	118	245	....	....	....	245	54	2	30	....	....	....	....	....	....
93 pt 92	23	Pleasant	51	51	137	125	262	....	....	....	262	49	....	31	....	....	....	....	....	....
......90	26	Troy	32	33	91	91	182	....	....	....	182	37	4	32	....	....	....	....	....	....
90 pt 91	23	Vernon	22	25	65	57	122	....	....	....	122	26	4	18	....	....	....	....	....	....
90 pt 91	24	Wall Lake	28	28	60	51	111	....	....	....	111	26	1	16	2	....	....	....	....	....
......90	24	Woodstock	14	14	47	38	85	....	....	....	85	15	....	14	....	....	....	....	....	....
....	......	Total	331	342	934	828	1762	2	1	3	1765	376	19	277	2	....	....	....	....	....

EXHIBIT

Showing the Population and various classifications thereof of the several incorporated Cities and Towns of Iowa, as returned by the Census of 1867 and 1869, alphabetically arranged.

Names of Towns and Cities.	Names of Counties.	Year when Census was taken.	No. of Dwelling Houses	No. of Families.	No. of White Males.	No. of White Females.	Total White Population	No. of Colored Males.	No. of Colored Females	No. of Colored Population.	Total Population.	No. entitled to Vote.	No. of Foreigners not Naturalized.	No. of Militia.
Adel	Dallas	1867	70	....	280	255	535	4	4	8	543	82	....	47
Adel	Dallas	1869	112	112	367	332	699	3	2	5	704	180	3	136
Agency City	Wapello	1867	90	....	290	298	588	....	....	....	588	124	3	64
Agency City	Wapello	1869	149	149	312	320	632	....	....	....	632	139	4	91
Albia	Monroe	1867	173	....	468	469	937	19	8	27	964	233	2	131
Albia	Monroe	1869	256	271	639	616	1255	15	14	29	1284	328	....	280
Anamosa	Jones	1867	316	....	870	881	1751	8	4	12	1763	388	21	320
Anamosa	Jones	1869	341	390	928	937	1865	13	15	28	1893	421	7	320
Andrew	Jackson	1867	46	....	155	144	299	....	....	....	299	74	3	48
Andrew	Jackson	1869	75	75	182	174	356	1	....	1	357	78	5	69
Bellevue	Jackson	1867	217	....	560	614	1174	5	3	8	1182	248	11	170
Bellevue	Jackson	1869	294	294	749	790	1539	2	1	3	1542	338	29	255
Bentonsport	Van Buren	1867	90	....	246	268	514	....	1	1	515	109	2	82
Bentonsport	Van Buren	1869	88	92	219	235	454	....	....	....	454	105	1	62

Birmingham	Van Buren	1867	99	....	269	272	541	4	4	8	549	128	....	89
Birmingham	Van Buren	1869	105	105	300	295	595	13	11	24	619	131	....	101
Bloomfield	Davis	1867	118	....	313	297	610	2	1	3	613	131	....	102
Bloomfield	Davis	1869	141	141	400	349	749	3	3	6	755	207	....	178
Boonsboro	Boone	1867	267	....	813	811	1624	....	....	....	1624	340	....	238
Boonsboro	Boone	1869	345	345	886	859	1745	2	....	2	1747	398	68	302
Buffalo	Scott	1869	73	75	179	187	366	....	1	1	367	73	14	54
Burlington	Des Moines	1867	1717	....	5383	5097	10480	76	60	136	10616	2075	294	1476
Burlington	Des Moines	1869	1810	2144	6325	5535	11860	91	83	174	12034	2111	499	1286
Camanche	Clinton	1867	108	....	264	289	553	4	4	8	561	124	....	98
Camanche	Clinton	1869	161	177	344	371	715	4	2	6	721	115	15	109
Cedar Falls*	Black Hawk	1867	554	....	1709	1676	3385	4	2	6	3391	641	46	497
Cedar Falls*	Black Hawk	1869	528	567	1639	1565	3204	2	....	2	3206	616	66	508
Cedar Rapids	Linn	1867	482	....	1451	1445	2896	15	14	29	2925	615	95	470
Cedar Rapids	Linn	1869	593	625	1656	1686	3342	12	13	25	3367	738	108	561
Chariton	Lucas	1867	138	....	544	440	984	6	2	8	992	287	....	244
Chariton	Lucas	1869	220	220	580	573	1153	21	19	40	1193	310	6	236
Clarence	Cedar	1867	82	....	260	227	487	....	1	1	488	86	7	72
Clarence	Cedar	1869	127	127	393	341	734	....	....	....	734	185	21	157
Clinton	Clinton	1867	725	....	2271	2047	4318	12	6	18	4336	1132	....	559
Clinton	Clinton	1899	1051	1138	3315	2921	6236	42	29	71	6307	1247	109	761
Council Bluffs*	Pottawattamie	1867	698	....	2700	2102	4802	19	11	30	4832	1214	138	745
Council Bluffs*	Pottawattamie	1869	1153	1178	3144	2612	5756	21	16	37	5793	1392	197	1304
Davenport*	Scott	1867	2778	....	8987	8316	17303	118	129	247	17550	2838	973	1709
Davenport*	Scott	1869	3012	3589	10251	9631	19882	94	89	183	20065	3361	1011	1145

* For population by wards for Cedar Falls, see page 6. For Council Bluffs, page 49. For Davenport, page 51.

POPULATION OF INCORPORATED TOWNS AND CITIES—CONTINUED.

Names of Towns and Cities.	Nomes of Counties.	Year when Census was taken.	No. of Dwelling Houses	No. of Families.	No. of White Males.	No. of White Females.	Total White Population	No. of Colored Males.	No. of Colored Females	Total Colored Population.	Total Population.	No. entitled to Vote.	No. of Foreigners not Naturalized.	No. of Militia.
Decorah	Winneshiek	1867	245	....	850	805	1655	11	9	20	1675	371	37	265
Decorah	Winneshiek	1869	337	358	950	984	1934	13	12	25	1958	372	55	231
Des Moines*	Polk	1867	1551	....	5301	4995	10296	105	110	215	10511	1856	92	1463
Des Moines	Polk	1869	1821	1916	6222	5958	12180	99	100	199	12379	2443	97	1974
De Witt	Clinton	1867	246	....	725	714	1439	6	4	10	1449	313	24	230
De Witt	Clinton	1869	....	....	887	934	1821	10	8	18	1839	399	38	315
Drakeville	Davis	1867	33	....	123	124	247	....	....	....	247	49	1	39
Drakeville	Davis	1869	44	45	99	119	218	....	....	....	218	42	....	26
Dubuque*	Dubuque	1867	3055	....	11056	10077	21133	42	47	89	21222	3487	350	2608
Dubuque	Dubuque	1869	3542	3612	8988	8971	17959	60	65	125	18084	3448	364	2102
Durant	Cedar	1869	67	70	196	150	346	....	....	....	346	91	10	67
Eddyville	Wapello	1867	226	....	672	672	1344	3	8	11	1255	295	10	206
Eddyville	Wapello	1869	339	339	566	565	1131	5	6	11	1142	242	45	166
Fairfield	Jefferson	1867	320	....	958	1060	2018	6	9	15	2033	389	17	266
Fairfield	Jefferson	1869	354	361	853	922	1775	6	8	14	1789	411	11	274
Farmington	Van Buren	1867	115	....	363	349	712	....	....	....	712	153	....	81

Farmington	Van Buren	1869	133	143	336	321	657	....	....	....	657	141	2	82
Grinnell	Poweshiek	1867	165	....	495	474	969	10	14	24	993	199	1	200
Grinnell	Poweshiek	1869	220	220	604	641	1245	18	14	32	1277	270	21	212
Guttenberg	Clayton	1867	109	....	428	407	835	1	....	1	836	189	10	101
Guttenberg	Clayton	1869	208	208	525	482	1007	....	....	....	1007	222	21	111
Independence	Buchanan	1867	375	....	1254	1213	2467	1	....	1	2468	549	17	375
Independence	Buchanan	1869	476	505	1364	1355	2717	....	....	....	2717	591	5	440
Indianola	Warren	1867	193	....	512	511	1023	9	10	19	1042	238	3	196
Indianola	Warren	1869	330	330	678	662	1340	20	18	38	1378	333	3	294
Iowa City	Johnson	1867	1025	....	3221	3163	6384	12	22	34	6418	1200	37	802
Iowa City	Johnson	1869	1051	1051	3255	3293	6548	13	22	35	6583	1152	98	843
Jefferson	Greene	1869	159	159	371	332	703	....	....	....	703	189	5	154
Keokuk *	Lee	1867	1739	....	4719	4852	9571	437	481	918	10489	2079	115	1499
Keokuk	Lee	1869	1974	2085	5355	5378	10733	500	521	1021	11754	2362	238	1899
Keosauqua	Van Buren	1867	99	....	319	327	646	27	15	42	688	139	1	81
Keosauqua	Van Buren	1869	185	185	364	400	764	45	49	94	858	184	1	114
Knoxville	Marion	1867	164	....	543	557	1100	3	3	6	1106	248	1	201
Knoxville	Marion	1869	177	177	426	447	873	....	....	....	873	215	....	144
Lansing	Allamakee	1867	196	....	812	725	1537	1	....	1	1538	351	35	333
Lansing	Allamakee	1869	280	280	989	972	1961	3	2	5	1966	363	30	293
Le Claire	Scott	1867	254	....	675	636	1311	1	1	2	1313	298	29	215
Le Claire	Scott	1869	205	205	508	487	995	1	1	2	997	245	8	190
Lyons	Clinton	1867	501	....	1750	1708	3458	5	7	12	3470	691	276	289
Lyons	Clinton	1869	....	635	1804	1815	3619	4	9	13	3632	727	74	223

* For population of Des Moines by wards, see page 47–8. Dubuque, see page 20–21. For Keokuk, page 36.

POPULATION OF INCORPORATED TOWNS AND CITIES—Continued.

Names of Towns and Cities.	Names of Counties.	Year when Census was taken.	No. of Dwelling Houses	No. of Families.	No. of White Males.	No. of White Females.	Total White Population	No. of Colored Males.	No. of Colored Females	Total Colored Population.	Total Population.	No. entitled to Vote.	No. of Foreigners not naturalized.	No. of Militia.
Manchester	Delaware	1869	282	282	686	689	1375	....	....	....	1375	360	13	285
Maquoketa	Jackson	1867	274	....	669	717	1386	....	....	....	1386	329	12	209
Maquoketa	Jackson	1869	278	278	659	685	1344	1	3	4	1348	287	9	168
Marengo	Iowa	1867	187	....	524	523	1047	1	3	4	1051	271	5	210
Marengo	Iowa	1869	329	344	598	613	1211	1	3	4	1215	280	16	200
Marion	Linn	1867	313	....	935	927	1862	5	1	6	1868	449	14	328
Marion	Linn	1869	327	377	932	952	1884	8	1	9	1893	428	7	337
Marshalltown	Marshall	1867	500	....	1154	1103	2257	15	7	22	2279	562	25	....
Marshalltown	Marshall	1869	508	606	1618	1535	3153	10	9	19	3172	820	57	577
Mechanicsville	Cedar	1869	131	138	293	287	580	....	1	1	581	156	1	116
McGregor *	Clayton	1867	264	....	1058	983	2041	2	3	5	2046	520	30	480
McGregor	Clayton	1869	381	421	1130	1153	2283	4	7	11	2294	506	15	435
Montana *	Boone	1867	139	....	602	502	1104	3	....	3	1107	315	4	281
Montana	Boone	1869	346	351	1103	999	2102	5	10	15	2117	375	19	302
Montezuma	Poweshiek	1869	98	98	240	241	481	....	1	1	482	115	2	90

Monticello	Jones	1869	236	270	612	661	1273	1	....	1	1274	329	4	177
Montrose	Lee	1867	85	....	305	332	637	1	....	1	638	130	....	97
Montrose	Lee	1869	150	142	392	342	734	....	....	....	734	163	3	5
Morning Sun	Louisa	1869	53	54	139	140	279	....	....	....	279	60	....	48
Moscow	Muscatine	1869	70	77	165	166	331	....	....	....	331	66	7	36
Mt. Pleasant	Henry	1867	725	....	1998	2112	4110	126	101	227	4337	947	16	719
Mt. Pleasant	Henry	1869	819	840	2035	2148	4183	129	113	242	4425	968	21	676
Muscatine	Muscatine	1867	2042	....	3760	3800	7560	52	53	105	7765	1492	180	1219
Muscatine	Muscatine	1869	1656	1560	5056	4946	10002	91	85	176	10178	1855	252	1243
New London	Henry	1867	84	....	230	266	496	2	1	3	499	101	....	64
New London	Henry	1869	104	104	223	240	463	1	1	2	465	94	2	61
Newton	Jasper	1869	345	345	807	841	1648	15	16	31	1679	382	....	245
Onawa	Monona	1869	69	71	206	197	403	1	....	1	404	94	11	67
Oskaloosa	Mahaska	1867	438	....	1276	1391	2667	25	29	54	2721	580	6	432
Oskaloosa	Mahaska	1869	631	631	1374	1490	2864	42	36	78	2942	684	....	572
Ottumwa*	Wapello	1867	556	....	1470	1442	2912	21	21	42	2954	676	14	566
Ottumwa	Wapello	1869	781	785	2355	2116	4471	45	41	86	4557	1039	87	972
Pella	Marion	1867	375	....	923	910	1833	....	....	....	1833	353	62	209
Pella	Marion	1869	373	398	933	914	1847	....	....	....	1847	350	90	220
Princeton	Scott	1867	112	....	289	289	578	....	....	....	578	145	3	97
Princeton	Scott	1869	119	112	276	249	525	....	....	....	525	126	4	95
Sabula	Jackson	1867	144	....	319	310	629	....	....	....	629	137	1	89
Sabula	Jackson	1869	189	189	429	388	817	....	....	....	817	177	....	132

* For population by wards for McGregor, see page 15. For Montana, see page 7.]

POPULATION OF INCORPORATED TOWNS AND CITIES—Continued.

Names of Towns and Cities.	Names of Counties.	Year when Census was taken.	No. of Dwelling Houses	No. of Families.	No. of White Males.	No. of White Females.	Total White Population	No. of Colored Males.	No. of Colored Females	Total Colored Population.	Total Population.	No. entitled to Vote.	No. of Foreigners not Naturalized.	No. of Militia.
Salem	Henry	1867	99	....	258	253	511	2	2	4	515	124	....	90
Salem	Henry	1869	108	108	249	261	510	....	....	....	510	128	....	94
Sigourney	Keokuk	1867	151	....	433	471	904	1	....	1	905	215	3	157
Sigourney	Keokuk	1869	181	190	453	464	917	1	....	1	918	225	4	180
State Center	Marshall	1869	74	97	254	215	469	....	....	....	469	115	1	108
Tabor	Fremont	1869	45	45	120	129	249	2	....	2	851	664	....	44
Tipton	Cedar	1867	275	....	675	687	1362	6	8	14	1376	265	2	181
Tipton	Cedar	1869	280	290	614	665	1279	6	7	13	1292	307	....	185
Toledo	Tama	1867	128	....	380	379	759	22	24	46	805	181	....	139
Toledo	Tama	1869	198	197	462	440	902	17	24	41	943	224	20	155
Wapello	Louisa	1867	127	....	400	380	780	2	....	2	782	187	2	130
Wapello	Louisa	1869	156	162	433	412	845	4	2	6	851	180	8	111
Washington	Washington	1867	402	....	1207	1253	2460	26	28	54	2514	511	8	315
Washington	Washington	1869	412	422	1251	1320	2571	16	18	34	2605	533	12	370
Waterloo *	Black Hawk	1867	384	....	1172	1158	2330	3	1	4	2334	578	14	394
Waterloo *	Black Hawk	1869	732	736	1836	1818	3654	6	2	8	3662	843	36	363

Waverly	Bremer	1867	361	....	1102	1018	2120	....	....	....	2120	483	19	349
Waverly	Bremer	1869	483	517	1372	1309	2681	2	....	2	2683	568	....	320
West Liberty	Muscatine	1869	169	158	388	379	767	1	....	1	768	209	3	155
West Point	Lee	1867	144	....	411	422	833	....	....	....	833	164	7	107
West Point	Lee	1869	164	164	420	413	833	....	....	....	833	160	9	102
West Union	Fayette	1869	203	211	516	529	1045	2	2	4	1049	250	7	179
Milton	Muscatine	1867	139	....	504	481	985	1	1	2	987	184	22	173
Milton	Muscatine	1869	187	189	507	502	1009	....	....	....	1009	257	11	187
Winterset	Madison	1867	204	....	683	674	1357	1	1	2	1359	308	4	214
Winterset	Madison	1869	288	326	807	751	1558	1	1	2	1560	400	....	330

* For population by wards of Waterloo, see page 5-6.

NOTE —The number of families was not reported in the year 1867.

TABLE I.

Showing the Population by Counties, and the various classifications thereof. Also the number of Dwelling-Houses and Families, January 1st, 1869.

COUNTIES.	No. of Dwelling Houses	No. of Families.	No. of White Males.	No. of White Females.	Total White Population	No. of Colored Males.	No. of Colored Females	Total Colored Population.	Total Population.	No. entitled to Vote.	No. of Foreigners not Naturalized.	No. of Militia.	No. of Blind not in Asylum, Jan. 1, 1869.	No. of Deaf and Dumb not in Asy., Jan. 1, '69	No. of Insane not in Hospital, Jan. 1, 1869	No. of Colleges, Academies and Universities	No. of Teachers in Colleges, Universities, etc.	No. of Students in Colleges, Universities, etc.
Adair	410	427	1241	1070	2311	1	....	1	2312	557	10	444	....	6	....	....	....	....
Adams	589	611	1781	1515	3296	2	4	6	3302	760	8	583	....	1	....	....	....	....
Allamakee	2850	2908	8634	8112	16746	9	11	20	16766	3145	374	2112	12	5	4	1	....	381
Appanoose	2597	2662	7565	7031	14596	10	19	29	14625	3010	8	2249	6	7	9	....	....	1
Audubon	183	183	539	490	1029	2	1	3	1032	248	3	204	1	....	....	....	....	1
Benton	3256	2891	10232	9172	19404	12	4	16	19420	3869	342	2986	....	1	2	....	....	7
Black Hawk	3475	3565	9843	9095	18938	15	8	23	18961	3937	311	2734	....	7	2	....	....	....
Boone	2435	2594	7372	6521	13893	8	11	19	13912	2585	1315	2081	4	2	2	....	....	....
Bremer	2092	2146	5976	5368	11344	9	5	14	11358	2371	133	1533	1	....	1	....	....	....
Buchanan	2654	2757	7733	7238	14971	2	....	2	14973	3259	134	2440	1	6	6	....	1	6
Buena Vista	54	54	132	110	242	....	....	....	242	64	8	49	....	....	....	....	....	....
Butler	1509	1572	4263	3869	8132	4	3	7	8139	1862	66	1344	2	....	2	....	....	....
Calhoun	192	193	526	418	944	....	....	....	944	205	3	163	1	....	....	....	....	....
Carroll	241	238	672	778	1450	....	....	....	1450	256	23	234	....	....	....	....	....	1
Cass	662	671	1956	1644	3600	4	....	4	3604	820	34	713	1	....	2	....	....	4
Cedar	3296	3405	9475	8721	18196	24	19	43	18239	4030	290	2801	6	7	8	....	....	29
Cerro Gordo	442	483	1281	1185	2466	....	....	....	2466	581	25	398	....	3	....	....	....	....
Cherokee	92	97	253	206	459	....	....	....	459	117	1	101	....	....	....	....	....	....
Chickasaw	1475	1565	4495	4015	8510	2	1	3	8513	1821	114	1279	1	2	3	1	3	125

Clarke	1554	1583	4116	3879	7995	19	13	32	8027	1748	50	1339	....	....	2	....	....	4
Clay	90	100	255	195	450	....	....	....	450	109	....	91	....	1	....	....	....	....
Clayton*	4509	4449	13391	12425	25816	8	8	16	25832	5046	678	6510	12	8	4	1	4	18
Clinton	3803	4626	16723	15111	31834	68	50	118	31952	6140	1151	3924	4	9	6	1	17	47
Crawford	316	316	929	708	1637	2	1	3	1640	348	50	304	....	....	....	....	....	....
Dallas	1804	1856	5508	4831	10339	12	10	22	10361	2342	106	1909	1	5	....	....	....	3
Davis	2651	2668	7492	7387	14879	20	22	42	14921	3170	34	2387	1	6	11	1	1	25
Decatur	1904	1932	5264	5011	10275	40	24	64	10339	1969	44	1575	7	....	6	....	1	1
Delaware	2978	3000	8006	7538	15544	11	2	13	15557	3332	243	2360	5	1	2	1	5	111
Des Moines	4264	4628	13530	12218	25748	124	114	238	25986	4981	685	3309	7	8	8	1	6	114
Dickinson	111	118	310	252	562	....	....	....	562	134	....	81	....	....	....	....	....	....
Dubuque	6686	6779	18880	17937	36817	63	66	129	36946	7093	783	4526	3	19	9	....	21	273
Emmet	217	219	551	438	989	1	....	1	990	203	22	146	....	....	....	....	....	....
Fayette	3023	3079	8402	7841	16243	73	75	148	16391	3414	266	2369	3	1	....	1	6	1
Floyd	1486	1631	4385	4080	8465	....	....	....	8465	1941	156	1401	1	3	3	....	....	1
Franklin	567	575	1597	1468	3065	7	3	10	3075	666	15	495	....	1	....	....	....	....
Fremont	1501	1567	4194	3837	8031	11	9	20	8051	1821	12	1317	1	5	1	....	9	63
Greene	678	728	1784	1710	3494	....	....	....	3494	783	27	638	1	1	....	....	....	1
Grundy	718	745	2049	1799	3848	2	....	2	3850	798	99	688	....	....	....	....	....	....
Guthrie	964	967	2717	2497	5214	3	2	5	5219	1164	25	922	....	....	....	....	....	....
Hamilton	766	800	2233	2033	4266	1	1	2	4268	916	66	677	1	1	....	....	....	2
Hancock	110	111	295	277	572	....	....	....	572	132	....	103	....	....	....	....	....	....
Hardin	2077	2177	5693	5292	10985	12	10	22	11007	2458	153	1848	2	....	1	....	....	1
Harrison	1513	1523	4025	3384	7409	2	....	2	7411	1736	176	1389	5	....	1	....	....	1
Henry	3495	3297	10415	10168	20583	209	179	388	20971	4406	184	3176	4	12	2	6	23	554
Howard	1571	1592	2732	2413	5145	4	....	4	5149	1173	85	883	2	....	....	1	2	61
Humboldt	352	352	945	865	1810	....	....	....	1810	410	2	340	....	....	....	....	....	....
Ida	29	29	77	67	144	....	....	....	144	45	....	35	....	....	....	....	....	....
Iowa	2691	2796	7647	7085	14732	3	3	6	14738	3162	294	2248	3	1	3	....	....	4
Jackson	3812	3853	10521	10041	20562	10	7	17	20579	4146	437	2732	4	1	5	1	2	13

* These figures include the population of Clayton towship for the year 1867, no return having been made for 1869.

TABLE I—Continued.

COUNTIES.	No. of Dwelling-Houses.	No. of Families.	No. of White Males.	No. of White Females.	Total White Population	No. of Colored Males.	No. of Colored Females	Total Colored Population.	Total Population.	No. entitled to Vote.	No. of Foreigners not Naturalized.	No. of Militia.	No. of Blind not in Asylum, Jan. 1, 1869.	No. of Deaf and Dumb not in Asy. Jan. 1, '69	No. of Insane not in Hospital, Jan. 1, 1869	No. of Colleges, Academies and Universities	No. of Teachers in Colleges and Universities	No. of Students in Colleges and Universities
Jasper	4359	4405	10593	9493	20086	34	28	62	20148	4427	154	3375	4	10	8	....	....	29
Jefferson	3007	3096	8497	8221	16718	29	25	54	16772	3612	146	2483	4	4	7	1	3	95
Johnson	4060	4140	12140	11712	23852	47	49	96	23948	4427	558	3117	3	4	2	4	29	686
Jones	3255	3362	9336	8736	18072	23	18	41	18113	3907	216	2432	2	8	5	....	....	5
Keokuk	3054	3150	8894	8384	17278	2	....	2	17280	3676	138	2732	7	9	6	....	....	1
Kossouth	383	387	1021	927	1948	1	....	1	1949	461	15	359	....	....	....	....	....	....
Lee	4974	5140	17019	15629	32648	752	727	1479	34127	6928	451	4734	7	6	7	1	6	144
Linn	4849	4978	14110	13256	27366	55	46	101	27467	5824	402	4003	6	6	8	3	17	529
Louisa	2192	2246	6317	5844	12161	37	21	58	12219	2744	47	2020	3	....	1	2	3	44
Lucas	1733	1744	4711	4423	9134	30	21	51	9185	1901	48	1418	1	4	3	....	....	1
Lyon	......	Not	organi	zed.	....	....	....	....	....	......	......	......	....	....	....	....	....	....
Madison	2117	2158	6148	5666	11814	2	1	3	11817	2585	17	2055	5	2	2	....	1	....
Mahaska	3700	3769	10189	9757	19946	77	53	130	20076	4360	116	3390	3	....	8	1	1	20
Marion	4206	4270	12061	11340	23401	23	16	39	23440	4832	295	3743	9	8	8	1	5	146
Marshall	2774	2774	8161	7299	15460	32	22	54	15514	3581	181	2746	5	3	5	1	3	80
Mills	1248	1232	3675	3258	6933	2	....	2	6935	1506	76	1248	2	1	1	....	....	....
Mitchell	1291	1384	3806	3477	7283	5	....	5	7288	1724	136	1138	1	2	....	....	....	1
Monona	478	504	1432	1226	2658	11	10	21	2679	631	62	456	....	1	2	....	....	....
Monroe	2171	2208	6186	5738	11924	36	30	66	11990	2416	86	1784	4	7	2	....	....	13
Montgomery	533	539	1541	1351	2892	....	....	....	2892	661	10	527	....	1	1	....	....	....
Muscatine	4214	4133	12442	11678	24120	117	99	216	24336	4868	494	3514	7	8	4	5	11	204

O'Brien	7	12	30	21	51	....	....	....	51	15	1	13	....	....	....	....	....	....
Osceola	......	Not	Organ	ized..	......	....	....	....	......	....	....	....	....	....	....	....	....	....
Page	1378	1411	4011	3682	7693	73	77	150	7843	1579	40	1302	1	....	2	1	3	75
Palo Alto	111	111	291	244	535	....	....	....	535	118	5	85	....	....	....	....	....	....
Plymouth	32	32	94	85	179	....	....	....	179	45	......	37	....	....	....	....	....	....
Pocahontas	126	137	341	296	637	....	....	....	637	136	10	123	....	....	....	....	....	....
Polk	4565	4696	13581	12567	26148	133	127	260	26408	5354	227	4436	5	5	1	....	....	3
Pottawattamie	2083	2134	5890	5041	10931	24	19	43	10974	2479	286	2005	....	3	1	....	8	112
Poweshiek	2201	2201	6796	6078	12874	41	21	62	12936	2704	121	2064	2	7	4	1	9	298
Ringgold	853	929	2534	2490	5024	3	2	5	5029	996	19	792	1	1	2	....	....	....
Sac	146	143	412	428	840	....	....	....	840	198	......	155	....	....	....	....	....	....
Scott	6094	6711	19539	17859	37398	116	101	217	37615	6563	2052	3815	3	6	8	1	2	40
Shelby	317	322	888	845	1733	3	8	11	1744	349	31	305	2	....	....	....	....	....
Sioux*	......	......	......	......	......	....	....	....	......	....	....	....	....	....	....	....	....	....
Story	1671	1739	4789	4553	9342	4	1	5	9347	1805	199	1459	....	1	2	1	4	75
Tama	2457	2483	7391	6820	14211	19	24	43	14254	2959	327	2374	4	4	....	....	....	1
Taylor	*	*	2867	2655	5522	33	36	69	5591	1147	5	910	2	3	....	1	3	2
Union	702	696	1944	1867	3811	6	4	10	3821	841	16	655	....	1	....	....	....	....
Van Buren	3218	3273	8410	8230	16640	100	99	199	16839	3783	42	2659	3	2	11	....	....	45
Wapello	3936	3953	10591	9938	20529	71	72	143	20672	4444	347	3285	6	10	12	....	....	2
Warren	2857	2904	8015	7734	15749	35	26	61	15810	3244	30	2557	4	5	8	1	7	201
Washington	3347	3399	9457	9146	18603	26	19	45	18648	4010	168	3025	1	6	3	1	2	60
Wayne	1724	1769	4833	4732	9565	1	....	1	9566	1934	2	1461	3	4	6			
Webster	1332	954	4125	3678	7803	6	3	9	7812	1646	182	1216	....	3	5	....	....	2
Winnebago	139	210	563	509	1072				1072	203	24	94	....	....	....	....	....	....
Winneshiek	3563	3698	11002	10012	21014	20	13	33	21047	3581	1139	2660	7	13	12	1	6	93
Woodbury*	......	......	......	......	......	....	....	....	......	....	....	....	....	....	....	....	....	....
Worth	389	411	1106	1028	2134	1	....	1	2135	346	108	257	1	....	1	....	....	....
Wright	331	342	934	828	1762	2	1	3	1765	376	19	277	2	....	....	....	....	....
Total	183921	187407	537348	498126	1035474	2841	2504	5345	1040819	215209	18103	160465	223	288	268	43	204	4860

* Not reported.

TABLE II.

Showing the number of acres of land inclosed and in cultivation, also the number of acres in the various kinds of grain, etc., in the several counties, in the year 1868.

COUNTIES.	No. of acres of land inclosed.	No. of acres of land in cultivation.	No. of acres of Spring Wheat.	No. of acres of Winter Wheat.	No. of acres of Corn.	No. of acres of Oats.	No. of acres of Buckwheat.	No. of acres of Barley.	No. of acres of Rye.	No. of acres of Potatoes.	No. of acres of Onions.	No. of acres of tame Grass.	No. of acres of Flax.	No. of acres of Sorghum	No. of acres of Hops.	No. of acres planted for Timber.
Adair........	9852	10504	2331	......	5512	787	6	1	2	146	1	42	29	100	12	39
Adams.........	16647	14073	2726	1	6993	1002	16	......	36	146	1	242	......	188	2	57
Allamakee	138439	93698	41007	191	25992	8982	253	1000	214	1093	11	11204	9	158	65	2
Appanoose......	117874	92263	8972	4417	41807	11715	254	37	588	276	17	13881	1531	700	....	3
Audubon.......	6489	4639	980	5	1959	238	......	18	......	58	....	33	......	26	1	7
Benton.........	169683	139390	58548	77	34893	11738	376	784	82	919	7	6176	66	299	3	943
Black Hawk	161014	123801	62167	8	24523	11342	242	130	220	1123	18	4029	4	349	36	708
Boone	60521	46886	8108	......	18779	23714	82	64	28	676	3	717	......	296	4	66
Bremer	99418	64520	27550	6	13393	9168	225	183	123	810	3	2710	4	413	20	183
Buchanan.......	138806	98094	41262	3	22808	11680	280	208	28	1076	8	6284	2	363	3	374
Buena Vista.....	871	812	161	114	55	......	......	......	......	13	....	......	......	14	....	......
Butler	89672	60232	28442	......	14035	6750	127	58	51	539	16	1018	......	225	11	458
Calhoun	3014	4364	1210	......	1263	461	10	2	......	76	....	......	......	51	....	22
Carroll..........	4941	5164	1411	......	2249	263	12	2	40	56	....	......	2	65	....	97
Cass	21841	16973	3355	......	8768	1259	2	12	......	308	....	65	......	113	....	65
Cedar...........	241940	182356	53109	142	53027	19085	322	3188	485	822	55	27584	2837	291	....	493
Cerro Gordo	16101	11959	4005	......	2696	2239	7	49	1	180	....	186	......	48	16	85
Cherokee.......	1102	1012	147	......	596	64	5	......	......	34	....	......	......	28	....	9

Chickasaw	64090	41378	15718	......	8540	6046	263	146	95	542	....	2600	......	166	25	95
Clarke	59987	46283	7740	......	22423	6241	101	8	57	296	....	3746	231	762	....	67
Clay	2552	1682	371	......	498	118	......	......	......	32	....	5	......	38	....	14
Clayton	208858	143967	73198	1182	31904	17850	226	1276	212	1545	61	12895	......	204	47	34
Clinton	310306	217934	69632	8	59115	24689	471	3997	388	1366	21	26212	288	216	14	910
Crawford	9672	8953	2662	......	2942	1119	13	3	......	108	2	9	5	36	2	241
Dallas	72849	58309	11948	......	25179	4429	124	24	40	944	....	509	214	463	....	168
Davis	153449	109317	7356	9891	42603	12750	280	12	1635	286	17	17296	505	791	....	15
Decatur	73260	53672	5566	1168	24968	8132	593	18	703	406	3	7065	8	698	4	111
Delaware	192382	110978	40291	33	32287	16281	391	842	70	1078	3	12071	1	254	60	179
Des Moines	144824	124314	14901	6580	47507	11304	388	377	1155	873	1	22078	393	397	....	29
Dickinson	2927	1505	369	10	314	235	5	9	2	52	....	......	......	41	....	......
Dubuque	193208	133185	36050	85	42260	23227	142	1332	418	1497	26	19213	4	216	31	60
Emmet	3801	2823	966	......	765	272	4	15	10	92	2	3	......	38	....	20
Fayette	161686	99793	37685	26	23900	14477	283	675	36	1144	7	9550	27	331	209	388
Floyd	69267	52045	20485	......	8975	14512	56	143	14	506	3	1345	3	133	44	102
Franklin	26295	22527	8454	......	4899	2693	24	31	2	230	....	136	4	58	7	143
Fremont	53365	40812	5020	188	28992	1859	60	134	666	348	3	93	16	153	....	125
Greene	16886	14471	3554	8	6818	1151	86	18	1	176	....	......	2	146	....	31
Grundy	33817	49575	17502	......	7047	3731	55	129	29	254	1	657	......	47	3	349
Guthrie	35345	29961	7470	......	14135	1981	35	1	......	272	....	191	......	225	7	104
Hamilton	22912	15643	5137	......	6655	2442	91	129	12	306	2	207	......	253	8	109
Hancock	3168	2402	843	......	651	556	15	7	......	49	....	11	......	12	....	23
Hardin	85750	61549	23488	......	20918	7126	125	97	35	597	....	1604	1	326	4	464
Harrison	42933	32479	8095	10	15590	2239	127	31	......	469	10	195	......	197	....	107
Henry	152616	123980	14962	5391	44958	10810	455	190	1595	675	18	24965	985	835	6	130
Howard	45873	29906	14901	5	3888	5487	57	328	7	419	12	696	4	35	22	195
Humboldt	11150	7185	1819	......	2547	912	28	4	......	185	....	8	......	118	....	125
Ida	......	900	290	......	350	151	......	......	......	15	2	......	......	5	....	10
Iowa	127324	101269	36784	48	29413	8284	284	565	202	878	16	6861	11	338	3	166
Jackson	185589	137069	33395	680	41910	23751	739	422	541	1028	4	20623	48	340	18	3

TABLE II—CONTINUED.

COUNTIES.	No. of acres of land inclosed.	No. of acres of land in cultivation.	No. of acres of Spring Wheat.	No. of acres of Winter Wheat.	No. of acres of Corn.	No. of acres of Oats.	No. of acres of Buckwheat.	No. of acres of Barley.	No. of acres of Rye.	No. of acres of Potatoes.	No. of acres of Onions.	No. of acres of tame Grass.	No. of acres of Flax.	No. of acres of Sorghum.	No. of acres of Hops.	No. of acres planted for Timber.
Jasper	158649	131509	46154	29	47712	9772	209	77	117	1191	4	3100	....	496	....	237
Jefferson	154488	124071	11820	7225	42599	10663	621	69	3832	488	2	26241	108	613	....	2846
Johnson	205788	158076	38149	463	49117	16585	334	369	1308	1071	9	17079	5604	421	5	200
Jones	186851	127104	31073	40	45748	18651	296	279	280	967	3	17392	34	308	348	316
Keokuk	175018	122032	24987	3263	48904	10358	365	197	1537	595	7	16856	142	651	....	121
Kossuth	9986	9437	1900	....	2488	1520	36	36	....	216	....	3	2	98	....	94
Lee	176509	142206	16409	4734	48789	12985	49	1244	6701	1045	87	27135	11	743	....	178
Linn	229147	158089	44056	26	54180	19425	547	298	441	1886	25	18319	3	589	29	326
Louisa	124374	101890	23577	2654	38887	8117	366	25	1245	631	4	17377	548	469	....	47
Lucas	60293	48295	7770	107	22518	6227	294	21	247	383	....	5214	....	462	....	127
Lyon	Not	organ-	ized.	....	.....	.....	....	....	....	.....	....	.....	....	....	....	....
Madison	89839	69419	15223	14	33372	5927	66	3	99	649	5	2665	1	520	11	134
Mahaska	179222	136613	56464	1319	54065	10036	399	12	284	792	1	17938	505	634	32	348
Marion	163810	129904	32311	963	58427	10465	292	89	898	1083	17	11334	35	887	....	74
Marshall	135475	114116	45086	....	32563	8299	141	83	46	783	2	2584	362	194	21	1080
Mills	61874	42724	10713	4	23515	2365	28	237	100	414	8	356	....	119	....	235
Mitchell	56855	40213	19824	....	4907	6236	84	716	25	478	3	730	1	91	9	90
Monona	15835	11227	2713	....	4687	750	29	....	....	199	....	1	....	85	....	161
Monroe	92548	72975	11295	3190	29672	7842	300	45	1208	456	....	11930	485	557	....	42
Montgomery	16322	13850	2627	....	7447	838	11	....	7	142	....	114	....	82	....	39
Muscatine	193721	127216	34037	414	43422	13348	405	3369	1888	909	28	20074	357	371	2	733

O'Brien	355	300	65	......	85	89	......	2	......	3	....	......	......	......	....	......
Osceola	Not or-	organi-	zed.	......	......	......	......	......	......	......	....	......	......	......	....	......
Page	54477	40899	5175	9	24681	3454	18	51	47	328	1	537	20	285	....	153
Palo Alto	2308	2087	445	......	732	318	3	......	......	100	....	......	......	23	....	27
Plymouth	750	1276	399	......	150	92		23	......	27	....	......	......	6	....	9
Pocahontas	2677	3355	1226	......	981	400	......	......	......	99	....	11	2	45	....	19
Polk	120358	78058	21008	71	41831	6932	88	120	29	1137	1	1484	159	589	41	120
Pottawattamie	32895	26750	5964	35	13911	1880	37	91	15	548	3	34	4	133	....	1200
Poweshiek	114344	98676	36513	10	32332	5860	120	145	95	483	8	3577	......	197	....	223
Ringgold	29727	24651	2853	17	14077	3337	66	13	77	216	1	1165	21	341	....	56
Sac	5405	5279	1586	......	1281	485	......	......	......	90	....	......	......	40	....	10
Scott	225420	185632	62552	102	44803	16718	186	22426	188	2289	369	17012	5	95	20	256
Shelby	8999	7620	2074	......	3211	516	......	1	......	115	....	12	......	57	....	29
Sioux	Not re-	ported.	......	......	......	......	......	......	......	......	....	......	......	......	....	......
Story	74088	44492	11854	15	18570	5181	74	23	8	602	....	567	139	331	19	229
Tama	117605	101995	46958	......	26086	6837	135	132	46	747	15	2915	43	164	5	384
Taylor	36565	29700	4300	......	17014	3380	91	2	51	369	1	1033	......	413	....	224
Union	20672	17041	2589	5	8947	1886	38	77	49	142	1	768	8	164	....	245
Van Buren	146566	108096	9640	9938	37044	12174	302	38	3268	356	....	24432	366	566	3	14
Wapello	144540	113784	13891	6073	41091	8106	494	159	1330	587	10	17794	225	594	26	20
Warren	126616	95170	22270	413	45756	7731	165	72	89	834	11	64523	445	660	25	228
Washington	184474	147479	32799	1602	49187	12918	411	100	1506	467	1	22767	9	443	....	397
Wayne	74564	57443	7108	879	26409	7251	238	44	375	321	....	7676	588	531	....	53
Webster	41340	29147	8986	......	9962	3713	72	31	6	500	3	88	3	335	....	66
Winnebago	4551	2048	911	......	391	261	13	12	......	58	1	3	......	5	....	3
Winneshiek	225511	144789	73500	23	20503	17431	80	2106	104	1093	10	10469	......	57	15	57
Woodbury	Not re-	ported.	......	......	......	......	......	......	......	......	....	......	......	......	....	......
Worth	12913	7612	3490	......	1220	1060	10	22	1	140	....	30	......	58	1	22
Wright	11740	8992	3143	......	2666	1136	20	51	1	150	....	38	......	87	....	75
......	8174930	6109743	1730590	73914	2058239	657007	15264	49307	37371	54528	995	602316	17842	26243	1299	19675

TABLE III.

Showing the number of rods of Hedging planted, number of Fruit Trees and Grape Vines in bearing and not in bearing; also, the number of Horses Cattle, Hogs, Sheep, Mules and Asses, Milch Cows, Work Oxen, Dogs and Hives of Bees in the several Counties, January 1st, 1869.

COUNTIES.	No. of Rods of Hedging planted.	No. of Fruit Trees in bearing.	No. of Fruit Trees not in bearing.	No. of Grape Vines in bearing.	No. of Grape Vines not in bearing.	No. of Horses of all ages.	No. of Cattle of all ages	No. of Hogs of all ages.	No. of Sheep of all ages	No. of Mules and Asses of all ages.	No. of Milch Cows.	No. of Work Oxen.	No. of Dogs.	No. of Hives of Bees.
Adair	4410	997	3894	845	1762	1492	2849	2527	4090	52	906	114	387	203
Adams	9270	660	4383	358	3572	1399	3499	3235	5598	202	1189	228	498	293
Allamakee	276	9021	30385	1818	2324	5779	14846	18458	10836	42	5691	1208	2533	1110
Appanoose	75901	20407	73369	4755	15374	7610	17365	30683	41455	608	4975	543	2242	2520
Audubon	370	89	1267	106	411	662	1775	882	1804	137	855	48	168	37
Benton	66319	19515	94008	3831	25179	9567	19268	24562	11826	367	6746	513	2770	758
Black Hawk	18528	13203	121361	5670	11082	8532	16958	12549	8482	225	5783	353	2540	631
Boone	9410	3986	26558	3191	15920	4553	9753	9079	10846	256	3267	452	1526	490
Bremer	6737	3714	45338	1699	4098	5072	12015	8811	9350	58	4208	272	1483	559
Buchanan	27302	10044	45131	3242	9784	6530	15813	12489	16123	161	5660	564	1822	677
Buena Vista	......	......	15	9	9	68	305	85	170	....	106	73	23	1
Butler	12995	1827	18750	407	3081	4427	9173	7692	5817	117	3256	296	1217	324
Calhoun	952	51	576	33	56	335	1056	379	1045	14	331	189	145	14
Carroll	9901	137	859	5	45	435	941	912	801	21	329	112	178	5
Cass	3984	426	4173	511	2978	2138	4823	2593	4258	114	1460	84	634	240
Cedar	130418	50387	119905	10214	30868	12082	27849	39092	25720	505	8489	144	2598	1901
Cerro Gordo	4300	522	4236	220	339	1297	3115	1199	2583	24	1152	155	346	78
Cherokee	......	......	45	......	24	146	728	79	18	6	177	108	79	......

Chickasaw	2802	831	6423	537	2427	3444	11089	5312	6152	66	3866	700	1176	281
Clarke	45998	10798	33326	4317	8709	4742	8747	14503	16558	308	2523	126	1208	856
Clay	…	…	50	…	16	143	606	144	126	6	231	127	65	4
Clayton	679	14759	62562	6008	32972	9548	21589	28185	14765	327	8827	893	4035	1990
Clinton	116683	35136	342279	7634	29938	15617	33687	38288	15260	357	11370	88	3975	1343
Crawford	999	1603	6505	1372	3243	719	2429	886	2504	19	687	249	193	64
Dallas	26869	11432	29884	5284	9111	5120	9773	12570	16534	466	3350	265	1403	763
Davis	79281	33760	58968	10290	30073	8398	19878	31560	46896	1668	5637	261	2599	3148
Decatur	28251	16481	34851	4579	15091	5544	11738	19204	31764	466	3556	433	1600	2066
Delaware	10198	11680	66754	2695	10557	8696	22388	24578	18044	366	7705	287	2455	1221
Des Moines	129534	151701	101737	247319	158717	9462	19178	32082	21181	811	5989	50	3403	1774
Dickinson	80	…	366	6	18	185	672	86	119	…	215	135	85	…
Dubuque	519	30130	63884	19965	48832	11009	27355	37275	14914	289	11165	354	4685	1101
Emmet	188	7	193	84	2	269	1590	229	1187	8	452	237	141	8
Fayette	13229	6935	52849	2339	8981	7845	19025	18258	21277	200	6690	726	2194	1275
Floyd	7792	1522	24144	800	4101	4278	8617	5907	9183	90	3061	356	1087	384
Franklin	7727	329	7472	229	1194	1788	3490	2371	2769	19	1175	139	441	45
Fremont	46962	6967	20931	1586	3294	4067	11144	21164	10505	478	4496	272	1157	580
Greene	2599	388	4048	358	1023	1657	3223	2884	4320	64	1079	173	1038	124
Grundy	10992	1280	11720	373	1759	2489	4725	3357	4990	73	1785	169	813	10
Guthrie	34756	3252	18897	2458	3011	2837	5234	6060	10879	118	1844	186	1002	303
Hamilton	3563	762	7037	411	3034	2006	4798	2531	3533	45	1672	209	550	192
Hancock	1240	32	1676	17	144	299	726	206	702	10	251	62	88	9
Hardin	18029	7991	31627	1543	12562	5636	10148	11652	9063	166	3550	149	1368	581
Harrison	1203	564	7663	204	1704	3484	10206	8923	6588	136	3359	276	1039	667
Henry	132492	106283	135870	24834	39152	9573	19957	31136	52321	767	6482	152	2861	2275
Howard	7209	767	11392	211	896	2251	6891	2769	2206	42	2446	433	758	183
Humboldt	3020	376	2868	68	333	791	2057	572	992	14	830	274	257	2
Ida	200	…	300	…	50	96	307	33	88	…	…	…	…	…
Iowa	61925	10961	38076	5327	16458	7416	19434	22119	15173	412	6245	690	2459	1038
Jackson	11372	29160	71400	6079	12117	10988	28009	33481	18680	154	9401	257	3403	1326

TABLE III—Continued.

COUNTIES.	No. of Rods of Hedging planted.	No. of Fruit Trees in bearing.	No. of Fruit Trees not in bearing.	No. of Grape Vines in bearing.	No. of Grape Vines not in bearing.	No. of Horses of all ages.	No. of Cattle of all ages	No. of Hogs of all ages.	No. of Sheep of all ages	No. of Mules and Asses of all ages.	No of Milch Cows.	No. of Work Oxen.	No. of Dogs.	No. of Hives of Bees.
Jasper	65240	16042	63494	7481	23759	10247	20090	34288	31502	704	6616	366	2998	1594
Jefferson	82040	66939	86898	25925	42641	9209	18809	35296	45879	748	6326	115	2893	2435
Johnson	60404	43534	87293	28278	73341	11261	28691	40181	29711	667	8675	427	3507	1947
Jones	31963	17227	63452	3213	15705	10026	26451	35532	21143	301	8842	257	2580	1577
Keokuk	115937	29174	77080	7912	24225	9982	22168	34717	38791	739	6846	302	3085	1767
Kossuth	2511	138	4134	10	371	909	2792	870	814	28	993	270	328	5
Lee	193837	122760	121114	258887	179919	10659	23744	28336	36363	1032	7991	108	3842	2450
Linn	48051	25176	85365	15719	26838	12353	32496	44094	27189	478	10205	334	3451	2420
Louisa	94095	51392	118809	12167	18023	7572	19238	29986	21085	450	5595	134	2015	1707
Lucas	65767	7435	28944	2334	13631	4627	9991	15134	20417	394	3040	154	1351	1217
Lyon	Not or-	ganized	......	......	......	......	......	......	......	......	......	......	......	......
Madison	56039	14757	46319	11785	20796	6194	12453	19987	30171	548	3816	270	1891	1242
Mahaska	79361	54439	67485	10813	26347	11720	28117	41433	59139	991	6506	533	2574	2614
Marion	53640	27022	58546	11788	38233	10541	23986	48218	44580	860	7306	415	3626	2623
Marshall	57171	8656	58420	9989	33430	7879	15098	16467	14661	372	4713	270	1953	912
Mills	21952	6105	16291	1289	3188	4248	11197	8527	5223	452	2910	224	1355	558
Mitchell	5572	941	8411	305	1827	2927	7591	3042	4380	60	2780	525	904	460
Monona	74	421	1847	331	881	1354	4902	2372	5207	31	1352	285	290	275
Monroe	54092	20704	32439	10808	14823	5576	14404	23187	29596	418	4172	530	2026	1860
Montgomery	7575	344	2409	166	566	1514	3344	4099	5546	93	1096	232	531	206
Muscatine	175597	64364	88053	28017	49773	10316	22726	27857	15001	669	7603	67	2935	1919

County														
O'Brien	......	......	20	......	5	34	94	19	1	4	18	2	9	4
Osceola	Not or-	ganized	......	......	......	......	......	......	......	......	......	......	......	......
Page	30536	9495	19764	4484	9859	4494	10747	16055	12872	330	3012	138	1402	628
Palo Alto	515	......	966	20	24	205	1582	296	132	7	533	162	101	......
Plymouth	......	......	......	......	27	71	394	31	2	4	107	39	34	......
Pocahontas	641	10	893	12	65	269	1180	292	23	4	362	167	129	......
Polk	17293	32412	92123	54269	143155	8075	16720	24765	18271	696	5901	170	2494	1496
Pottawattamie	10088	1212	6590	995	1921	3578	7373	4270	4679	213	2987	98	1076	276
Poweshiek	58231	9206	65781	2607	19763	7417	14424	20344	16470	457	4821	266	1956	640
Ringgold	32115	2596	10092	867	2362	2659	5961	9362	16577	204	1795	116	919	220
Sac	1200	......	1663	......	265	453	1005	326	1362	2	321	213	119	6
Scott	170903	74355	117445	42011	188088	11258	23929	30713	9106	948	9682	78	4781	812
Shelby	730	274	1519	35	142	990	1932	1462	3598	63	676	71	247	196
Sioux	Not re-	ported.	......	......	......	......	......	......	......	......	......	......	......	......
Story	36420	5327	30322	2667	6348	4792	12160	9283	8529	153	3954	231	1256	501
Tama	37695	6801	57069	2107	9789	7804	14582	15625	9324	287	5239	618	2270	654
Taylor	22212	3533	17410	2149	2131	3128	6930	10891	11773	216	2207	180	912	682
Union	16630	2149	9270	1236	2579	1818	3514	4614	6607	217	1068	111	543	326
Van Buren	121465	68869	90386	23397	29622	8518	17767	29529	49989	876	5817	145	2615	4029
Wapello	83936	33661	59043	12130	21688	8555	17474	35322	44010	860	5760	291	2971	2619
Warren	70027	21040	59133	10780	30872	8438	17940	31284	35259	506	5219	249	2327	1980
Washington	138831	46542	105946	24437	42634	9856	24792	38128	41159	727	7658	372	2898	2043
Wayne	79485	7348	34724	3557	10919	5058	11969	17615	27172	479	3285	191	1685	999
Webster	6514	2137	16275	658	2943	2804	7570	3986	6538	88	2526	661	949	350
Winnebago	......	......	747	42	83	233	1335	338	801	7	435	201	127	8
Winneshiek	2620	3757	33045	1809	4885	9013	21944	17576	16065	129	8413	1407	2354	773
Woodbury	Not re-	ported.	......	......	......	......	......	......	......	......	......	......	......	......
Worth	350	58	624	15	118	686	3722	1208	2076	10	1164	388	314	1
Wright	2233	718	2547	1074	260	945	2498	1092	1218	7	840	149	274	23
Total	3393061	1539943	4100207	1132416	1950307	482786	2108667	2409679	2370106	28420	367602	26726	147623	82517

TABLE IV.

Showing the number of bushels of Grain, Roots and Seeds of the various kinds harvested; also the number of bushels Apples, pounds of Grapes, and gallons of Syrup from Sorghum in the several Counties for the year 1868.

COUNTIES.	No. of bushels Spring Wheat.	No. of bushels Winter Wheat.	No. of bushels Corn.	No. of bushels Oats.	No. of bushels Buck-wheat.	No. of bushels Barley.	No. of bushels Rye.	No. of bushels Irish Potatoes	No. of bushels Onions.	No. of bushels Clover Seed.	No. of bushels Grass Seed.	No. of bushels Flax Seed.	No. of bushels Apples.	No. of lbs Grapes.	No. of gallons Syrup from Sorghum.
Adair	19119	.....	165767	22393	271	5	4	19690	98	....	....	245	238	933	9448
Adams	28442	176	216452	27519	59	13	538	15992	240	....	14	....	41	1013	15732
Allamakee	709668	2617	647309	313486	3067	16237	3170	73684	669	7	95	1	1822	4354	14506
Appanoose	127902	50038	1312754	321022	2025	641	6921	15076	582	10	1040	9360	10482	12639	67686
Audubon	9262	.....	67395	6327	.....	149	....	7974	22	....	....	....	4	183	2017
Benton	1131410	284	1381979	400833	4874	20779	951	93596	793	6	611	450	2581	9193	36624
Black Hawk	1168107	.....	848801	477379	2378	3593	3019	97595	2458	45	108	....	2396	16469	30126
Boone	29802	.....	423731	35283	462	451	446	84010	206	....	....	....	1935	5596	33865
Bremer	454734	29	504345	362182	2339	6809	1613	71405	1072	2	192	32	264	7959	28244
Buchanan	761466	17	804068	453044	2978	5553	1389	107273	1149	3	363	3	1202	4266	44964
Buena Vista	1094	.....	5365	1047	....	.....	....	2514	....	....	....	....	.....	.....	646
Butler	451023	.....	471677	230407	1014	1236	1128	47178	454	....	164	1	314	1522	23750
Calhoun	6299	.....	31895	7372	10	.....	....	6428	6	....	....	....	2	38	4181
Carroll	38510	.....	51485	4120	127	5	....	7371	12	....	45	....	4	.....	3711
Cass	42183	.....	306680	38034	29	123	....	27691	54	....	13	....	40	1903	13415
Cedar	792454	2478	2304394	591782	3415	80067	8692	69312	10993	83	6755	16352	10256	20593	28337
Cerro Gordo	75567	.....	96207	96692	133	881	45	19611	454	11	35	....	36	330	5186
Cherokee	1257	.....	9930	155	....	.....	....	2956	.....	....	.....	.....	.....	.....	543

Chickasaw	260919		291393	228694	2976	4349	1575	43621	373		1555	1	129	1490	17249
Clarke	101503		775069	119777	1985	74	850	26444	508	5	397	659	2963	7994	36617
Clay	3800		11862	3359				3749							3016
Clayton	1034502	22060	1349051	535065	3153	31402	1848	130595	972	15	390		3873	9327	32663
Clinton	1066721	980	2146099	725811	2145	102896	3991	94208	1612	151	1783	1916	5426	17307	20139
Crawford	15622		96542	9661	45	10		13472	10			10			2628
Dallas	47343		719531	78068	579	176	255	55292	183		12	47	5007	6895	35701
Davis	101672	101814	1365505	281099	2695	460	20860	11053	648	1	2334	2332	15569	12191	84980
Decatur	75774	14342	699235	158325	1541	40	5918	25638	822	23	391	200	4396	10262	49196
Delaware	696702	628	1150429	573188	4225	20719	822	105991	665	50	509		2888	5843	28250
Des Moines	176344	112178	1888149	278526	3797	6260	13222	63485	1305	18	540	1548	80755	600236	46083
Dickinson	5865		7522	6912		292	22	5092	39						2495
Dubuque	600597	1206	1616484	683720	1014	33830	6472	119366	1264	16	168	22	10952	19935	18475
Emmet	12954		17870	5955	65	266	137	8193	103		2				2037
Fayette	658107	488	882183	499869	3048	15800	367	103639	1313	68	944	150	1187	6655	35957
Floyd	349587		328592	254585	868	3994	253	46457	760	4	55	17	248	850	14787
Franklin	132773		135252	87723	352	918		23740	138		16		24	402	8591
Fremont	52314	205	1030917	57640	230	1743	302	35854	528		34		3915	1136	14485
Greene	15386		206690	20563	775	345	3	25837	137			17	25	393	14231
Grundy	310136		144279	136518	375	3584	405	23349	296		1	2	162	207	4452
Guthrie	61270		490207	50714	476	30	10	42622	154			18	732	3711	23636
Hamilton	52957		242111	29715	459	894		32757	491		25		111	327	23672
Hancock	15627		23030	20039	155	147		4869	165					1	820
Hardin	434706		684656	250577	1297	2944	404	58331	285		70		1448	4632	33189
Harrison	41449		421269	50887	63	108		39015	53		77		160	127	18878
Henry	205782	79448	2080095	267518	4508	1629	23635	48750	759	75	3063	3876	53288	79031	58252
Howard	242442		147875	186573	462	7347	113	25956	570		11	2	71	384	2872
Humboldt	21229		78354	15399	288	250		24800	75				4	187	8806
Ida															
Iowa	556426	377	1198037	269827	3462	17024	4911	77856	833	67	590	116	2800	23212	35630
Jackson	606667	6982	1483213	698838	7208	10790	6716	79336	410	35	915	10	11224	11256	28917

TABLE IV—CONTINUED.

COUNTIES.	No. of bushels Spring Wheat	No. of bushels Winter Wheat.	No. of bushels Corn.	No. of bushels Oats.	No. of bushels of Buck-wheat.	No. of bushels Barley.	No. of bushels Rye.	No. of bushels of Irish Potatoes.	No. of bushels Onions.	No. of bushels Clover Seed.	No. of bushels of Grass Seed.	No. of bushels of Flax Seed.	No. of bushels Apples.	No. of lbs. Grapes.	No. gallons syrup from Sorghum.
Jasper	1367485	875	2108566	301129	2290	754	1850	161939	989	1	266	2	4061	16590	57161
Jefferson	156693	110793	1639252	251336	5656	1052	54281	16756	325	328	12828	460	56747	81493	66766
Johnson	575904	9267	2902278	495217	3554	8020	23229	76192	690	116	5717	33773	12532	26015	51591
Jones	564745	321	1733062	632468	3600	7738	3677	91785	495	12	643	380	5169	5409	30603
Keokuk	365729	40194	1799067	248448	3032	3555	22480	35462	1667	8	935	913	19130	18658	67587
Kossuth	28923	....	71917	50583	282	459	......	24767	178	....	.....	8	2	15	7821
Lee	260652	58276	1644601	311521	1160	20337	78841	33479	341	63	10823	69	56857	269710	60287
Linn	758266	3066	2064749	637863	7477	8977	7971	114187	2115	17	884	31	5733	20411	70988
Louisa	231883	99305	1679563	181480	2647	71	15015	39505	694	17	467	2797	40318	15529	52144
Lucas	135092	1115	796818	186257	3501	277	3781	33972	478	111	458	2	2728	8037	38296
Lyon	Not or-	ganized	....	....	.....	......	.....	......	......	....	.....	.....	......	....	....
Madison	134434	101	1018369	101887	326	217	899	76818	367	2	57	.....	6267	19552	45994
Mahaska	440594	17994	2187663	255373	3119	1131	7505	78449	828	23	654	3573	11834	35301	79616
Marion	596140	12334	2363664	302707	3189	1931	16306	123487	1329	15	393	351	15940	49538	113490
Marshall	928986	....	1201182	279361	1633	2974	847	108514	499	14	111	3	1254	23974	32770
Mills	52517	65	807697	56300	143	2457	446	29135	369	....	123	.....	1865	2335	11338
Mitchell	393314	73	189814	296387	909	19852	383	48408	900	....	231	4	90	498	7525
Monona	26130	....	89589	19387	.....	7	......	20254	10	....	.....	.....	66	234	6270
Monroe	161943	52099	1041961	195518	2382	615	13169	31013	775	57	479	3480	6770	27118	57534
Montgomery	26778	......	236308	19087	89	....	292	11347	203	....	1	1	46	620	10340
Muscatine	454478	4572	1717065	342150	3499	75176	23577	75687	4764	15	2108	2858	18190	91175	37926

O'Brien	522		375	830				190							
Osceola	Not orga	nized													
Page	36712	111	796790	88710	223	64	639	23972	450		17	25	1290	6012	29146
Palo Alto	5596		20256	7241				11760	14						1737
Plymouth	4866		1295	1415		420		830							
Pocahontas	3233		21830	2260		20		9220	2			5			3518
Polk	221185	828	1734785	119425	998	2028	307	153561	605		87	278	10247	105360	62338
Pottawattamie	35967		345081	48702	265	1675	257	42854	104		30	15	341	773	12065
Poweshiek	633586		1232569	171109	1886	4208	1556	59635	1236	24	173		3364	9047	21839
Ringgold	24482	10	426840	51401	335	99	498	18432	303		85	25	825	861	33516
Sac	9833		39199	11103				8618	17						2422
Scott	925571	1454	2006139	482695	1987	504879	2498	164545	54334	564	577	21	17160	147912	13256
Shelby	9217		85110	12041				14689	51		10		23		4618
Sioux	Not repo	rted													
Story	141198	233	664400	85913	793	129	50	78938	486		20	741	1174	3936	39126
Tama	860019	2000	913537	256699	1340	3159	761	32402	414	4	175	21	1452	9009	15116
Taylor	38681		499072	77293	210	4	1003	21627	252	1	78	4	443	3593	26120
Union	23798	56	330658	36861	401	137	848	20338	170		271	2	170	489	13868
Van Buren	118567	206624	1259070	282225	2511	656	43991	9880	647	635	7426	1539	50582	65637	67446
Wapello	210303	80350	1508391	190529	4569	2450	18826	33981	436	55	1342	1098	24658	54289	66925
Warren	305391	5890	1898804	198652	1940	1412	1334	94983	1007	105	161	3177	12459	39309	63920
Washington	512358	23636	1988507	336919	3885	3038	21543	25517	453	106	787	80	34097	45711	52394
Wayne	103493	11916	829302	179830	2055	456	5161	19839	420	17	797	3270	2686	7291	52637
Webster	31150		267901	19469	280	218		46096	154	8		1	104	745	37767
Winnebago	15272		12895	10207	113	399		8213	175						449
Winneshiek	1420749	230	816658	690393	1065	57127	1515	65920	845	25	1365		498	5160	4848
Woodbury	Not repo	rted													
Worth	65267		45316	48904	79	572		15283	228			1	2	17	5691
Wright	47435		107430	47118	70	780	3	16656	190					67	8899
Total	16823520	1140035	76507575	18596625	144920	1144454	496347	4417858	115742	3028	73896	96395	666148	2128472	2592393

TABLE V.

Showing the Number of Pounds Honey, Butter, Cheese, Wool and Hops, the Number of Tons of Hay of the various kinds, Value of Farm Produce raised, Value of Stock sold, Value of Manufactures and Mineral, not including Coal, and Number of Bushels Coal, for the year 1868; Also, the value of Agricultural Implements and Machinery on the 1st of January 1869, in the several Counties.

COUNTIES.	No. lbs. Honey.	No. lbs. Butter made.	No. lbs. Cheese made.	No. lbs. Wool shorn in 1868.	No. of Tons Hay from tame grass.	No. of Tons Hay from wild grasses.	No. lbs. Hops raised.	Value Farm Produce during year 1868.	Value of Stock sold during year 1868.	Value of Agricultural Implements Machinery and Wagons.	Value of Manufactures for 1868.	No bushels coal mined 80 lbs. per bushel, during the year 1868	Value of Minerals not including Coal, during 1868.
Adair	1853	50068	445	12016	110	6019	501	$498133	$51547	$34547	$1697	……	……
Adams	3793	63997	9220	17728	310	6216	12	164703	55569	52186	13745	5377	$251
Allamakee	10390	292492	12672	32541	11358	6291	8082	1123679	199039	163527	198857	……	……
Appanoose	19784	341877	7239	120810	17214	2937	27	783893	388213	155432	135793	152186	573
Audubon	957	31830	3909	3040	50	5076	……	45811	25608	16783	1290	……	……
Benton	4686	426400	6300	39060	7697	22933	218	1517569	322051	251000	26465	……	……
Black Hawk	6512	405194	10463	32177	5049	20732	3820	1636369	197579	261346	533475	……	100
Boone	5431	195283	8109	39270	644	20929	45	428517	145553	115853	74833	1573500	67
Bremer	3888	308140	9853	29523	3221	17664	2615	786691	123189	177425	194281	……	……
Buchanan	3262	380438	15523	55883	7006	20365	878	1267741	211619	227027	42645	……	687
Buena Vista	……	5650	……	76	……	1074	……	4020	332	1810	40	……	……
Butler	2861	251146	38960	16388	1384	17993	5080	761528	135022	138504	12512	……	……
Calhoun	100	19769	290	3348	……	3214	……	32624	7406	10712	173	……	……
Carroll	25	11947	……	4653	2270	……	……	28200	11818	7223	1162	……	……
Cass	1413	53817	6045	13116	50	9354	20	204625	67379	55520	29910	……	……
Cedar	5680	520024	19351	100997	28597	12288	120	2025953	629073	366898	13989	……	227
Cerro Gordo	302	76194	20180	6849	432	7727	……	75904	26429	26578	4894	……	15
Cherokee	……	9590	……	165	……	1901	……	17400	7976	4572	1040	……	……

Chickasaw	2619	299121	17067	19071	2583	20157	3432	476714	$90215	$116118	$31494		
Clarke	11034	162200	1215	57026	5117	7035	6	469592	181011	93122	32628		
Clay	30	16340		215		3174		21712	2096	4021			
Clayton	7767	549519	57672	72783	34208	15410	80967	2086428	373040	258628	469274		$852
Clinton	6593	681551	7371	44808	24594	23445	1555	2408943	598125	388920	240977		5135
Crawford	361	26577	950	8089		6277		62506	20517	10085	500		
Dallas	5117	211533	2050	54623	341	19794		536817	232302	152006	77303	13975	2040
Davis	25485	313252	6589	144726	17852	514	62	947531	372542	172180	115892	9182	390
Decatur	22697	192381	2281	91135	10678	6852	13	538092	239691	129847	385424		
Delaware	5146	535289	51368	56886	13990	23418	22806	1590301	327662	261304	153965		400
Des Moines	14269	368942	11647	91978	23338	1484	1109	1444797	399556	215538	1320511		24
Dickinson		13435	150	281		2145		14246	3544	5035	258		
Dubuque	5796	476829	27610	46395	20290	11570	82	1542758	427959	217741	1963579		176829
Emmet	90	30275	4630	3005	1	4237	2	36212	9489	6025	1950		
Fayette	7792	523280	23965	63563	10946	23535	27634	1216192	272410	249696	333832	300	
Floyd	1754	192039	2994	30825	1856	15671	5595	653835	94288	112222	120475		
Franklin	473	79260	9053	8299	64	7915	1862	282991	53872	39645	3737		
Fremont	4170	172731	6261	40584	399	16950	12	557926	264836	96336	22989		
Greene	906	58090	2240	12552	25	7803	4	177987	88490	27167	10837	200	
Grundy		103776	3200	19209	469	14214	5	421302	67897	82586	1009		
Guthrie	3086	118294	1251	41059	244	12009	2966	230334	110343	57719	33128	24500	
Hamilton	1823	115491	11895	12007	156	13652	940	196438	66435	58082	16172	2540	
Hancock	20	16310		2314	28	2138		36892	3252	6812			
Hardin	5140	238174	9669	34541	2434	16980	4288	844834	194538	155461	62486	112191	1424
Harrison	4557	147729	9160	24277	1097	22962		362424	162551	98203	22708		
Henry	5412	530260	5115	175611	22075	1786	102	1312969	460892	225018	27123	20300	55
Howard	807	182186	14513	7543	776	13273	2721	386631	59687	75083	6808		
Humboldt		54470	1785	4076		7705	3	114907	14330	9035	28973		
Ida													
Iowa	9134	313841	13074	62921	9071	23061	99	1110349	310287	224128	158590		
Jackson	9002	510384	41533	63253	22349	6681	2185	1719527	583082	274671	225731		

TABLE V—CONTINUED.

COUNTIES.	No. lbs. Honey	No. lbs. Butter made.	No. lbs. Cheese.	No. lbs. Wool shorn in 1868.	No. of tons of Hay from tame grass.	No. of tons of Hay from wild grasses.	No. lbs. Hops raised.	Value of Farm Produce during year 1868.	Value of Stock sold during year 1868.	Value of Agricultural Implements, Machinery, and Wagons.	Value of Manufactures for 1868.	No. bushels coal mined, 80 lbs. per bushel, during the year 1868.	Value of Minerals not including coal during 1868.
Jasper	13229	395542	10010	110810	4226	23578	75	$2121765	$ 523912	$ 296633	$ 89128	$219915	$ 580
Jefferson	9630	390107	5317	149537	24330	587	95	1166381	460073	271653	97580	331645	2459
Johnson	7692	425991	28405	119162	25478	17388	430	1591822	597329	275285	219753	....	2249
Jones	7136	562159	137248	85448	20057	17979	99699	1368869	503994	260257	96808	....	400
Keokuk	13816	414843	14206	118783	18870	10297	391	1195833	471923	227408	108595	24557	849
Kossuth	100	56585	4640	3725	20	9076	......	129420	21670	34330	22317	....	1
Lee	9408	353165	132497	124905	19797	733	3	1357018	347076	222455	1452448	10650	35
Linn	88918	594500	65832	86690	22276	22989	15064	1769990	545260	323862	647138	....	......
Louisa	6522	311336	8609	68950	17374	7403	282	1055216	445324	168616	72965	....	......
Lucas	9447	203657	5385	56257	6314	5850	9	641440	204682	107883	74140	37284	......
Lyon	Not or	ganized	......	......	......	......	......	......	......	......	......	......	......
Madison	11740	243879	5253	111224	2871	13396	26	612285	329225	142714	58996	85	478
Mahaska	18791	393973	3012	199571	27728	9516	228	1351444	704882	351733	243658	1181754	7962
Marion	28518	431326	12872	114654	14563	9424	57	1698577	521376	273229	236471	251258	314
Marshall	6416	376488	7410	64695	4525	19425	436	1448160	275873	268020	445121	35200	45
Mills	2000	156261	6562	21009	790	18439	......	476013	150602	104725	27115	1000	......
Mitchell	1080	194800	13536	14557	1644	15017	239	434229	76522	108491	20143	....	......
Monona	1934	43543	10772	19145	1	13807	......	33991	41990	21920	27246	....	......
Monroe	19550	234768	6332	82727	14916	3825	89	1169240	375362	147912	185747	177845	43
Montgomery	1679	56719	1823	18469	70	6288	2	161735	60454	33103	44975	....	......
Muscatine	4579	424184	28045	63696	20373	11134	330	1508402	442193	349398	1034350	39222	......

O'Brien	25	900	......	3	......	212	......	124	625	305	......	......	......
Osceola	Not or	ganized.	......	......	......	......	......	......	......	......	......	......	......
Page	8173	173000	3306	36063	367	13371	......	408511	222976	94612	34307	29400	2106
Palo Alto	......	29480	......	304	......	5898	......	14807	8906	90130	......	......	......
Plymouth	......	4450	......	......	......	1219	......	9045	2680	3635	......	......	......
Pocahontas	......	22683	3072	32	......	4062	......	16779	8438	7533	......	......	......
Polk	16502	373947	24631	35107	2030	24889	1431	714978	433732	214414	792670	569965	......
Pottawattamie	1505	142276	4620	12479	176	17889	......	284358	159594	89066	19455	......	......
Poweshiek	10512	303055	1975	59143	4793	19216	49	1052514	351952	228774	24789	100	......
Ringgold	8195	110472	11856	43445	1214	9537	......	237651	142206	47762	13397	......	......
Sac	......	16708	215	5973	......	3955	......	50831	11725	9541	......	......	......
Scott	4740	515479	30528	35916	16520	16653	9249	2669501	416231	409154	1096600	240300	1875
Shelby	640	30765	530	10766	336	6050	......	74980	34108	21697	3117	......	......
Sioux	Not re	ported.	......	......	......	......	......	......	......	......	......	......	......
Story	4965	283257	10565	25320	642	24225	10	471610	142890	119531	37269	......	1142
Tama	3575	316534	4599	38011	4991	22058	139	1179115	222652	214110	74181	......	......
Taylor	8598	119523	2503	32171	956	10337	2	335634	179200	59598	16605	......	......
Union	4535	75888	5526	20330	1406	5662	......	206487	75391	41478	9740	......	......
Van Buren	8001	345118	8061	149609	20420	568	70	1020669	340175	198743	280966	114345	270
Wapello	17328	274576	5066	131911	17950	2331	258	1080885	389873	151627	637640	687584	......
Warren	21106	336677	2260	103372	7377	14614	5551	1135262	461303	217272	174336	88880	236
Washington	7720	531821	11524	132806	30762	6000	220	1290474	585363	247277	84164	160	542
Wayne	11410	202597	4191	72176	9700	5233	17	486519	246723	117241	39535	28065	......
Webster	3626	166741	8726	18538	64	31187	119	228606	73896	76405	61210	52819	8057
Winnebago	147	24841	320	1502	4	4236	......	12531	4632	3575	......	......	......
Winneshiek	3907	605756	13759	51713	11526	30958	2731	1726217	193588	286906	289341	40	1903
Woodbury	Not re	ported.	......	......	......	......	......	......	......	......	......	......	......
Worth	......	64115	480	4415	62	968	117	102028	30296	32327	800	......	......
Wright	305	53824	7600	2520	15	7178	9	124032	20749	28422	5240	......	......
Total	639717	22065724	1188546	4478934	677907	1059117	317295	69471525	20549977	12895139	16061210	6036324	219763

TABLE VI.

Showing the statistics of assessment, valuation, and taxation, the amount of land inclosed, the number of dwelling houses, and miles of railroad, January 1, 1869, *in the several counties of the State.*

COUNTIES.	No. of Dwelling Houses, 1867.	No. of Dwelling Houses, 1869.	No. of acres of land inclosed, 1867.	No. of acres of land inclosed, 1869.	No. of acres of land assessed, 1867.	No. of acres of land assessed, 1869.	Assessed value of land per acre, 1869.	Assessed value of lands and town lots, 1869.	Assessed value of personal property, 1869.	Total assessed valuation, 1869.	State tax at two mills.	No. of miles Railroad, Jan. 1, 1869.
Adair	262	410	6034	9852	358808	368400	$ 5.40	$ 2001329	$ 150850	$ 2152179	$ 4304.36	3.120
Adams	390	589	12388	16647	259791	260732	3.47	944747	167616	1112363	2224.73	....
Allamakee	2762	2850	117620	138439	406163	396566	3.86	1785743	596550	2382293	4764.59	4.000
Appanoose	2072	2597	95920	117874	324648	296762	6 27	2039065	1121949	3161014	6322.03	....
Audubon	139	183	3429	6489	121096	225659	4.23	965470	110859	1076329	2152.66	....
Benton	2464	3256	118226	169683	459498	450321	6.50	3400509	1188954	4589463	9178.93	25.000
Black Hawk	2742	3475	98693	161014	351138	357397	7.32	3562631	1041289	4603920	9207.84	34.095
Boone	1482	2435	34147	60521	304104	352391	6.95	2898396	652294	3550690	7101.38	27.500
Bremer	1586	2092	70964	99418	267115	274933	5.25	1665100	451465	2116565	4233.13	19.471
Buchanan	2090	2654	96629	138806	359104	358125	7.03	3129899	1009761	4139660	8279.32	24.526
Buena Vista	29	54	344	871	141051	196692	3.00	590076	18444	608520	1217.04	....
Butler	1144	1509	57167	89672	360608	358989	4.57	1741143	405645	2146788	4293.58	24.912
Calhoun	114	192	1619	3014	297095	297551	2.96	884279	52469	936748	1873.50	....
Carroll	132	241	2371	4941	223680	366657	4.20	1583899	150434	1734333	3468.67	25.500
Cass	388	662	13309	21841	306452	351267	4.86	1775261	229436	2004697	4009.39	....
Cedar	2747	3296	177749	241940	364916	325990	12.02	4355220	1421176	5776396	11552.79	31.882
Cerro Gordo	326	442	13337	16101	359642	358602	4.44	1641188	118199	1759387	3518.77	......

Cherokee	40	92	208	1102	59980	77895	3.02	235324	25813	261137	522.27	......
Chickasaw	1048	1475	47399	64090	315022	317625	4.41	1493618	270208	1763826	3527.65	7.047
Clarke	1025	1554	45634	59987	270478	272890	5.28	1624483	658135	2282618	4565.24	26.250
Clay	58	90	751	2552	......	143330	2.00	287172	12780	299952	599.90	......
Clayton *	3918	4509	172415	208858	492294	483502	7.04	4127244	1512407	5639651	11279.30	22.700
Clinton	4810	3803	228389	310306	445078	438940	9.79	5772815	2081641	7854456	15708.91	38.250
Crawford	168	316	5347	9672	264382	460800	3.51	1653052	84109	1737161	3474.32	31.500
Dallas	1156	1804	34667	72849	367404	380588	6.61	2709369	848870	3558239	7116.48	17.520
Davis	2101	2651	117096	153449	315290	316497	6.82	2285299	1124817	3410116	6820.23	.500
Decatur	1400	1904	58141	73260	339593	328324	4.24	1472954	594815	2067769	4135.54	......
Delaware	2670	2978	156644	192382	363137	361649	7.28	2946721	911342	3858063	7716.13	32.399
Des Moines	4013	4264	126321	144824	256846	251649	12.71	5385088	2365253	7750341	15500.68	17.750
Dickinson	97	111	1435	2927	2991	40863	2.03	83247	28292	111539	223.08	......
Dubuque	6130	6686	169433	193208	381650	377981	8.02	6615830	3110224	9726054	19452.11	37.583
Emmet	114	217	1423	3801	16134	65442	2.13	130220	77216	216436	432.87	......
Fayette	2492	3023	128431	161686	460035	460134	5.16	2555624	727790	3283414	6566.83	......
Floyd	1189	1486	45460	69267	323084	315593	5.25	1913731	396338	2310069	4620.14	8.107
Franklin	407	567	12520	26295	322809	355847	3.96	1425737	112490	1538227	3076.45	1.099
Fremont	1148	1501	44366	53365	283199	320674	6.35	2229242	711387	2940629	5881.26	26.250
Greene	424	678	10548	16886	317851	323079	6.11	2093251	204045	2297296	4594.59	24.500
Grundy	367	718	20306	33817	317692	332352	4.75	1584164	246702	1830866	3661.73	.164
Guthrie	654	964	24115	35345	333910	359596	5.39	1996381	391164	2387545	4775.09	13.050
Hamilton	546	766	15781	22912	336915	348640	3.71	1421639	510046	1931685	3863.37	......
Hancock	63	110	1919	3168	344890	367185	2.51	924135	23552	947687	1895.37	......
Hardin	1721	2077	64476	85750	336921	360499	5.24	2111075	593869	2704944	5409.89	11.192
Harrison	1009	1513	24811	42933	355427	401248	5.28	2267628	650026	2917654	5835.31	57.650
Henry	3374	3495	132534	152616	265893	266177	10.04	3422459	1587590	5010049	10020.10	19.500
Howard	776	1571	3582	45873	291000	295944	3.70	1172825	169682	1342507	2685.01	26.700
Humboldt	237	352	4842	11150	156912	162719	3.22	530600	72352	602952	1205.90	......
Ida	18	29	115	......	......	*......	..250	......	......	......	......	......

* No report received by Auditor of State.
† No returns were received from the township of Clayton, in Clayton county.

TABLE VI—CONTINUED.

COUNTIES.	No. of Dwelling Houses 1867.	No. of Dwelling Houses 1869.	No. of acres of land inclosed, 1867.	No. of acres of land inclosed, 1869.	No. of acres of land assessed, 1867.	No. of acres of land assessed, 1869.	Assessed value of land per acre, 1869.	Assessed value of lands and town lots, 1869.	Assessed value of personal property, 1869.	Total assessed valuation, 1869.	State tax at two mills.	No. of miles Railroad, Jan. 1st, 1869.
Iowa	2090	2691	97789	127324	389101	368727	6.74	2698154	1050328	3748482	7496.96	25.161
Jackson	2575	3812	168152	185589	397578	396674	6.98	3325389	1439989	4765378	9530.76	
Jasper	2639	4359	107596	158649	449175	451490	7.31	3810048	1649394	5459442	10918.88	55.137
Jefferson	2811	3007	121471	154488	273326	273307	8.65	2516036	1036425	3552461	7104.92	25.750
Johnson	3634	4060	160821	205788	388507	371090	9.78	4577583	1510949	6088532	12177.06	27.165
Jones	2792	3255	158528	186851	353740	338106	9.11	3377208	1300929	4678137	9356.27	19.710
Keokuk	2611	3054	124118	175018	369089	365525	5.96	2347765	1151950	3499715	6999.43	....
Kossuth	259	383	4007	9986	165829	286651	2.30	669732	56803	726535	1453.07	....
Lee	5388	4974	164223	176509	320609	320967	9.37	5981655	2938357	8920012	17840.02	55.000
Linn	4148	4849	174320	229147	448306	452231	10.90	6190949	937316	7128265	14256.53	49.090
Louisa	2275	2192	108619	124374	247142	250362	8.17	2222245	997151	3219396	6438.79	18.915
Lucas	1213	1733	45128	60293	272285	264580	6.38	1963350	579537	2542887	5085.77	26.250
Lyon	Not	organ-	ized ...	....	....	....	.....	....	....	....	....	....
Madison	1562	2117	64333	89839	359173	366533	6.45	2564117	1235883	3800000	7600.00	8.480
Mahaska	3128	3700	141172	179222	359686	358225	9.26	3901337	1623762	5525099	11050.20	20.000
Marion	3556	4206	120276	163810	354104	358890	7.88	3188234	1487151	4675385	9350.77	16.000
Marshall	2102	2774	79230	135475	330938	366032	7.11	3084580	789595	3874175	7748.35	26.000
Mills	1249	1248	35950	61874	258660	256950	5.91	1678978	990352	2669330	5338.66	18.250
Mitchell	1025	1291	38947	56855	286436	292244	4.94	1599310	363116	1962426	3924.85	......
Monona	281	478	6937	15835	302255	368381	4.05	1554335	160586	1714921	3429.84	25.560

Monroe	1735	2171	70218	92548	270164	273531	6.83	2121835	906285	3028120	6056.24	27.750
Montgomery	344	533	9363	16322	173600	179366	3.98	762101	230951	993052	1986.10	....
Muscatine	6475	4214	149718	193721	272567	275420	12.13	5005338	1775197	6780535	13561.07	45.210
O'Brien	7	7	123	355	112589 *		2.00	....	....	....	....	....
Osceola	Not organized		......	....	....	....	.....	....	....	....	....	....
Page	956	1378	34191	54477	335689	335144	4.78	1726867	594989	2321856	4643.71	....
Palo Alto	71	111	951	2308	....	126231	2.50	315577	17107	332684	665.37	....
Plymouth	......	32	675	750	53813	91497	2.00	182994	28343	211337	422.67	....
Pocahontas	87	126	1424	2677	250063	256156	2.25	576351	20764	597115	1194.23	....
Polk	3436	4565	81801	120358	362098	358575	9.78	5767335	1864080	7631415	15262.83	43.700
Pottawattamie	1571	2083	22580	32895	458427	542621	6.41	6647078	1324019	7971097	15942.19	28.500
Poweshiek	1653	2201	69417	114344	356256	356256	7.30	2854820	983962	3838782	7677.56	25.530
Ringgold	610	853	23130	29727	343862	337498	3.53	1228312	260401	1488713	2977.42	....
Sac	103	146	2593	5405	166361	358919	2.96	1153844	40623	1194467	2388.93	....
Scott	5638	6094	193381	225420	284906	283944	13.24	6766752	2464492	9231244	18462.49	13.656
Shelby	204	317	4616	8999	208487	326357	4.55	1494755	127205	1621960	3243.92	....
Sioux	4 †		40 †		175454	186798	2.00	373596	1805	375401	750.80	....
Story	1111	1671	40373	74088	359241	346063	5.73	2103726	375277	2479003	4958.00	24.250
Tama	1891	2457	77354	117605	450773	457756	6.41	3252611	1120432	4373043	8746.09	25.500
Taylor	706	......	26941	36565	380540	329312	5.14	1738175	666815	2404990	4809.98	....
Union	655	702	18271	20672	271867	272615	3.89	1150005	306742	1456747	2913.49	10.333
Van Buren	2780	3218	123684	146566	305350	310644	10.53	3840895	1591605	5432500	10865.00	30.000
Wapello	3213	3936	113821	144540	272761	262621	9.44	3736124	1948262	5684386	11368.77	56.750
Warren	2154	2857	83074	126616	355408	360642	7.93	3110296	1104767	4215063	8430.13	....
Washington	3005	3347	155347	184474	357867	360241	7.98	3272249	1626103	4898352	9796.70	11.023
Wayne	1317	1724	57974	74564	333799	311492	5.44	1776912	929630	2706542	5413.08	....
Webster	1039	1332	27117	41340	438342	445194	4.57	2322386	290102	2612488	5224.98	....
Winnebago	128	139	1429	9551	344918	243013	2.35	571080	18577	589657	1179.31	....

* No report received by Auditor of State.
† No returns were received from Sioux county.

TABLE VI—CONTINUED.

COUNTIES.	No. of Dwelling Houses 1867.	No. of Dwelling Houses 1869.	No. of acres of land inclosed, 1867.	No. of acres of land inclosed, 1869.	No. of acres of land assessed, 1867.	No. of acres of land assessed, 1869.	Assessed value of land per acre, 1869.	Assessed value of lands and town lots, 1869.	Assessed value of personal property, 1869.	Total assessed valuation, 1869.	State tax at two mills.	No. of miles Railroad, Jan. 1st, 1869.
Winneshiek	3438	4563	179265	225511	438027	435781	4.35	2302436	903916	3206352	6412.70	31.200
Woodbury..............	346	†	3413	†......	221233	*	3.50	....	......	....	....	22.540
Worth	269	389	7593	12913	244639	241952	3.03	745098	84661	829759	1659.52	....
Wright.................	231	331	6832	11740	346634	352471	2.72	966626	74161	1040787	2081.57	....
Total...............	155558	183921	8263174	8174930	28773400	30109771	.....	222561061	71971191	294532252	589064.44	1451.127

* No report received by Auditor of State.

† No returns were received from Woodbury county.

NOTE.—The statistics of assessment, valuation and taxation in the above table, were prepared by the Auditor of State, and are here inserted for the purpose of reference and comparison, and the number of miles of railroad was obtained from the reports of the several companies made to the State Treasurer, pursuant to chapter 196, Laws 1868.—[SECRETARY OF STATE.

TABLE VII.

Showing the average yield per acre of certain Agricultural Products in the several Counties for the year 1868.

COUNTIES.	Bushels Wheat	Bushels Oats.	Bushels Corn.	Bushels Rye.	Bushels Barley.	Bushels Potatoes.	Gallons of Sorghum.	Pounds Wool per Sheep.
Adair	8.20	28.45	30.00	2.75	5.00	134.86	94.48	2.09
Adams	10.43	27.46	30.95	14.93	....	109.53	83.67	3.16
Allamakee	17.36	34.90	24.51	14.81	16.23	67.41	91.81	3.00
Appanoose	14.25	27.40	31.40	11.77	17.32	54.62	96.69	2.91
Audubon	9.45	26.58	34.40	....	9.16	137.48	77.57	1.67
Benton	19.32	34.13	39.60	11.54	26.50	101.84	122.49	3.30
Black Hawk	18.78	36.79	34.61	13.75	27.63	86.90	86.32	3.79
Boone	3.67	9.50	22.58	16.93	7.04	124.27	114.40	3.53
Bremer	16.56	39.51	37.57	13.22	37.20	88.15	68.38	3.15
Buchan.an	18.45	38.78	35.25	49.60	26.69	100.00	124.00	3.46
Buena Vista	6.79	....	97.54	....	....	193.15	46.00	....
Butler	15.85	32.62	33.60	21.69	21.31	87.52	105.12	2.82
Calhoun	5.25	16.00	25.25	....	....	84.56	83.62	3.20
Carroll	27.28	15.66	22.28	....	....	131.62	57.00	5.80
Cass	12.57	30.20	34.97	....	11.18	90.00	118.71	3.08
Cedar	14.92	31.00	43.45	18.00	25.11	84.32	97.37	3.92
Cerro Gordo	16.37	43.18	35.67	....	18.00	108.95	108.00	2.69
Cherokee	8.50	....	16.64	....	....	87.00	19.40	9.00
Chickasaw	16.60	37.82	34.12	16.57	29.78	80.48	103.90	3.10
Clarke	13.11	19.19	34.57	15.00	9.25	89.33	48.00	3.44
Clay	10.24	28.46	23.81	.....	.....	110.90	79.47	2.00
Clayton	14.13	30.00	42.27	8.70	24.60	84.52	160.00	4.92
Clinton	15.31	29.43	36.33	10.28	25.74	69.00	93.23	3.00
Crawford	5.85	8.66	32.81	....	.....	124.74	73.00	.....
Dallas	3.96	17.62	28.57	7.00	7.33	58.60	77.10	3.30
Davis	13.82	22.04	32.05	12.75	30.00	38.64	107.43	3.04
Decatur	13.61	109.21	28.00	8.41	.....	63.12	70.48	2.87
Delaware	17.29	35.20	35.63	12.00	24.60	98.32	111.11	3.15
Des Moines	11.16	24.63	31.84	11.44	16.60	72.72	116.07	4.34
Dickinson	16.90	29.41	23.95	11.00	32.00	94.46	59.40	2.09
Dubuque	16.66	25.13	28.25	15.48	25.40	80.00	85.53	3.11
Emmet	13.40	21.88	23.33	13.70	17.73	89.00	53.60	2.53
Fayette	17.46	34.52	36.91	10.00	23.40	90.00	108.63	2.98
Floyd	17.06	17.53	36.58	18.00	27.91	91.80	111.16	3.35
Franklin	19.70	32.57	27.60	.....	29.61	103.21	148.11	2.97
Fremont	10.41	31.02	35.55	.....	13.75	131.80	94.67	3.90
Greene	4.30	17.71	33.03	.....	19.00	146.80	100.00	2.90
Grundy	17.72	36.58	34.38	14.00	27.79	91·92	92.70	3.90
Guthrie	8.20	25.60	34.67	.....	.....	157.27	105.00	3.77

TABLE VII—AVERAGES—CONTINUED.

COUNTIES.	Bushels Wheat	Bushels Oats.	Bushels Corn.	Bushels Rye.	Bushels Barley	Bushels of Potatoes.	Gallons of Sorghum.	Pounds Wool per Sheep.
Hamilton	10.38	12.17	36.38	.....	7.00	107.04	93.56	3.39
Hancock	18.50	36.04	35.37	.....	21.00	100.00	68.33	3.02
Hardin	18.46	35.16	32.73	11.54	30.40	97.70	101.80	3.81
Harrison	5.12	22.72	27.02	.....	.....	64.06	95.82	3.68
Henry	13.75	24.74	46.26	14.81	8.57	47.22	70.00	3.35
Howard	16.27	34.00	38.06	16.00	22.40	61.94	82.00	3.41
Humboldt	12.27	16.88	30.76	.....	.....	123.40	74.62	4.10
Ida	.....	.....	.....	.....	.....	......	......	....
Iowa	15.12	32.50	30.73	24.33	30.13	88.65	105.41	4.14
Jackson	18.19	29.42	35.38	12.41	25.56	77.17	85.05	3.38
Jasper	29.58	30.81	44.18	15.81	10.00	136.00	115.24	3.51
Jefferson	13.25	23.57	38.48	14.16	15.24	34.40	108.91	3.26
Johnson	15.09	29.26	40.76	17.75	21.73	71.14	122.46	3.68
Jones	18.17	33.91	37.88	13.12	27.73	94.91	100.00	4.04
Keokuk	14.63	23.98	36.79	14.62	18.04	59.60	103.82	3.06
Kossuth	15.22	32.26	28.93	.....	13.00	114.66	80.63	4.57
Lee	15.88	24.00	33.70	11.76	16.34	31.75	81.13	3.43
Linn	14.94	37.98	38.10	18.07	30.12	60.54	120.47	3.17
Louisa	9.83	22.35	43.20	12.05	.....	62.60	111.18	3.27
Lucas	17.37	29.91	35.34	15.30	13.17	88.69	82.88	2.75
Lyon	.....	.....	.....	.....	.....	......	......	....
Madison	8.83	17.19	30.51	9.08	.....	118.36	88.45	3.64
Mahaska	7.80	25.44	40.46	26.50	94.25	86.42	125.57	3.37
Marion	18.45	28.92	40.45	18.15	21.68	114.02	127.90	2.57
Marshall	20.60	33.66	36.88	18.41	35.83	138.58	168.90	4.51
Mills	4.92	23.80	34.77	4.46	10.36	70.37	95.28	4.02
Mitchell	19.84	47.52	38.68	15.32	27.72	101.27	81.80	3.32
Monona	10.00	25.85	19.32	.....	.....	102.30	74.00	3.69
Monroe	14.33	24.93	35.11	10.90	13.66	70.00	103.31	2.80
Montgomery	10.01	22.77	31.73	.....	.....	80.00	126.09	3.33
Muscatine	14.15	25.63	39.52	12.48	22.34	82.26	102.22	4.24
O'Brien	8.00	9.54	10.30	.....	.....	63.33	......	3.00
Osceola	.....	.....	.....	.....	.....	......	......	....
Page	7.09	22.50	32.28	13.59	12.55	73.09	102.27	2.75
Palo Alto	12.48	22.77	27.67	.....	.....	117.60	76.00	2.30
Plymouth	12.20	15.39	8.62	.....	18.30	30.74	......	....
Pocahontas	2.63	5.50	22.25	.....	.....	93.13	78.17	....
Polk	10.52	17.37	41.46	10.62	16.90	135.00	105.83	3.01
Potawattamie	6.03	25.90	23.75	17.13	18.40	80.00	90.71	2.66
Poweshiek	17.35	29.19	38.12	16.40	29.00	123.47	110.85	3.53
Ringgold	8.58	15.43	30.30	6.46	7.61	85.33	98.28	2.62
Sac	6.20	22.70	30.60	.....	.....	95.75	60.55	4.38
Scott	14.79	28.87	44.77	13.30	22.51	71.88	139.53	3.94
Shelby	4.44	23.33	26.50	.....	.....	127.73	81.00	3.00

TABLE VII—AVERAGES—CONTINUED.

COUNTIES.	Bushels Wheat	Bushels Oats.	Bushels Corn.	Bushels Rye.	Bushels Barley	Bushels of Potatoes.	Gallons of Sorghum.	Pounds Wool per Sheep.
Sioux, (not reported.)	....	....	....	.....	.....	....	......	.....
Story	11.91	16.58	35.77	.....	6.00	131.12	109.14	2.97
Tama	18.31	37.50	35.00	4.00	24.00	83.53	92.10	4.07
Taylor	9.00	22.86	29.39	20.00	....	58.60	63.24	3.73
Union	9.57	19.59	36.95	17.30	.....	143.22	80.30	3.08
Van Buren	12.30	23.18	32.98	13.46	17.26	28.00	119.10	3.00
Wapello	15.13	23.50	36.70	14.15	15.40	57.88	112.67	2.99
Warren	13.71	25.68	41.49	15.00	20.00	113.90	96.84	2.94
Washington	15.62	26.08	40.42	14.30	30.38	54.64	118.30	3.22
Wayne	14.56	24.80	31.40	13.00	10.40	61.80	83.41	2.65
Webster	3.46	5.21	26.89	.....	9.00	92.00	112.70	2.82
Winnebago	16.76	39.00	33.00	.....	10.30	141.60	109.10	2.00
Winneshiek	19.46	39.60	40.00	14.56	27.20	60.31	87.30	3.21
Woodbury, (not reported.)	....	....	....	.....	.....	....	......	....
Worth	18.70	46.13	37.10	.....	26.00	109.00	100.00	2.13
Wright	15.09	41.47	40.30	.....	15.30	111.00	162.30	2.70

13

TABLE VIII.

Exhibiting the aggregates of the several items in the preceding Tables; and comparing them with those of the Census of 1865 *and* 1867.

ITEMS.	1865.	1867.	1869.
Number of dwelling houses	114351	155558	183921
Number of families	....	....	187407
Number of white males	379746	463537	537348
Number of white females	371379	433316	498126
Total white population	751125	897325	1035474
Number of colored males	1804	2508	2841
Number of colored females	1803	2203	2504
Total colored population	3607	4715	5345
Total population	754699	902040	1040819
Number entitled to vote	146427	181749	215209
Number of Militia	94734	125646	160465
Number of foreigners not naturalized	10594	13503	18103
Number of blind	*259	*412	223
Number of deaf and dumb	376	368	288
Number of insane	613	644	268
Number of miles railroad	793	1152	1900
Number of colleges, academies, and universities	41	62	43
Number of students attending college	2337	3951	4860
Number of acres land inclosed	5327053	8263174	8174930
Number of acres of land in cultivation	....	....	6109743
Number of acres sorghum	21452	25796	26243
Number of gallons syrup from sorghum	1443605	2094557	2592393
Number of acres tame grasses	302899	497460	602316
Number of tons hay from tame grasses	225349	537812	677907
Number of tons hay from wild grass	713119	823153	1059117
Number of bushels grass seed	62114	107532	73896
Number of bushels clover seed	....	....	3028
Number of acres spring wheat	827487	983906	1730596
Number of bushels harvested	7175784	13912368	16823520
Number of acres winter wheat	116965	73425	73914
Number of bushels harvested	1108781	723152	1140035
Number of acres oats	577540	504362	657007
Number of bushels harvested	15928777	15861494	18596625
Number of acres corn	1727777	1992326	2058239
Number of bushels harvested	48471133	56928938	76507575
Number of acres rye	48992	35604	37371
Number of bushels harvested	662388	492841	496347
Number of acres barley	51804	48013	49607
Number of bushels harvested	950696	1197729	1144454

* The number of blind in 1865 and 1869 does not include the inmates of the State Asylum for the blind at Vinton; the census of 1867, on the contrary, does include the inmates of that Institution. The number of Deaf and Dumb, and Insane for 1865 and 1867 include the number then in the Hospital for the Insane at Mt. Pleasant, and the Institution for the Education of the Deaf and Dumb at Iowa City, but the numbers given in 1869 does not include those in said Institutions.

TABLE VIII.—AGGREGATES—CONTINUED.

ITEMS.	1865.	1867.	1869.
Number of acres of Irish potatoes	40198	42493	54528
Number of bushels harvested	2730811	2666678	4417858
Number of acres onions	....	....	995
Number of bushels onions	207638	213285	115742
Number of acres flax	12111	11906	17842
Number of bushels seed harvested	75721	61917	96395
Number of acres buckwheat	....	....	15264
Number bushels buckwheat	....	....	144920
Number of fruit trees in bearing	636458	1075177	1539943
Number of fruit trees not in bearing	2523905	3629789	4100207
Number bushels apples	....	....	666148
Number of hogs of all ages	1037117	1620089	2409679
Number of cattle of all ages	901831	956169	2108667
Number of milch cows	310137	326559	367602
Number of pounds butter made	14538216	19192727	22065724
Number of pounds cheese made	1000738	1403864	1188546
Number of work oxen	37717	27246	26726
Number of pounds wool shorn in 1866 and 1868	....	5323385	4478934
Number of sheep	....	1708958	2370106
Number of horses of all ages	316702	425055	482780
Number of mules and asses of all ages	14303	22037	28420
Number of dogs	86060	125207	147623
Number of hives of bees	87118	85727	82517
Number of pounds honey taken	1128399	896745	639717
Number of grape vines in bearing	....	....	1132416
Number of pounds grapes raised	390409	549179	2128472
Number of grape vines not in bearing	....	....	1735293
Number of pounds hops raised	27847	48653	317295
Number of acres hops	....	....	1299
Number of acres planted for timber	20285	48774	19675
Number of rods hedging	331741	663063	3393061
Number of bushels coal mined, 80 lbs. per bushel	1666582	2483010	6036324
Value of minerals raised, not including coal	$ 31875	$ 320820	$ 219763
Value of manufactures	$7100465	$ 15957599	$ 16061210
Value of agricultural implements, machinery, etc	$7707027	$ 11362402	$ 12895139
Value of farm produce in 1868	....	....	$ 69471525
Value of stock sold in 1868	....	....	$ 20549977
Number of acres of land assessed	....	28773400	30109771
Assessed value of lands and town lots	....	$189550825	$222561061
Assessed value of personal property	....	$ 66966359	$ 71971191
Total assessed valuation	....	$256517184	$294532252

TABLE IX.

Showing the Population of the several Counties of Iowa at each enumeration since the organization of the Territory.

COUNTIES.	Iowa Territory.				State of Iowa.												
	1838.	1840.	1844.	1846.	1847.	1849.	1850.	1851.	1852.	1854.	1856.	1859.	1860.	1863.	1865.	1867.	1869.
Adair										150	663	1011	984	900	1071	1594	2312
Adams										339	1019	1413	1533	1638	1818	2317	3302
Allamakee						227	777	1300	2000	4266	7709	10843	12237	13465	13957	16003	16766
Appanoose				1300	948	1281	3131	3951	4243	6265	9075	11449	11931	11866	10748	13064	14625
Audubon											283	365	454	388	510	790	1032
Benton				297	312	312	673	753	1237	2623	6247	8063	8496	9561	11245	14772	19420
Black Hawk									315	2514	5538	7095	8244	10014	12306	16036	18961
Boone						419	756	890	1024	1678	3518	4018	4232	4607	5236	9861	13912
Bremer									309	1095	3228	4336	4915	5404	7224	9337	11358
Buchanan				149	250	406	519	1006	1023	2299	5125	6918	7906	8294	10037	12231	14973
Buena Vista													57			151	242
Butler									73		2141	3504	3724	4142	5006	6542	8139
Calhoun											119	136	147	170	224	546	944
Carroll											251	250	281	297	400	688	1450
Cass										416	815	1489	1612	1623	1895	2479	3604
Cedar	557	1225	2217	2862	2809	3183	3941	4084	4971	7643	9481	12175	12949	13274	14041	16076	18239
Cerro Gordo											632	855	940	1007	1311	1988	2466
Cherokee												85	58	20	64	209	459
Chickasaw									400	588	2651	3816	4336	4397	5355	6220	8513
Clarke									549	1626	3978	5006	5427	5693	5716	6244	8027
Clay													52			369	450
Clayton	274	1044	1200	1500	2176	3000	3873	5000	6318	9337	15187	18669	20728	21235	21922	22879	25832
Clinton	445	800	1201	1300	1570	2044	2835	3001	3822	7306	13441	17395	18938	19821	22405	27234	31952
Crawford											235	429	383	456	574	1070	1640
Dallas					164	635	812	925	1216	2392	3991	4058	5244	5088	5886	7538	10361

Davis			2622	3400	4464	4939	7264	7454	7553	9787	11258	13323	13764	13959	13123	13517	14921
Decatur							965	1016	1184	3025	6229	8238	8677	8373	8052	8501	10339
Delaware		171	300	781	1111	1300	1759	2000	2615	4637	8099	10024	11024	11667	12508	14463	15557
Des Moines	4605	5546	9109	9391	10071	11649	12914	14488	12575	16700	20198	20781	19611	21213	19894	23444	25986
Dickinson												121	180	189	309	509	562
Dubuque	2381	3056	4049	6030	7440	9185	10841	11000	12500	16662	25871	30581	31164	30839	33078	38860	36946
Emmet													105		368	708	990
Fayette							825	1200	2065	5042	8375	11391	12073	12739	13124	14992	16391
Floyd											2448	3458	3744	4018	4886	6731	8465
Franklin											780	1159	1309	1448	1899	2321	3075
Fremont							1244	1600	2044	3006	3368	4327	5074	4778	5698	7013	8051
Greene											1089	1424	1374	1416	1659	2353	3494
Grundy											435	680	793	1024	1332	2119	3850
Guthrie								222	300	772	2149	2754	3058	3205	3249	3906	5219
Hamilton												655	1699	1602	2023	3154	4268
Hancock												121	179	240	292	357	572
Hardin									300	1259	4033	3323	5440	5376	6813	9345	11007
Harrison										1065	1900	3132	3621	3663	4265	5836	7411
Henry	3058	3784	6017	6875	6759	7229	8707	8915	9633	10159	15395	16299	18701	16780	17816	20110	20971
Howard											444	3017	3168	3382	3871	4401	5149
Humboldt												519	332	394	606	1307	1810
Ida												38	43			90	144
Iowa					435	600	822	1000	1323	2307	4873	7098	8029	8544	10258	12390	14738
Jackson	881	1452	2000	4767	4639	5677	7210	7597	8231	12166	14077	17710	18493	19158	19097	19970	20579
Jasper					560	1223	1288	1492	1674	3466	7490	9195	9883	10627	12095	16239	20148
Jefferson		2780	5694	6000	8463	8825	9997	10081	10225	11117	13305	14478	15038	14649	14772	16420	16772
Johnson	237	1504	2949	3000	3387	4010	4474	5061	5788	8467	14457	16900	17573	17184	18778	21641	23948
Jones	241	475	1112	1758	1779	2140	3007	3400	4201	6075	9835	13475	13306	13495	14376	16228	18113
Keokuk					2918	3953	4822	5105	5306	7299	10646	12329	13271	13412	13996	15429	17280
Kossuth											377	310	416	365	694	1573	1949

TABLE IX—CONTINUED.

COUNTIES.	IOWA TERRITORY.				STATE OF IOWA.												
	1838.	1840.	1844.	1846.	1847.	1849.	1850.	1851.	1852.	1854.	1856.	1859.	1860.	1863.	1865.	1867.	1869.
Lee	2839	6095	9830	12860	13231	15000	18783	17625	20360	22590	27273	31242	29232	28523	28063	31417	34127
Linn	205	1385	2643	3411	3954	4762	5444	6160	6890	10802	14702	17720	18947	18700	20754	24549	27467
Louisa	1180	1925	3238	3644	3648	4155	5067	5100	5476	7341	9568	10805	10370	10673	10948	11885	12219
Lucas	.....	.....	.....	.....	.....	.....	471	1025	1046	1921	4408	5287	5766	6257	6352	7746	9185
Lyon	Not	orga	nized	.....	.....	.....	.....	.....	.....	.....	.....	.....	.....	.....	.....	.....	.....
Madison	.....	.....	.....	.....	.....	701	1174	1492	1832	3122	5508	7071	7379	7934	8214	9764	11817
Mahaska	.....	.....	.....	2942	3774	5559	5986	6758	7479	9093	13050	14515	14816	16249	17082	18693	20076
Marion	.....	.....	.....	1360	2350	3797	5412	5809	6289	9315	14060	16167	16813	17318	18719	20181	23440
Marshall	.....	.....	.....	.....	.....	.....	338	454	710	1607	4460	5713	6015	7550	8759	11513	15514
Mills	.....	.....	.....	.....	.....	.....	.....	.....	1463	2171	3102	4381	4481	6287	5218	6994	6935
Mitchell	.....	.....	.....	.....	.....	.....	.....	.....	.....	.....	1911	3291	3409	3375	4176	6150	7288
Monona	.....	.....	.....	.....	.....	.....	.....	.....	.....	222	459	885	832	931	1096	1664	2679
Monroe	.....	.....	386	400	1222	2000	2886	3125	3430	4577	6860	8377	8612	9322	9435	10208	11990
Montgomery	.....	.....	.....	.....	.....	.....	.....	.....	.....	233	872	1094	1256	1218	1535	2072	2892
Muscatine	1247	1942	2882	1485	3010	4516	5773	6170	6812	9555	12569	15503	16444	16989	17241	20699	24336
O'Brien	.....	.....	.....	.....	.....	.....	.....	.....	.....	.....	.....	.....	8	.....	.....	20	51
Osceola	Not	orga	nized	.....	.....	.....	.....	.....	.....	.....	.....	.....	.....	.....	.....	.....	.....
Page	.....	.....	.....	.....	.....	.....	551	534	636	1148	1964	3674	4419	4662	5211	6025	7843
Palo Alto	.....	.....	.....	.....	.....	.....	.....	.....	.....	.....	.....	131	132	142	216	413	535
Plymouth	.....	.....	.....	.....	.....	.....	.....	.....	.....	.....	.....	112	148	93	105	214	179
Pocahontas	.....	.....	.....	.....	.....	.....	.....	.....	.....	.....	.....	126	103	122	215	453	637
Polk	.....	.....	.....	1301	1792	4214	4444	6000	5939	5368	9417	11238	11625	12956	16473	22630	26408
Pottawattamie	.....	.....	.....	.....	.....	6552	7828	5758	5057	3060	3498	5012	4968	4737	5388	8733	10974
Poweshiek	.....	.....	.....	.....	.....	443	615	742	915	1953	4460	5338	5668	6370	7796	9888	12936
Ringgold	.....	.....	.....	.....	.....	.....	.....	.....	.....	.....	1472	2507	2923	3039	3089	3888	5029
Sac	.....	.....	.....	.....	.....	.....	.....	.....	.....	.....	251	269	246	234	304	595	840

Scott	1252	2193	2750	3000	3652	4837	5987	6016	8628	12671	21521	25861	25959	26327	28474	34362	37615
Shelby										328	456	784	818	828	900	1213	1744
Sioux													10			18	
Story									214	836	2868	3826	4051	4368	5918	6888	9347
Tama									262	1163	3520	5346	5285	7027	7882	11165	14254
Taylor							204	393	479	891	2079	3468	3590	3757	4299	4546	5591
Union									80	81	806	1993	2012	2420	2528	3010	3821
Van Buren	3174	6166	9019	9870	10203	11577	12269	13000	12753	13843	15921	15879	17081	15862	15599	16292	16839
Wapello			2814	4422	5660	7255	8479	8500	8888	10521	13246	15060	14518	16729	18794	18930	20672
Warren						649	943	1193	1488	4446	8000	9150	10281	10932	11150	13162	15810
Washington	283	1571	3120	3483	3518	4434	4991	5079	5881	7560	11113	13366	14235	15003	15739	17675	18648
Wayne							341	500	794	1665	4182	5860	6409	6522	6327	7657	9566
Webster									372	907	3088	2596	2504	2858	3772	5631	7812
Winnebago												188	168	204	298	785	1072
Winneshiek					182	300	546	800	1523	3315	7506	12211	13942	15421	15421	19302	21047
Woodbury										170	2000	1100	1119	1106	1295	1970	
Worth												759	756	895	1143	1543	2135
Wright											427	632	653	693	908	1332	1765
Total	22859	43114	75152	97588	116651	152988	191982	204774	230713	326013	519055	638775	674913	701732	754699	902040	1040819

NOTE.—Calhoun county was originally called Fox county; Lyon was called Buncombe; Monroe, Kishkehosh; Washington, Slaughter; and Woodbury, Wahkaw. Hamilton was created as Risley county, and subsequently formed a part of Webster. Humboldt county, originally erected under that name, was afterwards divided between Kossuth and Webster; more recently, the territory which had been annexed to Kossuth, with the northern half of that detached to Webster, was re-erected into the county of Humboldt. The northern part of Kossuth county was at first Bancroft county, which, with the northern half of Humboldt was united with Kossuth in 1855; subsequently the territory obtained from Humboldt was again detached. Webster county was at first called Yell county, which in 1855 was united with Risley and two tiers of townships in Humboldt to form Webster; in 1857, Hamilton county was detached, and also one tier of townships to Humboldt.

SURPLUS

Agricultural Productions of Iowa, for the year ending April 30th, 1869, *as shown by Shipments over the several Railways of the State.*

Believing that it would be a matter of interest, not only to the citizens of the State, but to citizens of other States, wishing to migrate to Iowa, to engage either in business or agricultural pursuits, to be able to ascertain the amount of surplus agricultural productions of the State, or of any particular locality therein, for the period of one year; and believing the desired information could be obtained with less labor and more accurately by procuring the shipments for that period by the several railways traversing the State, than by attempting to ascertain it through the assessors at the time of taking the Census, I made an arrangement early in the year, by permission of the Census Board, with Hon. J. M. Shaffer, the worthy and energetic Secretary of the State Agricultural Society, to procure, if possible, the shipments of agricultural productions from the various railroad stations in the State, as shown by the books of the several railroads, for the twelve months ending April 30th, 1869. The following exhibits of shipments by months show the result of his labor.

In addition to the Tables furnished by the several railroads, giving the shipments from the various stations thereon for each of the twelve months ending April 30th, 1869, I have caused to be prepared and published therewith, tables for each of the several roads, exhibiting the total shipments from each station thereon, and the total shipments of the road; also one table, showing the aggregate shipments by all the railroads for the year. This aggregate does not show the entire surplus agricultural productions of the State for the above named period, as it will be noticed that the shipments by railroad from the cities of McGregor and Dubuque are not included therein, and the shipments by the Des Moines Valley Railroad are for six months only—ending June 30, 1869.

In addition to the above, and to complete the tables, the shipments by river from the several towns on the Mississippi and Missouri should be included—an item of much importance, but one which it has been impossible to obtain.

IOWA STATE AGRICULTURAL SOCIETY,
SECRETARY'S OFFICE, FAIRFIELD, IOWA, OCT. 28, 1869.

Hon. Ed Wright, Secretary of State, Des Moines, Iowa:

SIR—I have the honor to transmit herewith certain railroad statistics, collected in accordance with the request of the State Census Board. In the absence of definite instructions from the Board in regard to the kind and character of the statistics, I consulted with prominent railroad statisticians, and the forms now presented were adopted. Instead of showing *all* the work of the roads, it was thought best to seleet only the principal products carried eastward from each station in Iowa, for the year ending April 30th, 1869.

My acknowledgments are due the following persons for their co-operation in this matter. The figures on the Des Moines Valley Road were furnished by John Given, General Freight Agent; Milo Smith, Superintendent. Those on the Burlington and Missouri River Road by E. A. Touzalin, General Passenger Agent; G. C. Morton, General Freight Agent; C. E. Perkins, Superintendent. Those on the Chicago, Rock Island and Pacific Road by Louis Viele, General Freight Agent; E. St. John, General Ticket Agent; P. A. Hall, Superintendent. Those on the Chicago and Northwestern Railroad, by M. M. Kirkman, General Accountant; Henry R. Pearson, Vice-President. Those on the Chicago, Burlington and Quincy Road by Wm. McCredie, Freight Auditor; Robert Harris, Superintendent. Those on the Illinois Central by Joseph F. Tucker, General Agent; M. Hughitt, Superintendent. Those on the Milwaukee and St. Paul Road, by J. P. Whaling, Freight Auditor.

The statistics to my mind are especially valuable because they show, more satisfactorily than any other set of figures, the resources of the several localities in the State. The citizen can see at a glance the amount and kind of produce that is carried from the particular station in those neighborhoods in which he is interested, and he will often find himself astonished. The emigrant seeking a home among us can learn which will be the best locality for him to select, according to his tastes, in stock, or grain, or other product. Again, capitalists who seek investment, can have something; and already these very tables have been called for by a company of men about to locate a railroad, to enable them to make some estimate of the resources and capacities of the country along the proposed route. Hoping that the figures will meet your approbation and will accomplish good results to our glorious State, I remain, Your obedient servant,

J. M. SHAFFER, *Sec.*

EXHIBIT A.

MILWAUKEE & ST. PAUL RAILWAY.

Statement of Agricultural Products carried Eastward from the several Stations on the Iowa Division of the Milwaukee & St. Paul Railway for each of the twelve months ending April 50th, 1869, *and the aggregate carried Northward.*

LIME SPRINGS STATION.

MONTHS.	No. of Horses.	No. of Cattle.	No. of Hogs.	No. of Sheep.	Pounds dressed Hogs.	Pounds of Lard and Pork.	Pounds Wool.	Bushels Wheat	Bushels Corn.	Bushels other grains.	Pounds other Agricultural Products.*	Pounds Animal Products not specified.†
1868.												
May								9671		11403	72320	1010
June							290	2530		4238	23260	2870
July							1170	1195		849	16000	3940
August								986				3080
September		3	95				110	15947		443		2030
October		69	20					21457		1706	4000	3250
November		21						13302		360	8800	3030
December					47450			19272		1156	28000	4460
1869.												
January					42390			35756		1844	19000	3350
February					2500			7452		156	2000	1020
March					2520			16766		479	40000	1120
April								6173		2436	4000	2950
Total east'rd		93	115		94860		1570	150507		25070	217380	32110
Total west'rd								14		4834	3300	1180

CRESCO STATION.

1868.	No. of Horses.	No. of Cattle.	No. of Hogs.	No. of Sheep.	Pounds dressed Hogs.	Pounds of Lard and Pork.	Pounds Wool.	Bushels Wheat	Bushels Corn.	Bushels other grains.	Pounds other Agricultural Products.*	Pounds Animal Products not specified.†
May								14611	3592	16938	159040	4240
June	1							7827	1820	7831	37620	10600
July							11790	3063	1239	2160	180	3670
August		36					150	8394		3644		20290
September		102	48					58394		13164	2800	19510
October		120	100	50			570	42234		13331	7800	20650
November		80	50					18806		4932	4000	13450
December					116050			24542		2181	11000	2690
1869.												
January					59820			30765		2614		10320
February					7100			7996		869	2000	6310
March					2260			17131		876	16800	1590
April								7316		388	78000	6840
Total east'rd	1	338	198	50	185230		12510	241079	6651	68928	319240	120160
Total west'rd		38	2		15810				3956	25178	6720	2000

*"Other Agricultural Products" includes Flour, Potatoes, and Beans,

†"Animal Products not specified" includes Eggs, Butter, Tallow, and Hides.

EXHIBIT A—CONTINUED.

MONTHS.	No. of Horses.	No. of Cattle.	No. of Hogs.	No. of Sheep.	Pounds dressed Hogs.	Pounds of Lard and Pork.	Pounds Wool.	Bushels Wheat	Bushels Corn.	Bushels other grains.	Pounds other Agricultural Products.	Pounds Animal Products not specified.
RIDGEWAY STATION.												
1868.												
September								11303		318		
October								19043		512		
November							180	9105		333		1350
December					22910		70	12679		191		640
1869.												
January					18280			11195				360
February					5100			5478		262		620
March								4994				1270
April								3644		204		350
Total east'rd					46290		250	77441		1820		4590
Total west'rd		1										1050
CONOVER STATION.												
1868.												
May						2200		15038		2726	58940	6840
June		16	50				1680	3825	691	1971	3160	9850
July		38					6770	3542		1446	5600	7490
August		37	96				3780	1509		83	3400	17050
September		40	149					30904		384	2400	17920
October			155				1250	24334		546	4840	11040
November			51					10975		273	6200	7240
December					201110			14250		275	6800	6280
1869.												
January					172570			18250		75		
February					10680			5900		1519	4000	5250
March			220					10345		911	14800	7000
April			55					5314		1116	19200	7310
Total east'rd		131	776		384360	2200	13480	145084	691	11325	129340	103270
Total west'rd	6	62	7		1750	162720			299	813	2240	15730
CALMAR STATION.												
1868.												
May								11821	362	2835	94560	540
June							2080	6266	1091	884		2620
July								1394	782	766	1800	6160
August	1	46						4283	131			2120
September		20	47					34314				10750
October			90					31730		436		20670
November	1							14802		80		9440
December					155540			6999		524	1000	9750
1869.												
January					118500	920		9957		90		6190
February					11750	400		1099		1039		5580
March	1					100		8152		147		1130
April								10573			760	4410
Total east'rd	3	66	137		285790	1420	2080	141390	2366	6801	98120	79360
Total west'rd		29			7120			593				

EXHIBIT A—Continued.

OSSIAN STATION.

MONTHS. 1868.	No. of Horses.	No. of Cattle.	No. of Hogs.	No. of Sheep.	Pounds dressed Hogs.	Pounds Lard and Pork.	Pounds Wool.	Bushels Wheat	Bushels Corn.	Bushels other Grains.	Pounds other Agricultural Products.	Pounds animal Products not specified.
May	..	1	....	..	......	160	.....	36950	5899	15105	172260	5350
June	..	39	55	..	......	......	.....	16928	10304	8638	....	30220
July	..	...	39	..	......	......	.....	4381	4561	4510	360	11150
August	..	...	50	..	......	300	420	16892	289	2545	....	26150
September	..	70	180	..	......	......	5320	69570	.....	8195	....	15170
October	..	...	51	..	......	......	.....	76973	.....	7275	1020	5790
November	..	...	155	..	......	......	.....	30646	.....	1286	....	14780
December	..	...	158	..	174670	......	.....	32067	.....	790	....	12530
1869.												
January	..	...	....	..	80500	......	.....	10309	.....	.....	....	4050
February	..	...	....	..	34550	......	500	8101	.....	20	18000	7950
March	..	19	....	..	......	......	1000	13209	.....	.....	....	3350
April	..	...	....	..	......	......	1450	7748	.....	691	18800	5240
Total east'rd	..	129	688	..	289720	460	8690	323774	21053	49049	210440	141730
Total west'rd	..	...	....	..	1000	......	......	.....	8550	2874	....	8350

CASTALIA STATION.

1868.	No. of Horses.	No. of Cattle.	No. of Hogs.	No. of Sheep.	Pounds dressed Hogs.	Pounds Lard and Pork.	Pounds Wool.	Bushels Wheat	Bushels Corn.	Bushels other Grains.	Pounds other Agricultural Products.	Pounds animal Products not specified.
May	..	3	30	..	......	......	.....	2610	1726	1109	57540	140
June	..	...	....	..	......	......	.....	1615	691	500	....	......
July	..	...	....	..	......	......	210	......	791	340	200	1300
August	..	...	....	..	......	......	100	2838	.....	.....	....	......
September	..	19	....	..	......	......	.....	7912	.....	495	....	......
October	..	13	21	..	......	......	.....	15255	.....	3852	600	1290
November	..	11	69	..	......	......	.....	2223	.....	.....	....	490
December	..	...	50	..	11410	......	.....	4838	.....	878	1520	1900
1869.												
January	..	...	....	..	11490	......	.....	872	.....	1357	....	450
February	..	...	....	..	5400	......	.....	659	.....	1225	....	770
March	..	...	....	..	300	......	.....	630	.....	.....	120	......
April	..	...	....	..	......	......	.....	1828	.....	4934	....	250
Total east'rd	..	46	170	..	28600	......	310	41280	3207	14690	59980	6590
Total west'rd	..	...	....	..	......	......	.....	.....	3227	819	....	......

POSTVILLE STATION.

1868.	No. of Horses.	No. of Cattle.	No. of Hogs.	No. of Sheep.	Pounds dressed Hogs.	Pounds Lard and Pork.	Pounds Wool.	Bushels Wheat	Bushels Corn.	Bushels other Grains.	Pounds other Agricultural Products.	Pounds animal Products not specified.
May	..	...	50	..	......	......	.....	4502	2276	2167	56080	460
June	..	...	40	..	......	......	.....	1777	3210	1175	19420	3930
July	..	...	40	..	......	......	1340	2485	1400	641	120	3300
August	..	...	45	..	......	......	410	5144	.....	46	260000	2570
September	..	56	275	..	......	......	.....	24330	.....	1573	520000	5540
October	..	...	604	..	......	......	1920	21542	.....	1096	623600	2970
November	..	60	433	..	......	......	.....	7022	.....	364	482520	3570
December	..	...	650	..	205440	......	120	7230	.....	1143	659800	1460
1869.												
January	..	...	....	..	353780	......	.....	3719	.....	515	300240	4490
February	..	...	....	..	43360	200	.....	587	.....	547	540000	2180
March	..	...	....	..	......	......	.....	3463	.....	90	700000	2210
April	..	36	....	..	......	15510	.....	5215	.....	27	424040	11400
Total east'rd	..	152	2137	..	602580	15710	3790	87016	6876	9384	4585820	44080
Total west'rd	..	27	....	1	......	......	.....	6	8282	5647	200	......

EXHIBIT A—Continued.

LUANA STATION.

MONTHS. 1868.	No. of Horses.	No. of Cattle.	No. of Hogs.	No. of Sheep.	Pounds dressed Hogs.	Pounds of Lard and Pork.	Pounds Wool.	Bushels Wheat	Bushels Corn.	Bushels of other Grains.	Pounds of other Agricultural Products.	Pounds Animal Products not specified.
May								664	3237	3032		
June		16	59					236	5124	1548		
July		50	114						696			
August		19	191					2178	725	523		
September		36	274					7264	758	468		
October		60	163					4515		1444		
November		139	906					2553				
December		30	404		32130			3927		500	540	
1869.												
January					53580			383				
February					22240							
March								1936		1034	1000	
April		69	325					1596		531		
Total east'rd		419	2436		107950			25252	10540	9080	1540	
Total west'rd									343			

MONONA STATION.

MONTHS. 1868.	No. of Horses.	No. of Cattle.	No. of Hogs.	No. of Sheep.	Pounds dressed Hogs.	Pounds of Lard and Pork.	Pounds Wool.	Bushels Wheat	Bushels Corn.	Bushels of other Grains.	Pounds of other Agricultural Products.	Pounds Animal Products not specified.
May								940	364	834		
June								482	2298	789		
July								325	330			
August							1120	11977	348			80
September								15666				
October								14127		1093		1550
November								6626		726		
December					3700			6252		442	2000	560
1869.												
January					19170			1363	306		660	80
February								1688				
March					1900			1270				
April								331		839		
Total east'rd					24770		1120	61047	3646	4733	2660	2270
Total west'rd		.12										

J. P. WHALING, *Auditor.*

EXHIBIT B.

ILLINOIS CENTRAL RAILROAD—IOWA DIVISION.

Statement of Agricultural Products carried Eastward from the several Stations on the Iowa Division of the Illinois Central Railroad for each of the twelve months ending April 30, 1869.

CEDAR FALLS & MINNESOTA RAILROAD.

CHARLES CITY STATION.

MONTHS.	No. of Horses.	No. of Cattle.	No. of Hogs.	No. of Sheep.	Pounds dressed Hogs.	Barrels of Lard and Pork.	Pounds Wool.	Bushels Wheat	Bushels Corn.	Bushels other grains.	Flour and oth'r Agri'l Products, bbls.	Hides and An'l Products not specified, lbs.
1868.												
October							4000	30970		1420	400	3800
November			52					9000		1650	1150	4000
December					85000			22300		800	1600	12300
1869.												
January					82700			62600		2900	1300	6800
February		32			7200			22310		1020	412	2800
March		42						17650		2270	1100	4400
April		28	42					9330			500	7300
Total		102	94		174900		4000	174160		10060	6462	41400

NASHUA STATION.

MONTHS.	No. of Horses.	No. of Cattle.	No. of Hogs.	No. of Sheep.	Pounds dressed Hogs.	Barrels of Lard and Pork.	Pounds Wool.	Bushels Wheat	Bushels Corn.	Bushels other grains.	Flour and oth'r Agri'l Products, bbls.	Hides and An'l Products not specified, lbs.
1868.												
October			58					9000	350	400		
November			118					10330		5170		
December			52		112200			8660		2500		2700
1869.												
January					58600			22640		3900	400	5000
February					12000			5330		2500	600	
March								6330		2200	700	
April		30						3660			120	2900
Total		30	228		182800			65950	350	16670	1820	10600

PLAINFIELD STATION.

MONTHS.	No. of Horses.	No. of Cattle.	No. of Hogs.	No. of Sheep.	Pounds dressed Hogs.	Barrels of Lard and Pork.	Pounds Wool.	Bushels Wheat	Bushels Corn.	Bushels other grains.	Flour and oth'r Agri'l Products, bbls.	Hides and An'l Products not specified, lbs.
1868.												
October		15						4000		1250		
November		15	52					4000		1870		
December			114		1400			3670		1028		
1869.												
January		35	10		6100			4000		620		
February		17	10					1330		620		
March								2000		620		
April										620		
Total		82	186		7500			19000		6620		

EXHIBIT B—Continued.

WAVERLY STATION.

MONTHS. 1868	No. of Horses.	No. of Cattle.	No. of Hogs.	No. of Sheep.	Pounds dressed Hogs.	Barrels of Lard and Pork.	Wool, pounds.	Wheat, bushels	Corn, bushels.	Other Grains, bushels.	Flour and oth'r Ag'l products barrels.	Hides and An'l products not specified, lbs.
May	..	...	150	..	......	......	1100	14980	6770	20630	300	2000
June	..	45	250	..	......	12	.....	9330	11070	8740	800	3500
July	..	17	208	75	......	......	34000	2330	7130	6250	100	5000
August	..	90	100	..	......	......	16500	42630	1780	1250	1000	7500
September	..	75	500	..	......	......	.....	87250	1430	5330	2300	10500
October	..	53	218	..	......	......	2400	70930	700	4520	2400	5200
November	..	...	310	..	......	......	.....	26970	700	3920	2710	7200
December	..	...	490	..	193700	......	.....	10330	.....	1650	4020	6300
1869												
January	..	30	....	..	101800	......	.....	25970	.....	7900	2900	9200
February	..	36	62	..	10800	......	.....	8990	.....	5390	1025	4400
March	..	75	200	..	1100	......	.....	11330	.....	5950	1805	7400
April	..	150	162	..	......	......	.....	7660	.....	15000	800	2400
Total	..	571	2650	75	307400	12	54000	318700	29580	86530	20160	70600

JANESVILLE STATION.

1868	No. of Horses.	No. of Cattle.	No. of Hogs.	No. of Sheep.	Pounds dressed Hogs.	Barrels of Lard and Pork.	Wool, pounds.	Wheat, bushels	Corn, bushels.	Other Grains, bushels.	Flour and oth'r Ag'l products barrels.	Hides and An'l products not specified, lbs.
May	..	...	50	..	......	......	.....	.....	1090	.....	200	......
June	..	...	....	..	......	......	.....	.....	350	.....	100	......
August	..	...	....	..	......	......	.....	1330	.....	.....	500	......
September	..	...	....	..	......	......	.....	670	.....	.....	1600	......
October	..	...	58	..	......	......	.....	3000	.....	400	2500	......
November	..	...	156	..	......	......	.....	1000	.....	400	1600	......
December	..	...	....	..	17600	......	.....	330	.....	.....	1700	......
1869												
January	..	...	....	..	......	......	.....	330	.....	330	600	......
February	..	...	....	..	......	......	.....	.....	.....	.....	1500	......
March	..	...	....	..	......	......	.....	.....	.....	.....	1000	......
April	..	...	15	..	......	......	.....	330	.....	1250	500	......
Total	..	...	279	..	17600	......	.....	6990	1420	2380	11800	......

DUBUQUE AND SIOUX CITY RAILROAD.

IOWA FALLS STATION.

1868	No. of Horses.	No. of Cattle.	No. of Hogs.	No. of Sheep.	Pounds dressed Hogs.	Barrels of Lard and Pork.	Wool, pounds.	Wheat, bushels	Corn, bushels.	Other Grains, bushels.	Flour and oth'r Ag'l products barrels.	Hides and An'l products not specified, lbs.
May	..	...	50	..	......	......	.....	3300	5000	2500	......	......
June	..	...	100	..	......	......	.....	1000	700	1880	......	......
July	..	16	....	..	......	......	10700	.....	350	.....	......	......
August	..	18	....	..	......	19	4700	10330	700	2490	......	......
September	..	34	48	..	......	......	3900	21640	.....	1870	300	1200
October	..	65	100	..	......	......	.....	16980	.....	1870	200	......
November	..	...	256	..	......	......	.....	7330	.....	1250	200	4400
December	..	15	92	..	......	......	.....	670	.....	.....	100	4700
1869												
January	..	...	....	..	104700	......	.....	2670	.....	.....	......	4900
February	..	...	....	..	4100	......	.....	6670	.....	1250	......	......
March	..	32	12	..	......	......	.....	670	.....	1250	105	5100
April	..	...	....	..	......	......	.....	.....	.....	.....	100	1300
Total	..	180	658	..	108800	19	19300	71260	6750	14360	1005	21600

EXHIBIT B—Continued.

ACKLEY STATION.

MONTHS. 1868.	No. of Horses.	No. of Cattle.	No. of Hogs.	No. of Sheep.	Pounds dressed Hogs.	Barrels of Lard and Pork.	Pounds Wool.	Bushels Wheat	Bushels Corn.	Bushels other grains.	Flour and oth'r Ag'l products barrels.	Hides and An'l products not specified lbs.
May	..	225	100	...	...	...	...	6330	14570	6880	...	...
June	..	15	150	...	...	...	...	1330	8570	3740	53	...
July	..	...	50	...	...	...	6900	...	4600	2900	55	...
August	..	60	50	...	...	...	5500	17670	1780	1250	50	...
September	..	30	400	...	...	...	...	46280	3210	1870	205	...
October	..	30	150	...	...	...	...	58940	...	1420	545	7000
November	..	...	600	...	...	...	...	18980	...	...	535	3000
December	..	...	505	...	30400	...	...	28630	...	1250	435	7300
1869.												
Januray	..	120	50	...	87600	...	...	21980	...	...	315	3100
February	..	15	50	...	9500	...	...	8670	...	620	215	5000
March	..	135	150	...	...	...	...	15960	...	1870	200	4000
April	..	45	350	225	...	...	...	3000	...	...	115	3800
Total	..	675	2605	225	127500	...	12400	227790	32730	21800	2723	33200

APLINGTON STATION.

1868.	No. of Horses.	No. of Cattle.	No. of Hogs.	No. of Sheep.	Pounds dressed Hogs.	Barrels of Lard and Pork.	Pounds Wool.	Bushels Wheat	Bushels Corn.	Bushels other grains.	Flour and oth'r Ag'l products barrels.	Hides and An'l products not specified lbs.
May	..	...	7	...	...	...	...	670	...	...	...	...
June	..	...	...	...	...	...	...	320	350	...	...	...
August	..	...	...	...	...	...	...	2330	350	620	...	...
September	..	...	...	...	...	...	...	7650	350	620	...	...
October	..	...	...	...	...	...	...	5000	...	...	...	...
November	..	...	...	...	...	...	...	3000	...	...	...	...
December	..	...	...	...	21500	...	...	2000	...	...	...	...
1869.												
January	..	...	...	...	4300	...	...	2330	...	...	...	...
February	..	...	...	...	...	...	...	2330	...	...	...	...
March	..	...	...	...	...	...	...	2000	...	...	...	...
April	..	...	...	...	...	...	...	330	...	...	...	...
Total	..	...	7	...	25800	...	...	27970	1050	1240	...	...

PARKERSBURG STATION.

1868.	No. of Horses.	No. of Cattle.	No. of Hogs.	No. of Sheep.	Pounds dressed Hogs.	Barrels of Lard and Pork.	Pounds Wool.	Bushels Wheat	Bushels Corn.	Bushels other grains.	Flour and oth'r Ag'l products barrels.	Hides and An'l products not specified lbs.
May	..	...	...	...	...	...	...	660	...	620	...	...
July	..	...	...	...	...	...	...	330	...	...	...	...
August	..	...	...	...	...	...	...	2670	...	...	...	...
September	..	...	50	...	...	...	...	7670	...	...	...	...
October	..	...	50	...	...	...	...	6670	...	...	...	...
November	..	...	...	...	...	...	...	7000	...	...	...	...
December	..	...	...	...	...	...	...	3660	...	...	...	...
1869					19800							
January	..	...	...	...	3100	...	...	1670	...	...	...	...
February	3	...	...	...	1500	...	...	3000	...	...	...	1000
March	15	30	...	...	1400	...	...	3340	...	620	...	...
April	..	15	...	...	...	...	...	1660	...	620	...	...
Total	18	45	100	...	25800	...	...	38330	...	1860	...	1000

EXHIBIT B.—Continued.

NEW HARTFORD STATION,

MONTHS. 1868.	No. of Horses.	No. of Cattle.	No. of Hogs.	No. of Sheep.	Pounds dressed Hogs.	Barrels of Lard and Pork.	Pounds Wool.	Bushels Wheat.	Bushels Corn.	Bushels other Grains.	Flour and oth'r Ag'l products, bbls.	Hides and An'l products not speified, lbs.
May								330	700	600		
June								300	2860			
July			35						350			
August								4000				
September		18	71					12000				
October		23						6000		1250		
November								5330		620		
December			58		4600			4000				
1869.												
January					11500			2670		620		
February								1000				
March		63						1330	350	1250		
April								2000				
Total		104	164		16100			38960	4260	4340		

CEDAR FALLS STATION.

MONTHS. 1868.	No. of Horses.	No. of Cattle.	No. of Hogs.	No. of Sheep.	Pounds dressed Hogs.	Barrels of Lard and Pork.	Pounds Wool.	Bushels Wheat.	Bushels Corn.	Bushels other Grains.	Flour and oth'r Ag'l products, bbls.	Hides and An'l products not speified, lbs.
May			50					4660	5700	1870	1727	
June								1560	3210	2500	655	
July							6400		3570	1250	300	3000
August			124					11000	1430	620	1700	7900
September		43	116					29640	2140		4100	5900
October		21	136					26640		1200	4390	9000
November		6	50					26630	350	1350	4200	14700
December		71	277		27000			12980		3450	5590	13600
1869.												
January					44000			13100		2500	4390	15100
February					13500			2670			3210	
March		36	32		3300			3340		3750	2400	6200
April		17	65					1330			1100	
Total		194	850		87800		6400	133550	16400	18490	33762	75400

WATERLOO STATION.

MONTHS. 1868.	No. of Horses.	No. of Cattle.	No. of Hogs.	No. of Sheep.	Pounds dressed Hogs.	Barrels of Lard and Pork.	Pounds Wool.	Bushels Wheat.	Bushels Corn.	Bushels other Grains.	Flour and oth'r Ag'l products, bbls.	Hides and An'l products not speified, lbs.
May		60	66					9980	16420	4360	1100	5100
June		15	100					3670	13920	3750	711	
July							25100	3300	3210	1240	122	
August		30	53				11500	49620	350		500	6300
September			153				5100	82350			4512	11700
October			98				5900	87910		800	5950	7000
November			170					67600		400	6200	7300
December			608		40800		1700	39630			6600	10100
1869.												
January			60		59800			86250		3120	2800	24300
February	14				50000			19980		620	2820	3400
March		30	58		5100			33630		4700	4575	12000
April		30						2000		620	5312	11200
Total	14	165	1366		155700		49300	485920	33900	19610	41202	98400

EXHIBIT B—CONTINUED.

RAYMOND STATION

MONTHS. 1868.	No. of Horses.	No. of Cattle.	No. of Hogs.	No. of Sheep.	Pounds dressed Hogs.	Barrels of Lard and Pork.	Pounds Wool.	Bushels Wheat	Bushels Corn.	Bushels other Grains.	Flour and oth'r Agri'l Products, bbls.	Hides and An'l Products not specified, lbs.
May								1630	700			
June								330	700			
August								8330				
September								11650				
October								13650				
November								11310		330		
December			218		1500			3670				
1869.												
January								3000				
February								2670				
March								2000				
April								2000				
Total			218		1500			60240	1400	330		

JESUP STATION.

1868.	No. of Horses.	No. of Cattle.	No. of Hogs.	No. of Sheep.	Pounds dressed Hogs.	Barrels of Lard and Pork.	Pounds Wool.	Bushels Wheat	Bushels Corn.	Bushels other Grains.	Flour and oth'r Agri'l Products, bbls.	Hides and An'l Products not specified, lbs.
May								1330	1050			
June		26	90					330	1070			
July		88	58				1000	330				
August		16	24					20670		620		
September		73	80					23980		1870		1400
October			63					23970		1020		1500
November			96	75				13980		3300		1600
December			223		22300			9000		1870		2100
1869.												
January					20700			13330	350	3120		1300
February					6800			14340		620		1000
March								8330	350	3120		
April		27	43					3340		620		
Total		230	677	75	49800		1000	132930	2820	16160		8900

INDEPENDENCE STATION.

1868.	No. of Horses.	No. of Cattle.	No. of Hogs.	No. of Sheep.	Pounds dressed Hogs.	Barrels of Lard and Pork.	Pounds Wool.	Bushels Wheat	Bushels Corn.	Bushels other Grains.	Flour and oth'r Agri'l Products, bbls.	Hides and An'l Products not specified, lbs.
May	6		356					11330	17850	13750		4300
June		70	314					3000	11070	6870		1200
July			217				15400	1000	6070	3120		3100
August		65	200				5900	24970	700	1250		4800
September		24	94				3100	49950	350	3120		
October		17	294				5600	52950	350	8750		8000
November			124					48280	350	13120		
December			1180		81400		1100	25310	350	6650		17000
1869.												
January		22	143		132600			58270		16240		7200
February			152	95	43000			32810		11870		2800
March		69	117		11400			36970		6870		6600
April		36	72					5340	300	13740	34	3700
Total	6	303	3263	95	268400		31100	350180	37390	105350	34	58700

EXHIBIT B—Continued.

WINTHROP STATION.

MONTHS. 1868.	No. of Horses.	No. of Cattle.	No. of Hogs.	No. of Sheep.	Pounds dressed Hogs.	Barrels of Lard and Pork.	Pounds Wool.	Bushels Wheat	Bushels Corn.	Bushels other grains.	Flour and oth'r Agri'l Products, bbls.	Hides and An'l Products not specified, lbs.
May	..	53	100	...	......	......	.....	5320	2850	4370	......	......
June	..	50	113	...	......	......	2300	3330	3920	5300	......	......
July	..	67	30	...	......	......	3900	300	3570	1650	......	......
August	..	...	100	...	......	......	.....	12000	1700	1870	......	......
September	..	55	307	...	......	......	.....	20650	700	6250	......	......
October	..	108	173	...	......	......	.....	22300	.....	3750	......	......
November	..	...	55	...	......	......	.....	17980	350	7900	......	......
December	..	28	172	208	9700	......	.....	14000	.....	7050	115	1300
1869.												
January	..	...	...	...	24600	......	.....	32300	.....	4370	112	2100
February	..	...	...	...	1300	......	.....	12330	.....	7830	......	......
March	..	95	92	...	1400	......	.....	11000	.....	14370	133	1000
April	..	...	...	...	......	......	.....	7000	710	3120	......	1300
Total	..	456	1142	208	37000	......	6200	158510	13800	67830	360	5700

MASONVILLE STATION.

1868.												
May	..	...	...	...	......	......	.....	330	.....	620	......	......
June	..	...	...	...	......	......	.....	......	.....	.....	......	......
July	..	...	...	...	......	......	.....	......	350	620	......	......
August	..	...	...	...	......	......	.....	2000	.....	620	......	......
September	..	...	...	...	......	......	.....	3000	350	1870	......	......
October	..	...	...	...	......	......	.....	4330	.....	1020	......	......
November	..	...	...	...	......	......	.....	2330	.....	1020	......	......
December	..	...	...	...	......	......	.....	1330	.....	.....	......	......
1869.												
January	..	...	...	...	......	......	.....	2330	.....	1250	......	......
February	..	...	...	...	......	......	.....	1330	.....	.....	......	......
March	..	...	...	...	......	......	.....	2000	.....	1250	......	......
April	..	...	...	...	......	......	.....	......	350	.....	......	......
Total	..	...	...	...	......	......	.....	18980	1050	8270	......	......

MANCHESTER STATION.

1868.												
May	..	40	223	...	......	......	.....	3000	10000	17500	600	......
June	..	257	343	...	......	......	6300	1670	16780	7500	215	......
July	..	13	175	...	......	......	21400	570	5710	4370	135	6300
August	..	...	456	...	......	......	1200	15650	1780	6870	430	......
September	..	153	860	...	......	......	1100	33970	3210	5000	1258	3400
October	..	39	290	...	......	......	.....	32300	.....	6250	1800	......
November	..	32	692	...	......	......	.....	15980	350	7500	800	3000
December	..	75	1227	...	151000	......	.....	12330	.....	5970	1370	5900
1869.												
January	..	64	72	...	209500	......	.....	21650	350	8070	700	8200
February	..	135	120	...	70400	......	.....	12310	710	6870	112	5000
March	..	124	107	...	2700	......	.....	13310	710	13120	610	5800
April	..	177	390	...	......	......	.....	4000	350	5000	700	5000
Total	..	1109	4955	...	433600	......	30000	166740	39950	94020	8730	42600

EXHIBIT B—Continued.

DELAWARE STATION.

MONTHS. 1868	No. of Horses.	No. of Cattle.	No. of Hogs.	No. of Sheep.	Pounds dressed Hogs.	Barrels of Lard and Pork.	Pounds Wool.	Bushels Wheat.	Bushels Corn.	Bushels of other Grains.	Flour and oth'r Agric'l Products bbls.	Hides and An'l products not specified, lbs.
May	..	...	....	..	......	......	.....	670	1430	3120	45	......
June	..	...	....	..	......	......	.....	330	1070	620	....	......
July	..	...	50	..	......	......	.....	300	350	620	12	......
August	..	...	163	..	......	......	.....	5000	700	2270	300	......
September	..	51	111	..	......	......	.....	8330	.....	1250	204	......
October	..	135	50	..	......	......	.....	7670	.....	7270	200	......
November	..	...	100	68	......	......	.....	1330	.....	1650	290	......
December	..	37	890	..	12900	......	.....	1330	.....	620	400	......
1869												
January	..	15	150	..	56100	......	.....	1000	.....	620	705	......
February	..	30	....	..	......	......	.....	330	.....	620	100	1200
March	7	45	....	..	......	......	.....	330	.....	.....	400	......
April	..	90	100	..	......	......	.....	670	.....	2500	400	......
Total	7	403	1614	68	69000	......	.....	27290	3550	21160	3056	1200

1868 *EARLVILLE STATION.*

MONTHS. 1868	No. of Horses.	No. of Cattle.	No. of Hogs.	No. of Sheep.	Pounds dressed Hogs.	Barrels of Lard and Pork.	Pounds Wool.	Bushels Wheat.	Bushels Corn.	Bushels of other Grains.	Flour and oth'r Agric'l Products bbls.	Hides and An'l products not specified, lbs.
May	..	4	128	..	......	......	.....	3320	2140	4990	....	......
June	..	15	74	..	......	......	.....	2660	5350	3120	32	......
July	..	...	52	..	......	......	.....	330	5000	620	....	......
August	..	24	144	..	......	......	.....	2330	.....	620	....	......
September	..	36	253	..	......	......	.....	13650	350	1780	....	......
October	..	20	53	14	......	......	.....	15980	700	7900	....	......
November	..	...	111	..	......	......	.....	5330	.....	3750	15	1300
December	..	43	238	..	18900	......	.....	7330	.....	1650	....	2100
1869												......
January	..	51	18	..	40500	......	.....	5000	.....	2900	....	
February	..	72	77	..	2100	......	.....	3670	.....	2270	....	1000
March	..	...	....	..	......	......	.....	7330	.....	620	....	1500
April	..	72	78	..	......	......	.....	3000	.....	5620	22	1000
Total	..	337	1226	14	61500	......	.....	69930	13540	35840	69	6900

1868 *DYERSVILLE STATION.*

MONTHS. 1868	No. of Horses.	No. of Cattle.	No. of Hogs.	No. of Sheep.	Pounds dressed Hogs.	Barrels of Lard and Pork.	Pounds Wool.	Bushels Wheat.	Bushels Corn.	Bushels of other Grains.	Flour and oth'r Agric'l Products bbls.	Hides and An'l products not specified, lbs.
May	..	71	128	..	......	......	.....	10890	2850	25300	500	......
June	..	9	30	..	......	......	.....	10000	11770	15580	235	......
July	..	...	58	..	......	......	.....	3000	7130	5620	245	1600
August	..	8	263	..	......	......	.....	3330	3550	1870	112	......
September	..	18	389	..	......	......	3300	12000	3210	6250	130	1100
October	..	...	450	..	......	......	.....	13330	700	10120	175	4200
November	..	18	304	..	......	......	.....	3000	700	3820	215	......
December	..	...	430	..	849600	47	.....	8330	1070	4500	110	4800
1869												
January	..	...	....	..	933300	82	.....	8980	.....	6600	125	5000
February	..	18	....	..	532900	......	.....	12320	.....	2450	255	1900
March	..	13	32	..	47300	......	.....	15320	2500	7670	222	2300
April	7	41	35	..	......	......	.....	3000	710	1020	510	1500
Total	7	196	2119	..	2363100	129	3300	103500	34190	90800	2834	22400

EXHIBIT B—CONTINUED.

FARLEY STATION.

MONTHS. 1868.	No. of Horses.	No. of Cattle.	No. of Hogs.	No. of Sheep.	Pounds dressed Hogs.	Barrels of Lard and Pork,	Pounds Wool.	Bushels Wheat	Bushels Corn.	Bushels other Grains.	Flour and oth'r Agric'l Products bbls.	Hides and An'l products not specified, lbs.
May	..	...	....	...	......	......	.....	330	350	1870	......	......
June	..	...	....	...	......	......	.....	1670	1430	5620	......	......
July	..	...	60	...	......	......	.....	330	3930	620	......	......
August	..	11	100	...	......	......	.....	1330	350	1870	......	......
September	..	13	118	...	......	......	.....	4000	1780	3750	......	1200
October	..	...	....	...	......	......	.....	2330	1070	8920	......	1200
November	..	...	....	...	......	......	.....	1330	.....	3520	......	......
December	..	...	....	...	52900	......	.....	3000	.....	6020	......	1000
1869												
January	..	...	....	...	21200	......	.....	1000	.....	3120	......	......
February	..	...	....	...	2300	......	.....	1670	1420	2900	......	......
March	..	36	....	...	......	......	.....	5330	1070	3120	......	......
April	4	...	....	...	......	......	.....	670	710	1870	......	......
Total	4	60	278	...	76400	......	.....	22990	12110	43200	......	3400

EPWORTH STATION.

1868.	No. of Horses.	No. of Cattle.	No. of Hogs.	No. of Sheep.	Pounds dressed Hogs.	Barrels of Lard and Pork,	Pounds Wool.	Bushels Wheat	Bushels Corn.	Bushels other Grains.	Flour and oth'r Agric'l Products bbls.	Hides and An'l products not specified, lbs.
May	..	...	....	...	......	......	.....	......	1400	3800	......	......
June	..	...	100	...	......	......	.....	......	700	1240	......	......
July	..	...	100	...	......	......	.....	......	.....	.....	......	......
August	..	30	....	...	......	......	.....	......	700	620	......	......
September	..	...	50	...	......	......	.....	330	1430	1250	......	......
October	..	...	....	...	......	......	.....	......	.....	1870	......	......
November	..	...	50	...	......	......	.....	......	.....	1240	......	......
December	..	...	50	...	11500	......	.....	......	.....	.....	......	......
1869												
January	..	...	....	...	......	......	.....	......	.....	620	......	......
March	..	...	....	...	......	......	.....	330	.....	620	......	......
April	..	...	....	...	......	......	.....	......	350	3120	......	......
Total	..	30	350	...	11500	......	.....	660	4580	14380	......	......

PEOSTA STATION.

1868.	No. of Horses.	No. of Cattle.	No. of Hogs.	No. of Sheep.	Pounds dressed Hogs.	Barrels of Lard and Pork,	Pounds Wool.	Bushels Wheat	Bushels Corn.	Bushels other Grains.	Flour and oth'r Agric'l Products bbls.	Hides and An'l products not specified, lbs.
May	..	...	....	...	......	......	.....	330	700	620	......	......
June	..	...	....	...	......	......	.....	330	700	620	......	......
July	..	36	327	...	......	......	1800	......	350	.....	......	......
August	..	...	170	...	......	......	.....	......	350	1870	......	......
September	..	...	122	...	......	......	.....	2330	.....	1250	......	......
October	..	15	130	...	......	......	.....	660	.....	620	......	......
November	..	...	185	...	......	......	.....	......	.....	.....	......	......
December	..	...	688	...	......	......	.....	......	.....	.....	......	......
1869												
January	..	...	660	...	......	......	.....	......	.....	.....	......	......
March	..	...	....	...	......	......	.....	330	.....	.....	......	......
April	..	...	....	...	......	......	.....	......	.....	.....	......	......
Total	..	51	2282	...	......	......	1800	3980	2100	4980	......	......

EXHIBIT C.

CHICAGO AND NORTHWESTERN RAILWAY.

Statement of Agricultural Products carried Eastward and Westward from the several Stations on the Iowa Division of the Chicago and Northwestern Railway for each of the twelve months ending April 30th, 1869.

MISSOURI RIVER STATION.

MONTHS.	No. of Horses.	No. of Cattle.	No. of Hogs.	No. of Sheep.	Pounds dressed Hogs.	Pounds of Lard and Pork.	Pounds Wool.	Bushels Wheat	Bushels Corn.	Bushels of other Grains.	Other Agricultural Products lbs.	An'l Prod's not specified, lbs.	Flour, Barrels.
1868.													
May	..	...	....	...	.....	2420	3670	366	.....	....	160	75850	....
June	..	...	....	...	.....	6920	14450	2	.....	....	......	61880	....
July	..	...	....	...	.....	.....	6650	700	.....	....	50310	.....	....
August	..	...	....	...	.....	3390	23840	......	.....	....	560	52250	162
September	5	...	....	...	.....	.....	.....	3	... .	22	13120	30750	....
October.. ..	..	...	....	...	2100	.....	22540	......	.....	....	6330	88400	..17
November .	2	...	....	...	.....	.....	.....	......	.....	....	......	53440	..54
December. .	3	...	....	...	.....	6270	370	......	.....	....	975	97870	2
1869.													
January ...	3	...	....	...	.....	.....	.....	......	.....	....	......	117820	....
February ..	..	...	....	...	.....	.....	430	310	.....	....	460	87300	....
March	..	...	....	...	.....	4300	1220	2	.....	....	1260	98420	....
April	..	96	45	...	.....	.....	.....	......	.....	....	250	61390	306
Total	13	96	45	....	2100	23300	73170	1383	....	22	73425	825370	541

COUNCIL BLUFFS STATION.

MONTHS.	No. of Horses.	No. of Cattle.	No. of Hogs.	No. of Sheep.	Pounds dressed Hogs.	Pounds of Lard and Pork.	Pounds Wool.	Bushels Wheat	Bushels Corn.	Bushels of other Grains.	Other Agricultural Products lbs.	An'l Prod's not specified, lbs.	Flour, Barrels.
1868.													
May	..	336	270	...	.....	1300	.....	......	29	....	11256	17190	2
June	2	320	1350	...	.....	633	9100	......	30	2	1570	2930	2
July	..	144	1170	...	.....	.....	9250	666	662	....	11700	.....	350
August	..	288	855	...	.....	600	11780	333	4736	....	9830	6230	8
September .	..	320	1215	...	.....	190	1120	3180	10687	37	8730	19210	100
October .. .	..	352	990	...	.....	1490	2170	3335	.....	565	76500	24470	12
November	..	128	....	220	.....	.....	.....	333	.....	....	62100	20650	103
December .	..	...	....	...	26220	2290	290	333	380	....	16810	21330	105
1869.													
January ...	..	...	225	...	13780	27240	.....	......	589	218	1130	40500	1
February ..	..	96	....	...	16590	1800	.....	......	716	50	19930	28860	....
March.	..	66	135	550	2600	1750	250	4	19	....	1300	21720	....
April.	.2	323	135	...	.....	15410	.....	......	3700	562	3750	30000	....
Total	4	2373	6345	770	59190	52703	32960	8184	21508	1434	224606	233090	683

EXHIBIT C—Continued.

MISSOURI VALLEY JUNCTION.

MONTHS. 1868.	No. of Horses.	No. of Cattle.	No. of Hogs.	No. of Sheep.	Pounds dressed Hogs.	Pounds of Lard and Pork.	Pounds Wool.	Bushels Wheat	Bushels Corn.	Bushels other grains.	Other Agricultural Products lbs.	An'l Prod's not specified, lbs.	Flour, barrels.
May								333			500	9180	31
June						200	4860	3833				2600	330
July							10350				8760		
August						370	15840	123		93	220	3450	418
September		192	45				1440	306			5770	3600	810
October		752					2920	942		625	77180	21040	490
November			94		2890	1520	220			2	1180	5240	200
December			90		2520		220				860	21220	610
1869.													
January			29		19760	2760	150	14			2980	21393	440
February					2660		900				540	18674	15
March	16	64				300	480				780	18330	15
April						530	130		11		2070	55070	10
Total	16	1008	258		27830	5680	37510	5551	11	720	100840	179797	3369

LOGAN STATION.

1868.	No. of Horses.	No. of Cattle.	No. of Hogs.	No. of Sheep.	Pounds dressed Hogs.	Pounds of Lard and Pork.	Pounds Wool.	Bushels Wheat	Bushels Corn.	Bushels other grains.	Other Agricultural Products lbs.	An'l Prod's not specified, lbs.	Flour, barrels.
May								330			1130		25
June											2320	2870	12
July								650			1850	450	40
August		48									380		26
September									28		120		
October										562			37
November						780					1800		112
December	4				52250	11060			188	50	470	390	86
1869.													
January					17150	4250			238				2
February						10450		24					163
March					3900	3680		5			1520	900	2
April						450					2450	20	8
Total	4	48			73300	30670		1009	454	612	12040	4630	513

WOODBINE STATION.

1868.	No. of Horses.	No. of Cattle.	No. of Hogs.	No. of Sheep.	Pounds dressed Hogs.	Pounds of Lard and Pork.	Pounds Wool.	Bushels Wheat	Bushels Corn.	Bushels other grains.	Other Agricultural Products lbs.	An'l Prod's not specified, lbs.	Flour, barrels.
May		16							157	38	16590		300
June						330			17	54	300		105
July		32					2100		97	293	250		585
August							3970				18500		255
September			12				1600		613	640	50010	620	1125
October			7				1980			419	162320	670	938
November		134			6380	370			291		36730		1213
December		16	113		21420	200			1395	41	41050	1160	1062
1869.													
January					14820	680			1245		60000	2750	866
February					6930				624		46100	810	475
March					4680	2660		103	1119		22000	470	931
April						1750			1050		68850	300	572
Total		193	132		54230	5990	9650	103	6608	1485	522700	6780	8427

EXHIBIT C.—Continued.

DUNLAP STATION.

MONTHS. 1868	No. of Horses.	No. of Cattle.	No. of Hogs.	No. of Sheep.	Pounds dress'd Hogs,	Pounds of Lard and Pork.	Pounds Wool.	Bushels Wheat	Bushels Corn.	Bushels other grain.	Other Agricultural Products, lbs.	Animal Prod's n't specified, lbs	Flour, Barrels.
May											18520	969	
June											10260	3130	
July											3510	1080	
August	2						840	972		278	7700	970	4
September	1	96	90					319			15850	1220	
October		56	67				220		241	201	63500	610	
November	1	1			3690			308			24250	2010	27
December					16290	470			352		90	940	20
1869.													
January					4680						150	3440	
February					5230				321			2150	
March			3		3380							1580	
April											11800	200	
Total	4	153	160		33270	470	1060	1599	914	479	155630	18290	51

DENISON STATION.

1868	No. of Horses.	No. of Cattle.	No. of Hogs.	No. of Sheep.	Pounds dress'd Hogs,	Pounds of Lard and Pork.	Pounds Wool.	Bushels Wheat	Bushels Corn.	Bushels other grain.	Other Agricultural Products, lbs.	Animal Prod's n't specified, lbs	Flour, Barrels.
May											130	410	
June							6560	333					
July	1										240		
August						80	2090				380	130	
September												300	1
October	1										21400	470	
November	3				1180	700					850		
December	14				3560						110	1020	
1869.													
January	2				780	380					170	2450	
February					330	280					410	280	
March								93	316			150	1
April								48	750		18390		
Total	21				5850	1440	8650	474	1066		42080	5210	2

CARROLL STATION.

1868	No. of Horses.	No. of Cattle.	No. of Hogs.	No. of Sheep.	Pounds dress'd Hogs,	Pounds of Lard and Pork.	Pounds Wool.	Bushels Wheat	Bushels Corn.	Bushels other grain.	Other Agricultural Products, lbs.	Animal Prod's n't specified, lbs	Flour, Barrels.
May											600	240	
June											570	360	
July											100	590	
August											90	360	
September							210					560	
October												500	
November												120	
December												550	
1869.													
January						400						1660	
February	4											3120	1
March												660	
April						400						3940	
Total	4					800	210				1360	12660	1

EXHIBIT C—CONTINUED.

GLIDDEN STATION.

MONTHS. 1868	No. of Horses.	No. of Cattle.	No. of Hogs.	No. of Sheep.	Pounds dressed Hogs.	Pounds of Lard and Pork.	Pounds Wool.	Bushels Wheat.	Bushels Corn.	Bushels Other Grains.	Other Agricultural Products lbs.	Animal Prod'ts n't spe'fi'd, lbs	Flour, barrels.
May								326			2750	290	
June											50	570	
July											340	860	
August											490	90	
September								333					
October											230	190	
November		16											
December	2				2790							260	
1869													
January							110						
February											60	150	
March					260							450	
April											5160	560	
Total	2	16			3050		110	659			9080	3420	

JEFFERSON STATION.

1868	No. of Horses.	No. of Cattle.	No. of Hogs.	No. of Sheep.	Pounds dressed Hogs.	Pounds of Lard and Pork.	Pounds Wool.	Bushels Wheat.	Bushels Corn.	Bushels Other Grains.	Other Agricultural Products lbs.	Animal Prod'ts n't spe'fi'd, lbs	Flour, barrels.
May			45					300			500	830	15
June		16		110			8260				250		33
July							7500	313				600	14
August	1	48	45			1730	430			366	980	620	16
September		34									400		14
October		78	48								1160	2810	18
November		32	110			120					450	740	8
December			180		18750						1190	2570	7
1869													
January			144			180					200		22
February	4											1570	30
March	1	1						154	2		590	2950	37
April	14	64						172				22870	55
Total	20	273	572	110	18750	2030	16190	939	2	366	5720	35560	269

OGDEN STATION.

1868	No. of Horses.	No. of Cattle.	No. of Hogs.	No. of Sheep.	Pounds dressed Hogs.	Pounds of Lard and Pork.	Pounds Wool.	Bushels Wheat.	Bushels Corn.	Bushels Other Grains.	Other Agricultural Products lbs.	Animal Prod'ts n't spe'fi'd, lbs	Flour, barrels.
May		48				220							
June			180								680	1030	
July			45										
September		64	45										
October												680	
December		32			2230	100			6			470	
1869													
January	2					480						320	
February												430	
March											460	700	
April												160	
Total	2	144	270		2230	800			6		1140	3790	

EXHIBIT C—Continued.

MOINGONA STATION.

MONTHS. 1868.	No. of Horses.	No. of Cattle.	No. of Hogs.	No. of Sheep.	Pounds dressed Hogs.	Pounds of Lard and Pork.	Pounds Wool.	Bushels Wheat	Bushels Corn.	Bushels other Grain.	Other Agricultural Products lbs.	Animal Prod'ts n't spe'fied lbs	Flour, barrels.
May.......	..	...	....	...	.....	780	.....	......	.....	....	400	1090	2
June	1	...	....	...	.....	.....	.....	......	.....	....	......	.....	....
July.......	..	...	....	...	.....	.....	890	......	.....	....	......	290	10
August. ...	..	...	....	...	.....	.....	1060	......	.....	....	340	.....	1
September .	..	...	....	...	.....	.....	.....	......	.....	....	1210	.....	5
October .. .	..	...	....	...	.....	.....	280	......	.....	....	1950	1300	37
November .	..	...	....	...	.....	970	.....	......	.....	....	......	.....	20
December ..	..	...	....	...	.....	.....	.....	......	.....	....	1460	.....	....
1869.													
February ..	..	...	....	...	.....	.....	.....	......	.....	....	240	1730	....
March.	..	...	....	...	.....	300	.....	......	.....	....	20000	.....	34
April.	..	...	....	...	.....	370	.....	......	.....	....	900	.....	36
Total......	1	...	....	...	.....	2420	2230	......	.....	....	26500	4410	145

BOONE STATION.

MONTHS. 1868.	No. of Horses.	No. of Cattle.	No. of Hogs.	No. of Sheep.	Pounds dressed Hogs.	Pounds of Lard and Pork.	Pounds Wool.	Bushels Wheat	Bushels Corn.	Bushels other Grain.	Other Agricultural Products lbs.	Animal Prod'ts n't spe'fied lbs	Flour, barrels.
May.	1	33	....	...	.....	3810	290	......	258	11	10440	9630	49
June.	5	...	....	...	.....	7450	10690	......	.....	10	27930	7210	95
July	..	179	....	...	.....	.....	10470	......	.....	....	2410	8990	....
August.....	..	...	....	...	.....	6260	25080	......	6781	....	9580	9400	101
September .	6	184	....	...	.....	.....	2340	......	7	....	27020	18310	101
October....	..	229	....	...	.....	370	2020	......	8	....	316460	14000	17
November .	..	...	240	...	.....	14110	160	......	.....	....	63390	20140	15
December. .	1	54	135	...	73780	20720	450	......	.....	....	5130	7830	1
1869.													
January. ..	2	...	....	...	34320	14740	90	......	20	....	2100	24700	13
February. .	..	126	....	...	210	340	150	98	.....	....	10530	17900	2
March.	2	17	65	...	.....	9260	.....	129	.....	....	12080	9530	....
April......	13	13	1	...	.....	3490	.....	23	.....	....	77310	16550	73
Total..........	30	835	441		108310	80550	51740	250	7074	21	564380	164190	467

AMES STATION.

MONTHS. 1868.	No. of Horses.	No. of Cattle.	No. of Hogs.	No. of Sheep.	Pounds dressed Hogs.	Pounds of Lard and Pork.	Pounds Wool.	Bushels Wheat	Bushels Corn.	Bushels other Grain.	Other Agricultural Products lbs.	Animal Prod'ts n't spe'fied lbs	Flour, barrels.
May.......	..	...	....	...	......	......	.....	350	.....	....	8920	830	....
June..... ..	..	...	45	...	......	......	.....	660	.....	....	3120	490	....
July..... ..	..	64	....	...	......	......	3380	......	.....	....	1610	920	....
August	..	...	45	...	......	......	3570	1649	1303	....	4320	1480	....
September. .	..	7	90	220	......	......	.....	993	321	....	210	980	....
October....	..	...	90	...	......	540	220	673	.....	....	170200	1250	....
November .	..	...	90	...	......	410	30	......	.....	31	21150	3640	....
December..	..	16	45	...	......	720	20	1000	.....	....	5330	3180	1
1869.													
January. ..	..	16	46	...	26520	210	.....	......	.....	....	450	2270	....
February ..	4	66	....	...	......	......	.....	......	.....	....	220	.....	....
March......	1	...	45	...	390	......	.....	16	.....	....	360	1820	....
April......	..	...	98	...	......	170	.....	......	.....	....	2470	1350	....
Total..........	5	169	594	220	26910	2050	7220	5341	1624	31	218360	18210	1

EXHIBIT C—Continued.

NEVADA STATION.

MONTHS. 1868.	No. of Horses.	No of Cattle.	No. of Hogs.	No. of Sheep.	Pounds dressed Hogs.	Pounds of Lard and Pork.	Pounds Wool.	Bushels Wheat.	Bushels Corn.	Bushels of other Grains.	Other Agricultural Products, lbs.	Animal Prod'ts n't specified, lbs.	Flour, Barrels.
May	3	34	....	...	.....	4430	.....	510	.....	....	12140	440	2
June	3	...	....	...	.....	990	40	2	102	....	17972	.....	4
July	..	17	45	...	.....	.....	800	351	1246	190	450	1710	....
August	..	16	135	...	.....	13520	530	7660	2287	....	2240	410	....
September	..	32	180	...	.....	.....	.....	5974	1824	....	29630	30670	....
October	..	...	....	...	.....	.....	550	6854	322	654	285640	1380	....
November	..	...	90	...	.....	2570	80	699	.....	90	21150	3210	2
December	1	...	135	...	110960	4360	200	1390	.....	113	230	5940	33
1869.													
January	14	...	....	...	62400	.....	.....	330	.....	....	370	4630	146
February	6	...	....	...	14890	.....	.....	1020	.....	42	3710	1410	90
March	..	64	45	...	7020	7580	.....	1770	376	6	6510	1470	330
April	..	39	164	...	360	520	60	20	.....	1247	10110	490	238
Total	27	202	794	......	195630	33970	2260	26580	6157	2342	390152	51760	845

COLO STATION.

MONTHS. 1868.	No. of Horses.	No of Cattle.	No. of Hogs.	No. of Sheep.	Pounds dressed Hogs.	Pounds of Lard and Pork.	Pounds Wool.	Bushels Wheat.	Bushels Corn.	Bushels of other Grains.	Other Agricultural Products, lbs.	Animal Prod'ts n't specified, lbs.	Flour, Barrels.
May	..	64	135	...	.....	250	1910	1370	321	....	9680	3350	....
June	..	...	45	...	.....	660	1060	328	.....	....	6760	3080	....
July	..	...	....	...	.....	.....	.....	1017	.....	....	7180	3770	....
August	..	32	180	...	.....	.....	1120	5255	711	722	10270	510	....
September	..	16	90	...	.....	31550	190	2673	321	1125	11420	1080	....
October	..	...	....	...	.....	.....	240	4356	.....	562	49740	1630	....
November	..	...	360	...	.....	3560	.....	682	.....	563	1410	2380	....
December	..	...	225	...	2110	4510	.....	650	.....	....	500	5680	....
1899.													
January	..	16	90	...	1560	1970	.....	2371	.....	....	720	1970	....
February	..	50	90	...	.....	.....	.....	995	.....	....	3500	2400	....
March	..	34	....	...	.....	1320	.....	680	.....	....	8480	1310	....
April	..	96	90	...	.....	4060	.....	339	.....	....	20400	720	....
Total	...	308	1305	......	3670	47880	4520	20716	1353	2972	130060	27880	......

STATE CENTER STATION.

MONTHS. 1868.	No. of Horses.	No of Cattle.	No. of Hogs.	No. of Sheep.	Pounds dressed Hogs.	Pounds of Lard and Pork.	Pounds Wool.	Bushels Wheat.	Bushels Corn.	Bushels of other Grains.	Other Agricultural Products, lbs.	Animal Prod'ts n't specified, lbs.	Flour, Barrels.
May	..	...	180	...	......	......	......	5600	2988	....	1390	2050	....
June	..	128	360	...	......	......	230	4149	1361	....	3030	4100	....
July	..	64	....	...	......	......	......	1672	1063	1240	1160	2010	....
August	..	...	159	...	......	......	420	18354	776	....	110	1010	24
September	..	15	135	...	......	340	......	32525	351	580	540	.....	1
October	..	...	121	...	......	......	750	20735	321	562	102700	2240	....
November	..	...	180	...	......	330	340	8783	362	....	184160	2700	....
December	..	...	482	109	......	1240	......	5485	13446	763	840	4950	....
1869.													
January	..	49	225	...	......	......	......	8220	6400	641	230	3500	2
February	7	19	200	103	1840	......	2480	3625	744	636	790	1610	....
March	19	32	135	66	......	4370	1200	3041	1512	....	720	1290	....
April	..	...	90	312	......	1000	.....	1455	1388	....	141800	1990	2
Total	26	307	2267	590	1840	7280	5420	113644	30712	4422	437470	27460	29

EXHIBIT C—Continued.

LA MOILLE STATION.

MONTHS. 1868.	No. of Horses.	No. of Cattle.	No. of Hogs.	No. of Sheep.	Pounds dressed Hogs.	Pounds of Lard and Pork.	Pounds Wool.	Bushels Wheat	Bushels Corn.	Bushels other grains.	Other Agricultural Products lbs.	An'l Prod's not specified, lbs.	Flour, barrels.
June	..	....	....	....	......	......	......	333	......	....	......	......	....
August	..	....	....	....	......	......	......	5683	......	....	50	......	....
September	..	....	....	....	......	200	......	6184	......	....	950	2700	....
October	..	....	....	....	......	......	......	6607	......	....	......	......	....
November	..	....	....	....	......	......	......	1382	......	....	......	......	....
December	..	....	....	....	......	....	......	975	339	...	......	400	....
1869.													
January	..	...	..	....	......	......	....	1440	...	...	....	.....	....
February	..	...	....	....	......	.....	....	1719	....		.....	.....	....
March	..	...	....	..	....	....	....	2176	736	668	....	....	....
April	..	...	....	...	....	...	....	42	366	.	.	....	....
Total	...	...	......	....	......	200	....	26541	1441	668	1000	3100	......

MARSHALLTOWN STATION.

1868.	No. of Horses.	No. of Cattle.	No. of Hogs.	No. of Sheep.	Pounds dressed Hogs.	Pounds of Lard and Pork.	Pounds Wool.	Bushels Wheat	Bushels Corn.	Bushels other grains.	Other Agricultural Products lbs.	An'l Prod's not specified, lbs.	Flour, barrels.
May	..	113	540	...	.....	1740	....	8432	22848	2464	298160	3500	11
June	34	85	765	..	....	460	....	7763	20648	2583	116350	.....	226
July	1	16	411	...	.....	.....	27330	2362	16159	4382	2018	5920	189
August	2	...	134	...	....	3810	11590	161761	7630	2701	25660	5170	49
September	14	72	225	110	.....	...	3240	115559	2064	1293	6310	6100	25
October	2	...	270	...	....	....	1490	101133	386	1557	269040	16000	302
November	2	..	540	...	400	5840	1200	24561	1437	3398	135100	12000	358
December	1	16	1440	...	40500	1120	....	28521	10246	1923	8020	20740	370
1869.													
January	..	...	45	110	158600	5280	18240	29165	10691	3170	35470	25780	480
February	2	35	63	230	:8340	240	1420	21028	2884	2555	29160	11310	295
March	17	3	161	110	11640	1930	....	31019	7740	4069	44540	6300	1112
April	..	272	135	..	....	....	720	12148	2273	1263	145640	7430	636
Total	75	612	4729	560	229480	20420	65230	543452	105006	31358	1115468	120250	4053

QUARRY STATION.

1868	No. of Horses.	No. of Cattle.	No. of Hogs.	No. of Sheep.	Pounds dressed Hogs.	Pounds of Lard and Pork.	Pounds Wool.	Bushels Wheat	Bushels Corn.	Bushels other grains.	Other Agricultural Products lbs.	An'l Prod's not specified, lbs.	Flour, barrels.
June	..	...	....	...	....	....	.....	......	....	....	600	....	....
August	..	. .	....	...	.....	....	.....	......	.....	..	......	...	148
September	..	..	...	...	.....	....	.....	2942	...		50	....	247
October	..	...	..	...	......	......	......	2746	....	638	21380	.. .	293
November	..	...	....	...	...	......	......	1353	....	....	25700	.....	158
December	..	...	....	...	640	....	.....	333	727	...	... ..	200	395
1869.													
January	..	...	....	...	1040	.....	.....	335	721	625	9400	450	422
February	..	...	....	...	200	.....	.....	1036	727	..	6230	....	120
March	..	...	....	...	.....	....	.....	1690	1457	..	2590	170	290
April	..	...	....	...	.....	..	.	1363	630	..	2570	.. .	...
tal	...	......	......	....	1880	....	....	11798	4262	1263	68520	820	2073

EXHIBIT C—Continued.

LE GRAND STATION.

MONTHS. 1868	No. of Horses.	No. of Cattle.	No. of Hogs.	No. of Sheep.	Pounds dressed Hogs.	Pounds of Lard and Pork.	Pounds Wool.	Bushels Wheat	Bushels Corn.	Other Grains, bushels.	Other Ag'l products, lbs.	Animal Prod'ts n't spe'fi'd, lbs	Flour, barrels.
May.......	..	112	135	...	.....	.....	.....	338	.....	....	290	1010	....
June......	..	...	90	...	.....	.....	.....	8395	.....	...	.....	880	....
July......	..	18	135	...	....	.....	.....	333	.....	....	1930	8640	....
August...	..	...	90	...	.....	.....	3400	6825	394	....	......	700	....
September	..	...	45	..	....	.....	1420	11724	.....	....	......	2000	75
October...		...	....	...	.....	.....	.....	9769	383	....	... .	700	...
November.	..	...	....	...	....	.....	.....	1284	.....	....	1400	1390	...
December.	..	...	180	...	....	330	.....	959	.....	....	4890	1360	....
1869.													
January..	..	...	...	...	5980	....	.....	....	.....	....	......	2080	....
February..	..	...	90	..	5640	....	.....	336	....	...	.....	720	..15
March	..	128	90	...	.....	.....	60	705	.....	....	......	360	....
April......	..	15	. .	..	....	....	....	692	.....	....	320	990	40
Total....	..	273	855	...	11620	330	4880	41360	777	...	8830	20830	130

1868. *ORFORD STATION.*

MONTHS.	No. of Horses.	No. of Cattle.	No. of Hogs.	No. of Sheep.	Pounds dressed Hogs.	Pounds of Lard and Pork.	Pounds Wool.	Bushels Wheat	Bushels Corn.	Other Grains, bushels.	Other Ag'l products, lbs.	Animal Prod'ts n't spe'fi'd, lbs	Flour, barrels.
May.......	..	...	90	...	....	.....	.....	370	.....	....	930	490	30
June... ..	..	...	45	..	.....	.....	.....	2029	....	....	660	970	32
July.......	..	...	45	...	.....	.....	.....	1795	.....	....	860	.....	45
August....	..	...	45	...	.....	460	....	14711	706	....	530	1700	36
September.	..	17	46	..	.....	.....	30	16950	.....	....	......	660	63
October ...	..	...	....	...	.....	....	60	8405	....	....	3970	1750	108
November.	..	...	205	...	.....	.....	....	2410	188	....	18150	760	35
December.	..	32	135	...	370	.....	....	6024	.....	....	100	2120	83
1869													
January...	.	...	45	...	15600	.....	.....	5957	.....	..	170	1190	71
February..	14	...	....	...	8060	.....	.....	1641	.....	...	......	260	47
March.....	..	32	....	...	2600	.. .	....	4441	.. .	....	170	1070	56
April.....	7	17	116	...	.....	.....	.....	962	.....	....	2000	790	51
Total....	21	98	772	...	26630	460	90	65695	894	....	27540	11760	657

1868. *TAMA CITY STATION.*

MONTHS.	No. of Horses.	No. of Cattle.	No. of Hogs.	No. of Sheep.	Pounds dressed Hogs.	Pounds of Lard and Pork.	Pounds Wool.	Bushels Wheat	Bushels Corn.	Other Grains, bushels.	Other Ag'l products, lbs.	Animal Prod'ts n't spe'fi'd, lbs	Flour, barrels.
May.	..	...	45	110	.....	8720	1600	6601	2290	604	79260	3100	....
June.. ..	..	1	225	...	.....	10892	3820	3720	3668	286	49808	1930	43
July,......	..	...	99	...	.....	.... .	7400	1025	1507	473	9980	3910	7
August....	..	16	195	110	.....	4560	3500	33475	2162	....	2640	2530	30
September.	..	48	45	...	.....	.....	830	44674	1114	42	4870	6290	38
October...	.	80	....	...	.....	. ...	200	50830	.....	825	8430	7370	59
November.	..	16	315	...	3170	1050	120	19906	.....	....	1990	5190	317
December.	..	...	765	...	34510	950	210	32309	324	16	4630	7580	339
1869													
January...	..	...	90	110	93340	2130	660	18816	.....	562	1220	5488	450
February..	..	16	90	..	12990	.....	.....	11768	.....	....	18000	6020	345
March.....	..	...	180	210	12220	400	....	18249	.....	44	1340	4070	215
April......	..	...	97	...	.....	.....	.....	4512	....	625	10340	2480	246
Total......	....	177	2146	540	156230	28702	18340	245885	11065	3477	192508	55958	2089

EXHIBIT C—Continued.

CHELSEA STATION.

MONTHS. 1868.	No. of Horses.	No. of Cattle.	No. of Hogs.	No. of Sheep.	Pounds dressed Hogs.	Pounds of Lard and Pork.	Pounds Wool.	Bushels Wheat	Bushels Corn.	Bushels Other Grains.	Other Ag'l products, lbs.	Animal Prod'ts n't spe'fi'd, lbs	Flour, barrels.
May	..	...	90	...	.....	.....	.....	1698	....	....	800	350	...
June	..	32	90	...	.....	...	.....	972	...	...	......	1240	....
July.	..	...	...	...	....	.. .	.....	372	.....	...	1270	430	....
August....	..	1	125	...	.....	.....	.....	7071	.....	....	400	....	....
September.	..	...	....	...	.....	.....	.....	8910	.....	....	......	520	....
October ...	2	...	...	...	.....	.....	.....	16195	....	...	250	230	....
November.	..	...	158	...	.....	.....	.....	2407	.....	34	......	600	....
December .	..	16	225	...	8150	....	.....	3051	.....	....	100	270	....
1869													
January...	..	161	134	100	52520	.....	.....	5108	.....	63	100	1990	....
February...	..	134	54	...	3560	.....	.....	1715	.....	....	......	500	15
March.....	..	34	125	...	1820	.....	.....	2724	.....	...	.....	.....	....
April.. ...	..	16	56	...	.....	....	.....	1025	.....	....	......	800	....
Total....	2	394	1057	100	66050	.....	. ...	51248	.....	97	2920	6930	15

BELLE PLAINE STATION.

MONTHS.	No. of Horses.	No. of Cattle.	No. of Hogs.	No. of Sheep.	Pounds dressed Hogs.	Pounds of Lard and Pork.	Pounds Wool.	Bushels Wheat	Bushels Corn.	Bushels Other Grains.	Other Ag'l products, lbs.	Animal Prod'ts n't spe'fi'd, lbs	Flour, barrels.
May.......	..	...	45	...	.....	2670	....	2029	3452	....	21410	1130	15
June	..	...	225	...	.....	12430	3240	2417	2170	75	830	300	10
July	.	96	90	...	.....	.....	3850	1007	365	1306	4430	2170	23
August....	..	...	90	...	.....	2060	4010	35508	68050	437	560	3290	5
September..	..	...	90	...	.....	....	.....	41999	....	775	720	1160	....
October ...	..	16	180	...	.....	.....	6610	42639	.....	1034	23200	1710	1
November.	..	...	270	...	.....	830	....	13544	.....	129	3360	8970	10
December .	..	...	270	...	34690	1340	.....	18566	.....	1800	3000	1850	11
1869.													
January ...	..	16	....	...	104520	1010	.....	20276	.....	....	1200	6630	30
February..	3	80	45	. .	12000	.....	.....	7297	.....	23	120	2170	....
March.....	..	17	90	110	.....	600	.....	10826	3	667	720	2950	...
April......	9	...	90	...	.....	.....	70	6960	.....	....	5930	9990	....
Total.........	12	225	1485	110	151210	20940	17780	203068	74040	6246	65480	42320	105

1868. *LUZERNE STATION.*

MONTHS.	No. of Horses.	No. of Cattle.	No. of Hogs.	No. of Sheep.	Pounds dressed Hogs.	Pounds of Lard and Pork.	Pounds Wool.	Bushels Wheat	Bushels Corn.	Bushels Other Grains.	Other Ag'l products, lbs.	Animal Prod'ts n't spe'fi'd, lbs	Flour, barrels.
May	..	...	...	...	.....	770	.....	3047	.....	2320	1160	570	...
June......	..	...	45	...	.....	410	.....	2027	.....	562	430	720	....
July	..	...	90	...	.....	200	.....	1025	.....	....	460	520	....
August....	..	...	65	...	... .	.....	.....	12916	600	367	1180	......	....
September	..	...	.....	...	.....	2840	.....	15378	.....	1500	403	220	....
October ...	.	...	....	...	....	....	....	14007	.....	1542	450	70	....
November.	..	...	45	...	.....	170	.....	4872	....	375	190	580	....
December .	..	...	.....	..	4490	1040	.....	5533	.....	1181	1460	670	....
1869.													
January. .	..	18	29	85	.....	......	...	5577	.....	...	300	630	...
February..	..	...	.....	...	3280	.....	.....	3901	.....	..	1000	330	...
March	..	...	.....	..	520	370	... .	3428	.....	....	1320	350	...
April......	..	...	...	...	.....	100	....	2239	....	....	3170	350	...
Total....	..	18	274	85	8290	5900	.....	73950	600	7847	11523	5010	....

EXHIBIT C—Continued.

BLAIRSTOWN STATION.

MONTHS. 1868.	No. of Horses.	No. of Cattle.	No. of Hogs.	No. of Sheep.	Pounds dressed Hogs.	Pounds of Lard and Pork.	Pounds Wool	Bushels Wheat	Bushels Corn.	Bushels other Grains.	Other Agricultural Products lbs.	Animal Prod'ts n't spe'fi'd, lbs	Flour, Barrels.
May	..	..	225	...	.....	2660	....	2387	.....	953	13900	16870	73
June......	.	...	180	...	.....	1670	.....	2025	....	381	9160	11650	128
July	..	...	....	...	.. ...	1210	....	987	....	375	13290	11660	80
August ..	..	32	225	..	....	.....	....	16821	....	...	370	160	155
September.	1	16	315	...	.....	1630	....	32140	....	1264	5550	2790	40
October ..	..	32	157	55	.....	.....	.....	51293	358	1222	3000	1360	76
November.	..	16	495	...	.....	970	.....	12695	.....	1294	30570	2410	131
December .	1	16	445	...	16320	690	.....	22707	1	911	1740	3830	232
1869.													
January...	..	16	135	...	26260	....	.....	17542	.....	2348	14870	2460	221
February..	..	112	90	..	6070	.....	.....	10015	.....	562	3830	2980	228
March	1	18	90	...	780	250	2800	12160	46	156	580	1330	
April	2	112	225	...	.....	....	....	662	...	213	37000	920	121
Total ...	5	370	2582	55	49430	9080	2800	181434	405	9679	133860	58420	1485

1868. *NORWAY STATION.*

MONTHS.	No. of Horses.	No. of Cattle.	No. of Hogs.	No. of Sheep.	Pounds dressed Hogs.	Pounds of Lard and Pork.	Pounds Wool	Bushels Wheat	Bushels Corn.	Bushels other Grains.	Other Agricultural Products lbs.	Animal Prod'ts n't spe'fi'd, lbs	Flour, Barrels.
May	..	48	135	...	.....	150	....	3583	....	....	550	530	....
June......	..	180	....	...	.....	.....	.....	10390	.....	...	1290	.....	....
July	..	90	....	...	.....	.....	.....	358	....	...	1160	...	....
August ...	..	...	135	...	.....	.....	....	12260	384	1250	530	370	....
September.	..	...	135	...	....	.....	.....	24224	1075	416	......	680	....
October. ..	..	...	135	...	.....	.....	.....	30764	....	....	1360	1090	...
November.	..	...	90	...	.....	.....	....	8610	.....	...	2120	60	....
December .	.	16	225	...	4990	470	.....	8595	.....	1187	......	...	....
1869.													
January...	..	...	180	...	4420	580	620	5634	.....	....	......	.....	....
February..	3	64	135	...	.....	170	.....	2104	.....	145	......	.....	....
March	..	20	68	...	780	380	.....	2691	....	...	2370	570	....
April.	3	...	135	...	...	.....	.....	1516	4	...	1830	270	...
Total........	6	418	1373	... ..	10190	1750	620	110729	1463	2998	11210	3570	......

1868. *FAIRFAX STATION.*

MONTHS.	No. of Horses.	No. of Cattle.	No. of Hogs.	No. of Sheep.	Pounds dressed Hogs.	Pounds of Lard and Pork.	Pounds Wool	Bushels Wheat	Bushels Corn.	Bushels other Grains.	Other Agricultural Products lbs.	Animal Prod'ts n't spe'fi'd, lbs	Flour, Barrels.
May......	..	...	45	...	....	1250	....	3410	.....	....	1120	350	4
June......	..	...	135	..	....	680	.....	2322	....	...	480	850	2
July......	..	48	45	...	....	1340	....	2067	.....	...	1050	200	....
Augnst....	..	32	90	...	.....	.....	.....	11467	567	....	380	.....	....
September.	..	16	45	...	.....	.....	.....	17270	.....	562	480	.....	....
October...	..	...	....	...	.....	.....	.....	12273	.....	...	......	.....	....
November.	..	...	135	...	.....	.....	.....	1752	....	..	......	.....	....
December .	..	...	270	...	.....	.. .	....	1684	.....	...	......	.....	....
1869.													
January...	..	...	45	...	.....	....	... .	1741	.....	....	......	.....	....
February..	..	...	....	..	.....	.....	.....	495	387	1240	... ..	.....	....
March.....	..	48	90	220	....	220	....	1099	368	....	190	.....	....
April.... .	...	...	45	...	.....	.....	....	301	.....	20	660	.....	....
Total.........	...	144	945	220	....	3490	....	55881	1322	1822	4360	1400	6

EXHIBIT C—CONTINUED.

CEDAR RAPIDS STATION.

MONTHS.	No. of Horses.	No. of Cattle.	No. of Hogs.	No. of Sheep.	Pounds dressed Hogs.	Pounds of Lard and Pork.	Pounds Wool.	Bushels Wheat	Bushels Corn.	Bushels other Grains.	Other Agricultural Products lbs.	An'l Prod's not specified, lbs.	Flour, Barrels.
1868.													
May.... ..	8	197	675	..	.....	27790	.....	15334	20136	10915	109500	5740	670
June......	1	18	451	...	.....	41090	3900	9604	43667	8830	38280	640	396
July.......	5	2	560	...	....	.....	16050	2115	18982	9319	47790	19790	123
Augnst....	1	...	140	...	.....	52318	2600	22594	17533	8181	37648	520	705
September.	..	89	149	...	.....	1160	2500	112266	6468	20963	8320	11670	1920
October ...	3	65	168	...	.....	.... .	4250	48045	2670	9514	96760	64380	3675
November.	8	16	315	...	.....	16172	10370	12002	1098	4684	57390	2300	3684
December .	1	106	880	...	458130	22226	500	24555	1812	4406	119100	28100	3709
1869.													
January...	1	48	....	...	804700	19641	330	16020	5015	3125	26030	27470	2903
February. .	23	37	68	...	63480	630	160	8321	2174	2637	13320	25820	2125
March	13	86	173	...	18720	10550	.....	12612	5950	6421	14190	4830	3210
April	35	4	11	388	635	6860	....	6580	3401	10338	85750	47270	1908
Total........	99	668	3590	388	1345665	198437	26260	290048	128906	99333	654078	238530	25028

BERTRAM STATION.

MONTHS.	No. of Horses.	No. of Cattle.	No. of Hogs.	No. of Sheep.	Pounds dressed Hogs.	Pounds of Lard and Pork.	Pounds Wool.	Bushels Wheat	Bushels Corn.	Bushels other Grains.	Other Agricultural Products lbs.	An'l Prod's not specified, lbs.	Flour, Barrels.
1868.													
June......	..	...	....	...	.....	....	.....	......	.....	...	7270	700	....
July......	..	...	....	...	.....	....	.....	......	.....	....	200	.....	....
August....	3	4	....	...	.....	....	.....	......	.....	....	250	.....	....
September.	..	...	...	...	.....	....	.....	......	.....	....	210	.....	....
November.	..	18	....	...	.....	....	.....	......	.....	...	......	.....	....
December.	..	...	....	400	.....	....	.....	......	.....	....	50	210	...
1869.													
January...	..	32	180	...	.....	....	.....	......	.....	....	......	.....	....
February..	..	...	....	...	.....	....	.....	......	.....	....	190	.....	....
March	..	32	...	990	.....	....	.....	50	.....	...	......	.....	.
April.....	..	16	180	...	.....	....	.....	... ..	.....	....	180	.....	....
Total ...	3	102	360	1390	. ..	....	.....	50	.....	....	8350	910	....

MOUNT VERNON STATION.

MONTHS.	No. of Horses.	No. of Cattle.	No. of Hogs.	No. of Sheep.	Pounds dressed Hogs.	Pounds of Lard and Pork.	Pounds Wool.	Bushels Wheat	Bushels Corn.	Bushels other Grains.	Other Agricultural Products lbs.	An'l Prod's not specified, lbs.	Flour, Barrels.
1868													
May.......	..	64	45	...	.....	3098	.....	4104	....	1827	16340	10690	...
June	..	...	....	...	.....	5030	.....	2394	....	1273	13795	6985	3
July	..	48	45	...	.....	6620	780	689	.....	1158	20980	1000	....
August....	..	...	...	...	.....	.....	....	4091	708	1283	1170	380	...
September.	..	1	....	...	.....	.....	...	1697	.....	1688	240	4010	...
October ...	3	...	....	...	.....	....	5150	1708	.....	3028	31300	.....	....
November	..	...	45	...	.....	330	....	......	.....	.	8760	2480	1
December	..	...	225	...	350	490	...	373	.....	688	900	4960	....
1869.													
January...	..	...	45	220	59020	1120	....	317	.....	656	.. ..	5330	....
February.	..	22	63	...	.....	530	110	368	.....	....	.....	2940	....
March ..	..	..	45	79	33800	1370	....	2816	5	....	.....	.....	...
April......	.	..	135	...	.....	8945	....	1805	.....	....	16290	4470	21
Total	3	135	648	299	93170	22533	6040	20662	713	11551	109775	43245	25

EXHIBIT C—Continued.

LISBON STATION.

MONTHS.	No. of Horses.	No. of Cattle.	No. of Hogs.	No. of Sheep.	Pounds Dress'd Hogs.	Pounds of Lard and Pork.	Pounds Wool.	Bushels Wheat.	Bushels Corn.	Bushels Other Grain.	Other Agricultural Products, lbs.	An'l prod'ts not specified, lbs.	Flour, Barrels
1868.													
May	..	176	360	...	.....	480	.....	4590	2366	3152	2520	1530	21
June	..	32	45	...	.....	1950	.....	4918	1335	2290	5150	3700	11
July	..	...	360	...	....	760	.....	1591	703	1184	1120	1140	56
August	..	...	45	...	.....	.....	.....	7824	2446	6756	1130	610	51
September	..	16	45	...	....	1830	.....	12241	1106	10206	1240	2770	25
October	..	...	540	...	.....	1760	.....	8041	2987	4535	4370	4480	20
November	..	...	765	...	.....	370	70	678	...	1156	4620	1000	33
December	..	...	1485	...	.....	1680	.....	1779	709	1359	9230	1010	47
1869.													
January	..	17	2205	...	17940	3940	280	3652	.....	4133	410	5770	42
February	2	2	180	...	.....	870	.....	1055	.....	642	.....	920	..
March	..	32	45	...	.....	590	770	3861	353	1058	1210	580	6
April	..	96	180	...	.....	550	.....	933	....	589	9360	1340	40
Total	2	371	6255	...	17940	14780	1120	51163	12005	37060	40360	24850	352

MECHANICSVILLE STATION.

MONTHS.	No. of Horses.	No. of Cattle.	No. of Hogs.	No. of Sheep.	Pounds Dress'd Hogs.	Pounds of Lard and Pork.	Pounds Wool.	Bushels Wheat.	Bushels Corn.	Bushels Other Grain.	Other Agricultural Products, lbs.	An'l prod'ts not specified, lbs.	Flour, Barrels
1868.													
May	..	80	270	...	.....	80	.....	2953	5585	5445	4030	700	..
June	2	48	360	110	...	7070	6470	4280	12699	6626	3330	590	..
July	..	...	135	220	.....	.....	6210	1585	5041	2702	6580	1690	..
August	..	48	270	220	.....	2420	1220	20429	6043	9608	3480	1030	..
September	..	16	270	...	.....	.....	.....	24515	2125	15940	3820	9760	..
October	..	..	405	...	.....	.....	11230	19662	.....	18251	3380	2110	..
November	..	16	810	...	.....	1500	260	2147	755	3177	490	2880	..
December	..	..	1440	...	11580	2750	110	7276	11624	7921	3310	5290	3
1869.													
January	..	96	585	110	12220	1830	.....	4077	702	9154	880	5180	..
February	..	64	540	...	3500	440	.....	5953	2700	2600	1730	20140	..
March	..	256	270	...	3120	1030	.....	9151	6218	6188	3710	2150	..
April	1	197	212	...	.....	....	.....	3973	2420	1849	14950	980	..
Total	3	821	5567	660	30420	17120	25500	106001	55912	89461	49690	52500	3

CLARENCE STATION.

MONTHS.	No. of Horses.	No. of Cattle.	No. of Hogs.	No. of Sheep.	Pounds Dress'd Hogs.	Pounds of Lard and Pork.	Pounds Wool.	Bushels Wheat.	Bushels Corn.	Bushels Other Grain.	Other Agricultural Products, lbs.	An'l prod'ts not specified, lbs.	Flour, Barrels
May	14	16	360	110	.....	11940	.....	4140	10327	4534	3930	3850	2
June	..	64	135	...	.....	16230	26470	4201	19589	3948	3770	1780	..
July	..	48	135	...	.....	....	38990	1049	9977	2374	6890	1000	..
August	..	...	90	...	.....	11768	2940	10102	2087	3383	3262	2120	..
September	..	...	180	...	.....	.....	1650	27185	1469	14105	1160	20010	..
October	..	32	45	...	.....	.....	.....	26589	1006	17028	23042	4480	1
November	4	..	180	...	.....	7060	2120	9896	.....	4865	19070	2980	6
December	14	...	990	220	27210	8450	.....	15990	4	9123	1710	8980	4
1869.													
January	..	...	360	...	28860	8350	.....	13615	2179	4934	2700	93160	17
February	..	..	135	110	9000	....	2160	10455	3920	5905	13800	17980	10
March	..	48	225	330	12220	12191	340	8639	6719	4548	9320	3600	1
April	24	79	236	..	.....	....	.....	2653	....	605	66640	2560	..
Total	56	287	3071	770	77290	75989	74670	134514	57277	75352	155294	162500	41

EXHIBIT C—Continued.

LOUDEN STATION.

MONTHS. 1868.	No. of Horses.	No. of Cattle.	No. of Hogs.	No. of Sheep.	Pounds dressed Hogs.	Pounds of Lard and Pork.	Pounds Wool.	Bushels Wheat	Bushels Corn.	Bushels other grains.	Other Agricultural Prod's, lbs.	An'l Prod's not specified, lbs.	Flour, barrels.
May........	..	144	450	110	......	100	....	1629	2825	1313	4157	.....	15
June	..	1	135	....	......	7303	1140	1040	3742	3226	1850	360	...
July........	..	....	315	....	......	......	600	319	3391	940	6500	1080	...
August	..	32	180	....	......	5240	....	6185	7481	6167	4900	320	...
September ..	..	....	360	....	......	......	....	16508	348	14095	2200	3020	...
October	1	44	135	....	......	......	480	17111	.....	7733	24550	2950	...
November ..	..	....	405	....	......	17540	....	2678	215	2214	1870	1341	...
December ..	..	....	1395	....	43960	2660	300	6161	1056	3338	1830	3480	2
1869.													
January	..	48	675	....	15080	4830	....	4139	1428	4260	380	3700	...
February . .	..	32	495	....	4020	......	....	3651	2693	1411	3240	2050	...
March..	..	32	135	....	1820	8010	....	4009	728	4581	700	830	...
April	..	....	315	....	......	150	....	3647	334	1246	11960	1610	...
Total.	1	333	4995	110	64880	45833	2520	67077	24241	50524	64137	20741	17

WHEATLAND STATION.

1868.	No. of Horses.	No. of Cattle.	No. of Hogs.	No. of Sheep.	Pounds dressed Hogs.	Pounds of Lard and Pork.	Pounds Wool.	Bushels Wheat	Bushels Corn.	Bushels other grains.	Other Agricultural Prod's, lbs.	An'l Prod's not specified, lbs.	Flour, barrels.
May........	70	32	270	...	......	60	1100	958	1388	1972	3200	1200	...
June........	..	16	225	...	......	4840	2988	2110	4170	3040	1790	750	...
July........	..	...	270	...	......	......	2630	650	2364	1332	7000	2172	...
August	..	...	90	...	......	5060	....	8830	1724	16390	2840	2440	...
September ..	1	...	98	110	......	......	....	23477	1836	14480	......	1500	...
October	7	8	288	...	......	......	....	29701	191	12052	4610	2470	...
November ..	..	20	539	...	700	1530	....	10725	324	5429	8420	4540	21
December ..	2	7	1120	...	47020	970	....	18280	340	7902	330	3640	2
1869.													
January	..	18	115	...	138840	3120	....	7407	819	2462	1130	2880	21
February ...	1	91	452	181	30150	......	....	4196	1377	2549	2530	6330	20
March	17	101	199	...	2600	3940	....	5910	1130	2565	4560	980	32
April	..	52	452	...	......	660	....	956	.....	1128	19930	3670	109
Total.	98	345	4118	291	219310	20180	6718	113200	15663	71301	56340	32572	205

CALAMUS STATION.

1868.	No. of Horses.	No. of Cattle.	No. of Hogs.	No. of Sheep.	Pounds dressed Hogs.	Pounds of Lard and Pork.	Pounds Wool.	Bushels Wheat	Bushels Corn.	Bushels other grains.	Other Agricultural Prod's, lbs.	An'l Prod's not specified, lbs.	Flour, barrels.
May........	..	...	....	...	......	1520	....	758	355	198	6230	3810	...
June........	..	...	45	...	......	......	....	2185	.....	.....	9230	2850	5
July	..	...	45	...	......	350	....	1290	675	.....	13870	2220	...
August	..	32	135	...	......	......	....	1660	596	3729	2870	30	...
September ..	..	...	90	...	......	200	....	6263	.....	1270	1520	700	...
October	..	...	....	...	......	2140	....	3902	1715	903	4294	2797	...
November ..	..	...	....	...	......	330	....	......	.....	610	......	340	...
December ..	..	...	242	...	2100	630	....	2724	1101	645	90	670	3
1869.													
January	..	...	....	...	8580	420	....	2060	405	667	......	490	2
February ...	14	32	....	...	3690	......	....	1925	769	594	560	1370	...
March	14	...	....	...	520	880	....	1687	2655	632	1850	631	2
April.......	2	...	....	...	......	......	....	670	.....	.....	4380	1630	...
Total.	30	64	557	...	14890	6470	....	25124	8271	9248	44894	17538	12

EXHIBIT C—Continued.

GRAND MOUND STATION.

MONTHS. 1868.	No. of Horses.	No. of Cattle.	No. of Hogs.	No. of Sheep.	Pounds dressed Hogs.	Pounds of Lard and Pork.	Pounds Wool.	Bushels Wheat	Bushels Corn.	Bushels other Grains.	Other Agricultural Products lbs.	An'l Prod's not specified, lbs.	Flour, Barrels.
May						610		2040		617	610	930	
June						200		1373	339	1210	1850	610	
July						820		642			2820	1250	15
August								1005	730		260		
September						300		3375	512	1056	500		
October						280		1754	1033	2299	2260		
November						80		1361		1100		160	
December						680		2038	364	622	4130		
1869.													
January			48			330		3796		1609		720	
February					1380			1789	734	1130	290		
March					26780	990		1103	796	605			
April	4	16				570			2		3220	210	
Total	4	16	48		28160	4860		38278	4510	10248	15940	3880	15

DE WITT STATION.

1868.	No. of Horses.	No. of Cattle.	No. of Hogs.	No. of Sheep.	Pounds dressed Hogs.	Pounds of Lard and Pork.	Pounds Wool.	Bushels Wheat	Bushels Corn.	Bushels other Grains.	Other Agricultural Products lbs.	An'l Prod's not specified, lbs.	Flour, Barrels.
May	6	2	405			7640		12252	9493	7299	2900	2590	90
June	1	96	405			33071	18950	15615	18382	9504	4940	2580	8
July	1	48	315				14680	3370	11196	2483	24030	6100	7
August		48	585			27920	1460	18002	4096	2771	920	2330	
September	1	64	675				1440	38312	3652	7000	910	42220	
October			495		300		720	30005	1487	13491	40440	5650	1
November	2	3	1215		850	7980	3670	9459	1382	2954	4500	2900	
December	2	16	2835		48730	5870		25543	715	7187	730	8730	1
1869.													
January		64	660		34840			30706	650	5154		8110	2
February	3	240	450		12290	200		18920		1285	11780	6840	1
March	18	256	342	110	13260	6270		19254	2716	5775	5650	3400	3
April	2	192	405			660		9616	4714	1039	17150	3000	4
Total	36	1029	8787	110	110270	89611	40920	231054	58483	65942	113950	94450	117

MALONE STATION.

1868.	No. of Horses.	No. of Cattle.	No. of Hogs.	No. of Sheep.	Pounds dressed Hogs.	Pounds of Lard and Pork.	Pounds Wool.	Bushels Wheat	Bushels Corn.	Bushels other Grains.	Other Agricultural Products lbs.	An'l Prod's not specified, lbs.	Flour, Barrels.
May						650		1309	365	650	200		
June								3627	1455	1866	2500		
July								3089	1346	1370			
August								743	1744	2324			
September								1963					
October								651	356	578	100		
November								433		1175			
December								900		611			
1869.													
January								960	355		1260		
February								1259	716	567			
March								642	1437				
April						50					950		
Total						700		15576	7774	9141	5010		

EXHIBIT C—Continued.

LOW MOOR STATION.

MONTHS. 1868.	No. of Horses.	No. of Cattle.	No. of Hogs.	No. of Sheep.	Pounds dressed Hogs.	Pounds of Lard and Pork.	Pounds Wool.	Bushels Wheat.	Bushels Corn.	Bushels other Grains.	Other Agricultural Products lbs.	An'l Prod's not specified, lbs.	Flour, Barrels.
May	.	...	45	...	.....	450	.....	999	.....	.....	5220	.....	....
June	..	...	135	...	.....	.....	.....	3811	2157	2779	1360	....	5
July	..	...	90	...	.....	630	1800	1710	1230	1133	420	.....	....
August	..	...	180	...	.....	.....	1020	2284	2706	1586	......	.....	....
September .	..	...	191	...	.....	.....	690	3019	6324	1747	......	.....	....
October ...	..	...	90	...	.....	340	1100	1885	1071	....	3480	....	....
November .	..	...	225	...	1310	300	.....	635	642	....	380	.....	....
December .	..	...	270	...	3360	560	.....	1069	1367	571	2760	.....	....
1869.													
January ...	..	...	450	...	7280	....	.....	998	1036	763	....	.....	...
February ..	..	..	....	...	.....	.....	.....	354	.....	.....	......	.....	....
March	..	96	45	...	....	.....	.....	1728	.....	1860	.....	.....	....
April......	..	...	45	...	.....	....	.....	.....	97	.....	1150	....	....
Total....	..	96	1766	...	11950	2280	4610	18492	16630	10439	14770	.....	5
1868.							***CAMANCHE STATION.***						
May	..	...	....	...	.....	600	.....	2757	1513	....	......	.....	....
June	..	...	....	...	.....	.....	.....	2437	3440	3789	700	.....	....
July	..	..	....	...	.....	.....	.....	2054	660	....	50	....	....
August....	..	...	....	...	.....	.....	.....	958	4136	1204	150	....	2
September .	..	...	....	...	....	....	.....	4011	2534	1191	......	.....	....
October ...	..	...	....	...	.....	800	.....	1302	321	....	......	.....	....
November .	..	...	45	...	....	280	.....	321	.....	1312	......	.....	....
December .	..	.	90	...	1590	240	.....	346	.....	578	......	.....	10
1869.													
January ...	..	..	....	...	2860	1490	.....	325	.....	.....	540	.....	....
February ..	..	.	45	...	.....	.....	.....	885	938	....	......	....	12
March.....	..	16	....	...	.....	.....	.....	.....	2295	....	......	....	11
April......	..	37	....	...	....	.....	.....	.....	666	....	1660	....	....
Total	..	53	180	...	4450	3410	.....	15396	16503	8074	3100	.....	35
1868.							***CLINTON STATION.***						
May.......	25	176	281	...	....	2370	.....	3655	1418	4457	8320	6500	627
June......	3	32	315	...	.....	2770	....	1338	3641	1967	1863	6460	160
July......	..	...	180	.	.....	500	550	.....	3187	27	9458	13050	144
August . ..	3	48	270	110	.....	15386	1080	658	3264	1775	6574	5140	196
September .	2	32	135	..	.....	.....	.....	5780	716	2394	5550	5970	488
October. ..	57	47	234	39	.....	....	900	9100	.....	3958	22690	7770	750
November .	14	...	135	...	.....	6867	.....	81	361	635	101364	11110	151
December .	31	16	270	...	26170	5365	.....	6802	4	12845	13540	6300	888
1869.													
January ...	8	57	90	...	.....	.....	.....	5189	.....	2	......	11510	1018
February ..	99	370	180	110	54420	2150	.....	2384	.....	871	3830	11760	334
March	180	..	90	...	5720	2490	....	7269	13	9511	23170	9810	2832
April......	33	218	135	...	.....	27970	.....	1851	35	981	11920	4410	221
Total	455	996	2315	259	86310	65868	2530	44107	12639	39423	208279	99790	7809

EXHIBIT D.

CHICAGO, ROCK ISLAND AND PACIFIC RAILROAD.

Statement of Agricultural Products carried Eastward from the several Stations on the Chicago, Rock Island and Pacific Railroad, for each of the twelve months, ending April 30, 1869.

DE SOTO STATION.

MONTHS.	No. of Horses.	No. of Cattle.	No of Hogs.	No. of Sheep.	Pounds dressed Hogs.	Pounds of Lard and Pork.	Pounds Wool.	Pounds Wheat.	Pounds Corn.	Pounds other Grains.	Pounds other Ag'l Prod'ts.	Flour Barrels.	An'l Prod'ts n't specified, lbs.
1868.													
Novemb'r	..	...	770	...	...	...	...	...	...	...	...	...	...
December	..	...	630	460	...	...	...	...	...	...	...	...	1500
1869.													
January..	..	...	255	...	600	...	...	...	...	...	...	...	1200
February.	..	...	150	...	200	...	...	...	...	...	...	...	700
March ...	..	32	100	...	...	...	...	...	...	...	...	...	...
April	1	256	800	100	...	...	...	...	...	...	...	...	...
Total ..	1	288	2405	560	800	...	...	...	...	...	...	...	3400

DES MOINES STATION.

MONTHS.	No. of Horses.	No. of Cattle.	No of Hogs.	No. of Sheep.	Pounds dressed Hogs.	Pounds of Lard and Pork.	Pounds Wool.	Pounds Wheat.	Pounds Corn.	Pounds other Grains.	Pounds other Ag'l Prod'ts.	Flour Barrels.	An'l Prod'ts n't specified, lbs.
1868.													
May.....	1	765	2915	200	...	...	215	20200	60000	11000	21000	...	14000
June	2	144	2035	200	...	1150	19375	242160	24080	...	27700	...	10400
July.....	2	216	1715	...	...	...	116826	343270	363000	43000	...	...	2425
August...	..	96	385	90	...	...	67125	1341340	1160000	120460	...	...	5900
Septemb'r	..	304	880	380	...	338700	30546	641670	241700	86100	1600	201	2800
October ..	3	256	3005	385	...	150800	10410	624190	48200	20900	92200	100	18200
Novemb'r	..	180	2850	...	...	179500	2876	20060	...	21300	800	...	7800
December	..	280	2310	200	81875	450200	2128	...	...	38000	5400	...	30100
1869.													
January..	..	165	800	...	134100	2900	1050	22100	221000	...	55400	...	36300
February.	..	1168	350	100	129250	157200	...	...	420500	...	...	100	17000
March....	1	352	600	700	27500	1105000	1036	18550	141200	7800	500	100	29500
April	1	292	1350	600	...	780600	...	...	...	...	...	...	26400
Total	10	4218	19195	2855	372725	3166050	251587	3273540	2679680	348560	197600	501	200825

ALTOONA STATION.

MONTHS.	No. of Horses.	No. of Cattle.	No of Hogs.	No. of Sheep.	Pounds dressed Hogs.	Pounds of Lard and Pork.	Pounds Wool.	Pounds Wheat.	Pounds Corn.	Pounds other Grains.	Pounds other Ag'l Prod'ts.	Flour Barrels.	An'l Prod'ts n't specified, lbs.
1868.													
Septemb'r	..	...	...	...	...	...	...	63400	...	...	...	...	...
October ..	..	...	...	...	...	...	...	18640	...	12800	...	...	...
Novemb'r	..	...	...	...	...	...	...	...	...	...	...	...	...
December	..	...	...	...	...	...	...	...	...	...	...	...	...
1869.													
January..	..	...	...	...	...	...	...	...	...	...	...	...	...
February	..	16	...	...	...	...	...	...	...	...	...	...	...
March ...	..	...	...	...	...	...	...	...	...	...	...	...	...
April	..	128	300	...	...	...	...	...	...	...	...	...	...
Total...	..	144	300	...	...	...	...	82040	...	12800	...	...	...

EXHIBIT D—Continued.

MITCHELLVILLE STATION.

MONTHS. 1868.	No. of Horses.	No. of Cattle.	No. of Hogs.	No. of Sheep.	Pounds dressed Hogs.	Pounds of Lard and Pork.	Pounds Wool.	Pounds Wheat.	Pounds Corn.	Pounds other Grains.	Pounds other Ag'l Prod'ts.	Flour, Barrels.	An'l Prod'ts n't specified, lbs.
May	..	177	960	...	...	...	...	20000	120000	...	...	...	...
June	..	204	320	96	...	...	...	...	...	...	...	...	1475
July	..	240	56	280	...	...	...	...	...	...	...	...	...
August	..	75	...	100	...	...	...	401190	20000	20300	...	...	...
Sept'mb'r	..	...	...	...	...	...	...	206090	...	42700	300	...	...
October	..	...	557	115	...	...	...	80190	...	21300	800	...	...
Novemb'r	..	18	674	163	...	...	...	...	...	...	...	...	1150
December	..	...	...	...	1325	...	...	...	...	...	1450	...	2200
1869.													
January	..	...	122	...	1615	...	...	...	...	...	...	...	1460
February	.	16	119	...	...	...	...	...	...	21800	...	...	505
March	..	48	...	182	...	...	...	...	...	1500	...	...	750
April	..	153	297	...	...	...	...	...	...	...	10700	...	1450
Total	..	931	3105	936	2940	...	...	707470	140000	107600	13250	...	8990

COLFAX STATION.

1868.	No. of Horses.	No. of Cattle.	No. of Hogs.	No. of Sheep.	Pounds dressed Hogs.	Pounds of Lard and Pork.	Pounds Wool.	Pounds Wheat.	Pounds Corn.	Pounds other Grains.	Pounds other Ag'l Prod'ts.	Flour, Barrels.	An'l Prod'ts n't specified, lbs.
May	..	...	400	...	...	...	...	41140	...	...	...	1	100
June	..	...	206	...	...	...	...	40060	260120	20210	...	...	100
July	..	...	60	...	...	...	...	40110	40240	...	...	...	...
August	..	...	52	...	...	...	...	981120	21160	60060	...	...	...
Sept'mb'r	..	...	260	...	...	...	...	562040	82360	18960	...	...	300
October	..	...	300	...	...	...	...	326410	143060	...	800	...	340
Novemb'r	..	...	880	...	...	...	...	227960	41090	...	...	...	230
December	..	...	550	...	1600	...	...	61060	80150	20120	...	...	1270
1869.													
January	..	...	18	500	...	...	...	80090	40160	...	...	...	1100
February	..	...	120	100	...	250	...	122070	...	20090	...	...	1000
March	..	32	110	480	...	...	...	106030	90240	39640	...	...	215
April	..	160	...	...	...	...	...	104210	32260	8000	...	...	250
Total	...	192	2956	1080	1600	250	...	2692300	830840	187080	800	1	4905

NEWTON STATION.

1868.	No. of Horses.	No. of Cattle.	No. of Hogs.	No. of Sheep.	Pounds dressed Hogs.	Pounds of Lard and Pork.	Pounds Wool.	Pounds Wheat.	Pounds Corn.	Pounds other Grains.	Pounds other Ag'l Prod'ts.	Flour, Barrels.	An'l Prod'ts n't specified, lbs.
May	..	...	250	...	...	...	7208	262090	420120	...	...	...	2800
June	..	98	540	...	...	1225	...	261090	440240	...	...	...	600
July	..	16	300	...	...	...	...	78080	281360	2000	...	...	1900
August	..	32	400	...	...	...	2110	1803130	...	...	...	½	6500
Sept'mb'r	..	16	400	...	...	...	4650	1610520	...	20000	...	...	3800
October	..	16	450	200	...	...	920	1401170	60120	...	25000	½	7500
Novemb'r	2	...	210	100	...	...	...	302270	...	10010	2630	...	6730
December	..	...	300	...	6200	...	...	420030	...	20720	880	½	8100
1869.													
January	..	32	150	400	3750	...	...	522540	...	20600	...	102	8500
February	..	32	60	...	1620	...	...	280450	16000	20400	800	½	6550
March	..	112	110	...	...	...	...	525060	60200	...	...	...	6400
April	..	176	160	90	...	...	...	281070	...	20120	230	...	10100
Total	2	530	3330	790	11570	1225	14888	7747470	1278040	111850	48540	104	69480

EXHIBIT D—Continued.

KELLOGG STATION.

MONTHS. 1868.	No. of Horses.	No. of Cattle.	No. of Hogs.	No. of Sheep.	Pounds dressed Hogs.	Pounds of Lard and Pork.	Pounds Wool.	Pounds Wheat.	Pounds Corn.	Pounds other Grains.	Pounds other Ag'l Prod's.	Flour, barrels.	An'l Prod's not specified, lbs.
May		336	350					21200	81210				
June		240	100					10000	80310		600		
July		64	205					823410	78690				
August			155							41100			
Sept'mb'r			50					561360	28900		150		
October			104					411240		21120	880		
Novemb'r			100					143120			150		1200
December		16	250					222190			110		600
1869.													
January			53	200	250			143160					150
February		176						40190					1000
March		96	100					161210		20310			1600
April		192	51					40160					1250
Total		1120	1518	200	250			2577240	269110	82530	1890		5800

GRINNELL STATION.

1868.	No. of Horses.	No. of Cattle.	No. of Hogs.	No. of Sheep.	Pounds dressed Hogs.	Pounds of Lard and Pork.	Pounds Wool.	Pounds Wheat.	Pounds Corn.	Pounds other Grains.	Pounds other Ag'l Prod's.	Flour, barrels.	An'l Prod's not specified, lbs.
May		16	200					40150	21000	20390			225
June		84	50					62290	100240		1300		500
July		80					4500	6000	57600				2700
August		64					560	1243120	43150		650		2500
Septemb'r		64						1482260	224410	80940	400		4860
October		128	100				2200	1012390	20960	41160			
Novemb'r		272					6660	663190		18980	530		6200
December		80						286400			1000		3900
1869.													
January		32			1350			223210		20110			3100
February		84	150					180500	40690	20070			2200
March		128	50	100				120500					3800
April			50	100				143170	21070				3100
Total		1032	600	200	1350		13920	5463180	529120	191650	3880		33085

MALCOM STATION.

1868.	No. of Horses.	No. of Cattle.	No. of Hogs.	No. of Sheep.	Pounds dressed Hogs.	Pounds of Lard and Pork.	Pounds Wool.	Pounds Wheat.	Pounds Corn.	Pounds other Grains.	Pounds other Ag'l Prod's.	Flour, barrels.	An'l Prod's not specified, lbs.
May			54					60690	410740				2450
June		128	150	100				52700	385640				3200
July							700		180220				2500
August			150					565160					3400
Sept'mb'r			350					1143090	107940	41400	4200		7050
October		48	555					887640			1600		2500
Novemb'r			1220					521460					4550
December		32	1250	200	9100		1400	626750					9100
1869.													
January		18	254		5150			621570		20640			2000
February					3300			228740	260490				3100
March		56	175		1650			367470	126970	40160			3000
April		8	230					230780					7800
Total		290	4388	300	19200		2100	5306050	1472000	102200	5800		50650

EXHIBIT D—CONTINUED.

1868. BROOKLYN STATION.

MONTHS. 1868.	No. of Horses.	No. of Cattle.	No. of Hogs.	No. of Sheep.	Pounds dressed Hogs.	Pounds of Lard and Pork.	Pounds Wool.	Pounds Wheat.	Pounds Corn.	Pounds other Grains.	Pounds other Agri'l Prod's	Flour, Barrels.	An'l Prod's not specified, lbs.
May	..	...	250	...	......	......	.....	20000	42100	.....	.....	...	1120
June	..	96	150	...	......	......	.....	41200	61300	.....	.....	...	2900
July	..	...	...	...	......	......	360	642100	......	.....	.....	...	820
August	..	...	150	...	......	......	.....	1020100	......	.....	.....	...	7600
Sept'mb'r	..	...	...	...	......	......	.....	1410000	......	.....	300	...	800
October	..	...	105	...	......	......	.....	186000	......	20800	.....	...	2900
Novemb'r	..	...	210	...	......	......	.....	45800	......	27000	150	...	4300
December	..	...	155	...	7660	......	....	42000	......	.....	510	...	4600
1869.													
January	..	16	53	...	9500	......	.....	126250	......	.....	.....	...	3730
February	..	...	...	...	5560	......	.....	49600	40900	26100	220	...	1090
March	..	32	...	...	1000	......	.....	40310	205000	.....	.....	...	800
April	..	16	...	...	......	......	.....	......	......	.....	.....	...	5500
Total	..	160	1073	.....	23720	....	360	3623360	349300	73900	880	.....	36070

1868. VICTOR STATION.

MONTHS.	No. of Horses.	No. of Cattle.	No. of Hogs.	No. of Sheep.	Pounds dressed Hogs.	Pounds of Lard and Pork.	Pounds Wool.	Pounds Wheat.	Pounds Corn.	Pounds other Grains.	Pounds other Agri'l Prod's	Flour, Barrels.	An'l Prod's not specified, lbs.
May	..	64	...	...	......	......	125	122100	80650	.....	.....	...	500
June	..	...	200	...	..	......	.....	40900	43000	.....	.....	...	2615
July	..	144	150	...	......	......	.....	41000	21420	6900	.....	...	500
August	..	18	200	...	......	......	.....	460710	......	45150	.....	...	2430
Sept'mb'r	..	16	50	...	......	......	.....	1440000	......	.....	.....	...	2100
October	..	...	450	...	......	......	.....	1443000	......	20700	.....	...	1200
Nov'm'b'r	..	...	400	...	......	......	.....	63500	......	.....	300	...	1900
December	..	18	400	...	500	......	.....	481000	......	.....	200	...	7400
1869.													
January	..	36	250	...	6850	......	.....	424300	......	.....	.....	...	2625
February	..	108	156	...	1700	......	.....	141640	......	.....	.....	...	1250
March	..	...	...	...	2900	285	.....	260900	20900	.....	.....	...	1400
April	..	...	200	310	......	......	.....	283800	......	.....	.....	...	3660
Total	....	404	2456	310	11950	285	125	5201850	165970	72750	500	.....	27520

1869. LADORA STATION.

MONTHS.	No. of Horses.	No. of Cattle.	No. of Hogs.	No. of Sheep.	Pounds dressed Hogs.	Pounds of Lard and Pork.	Pounds Wool.	Pounds Wheat.	Pounds Corn.	Pounds other Grains.	Pounds other Agri'l Prod's	Flour, Barrels.	An'l Prod's not specified, lbs.
May	..	...	....	...	......	......	.....	......	......	.....	.....	...	200
June	..	...	....	...	......	......	.....	21070	......	2040	.....	...	200
July	..	...	....	...	......	......	.....	......	21100	.....	.....	...	175
August	..	...	....	...	......	......	.....	63100	10350	.....	.....	...	.....
Sept'mb'r	..	...	....	...	......	......	.....	260300	......	.....	.....	...	100
October	..	...	....	...	......	......	.....	321040	......	.....	.....	...	.....
Nov'mb'r	..	...	....	...	......	......	.....	20900	......	.....	.....	...	3868
December	..	...	....	.	8200	......	.....	62100	21200	.....	.....	...	1950
1868.													
January	..	...	....	...	900	......	.....	144090	......	.....	.....	...	2850
February	..	...	....	...	......	......	.....	......	......	.....	.....	...	1180
March	..	...	....	...	540	......	.....	......	......	.....	.....	...	2050
April	..	...	....	...	......	......	.....	20200	......	.....	.....	...	3070
Total	..	...	....	...	9640	......	.....	912800	51650	2040	.....	...	13543

EXHIBIT D—Continued.

MARENGO STATION.

MONTHS. 1868.	No. of Horses.	No. of Cattle.	No. of Hogs.	No. of Sheep.	Pounds dressed Hogs.	Pounds of Lard and Pork,	Pounds Wool.	Pounds Wheat	Pounds Corn.	Pounds other Grains.	Pounds other Ag'l Prod'ts.	Flour, Barrels.	An'l Prod's not specified, lbs.
May	..	16	154	...	...	...	...	163200	41300	...	500	...	2430
June	..	32	206	...	...	...	...	161310	...	...	...	...	175
July	..	16	155	...	...	...	18500	85100	12600	8100	...	...	3250
August	..	48	53	...	...	...	2200	360730	...	23000	...	...	6960
Sept'mb'r	..	...	210	200	...	...	...	904400	...	...	2578	...	4000
October	..	16	152	...	...	...	...	960080	...	34800	...	...	600
Novemb'r	..	...	860	100	...	...	...	263600	...	20060	340	...	8700
December	..	...	858	200	28100	...	...	221000	...	56200	600	1	3450
1869.													
January	..	...	309	...	40430	...	2800	487050	...	43060	...	...	3800
February	..	...	...	...	19036	...	...	309000	...	20900	2400	...	...
March	..	112	...	...	14700	...	...	341500	...	41080	...	...	4825
April	..	...	153	...	...	...	...	282130	...	80410	...	...	5864
Total	....	240	3110	500	102266	...	23500	4539100	53900	327610	6418	1	44054

HOMESTEAD STATION.

1868.	No. of Horses.	No. of Cattle.	No. of Hogs.	No. of Sheep.	Pounds dressed Hogs.	Pounds of Lard and Pork,	Pounds Wool.	Pounds Wheat	Pounds Corn.	Pounds other Grains.	Pounds other Ag'l Prod'ts.	Flour, Barrels.	An'l Prod's not specified, lbs.
May	..	32	55	...	...	...	...	21350	...	...	...	...	2920
June	..	...	53	...	...	...	...	72800	...	...	...	...	2420
July	..	...	56	...	...	...	...	41080	...	...	...	...	860
August	..	32	...	...	...	...	...	141000	...	...	...	...	1305
Sept'mb'r	..	...	52	...	...	...	...	980360	...	...	...	...	2895
October	..	...	158	...	...	...	...	516000	...	...	...	...	9200
Novemb'r	..	16	206	...	...	...	...	204500	...	21000	...	...	2348
December	..	...	400	...	...	...	...	460900	...	20600	...	...	840
1869.													
January	..	32	50	...	10140	...	...	306100	...	...	1500	...	2710
February	..	16	...	100	1640	3930	300	264700	...	19350	4350	...	2905
March	..	36	...	...	2730	...	450	143090	...	...	...	...	3560
April	..	64	...	...	...	...	...	224630	...	...	375	...	8200
Total	...	228	1030	100	14510	.3930	750	3376510	...	60950	6225	...	40163

OXFORD STATION.

1868.	No. of Horses.	No. of Cattle.	No. of Hogs.	No. of Sheep.	Pounds dressed Hogs.	Pounds of Lard and Pork,	Pounds Wool.	Pounds Wheat	Pounds Corn.	Pounds other Grains.	Pounds other Ag'l Prod'ts.	Flour, Barrels.	An'l Prod's not specified, lbs.
October	..	...	...	...	...	...	...	...	...	...	...	...	...
Novemb'r	..	...	...	...	...	...	...	80000	...	...	...	...	...
December	..	...	...	...	12170	...	...	300850	...	...	...	...	...
1869.													
January	..	...	...	...	...	...	...	261300	...	40250	...	...	...
February	..	...	...	...	...	...	...	62100	41600	23680	...	...	...
March	..	...	...	...	5200	...	...	43060	20850	...	...	...	...
April	..	...	...	...	...	...	...	60780	...	...	...	...	...
Total	....	...	...	...	17370	...	...	808090	62450	63930	...	...	...

EXHIBIT D.—Continued.

CLEAR CREEK STATION.

MONTHS. 1868	No. of Horses.	No. of Cattle.	No. of Hogs.	No. of Sheep.	Pounds dress'd Hogs.	Pounds of Lard and Pork.	Pounds Wool.	Pounds Wheat	Pounds Corn.	Pounds other Grains.	Pounds other Agri'l Prod's	Flour, Barrels.	Animal Prod's n't specified, lbs
August..	..	...	....	...	......	......	.....	196220	......	17450	....	...	.....
October..	..	...	....	...	......	......	.....	106860	......	......	....	...	.....
December	..	...	....	...	......	......	.....	80000	......	......	....	...	.....
1869.													
February.	..	...	....	...	......	......	.....	40000	......	......	....	...	.....
March....	..	...	....	...	......	......	.....	60000	......	......	....	...	.....
Total...	..	...	....	...	......	......	.....	483080	......	17450	....	...	.....

1868. *IOWA CITY STATION.*

MONTHS.	No. of Horses.	No. of Cattle.	No. of Hogs.	No. of Sheep.	Pounds dress'd Hogs.	Pounds of Lard and Pork.	Pounds Wool.	Pounds Wheat	Pounds Corn.	Pounds other Grains.	Pounds other Agri'l Prod's	Flour, Barrels.	Animal Prod's n't specified, lbs
May......	1	...	600	...	......	......	.....	520000	255110	179670	....	100	44165
June.....	..	176	....	...	......	......	820	465740	200470	221820	....	250	44310
July.....	..	112	200	...	......	4810	1650	79740	154020	144260	....	200	27220
August...	..	80	150	...	......	14440	4426	1012650	188350	201480	....	400	.....
Septemb'r	..	96	600	100	......	6790	17208	1759340	189943	358950	2350	800	40320
October..	..	32	850	...	......	7126	.....	1811228	20880	445130	....	1000	36270
Novemb'r	..	...	2050	...	1413	1530	3785	203970	14600	259670	....	400	28240
December	..	...	5400	...	416611	3470	.....	620290	257630	......	....	650	21630
1869.													
January,.	1	26	4200	...	326210	6775	.....	180280	93350	360961	....	500	23190
February.	1	16	1200	...	123037	6500	420	420000	......	319300	....	200	33060
March ...	..	320	650	...	46290	3600	750	286290	42750	110670	....	400	13000
April....	..	448	510	...	3500	5610	.....	1160230	40000	210650	....	700	106270
Total...	3	1316	16410	100	917061	60651	29059	8519758	1457103	2812561	2350	5600	417675

1868. *DOWNEY STATION.*

MONTHS.	No. of Horses.	No. of Cattle.	No. of Hogs.	No. of Sheep.	Pounds dress'd Hogs.	Pounds of Lard and Pork.	Pounds Wool.	Pounds Wheat	Pounds Corn.	Pounds other Grains.	Pounds other Agri'l Prod's	Flour, Barrels.	Animal Prod's n't specified, lbs
May......	..	160	500	100	......	......	.....	......	185470	9680	....	...	2410
June.....	2	32	150	...	......	......	.....	24370	132960	......	....	...	1790
July.....	..	...	150	...	......	......	.....	139100	32850	......	....	...	2008
August...	..	...	109	...	......	......	.....	400660	38500	105990	....	...	925
Septemb'r	..	...	155	...	......	......	.....	237050	66000	98080	....	...	1790
October	..	...	250	...	......	......	3167	9530	40600	186890	....	...	900
Novemb'r	..	...	453	...	......	......	.....	55670	16000	63620	....	...	600
December	..	...	550	...	250	......	.....	......	138510	32980	....	...	.....
1869.													
January..	..	112	....	100	300	......	.....	94290	156000	67220	....	...	.....
February.	..	32	100	100	......	......	.....	98120	82000	38000	....	...	.....
March ...	..	112	250	...	......	......	.....	40000	83420	12700	....	...	400
April....	..	32	150	98	......	......	.....	19039	......	......	....	...	2550
Total....	2	480	2817	398	550	......	3167	1117829	972310	615160	....	...	13373

EXHIBIT B—Continued.

WEST LIBERTY STATION.

MONTHS. 1868.	No. of Horses.	No. of Cattle.	No. of Hogs.	No. of Sheep.	Pounds dressed Hogs.	Pounds of Lard and Pork.	Pounds Wool.	Pounds Wheat.	Pounds Corn.	Pounds Other Grains.	Pounds other Ag'l Prod'ts.	Flour, Barrels.	An'l Prod'ts n't specified, lbs.
May	..	16	250	...	......	......	.....	18600	196100	61800	....	...	7545
June	..	64	250	...	......	......	.....	91450	846090	123550	....	...	9375
July	..	...	50	...	......	285	.....	20270	403060	22300	....	100	3285
August	..	...	100	...	......	1130	1830	279550	4230	188680	....	...	4550
Septemb'r	..	...	50	...	......	725	8779	424660	211320	472120	....	...	1970
October	..	...	150	...	......	300	2275	423060	84612	428990	....	100	1920
Novemb'r	..	...	850	...	......	525	.....	17000	54970	119510	....	...	8260
December	..	16	1200	...	24295	280	.....	......	211530	80530	....	...	.....
1869.													
January	..	148	450	...	1640	......	.....	181680	96240	55520	....	100	.....
February	..	108	350	300	......	......	.....	20250	86220	100330	....	100	2565
March	..	432	250	...	......	......	.....	40000	323295	21540	....	...	8300
April	..	112	100	300	......	......	.....	......	21550	......	....	100	19515
Total	..	896	4050	600	25935	8245	12884	1516520	2577287	1074870	......	500	67285

1868. *ATALISSA STATION.*

MONTHS. 1868.	No. of Horses.	No. of Cattle.	No. of Hogs.	No. of Sheep.	Pounds dressed Hogs.	Pounds of Lard and Pork.	Pounds Wool.	Pounds Wheat.	Pounds Corn.	Pounds Other Grains.	Pounds other Ag'l Prod'ts.	Flour, Barrels.	An'l Prod'ts n't specified, lbs.
May	..	...	100	...	......	......	.....	27500	238860	42050	....	...	1661
June	..	...	250	...	......	......	.....	37350	100850	146880	....	...	1533
July	..	...	200	...	......	......	.....	......	236780	......	....	...	1422
August	..	...	150	...	......	......	1141	58370	438560	98816	....	...	1550
Septemb'r	..	...	50	...	......	......	4335	145100	130120	131098	....	...	2200
October	..	...	....	...	......	......	4312	19380	477990	154380	....	...	400
Novemb'r	..	...	150	...	......	......	.....	......	......	41995	....	...	.....
December	..	...	250	...	......	......	.....	......	......	......	....	...	.....
1869.													
January	..	16	600	...	2616	......	.....	......	......	......	....	...	....
February	..	48	150	...	......	......	.....	......	......	......	....	...	200
March	..	16	50	200	......	......	.....	......	......	6200	....	...	765
April	..	48	100	600	......	......	.....	......	......	......	....	...	600
Total	..	128	2050	800	2616	....	9788	297700	1623160	621419	....	......	10331

1868. *MOSCOW STATION.*

MONTHS. 1868.	No. of Horses.	No. of Cattle.	No. of Hogs.	No. of Sheep.	Pounds dressed Hogs.	Pounds of Lard and Pork.	Pounds Wool.	Pounds Wheat.	Pounds Corn.	Pounds Other Grains.	Pounds other Ag'l Prod'ts.	Flour, Barrels.	An'l Prod'ts n't specified, lbs.
May	..	...	....	...	......	......	.....	......	......	21300	....	...	.....
July	..	...	....	...	......	......	.....	......	18450	......	....	...	.....
August	..	...	....	...	......	......	.....	......	56250	......	....	...	.....
Septemb'r	..	...	....	...	......	......	.....	20450	49730	111950	....	...	.....
October	..	...	....	...	......	......	.....	......	......	18850	....	...	.....
1869.													
February	..	...	50	...	......	......	.....	......	......	......	....	...	.....
March	..	32	....	...	......	......	.....	......	......	20450	....	...	.....
April	..	80	50	...	......	......	.....	......	......	......	....	...	.....
Total	..	112	100	...	......	......	.....	20450	124430	172550	....	...	.....

EXHIBIT D—Continued.

WASHINGTON STATION.

MONTHS 1868.	No. of Horses.	No. of Cattle.	No. of Hogs.	No. of Sheep.	Pounds dressed Hogs.	Pounds of Lard and Pork.	Pounds Wool.	Pounds Wheat	Pounds Corn.	Pounds other Grain.	Pounds other Agri'l Prod's	Flour, barrels.	An'l Prod'ts n't specified, lbs.
May.	32	336	1700	300	......	......	.....	420000	650790	178650	....	...	23530
June	..	400	900	100	......	3095	5295	500970	247070	397810	....	...	23090
July.	..	176	500	...	......	1740	24340	99800	98520	142770	....	...	13880
August. .	..	64	800	100	......	......	2800	999420	325230	578350	....	...	16130
Septemb'r	16	352	400	...	......	2880	33790	1232500	100555	344200	....	...	14270
October .	17	240	1950	100	......	7210	2590	2557200	38980	1174360	....	...	17250
Nov'mb'r.	..	80	2750	...	......	22810	260	520750	75490	190380	....	...	11560
December	..	112	3900	...	57376	4305	140	1160000	379910	40000	....	78	30670
1869.													
January..	..	144	4000	...	114370	......	200	727200	199020	575850	....	100	7650
February.	..	320	1250	400	67930	5120	.....	20000	164150	85250	1300	...	10500
March. ..	..	336	800	...	11400	1520	.....	1080190	139630	143250	....	100	12300
April. ...	2	656	900	500	......	......	.....	624150	......	57780	....	100	52750
Total... ...	67	3216	19850	1500	251076	48680	69415	9942180	2419345	3608620	1300	378	233580

AINSWORTH STATION.

1868.	No. of Horses.	No. of Cattle.	No. of Hogs.	No. of Sheep.	Pounds dressed Hogs.	Pounds of Lard and Pork.	Pounds Wool.	Pounds Wheat	Pounds Corn.	Pounds other Grain.	Pounds other Agri'l Prod's	Flour, barrels.	An'l Prod'ts n't specified, lbs.
May. ...	..	...	250	...	......	......	.....	......	......	45970	....	...	2650
June. ...	..	...	310	...	......	......	.....	61100	87500	88900	....	...	4000
July	..	...	53	...	......	......	.....	22400	33320	......	....	...	4600
August...	..	...	50	...	......	......	.....	301700	......	57920	....	...	4757
Septemb'r	..	32	104	...	......	......	.....	389240	191910	......	....	...	6000
October..	..	16	200	...	......	......	.....	305800	13300	167330	....	...	3986
Novemb'r	..	...	500	...	......	......	.....	73420	62380	49800	....	...	2450
December	..	...	1600	...	2416	......	.....	76150	183520	56190	....	...	1149
1869.													
January .	..	64	510	...	3820	......	.....	115090	316850	19030	....	...	.....
February	..	48	150	...	607	......	.....	100996	174650	40520	....	...	5181
March. ..	..	32	155	...	......	......	.....	207442	229510	18970	....	...	4383
April. ...	..	32	400	...	......	......	.....	56530	20900	18150	....	...	9332
Total... ...	..	224	4282	......	6943	....	... .	1709868	1313840	562780	....	......	48488

CLIFTON STATION.

1868.	No. of Horses.	No. of Cattle.	No. of Hogs.	No. of Sheep.	Pounds dressed Hogs.	Pounds of Lard and Pork.	Pounds Wool.	Pounds Wheat	Pounds Corn.	Pounds other Grain.	Pounds other Agri'l Prod's	Flour, barrels.	An'l Prod'ts n't specified, lbs.
May.	2	32	160	...	......	......	5590	33600	......	19570	....	...	1000
June	..	16	250	...	......	......	.....	130900	184710	50310	....	...	200
July.	..	...	155	...	......	......	16150	......	68100	......	....	...	.....
August ..	..	...	53	...	......	......	450	176250	39300	86050	....	...	1100
Septemb'r	..	...	50	...	......	800	.....	527530	93310	173360	....	...	2200
October..	..	...	250	...	......	9600	100	354840	75220	204400	....	...	800
Novemb'r	..	16	108	200	......	1100	.....	50910	......	39840	....	...	.....
December	..	80	2650	100	6070	800	.....	......	......	20100	....	...	1600
1869.													
January .	..	48	1000	100	12970	......	.....	......	......	......	....	...	.....
February.	..	160	200	400	2970	......	.....	35520	20070	23930	....	100	370
March....	..	128	210	300	320	......	.....	31850	......	18070	....	...	3150
April	1	18	350	100	......	......	.....	......	......	16520	....	100	7860
Total... ...	3	498	5436	1200	22332	12300	22290	1341400	480710	652150	....	200	18280

EXHIBIT D—Continued.

FREDONIA STATION.

MONTHS. 1868.	No. of Horses.	No. of Cattle.	No. of Hogs.	No. of Sheep.	Pounds dressed Hogs.	Pounds of Lard and Pork.	Pounds Wool.	Pounds Wheat.	Pounds Corn.	Pounds other Grains.	Pounds other Agri'l Prod's	Flour, barrels.	An'l Prod's not specified, lbs.
May	128								288100				
June									397930				
July								18500	121160	33270			
August								150470	113550	177090			
Sept'mb'r								94310	62740	105120			
October			100					41080		55200			
Novemb'r			200										
Decemb'r			100										
1869.													
January			50						39480				
February	16		103						34390				
March			55						155750				
April		240	160	100					21230	18270			600
Total	144	240	768	100				304360	1234330	388950			600

ONONWA STATION.

1868.	No. of Horses.	No. of Cattle.	No. of Hogs.	No. of Sheep.	Pounds dressed Hogs.	Pounds of Lard and Pork.	Pounds Wool.	Pounds Wheat.	Pounds Corn.	Pounds other Grains.	Pounds other Agri'l Prod's	Flour, barrels.	An'l Prod's not specified, lbs.
May		16	200						121790				
June		32	100						87640				
July		64	150				1585		98120				
August			50					99150	38270	169340			
Sept'mb'r		128	100					52000	196150	135520			
October		128							20700	35930			
Novemb'r		272	550					39780		16920			
Decemb'r			800							16280			
1869.													
January		64			2620								
February		160	150							39220			
March		64	100		2600								
April		32	100										
Total		960	2300		5220		1585	190930	562670	413210			

MUSCATINE STATION.

1868.	No. of Horses.	No. of Cattle.	No. of Hogs.	No. of Sheep.	Pounds dressed Hogs.	Pounds of Lard and Pork.	Pounds Wool.	Pounds Wheat.	Pounds Corn.	Pounds other Grains.	Pounds other Agri'l Prod's	Flour, barrels.	An'l Prod's not specified, lbs.
May	1	32	150				2730	194950	469250	21650			140
June		32	150				2900	572250	797410	12700			
July		16	50				13640	176660	864820	212590		185	
August			300				7030	964770	615930	316790	100400	395	
Sept'mb'r	1		310			3790	12370	790690	497670	1024390	61200	65	
October			309				1860	1134020	212610	243220			
Novemb'r	1	16	550		6360		1040	60000	68550	28320		2	
Decemb'r	1		700		482220	386640	3370	340410	120820	72030	12480		
1869.													
January			250		284950	144190		870530	256910				3160
February					49920			498980	393470			600	3910
March	4	68	50		22360	3200		440000	207110	200300		600	390
April			50					60000	79120	353598		500	1100
Total	8	164	2869		845810	537820	44940	6103260	4583670	2485588	174080	2347	8700

EXHIBIT D—Continued.

WILTON STATION.

MONTHS. 1868.	No. of Horses.	No. of Cattle.	No. of Hogs.	No. of Sheep.	Pounds dressed Hogs.	Pounds of Lard and Pork.	Pounds Wool.	Pounds Wheat	Pounds Corn.	Pounds Other Grains.	Pounds Other Ag'l Prod'ts.	Flour, barrels.	Animal Prod'ts n't spe'fi'd, lbs
May	..	64	250	...	...	...	...	298273	292450	177816	240	..	1000
June	..	...	...	...	...	...	...	160000	...	...	...	..	...
July	..	...	150	...	...	...	935	...	592310	51120	...	..	800
August	..	...	150	...	...	...	...	590140	310890	248890	...	..	...
Septemb'r	..	...	100	...	...	...	1500	1151340	284270	381350	...	..	200
October	..	...	350	...	...	...	...	1110950	46490	574685	...	..	...
Novemb'r	..	160	1250	...	175	...	...	337180	194520	88120	...	..	...
December	..	32	2300	...	21200	...	...	698300	508870	87850	...	..	...
1869.													
January	..	272	300	...	30880	...	...	516000	78820	23765	...	..	300
February	..	96	100	...	7410	525	...	344526	213240	20400	...	..	1780
March	..	224	100	...	9965	...	...	184900	282230	20250	...	2	1000
April	2	32	200	...	...	...	...	147260	119280	339350	...	..	7300
Total	2	880	5250	...	69630	525	2435	5538869	2923370	1813596	240	2	12380
1868.						***DURANT STATION.***							
May	..	16	150	...	...	...	...	181270	121720	18500	415	..	360
June	..	...	...	...	...	...	...	...	...	...	...	..	...
July	..	16	150	...	...	...	164	...	209770	...	...	..	...
August	..	...	100	...	...	...	...	376630	223910	151960	...	..	...
Septemb'r	..	...	300	...	...	170	...	335980	20850	90700	20000	..	...
October	..	...	200	200	...	...	...	226460	41605	632860	382000	..	...
Novemb'r	..	...	250	...	...	...	...	...	...	...	20000	..	...
December	..	...	500	...	4240	...	...	84170	59100	42700	...	..	...
1869.													
January	..	112	100	...	3505	...	...	17500	68900	100970	...	..	600
February	..	16	...	...	26700	...	...	19600	33400	63500	...	..	...
March	..	48	200	...	1510	...	...	121550	92250	122330	...	..	...
April	..	16	100	...	140	...	...	...,...	47285	...	...	..	2120
Total	..	224	2050	200	36095	170	164	1363160	918790	1393520	422415	...	3080
1868.						***FULTON STATION.***							
May	..	32	...	100	...	...	...	...	...	...	...	..	...
June	..	32	...	100	...	...	...	20370	20200	...	...	..	...
July	..	16	100	...	...	...	226	...	148530	...	...	..	...
August	..	...	50	...	...	...	...	...	...	20300	...	..	...
October	..	...	50	...	...	...	...	...	...	...	220000	..	...
Novemb'r	..	...	100	...	...	...	...	...	...	...	...	..	...
1869.													
February	..	...	50	...	...	...	...	...	...	...	...	..	...
Total	..	80	350	200	...	...	226	20370	168730	20300	220000	..	...

EXHIBIT D—Continued.

WALCOTT STATION.

MONTHS. 1868.	No. of Horses.	No of Cattle.	No. of Hogs.	No. of Sheep.	Pounds dressed Hogs.	Pounds of Lard and Pork.	Pounds Wool.	Pounds Wheat.	Pounds Corn.	Pounds of other Grains.	Other Agricultural Prod's lbs.	Flour, Barrels.	Animal Prod'ts n't specified, lbs
May	..	...	55	...	......	.....	.....	20000	140900	......	.....	....	....
June	..	...	52	...	......	.....	356	......	81750	......	.....	....	....
July	..	16	50	...	......	.....	226	......	120100	......	.....	....	....
August ..	..	...	....	...	......	.....	.....	240070	200650	144740	.....	....	....
Septemb'r	..	...	....	...	......	.....	.....	250110	61120	240050	40700	....	....
October..	..	...	....	...	......	.....	.....	141130	41200	141110	40000	....	....
Novemb'r	..	...	....	...	......	.....	.....	162020	62150	188120	20000	....	....
December	..	...	....	...	12475	.....	.....	457670	99293	237105	.....	....	....
1869.													
January .	..	...	....	...	7395	.....	.....	477080	77050	110715	.....	....	....
February.	..	...	....	...	2114	.....	....	198230	34870	136850	.....	....	....
March...	..	...	....	...	......	.....	.....	161275	81190	60270	.....	....	....
April.....	..	...	....	...	......	.....	.....	173211	......	......	.....	....	....
Total	..	16	157	...	21984	.....	582	2280796	1000273	1258060	100700	....	....

1868. *DAVENPORT STATION.*

MONTHS. 1868.	No. of Horses.	No of Cattle.	No. of Hogs.	No. of Sheep.	Pounds dressed Hogs.	Pounds of Lard and Pork.	Pounds Wool.	Pounds Wheat.	Pounds Corn.	Pounds of other Grains.	Other Agricultural Prod's lbs.	Flour, Barrels.	Animal Prod'ts n't specified, lbs
May	..	64	450	...	......	.....	3932	230000	1620100	220260	89400	1121	....
June	..	64	400	...	......	.....	.....	2514220	1310470	275000	160	2307	....
July....	..	16	350	...	......	.....	20586	1240000	1640000	488700	365	2150	....
August ..	2	64	750	...	......	.....	10612	227200	2001300	501700	.....	600	....
Septemb'r	1	...	500	...	......	.....	27590	204000	84600	610000	61400	8761	....
October..	1	50	250	...	......	.....	.....	101060	109000	360700	1110250	9100	....
Novemb'r	17	112	1000	...	......	.....	1350	500800	1302000	2302000	212950	16550	....
December	32	240	2250	...	138370	.....	1300	803000	160100	1301350	321320	12350	....
1869.													
January .	2	48	1000	...	......	.....	3772	2640900	48070	781974	123000	5000	....
February.	1	48	250	100	30000	322126	.....	3010000	61000	1204000	660	3800	....
March....	1	112	200	900	10620	72140	.....	1905070	60500	701000	.....	6600	....
April.....	2	128	350	...	......	.....	.....	429000	44090	403050	.....	3404	....
Total	59	946	7750	1000	178990	394266	69142	13805250	8541230	9149734	1919505	71743	....

EXHIBIT E.

BURLINGTON AND MISSOURI RIVER RAILROAD.

Statement of Agricultural Products carried Eastward from the several Stations on the Burlington and Missouri River Railroad for each of the twelve months ending April 30th, 1869.

AFTON STATION,

MONTHS. 1868.	No. of Horses.	No. of Cattle.	No. of Hogs.	No. of Sheep.	Pounds dressed Hogs.	Pounds of Lard and Pork.	Pounds Wool.	Bushels Wheat.	Bushels Corn.	Bushels other Grains.	Pounds other Ag'l Prod'ts.	An'l Prod's not specified, lbs.
September	..	....	420	....	....	....	1665	....	....	....	......	3800
October	..	666	1320	160	....	....	12300	300	....	....	21300	3280
November	..	90	600	....	....	....	670	....	....	....	300	6115
December	..	18	2160	....	1220	....	......	....	....	....	13350	18040
1869.												
January	..	126	660	....	1500	....	200	....	....	....	5200	5070
February	..	162	540	....	....	....	......	....	....	....	4340	......
March	..	144	......	220	....	....	1270	....	....	....	1180	3400
April	..	342	1200	....	....	....	1540	....	....	....	140	11660
Total	..	1548	6900	380	2720	....	17645	300	....	....	45810	51365

MURRAY STATION.

MONTHS. 1868.	No. of Horses.	No. of Cattle.	No. of Hogs.	No. of Sheep.	Pounds dressed Hogs.	Pounds of Lard and Pork.	Pounds Wool.	Bushels Wheat.	Bushels Corn.	Bushels other Grains.	Pounds other Ag'l Prod'ts.	An'l Prod's not specified, lbs.
July	..	....	......	....	....	....	22320	....	....	....	......	2200
August	..	90	60	80	....	....	1850	....	....	....	......	......
September	..	36	189	320	....	....	......	300	....	....	......	......
October	..	....	369	....	....	....	......	300	....	....	970	1075
November	..	....	360	....	....	....	......	....	....	....	5760	......
December	..	18	780	....	....	....	......	....	....	....	......	......
1869.												
February	..	18	120	....	....	....	......	....	....	....	655	......
March	..	....	120	240	....	....	......	....	....	....	1000	......
April	..	18	480	320	....	....	......	....	....	....	......	330
Total	..	150	2478	960	....	....	24170	600	....	....	8385	3605

EXHIBIT E—Continued.

OSCEOLA STATION.

MONTHS. 1868.	No. of Horses.	No. of Cattle.	No. of Hogs.	No. of Sheep.	Pounds dressed Hogs.	Pounds of Lard and Pork.	Pounds Wool.	Bushels Wheat	Bushels Corn.	Bushels other Grains.	Pounds other Agri'l Prod's	An'l Prod'ts n't specified, lbs.
May........	..	1116	3180	160	....	....	325	635	360	23360	36710	2160
June........	..	936	1260	560	....	....	17725	300	.....	2285	1100	4325
July........	..	630	900	1280	....	1030	64715	1200	2395	2250	......	3000
August......	..	576	600	240	....	....	14300	9300	5605	9605	37350	3060
September...	..	882	420	640	....	....	4000	2100	1930	6750	36500	500
October.....	..	882	660	240	....	....	11315	900	.....	3440	42800	5300
November....	..	90	1620	....	....	....	1460	.....	.....	.....	14600	2450
December....	..	126	4680	....	5700	....	1175	.....	.....	530	11400	5200
1869.												
January.....	..	108	540	240	3600	....	2740	300	.....	560	......	8900
February....	..	126	600	160	....	....	......	.....	.....	.....	3600	4800
March.......	..	432	840	160	....	....	460	.....	.....	1120	4430	4060
April.......	..	306	1000	240	....	....	......	.....	.....	.....	8065	3360
Total.......	..	6210	16300	3920	9300	1030	118215	14735	10290	40900	196555	48115

WOODBURN STATION.

1868.	No. of Horses.	No. of Cattle.	No. of Hogs.	No. of Sheep.	Pounds dressed Hogs.	Pounds of Lard and Pork.	Pounds Wool.	Bushels Wheat	Bushels Corn.	Bushels other Grains.	Pounds other Agri'l Prod's	An'l Prod'ts n't specified, lbs.
May........	..	18	60	....	....	....	......	200	.....	.....	......	......
June........	..	72	......	....	....	....	......	.....	.....	.....	......	......
July........	..	18	60	....	....	....	560	335	360	.....	......	......
August......	..	....	......	....	....	....	......	970	.....	.....	......	165
September...	..	....	......	....	....	....	......	870	.....	625	50	......
October.....	..	....	......	....	....	....	......	325	.....	1780	......	715
November....	..	....	720	....	....	....	360	.....	.....	560	......	......
December....	..	....	840	....	....	....	......	.....	.....	.....	......	1600
1869.												
January.....	..	....	......	....	....	....	......	.....	.....	.....	......	......
February....	..	....	......	....	....	....	......	.....	.....	.....	......	200
March.......	..	72	240	160	....	....	......	.....	.....	560	......	350
April.......	..	90	180	80	....	....	......	.....	.....	.....	100	50
Total.......	..	270	2100	240	....	....	920	2700	360	3525	150	3080

LUCAS STATION.

1868.	No. of Horses.	No. of Cattle.	No. of Hogs.	No. of Sheep.	Pounds dressed Hogs.	Pounds of Lard and Pork.	Pounds Wool.	Bushels Wheat	Bushels Corn.	Bushels other Grains.	Pounds other Agri'l Prod's	An'l Prod'ts n't specified, lbs.
August......	..	....	......	....	....	....	......	1995	.....	1815	......	......
September...	..	....	......	....	....	....	......	1655	.....	680	......	......
October.....	..	....	......	....	....	....	......	320	.....	590	......	......
November....	..	....	60	....	....	....	......	.....	.....	.....	......	......
December....	..	....	300	....	....	....	......	.....	.....	.....	......	......
1869.												
February....	..	....	......	....	....	....	......	.....	.....	600	......	......
March.......	..	....	......	....	....	....	......	.....	.....	630	......	......
Total.......	..	....	360	....	....	....	......	3970	.....	4315	......	......

EXHIBIT E—CONTINUED.

CHARITON STATION.

MONTHS. 1868.	No. of Horses.	No. of Cattle.	No. of Hogs.	No. of Sheep.	Pounds dressed Hogs.	Pounds of Lard and Pork.	Pounds Wool.	Bushels Wheat	Bushels Corn.	Bushels other grains.	Other Agricultural Products lbs.	An'l Prod's not specified, lbs.
May......	..	108	1020	....	....	8265	......	600	.....	285	19420	9620
June......	..	540	780	800	....	....	23265	......	1930	5250	1605	9225
July......	..	234	480	320	....	....	37385	300	2930	1690	1965	4680
August....	..	306	300	720	....	....	29875	27435	3215	25940	1240	4960
September.	..	738	300	80	....	....	3170	14425	4250	16120	2245	24410
October...	..	468	900	80	....	....	3100	5175	.....	27845	118980	11575
November	..	54	2220	80	....	....	675	450	.....	3410	27500	6750
December.	..	18	2520	....	4230	....	420	......	320	560	1485	9820
1869.												
January..	..	36	420	80	....	....	1750	930	960	3375	3500	10400
February..	..	216	660	560	....	....	......	480	.....	2535	4670	12825
March.....	..	270	360	160	....	....	300	1275	680	5530	4875	11470
April......	..	378	420	240	....	....	......	670	.....	1190	2880	20950
Total....	..	3366	10380	3120	4230	8265	99940	51740	14285	93730	190365	136685

RUSSELL STATION.

1868.	No. of Horses.	No. of Cattle.	No. of Hogs.	No. of Sheep.	Pounds dressed Hogs.	Pounds of Lard and Pork.	Pounds Wool.	Bushels Wheat	Bushels Corn.	Bushels other grains.	Other Agricultural Products lbs.	An'l Prod's not specified, lbs.
May......	..	54	......	....	....	....	......	......	.....	.....	......	60
June......	..	....	180	....	....	....	......	......	750	560	......	......
July......	..	....	60	....	....	....	......	......	.....	.....	......	......
August....	..	....	......	....	....	....	......	1335	730	.....	......	......
September.	..	....	......	....	....	....	......	6665	.....	4690	......	......
October...	..	....	60	....	....	....	......	......	.....	1250	......	......
November.	..	....	60	....	....	....	......	......	.....	.....	20000	......
December.	..	54	60	....	....	....	......	......	.....	.....	......	......
1869.												
January..	..	....	60	....	....	....	......	......	.....	.....	......	......
February..	..	....	......	....	....	....	......	350	.....	.....	......	1800
March.....	..	36	......	....	....	....	......	......	720	.....	......	550
April......	..	....	......	....	....	....	......	......	.....	630	......	......
Total...	..	144	480	....	....	....	......	8350	2200	7130	20000	2410

MELROSE STATION.

1868.	No. of Horses.	No. of Cattle.	No. of Hogs.	No. of Sheep.	Pounds dressed Hogs.	Pounds of Lard and Pork.	Pounds Wool.	Bushels Wheat	Bushels Corn.	Bushels other grains.	Other Agricultural Products lbs.	An'l Prod's not specified, lbs.
May......	..	306	1980	....	....	....	......	......	340	565	2400	610
June......	..	576	720	640	....	....	......	......	650	560	......	975
July......	..	342	1020	640	....	....	......	......	.....	.....	......	......
August....	..	270	420	....	....	....	......	1885	665	6710	......	......
September	..	666	960	....	....	....	......	1935	.....	2435	20000	925
October...	..	360	1560	160	....	....	......	950	.....	5425	2500	645
November.	..	36	1980	80	....	....	......	......	.....	1115	......	155
December.	..	....	4980	....	....	....	......	......	.....	.....	......	3000
1869.												
January...	..	216	420	80	....	....	......	......	.....	570	......	2300
February..	..	378	780	160	....	....	......	......	.....	1190	......	2160
March.....	..	378	420	480	....	....	......	......	2860	1150	450	1000
April......	..	360	1320	560	....	....	......	......	.....	560	......	2100
Total....	..	3888	16660	2800	....	....	......	4770	4515	20280	25350	13870

EXHIBIT E—Continued.

TYRONE STATION.

MONTHS. 1868.	No. of Horses.	No. of Cattle.	No. of Hogs.	No. of Sheep.	Pounds dressed Hogs.	Pounds of Lard and Pork.	Pounds Wool.	Bushels Wheat	Bushels Corn.	Bushels other grains.	Other Agricultural Products lbs.	An'l Prod's not specified, lbs.
May	..	....	....	....	....	....	....	....	....	....	500	....
June	..	....	....	....	....	....	....	....	715	....	....	....
July	..	....	....	....	....	....	....	....	360	....	....	....
August	..	....	....	....	....	....	....	....	715	....	....	....
September	..	....	....	....	....	....	....	335	....	570	....	....
October	..	....	....	....	....	....	....	....	....	625	....	....
November	..	....	300	....	....	....	....	....	....	565	1000	....
December	..	....	420	....	....	....	....	....	....	....	1200	....
1869.												
April		....	....	....	....	....	....	....	....	560	....	....
Total		....	720	....	....	....	....	335	1790	2320	2700	....

ALBIA STATION.

MONTHS. 1868.	No. of Horses.	No. of Cattle.	No. of Hogs.	No. of Sheep.	Pounds dressed Hogs.	Pounds of Lard and Pork.	Pounds Wool.	Bushels Wheat	Bushels Corn.	Bushels other grains.	Other Agricultural Products lbs.	An'l Prod's not specified, lbs.
May	..	504	1140	80	....	....	1465	300	705	5780	29200	15660
June	..	162	2400	480	....	....	16400	....	355	5205	2205	21600
July	..	72	120	320	....	....	20400	....	660	1815	500	5800
August	..	342	360	80	....	....	3325	12385	....	12780	231885	2320
September	..	288	1080	80	....	....	10285	7650	2270	17750	398940	9155
October	..	108	1260	320	....	....	....	4215	....	35030	134405	16210
November	..	126	3900	....	....	....	1270	300	....	1670	15740	5200
December	..	....	6060	....	54000	....	350	1200	....	3400	470	7500
1869.												
January	..	....	480	....	11200	1200	10190	600	....	3400	600	18130
February	..	252	300	80	11400	....	....	300	....	560	440	8700
March	..	432	540	....	....	....	....	3050	320	15560	6600	12700
April	..	126	900	....	....	....	....	600		1120	5375	11730
Total	..	2412	18540	1400	76600	1200	63685	30600	4310	104070	826360	134705

FREDERIC STATION.

MONTHS. 1868.	No. of Horses.	No. of Cattle.	No. of Hogs.	No. of Sheep.	Pounds dressed Hogs.	Pounds of Lard and Pork.	Pounds Wool.	Bushels Wheat	Bushels Corn.	Bushels other grains.	Other Agricultural Products lbs.	An'l Prod's not specified, lbs.
June	..	....	....	....	....	....	....	....	....	....	110	....
July	.	18	....	....	....	....	....	....	....	....	....	....
August		342	360	80	....	....	....	....	....	....	....	....
September	..	....	60	80	....	....	....	300	....	1125	....	....
October	..	18	60	....	....	....	....	....	....	1255	970	....
November	..	....	780	....	....	....	....	....	....	....	....	....
December	..	....	240	....	....	....	....	....	....	600	390	....
1869.												
January	..	90	....	....	....	....	....	300	....	....	5110	110
February	..	60	....	....	....	....	....	....	....	....	20000	....
March		..	60	480	....	....	....	....	....	1120	....	....
Total	..	528	1560	640	....	....	....	600	...	4100	26580	110

EXHIBIT E—Continued.

OTTUMWA STATION.

MONTHS. 1868.	No. of Horses.	No. of Cattle.	No. of Hogs.	No. of Sheep.	Pounds dressed Hogs.	Pounds of Lard and Pork.	Pounds Wool.	Bushels Wheat	Bushels Corn.	Bushels other Grains.	Other Agricultural Products lbs.	An'l Prod's not specified, lbs.
May	..	810	3240	640	...	...	5200	5335	...	260	61015	30445
June	..	504	3360	240	...	...	50050	7115	2700	6395	8785	19420
July	..	324	2880	480	...	...	112925	10725	6545	5145	...	27995
August	..	468	2340	160	...	...	123270	30785	6380	7800	124200	35350
September	..	522	2340	240	...	...	18800	35935	890	7125	228235	55815
October	14	288	3240	320	...	...	14230	11500	...	20440	403285	66600
November	..	18	3431	320	...	...	5060	1710	...	10045	40500	59330
December	..	108	2880	160	7400	144300	1640	910	...	600	22240	41060
1869.												
January	..	162	2940	...	17840	153450	...	3830	...	630	61000	58230
February	..	108	1320	400	...	516650	175	2800	...	...	25300	35670
March	..	720	2040	960	500	358000	250	2900	1900	560	1950	14300
April	..	1008	1800	1280	...	301550	...	3260	...	...	205170	29900
Total	14	5040	31811	5200	25740	1473950	331600	116805	18415	59000	1181680	477115

AGENCY CITY STATION.

1868.	No. of Horses.	No. of Cattle.	No. of Hogs.	No. of Sheep.	Pounds dressed Hogs.	Pounds of Lard and Pork.	Pounds Wool.	Bushels Wheat	Bushels Corn.	Bushels other Grains.	Other Agricultural Products lbs.	An'l Prod's not specified, lbs.
May	..	36	420	320	...	...	...	...	320	...	...	920
June	..	108	240	...	...	...	7270	...	...	...	350	1070
July	..	36	120	320	...	...	11320	...	...	...	...	700
August	..	36	180	...	...	...	6315	...	1785	...	155	250
September	..	72	60	...	...	...	5000	3600	360	1750	200	80
October	..	18	120	160	...	...	...	320	...	560	2050	50
November	..	18	1380	80	...	...	...	...	...	...	2940	550
December	..	90	960	...	...	...	450	...	...	...	...	7810
1869.												
January	..	90	780	...	2600	...	...	335	...	600	5100	2250
February	..	36	180	80	815	...	15500	...	...	560	3230	900
March	..	36	240	...	...	...	...	1000	...	...	5000	1320
April	..	252	240	320	...	...	...	670	...	...	5775	700
Total	..	828	4920	1280	3415	...	45855	5925	2465	3470	24800	16600

BATAVIA STATION.

1868.	No. of Horses.	No. of Cattle.	No. of Hogs.	No. of Sheep.	Pounds dressed Hogs.	Pounds of Lard and Pork.	Pounds Wool.	Bushels Wheat	Bushels Corn.	Bushels other Grains.	Other Agricultural Products lbs.	An'l Prod's not specified, lbs.
May	..	198	120	...	...	...	...	300	700	625	...	...
June	..	...	600	...	...	...	225	...	7100	2370	1050	270
July	..	...	180	...	...	...	1900	...	...	710	...	...
August	..	...	60	...	...	...	...	4275	360	9275	...	130
September	..	18	120	...	...	...	...	2600	170	4850	700	1750
October	..	...	420	160	...	...	...	300	325	3700	...	...
November	..	...	1620	...	...	...	...	600	...	1115	...	40
December	..	...	1260	...	...	...	...	...	...	570	2460	400
1869.												
January	..	36	300	...	2000	...	...	...	...	1680	500	2300
February	..	108	480	...	150	...	...	600	...	1750	5600	600
March	10	120	160	...	...	...	...	...	1040	...	5140	525
April	..		360	...	...	...	...	...	...	3080	56570	4770
Total	10	480	5680	160	2150	...	2125	8675	9695	29725	72020	10685

EXHIBIT E—Continued.

WHITFIELD STATION.

MONTHS. 1868.	No. of Horses.	No. of Cattle.	No. of Hogs.	No. of Sheep.	Pounds dressed Hogs.	Pounds of Lard and Pork.	Pounds Wool.	Bushels Wheat	Bushels Corn.	Bushels other Grains.	Other Ag'l products, lbs.	Animal Prod'ts n't spe'fi'd, lbs
May	..	....	60	....	....	....	......	.....	340	....	......	......
July	..	....	......	160	....	....	......	.....	.....	....	......	......
August	..	....	......	....	....	....	......	.....	370	....	......	......
October	..	....	60	....	....	....	......	.....	.....	....	......	......
November	..	....	240	....	....	....	......	.....	.....	....	......	......
December	..	....	360	....	....	....	......	.....	.....	....	......	......
1869.												
January	..	....	120	....	....	....	......	.....	.....	....	......	......
March	..	126	60	....	....	....	......	.....	.....	....	......	......
Total	..	126	900	160	....	....	......	.....	710	....	......	......

FAIRFIELD STATION.

MONTHS. 1868.	No. of Horses.	No. of Cattle.	No. of Hogs.	No. of Sheep.	Pounds dressed Hogs.	Pounds of Lard and Pork.	Pounds Wool.	Bushels Wheat	Bushels Corn.	Bushels other Grains.	Other Ag'l products, lbs.	Animal Prod'ts n't spe'fi'd, lbs
May	..	126	540	....	....	....	745	900	340	5745	55090	13440
June	..	90	600	....	....	....	14356	900	.....	4000	14420	13460
July	..	36	120	80	....	....	19005	300	320	2340	......	9670
August	..	....	120	....	....	....	28070	11080	.....	15190	5435	18400
September	..	18	360	240	....	....	29590	7130	360	21150	195300	11105
October	..	90	780	....	....	....	5395	1570	1715	20500	28460	15150
November	..	72	3000	....	....	....	......	635	.....	1875	13520	12260
December	..	72	3540	....	....	....	550	320	.....	1170	22450	17800
1869.												
January	..	90	300	....	1750	....	1170	1200	.....	1335	64400	17600
February	..	144	540	240	2750	....	......	.....	320	630	72700	11420
March	15	234	480	740	....	....	......	1500	.....	750	21430	16500
April	..	198	780	480	....	....	100	2130	....	2835	23400	29050
Total	15	1170	11160	1780	4500	....	128981	27665	3055	77520	576605	185855

GLENDALE STATION.

MONTHS. 1838.	No. of Horses.	No. of Cattle.	No. of Hogs.	No. of Sheep.	Pounds dressed Hogs.	Pounds of Lard and Pork.	Pounds Wool.	Bushels Wheat	Bushels Corn.	Bushels other Grains.	Other Ag'l products, lbs.	Animal Prod'ts n't spe'fi'd, lbs
May	..	....	......	....	....	....	......	.....	.....	.....	......	2490
June	..	36	......	....	....	....	......	.....	.....	.....	......	1810
July	..	....	......	....	....	....	......	.....	.....	.....	......	3620
August	..	....	......	....	....	....	......	670	.....	1260	......	1200
September	..	....	120	....	....	....	......	1100	.....	2490	......	1000
October	..	18	180	....	....	....	......	'330	.....	2875	15000	......
November	..	36	660	80	....	....	......	.....	.....	550	......	......
December	..	....	1320	....	....	....	......	.....	.....	.....	100	1500
1869.												
Jauuary	..	....	120	....	....	....	......	200	.....	.....	200	1400
February	..	....	......	....	....	....	......	.....	.....	.....	......	2585
March	..	198	......	....	....	....	......	.....	.....	.....	......	4175
April	..	....	......	....	....	....	......	.....	.....	.....	8900	......
Total	..	288	2400	80	....	....	......	2300	.....	7175	14200	19780

EXHIBIT E—Continued.

ROME STATION.

MONTHS.	No. of Horses.	No. of Cattle.	No. of Hogs.	No. of Sheep.	Pounds dressed Hogs.	Pounds of Lard and Pork.	Pounds Wool.	Bushels Wheat	Bushels Corn.	Bushels other Grains.	Other Ag'l products, lbs.	Animal Prod'ts n't spe'fi'd, lbs
1868.												
May			60								16500	
June											15200	
July											9600	
August			60								37600	
September								135			36800	
October							310			1700	39800	
November			60								40000	
December			300				350				60630	
1869.												
January											67000	300
February		36										23220
March											68550	
April			60								48610	
Total		36	540				660	135		1700	440290	23520

MOUNT PLEASANT STATION.

MONTHS.	No. of Horses.	No. of Cattle.	No. of Hogs.	No. of Sheep.	Pounds dressed Hogs.	Pounds of Lard and Pork.	Pounds Wool.	Bushels Wheat	Bushels Corn.	Bushels other Grains.	Other Ag'l products, lbs.	Animal Prod'ts n't spe'fi'd, lbs
1868.												
May		18	660	80		6470	2225		100	350	7785	7750
June		54	600				32370			600	1200	10550
July		72	840				36100	3400		560	20000	9650
August			300				76320	7750	350	6700	60800	9000
September		16	360				55890	7000	1070	7850	101400	12050
October		36	1140				15120	2000	320	8100	17550	22000
November		54	1740				9570			1900	12400	8800
December			3900					335		1190	900	23360
1869.												
January		198	840		1380	61800		335	360	630	32400	10800
February		234	1280	80							28800	21070
March		594	840	320		42450				1260	51160	14100
April		234	840	560			16330		320	650	7300	24980
Total		1510	13340	1040	1380	110720	263925	20820	2520	29290	341695	174110

NEW LONDON STATION.

MONTHS.	No. of Horses.	No. of Cattle.	No. of Hogs.	No. of Sheep.	Pounds dressed Hogs.	Pounds of Lard and Pork.	Pounds Wool.	Bushels Wheat	Bushels Corn.	Bushels other Grains.	Other Ag'l products, lbs.	Animal Prod'ts n't spe'fi'd, lbs
May			120							1940	18450	1500
June			180					310	965	2400	2000	
July			60						1385	270	3400	
August								1000	2070	1225	1665	
September			60					2560	370	3050	1100	820
October		54	60					310		5800	29800	
November			360					335		1100	4710	350
December			960							600	1165	
1869.												
January			600		1000						130	2900
February		36			7200						1600	425
March		234	120	160						1160	46525	1150
April		18	60	80				1300		1780	71600	350
Total		342	2580	240	8200			5815	4790	19325	182145	7495

EXHIBIT E—CONTINUED.

DANVILLE STATION.

MONTHS. 1868.	No. of Horses.	No. of Cattle.	No. of Hogs.	No. of Sheep.	Pounds dressed Hogs.	Pounds of Lard and Pork.	Pounds Wool.	Bushels Wheat	Bushels Corn.	Bushels of other Grains.	Pounds Other Ag'l Prod'ts.	An'l Prod's not specified, lbs.	Flour, Barrels.
May....	..	18	60	80	......	......	.....	.....	.....	120	.....	.....	....
June ...	..	19	120	....	......	......	.....	.....	.....	4230	74000	3850	....
July....	..	....	120	....	......	......	41760	.....	1170	560	18000	.....	....
August .	..	....	60	....	......	......	470	.....	2400	6125	.....	.....	....
Sept. ...	..	....	120	80	......	......	.....	.....	1400	1020	3080	160	....
October.	..	....	....	....	......	......	.....	.....	.....	4710	30700	.....	....
Nov	..	....	240	....	......	......	.....	.....	.....	590	36450	640	....
Dec	..	....	1980	....	......	......	.....	.....	.....	.....	50000	.....	....
1869.													
Jan......	..	72	660	....	......	......	.....	.....	.....	.....	30000	3550	....
Feb	..	....	60	....	2000	......	.....	.....	.....	.....	20000	700	....
March ..	..	108	180	160	1340	......	.....	.....	.....	630	820	10270	....
April ...	..	72	240	160	......	......	.....	.....	.....	625	41280	.....	....
Total .	..	289	3840	480	3340	......	42230	.....	4970	18610	304330	19170	....

G. C. MORTON.

Statistics of Products Carried Eastward from Burlington Station, for the 12 *months ending April* 30, 1869, *not including Freight received from the B. & M. R. R. R.*

1868.	No. of Horses.	No. of Cattle.	No. of Hogs.	No. of Sheep.	Pounds dressed Hogs.	Pounds of Lard and Pork.	Pounds Wool.	Bushels Wheat	Bushels Corn.	Bushels of other Grains.	Pounds Other Ag'l Prod'ts.	An'l Prod's not specified, lbs.	Flour, Barrels.
May....	2	53	630	82	......	......	1490	.....	7324	494	.....	2250	5400
June....	1	408	311	387	......	......	13197	1660	8513	.....	12390	.....	4600
July....	7	40	331	....	......	35500	18075	.....	3492	.....	.....	33099	3300
August .	3	34	462	97	......	3695	11877	15947	28733	34127	.....	20465	6400
Sept....	3	77	283	....	......	3420	6580	11430	9821	19992	38510	20865	8609
October.	7	114	232	....	......	3680	5426	1018	2727	28342	2900	38080	8201
Nov....	1	132	646	....	......	......	7220	.....	356	1454	4920	28005	6301
Dec	3	252	2317	....	26720	169872	1585	.....	1384	1207	980	33820	1508
1869.													
Jan	2	137	2291	....	145660	3000	550	.....	3602	660	.....	54655	903
Feb	5	327	165	255	28525	70000	2790	.....	2953	926	2100	4690	400
March ..	16	443	289	184	6240	45020	200	.....	7345	371	4600	54805	1321
April ...	2	194	471	158	......	399545	660	1423	1751	625	12950	19300	2406
Total ...	52	2211	8428	1163	207145	738732	69650	31478	77641	88198	79350	380034	49349

W. McCREDIE, *Freight Auditor.*

Statistics of Products Carried Eastward from Keokuk Station, for the 6 *months ending Oct.* 31, 1868, *via the T. P & W. R. R., and C. B. & Q. R. R., and not received from the D. V. R, R.*

1868.	No. of Horses.	No. of Cattle.	No. of Hogs.	No. of Sheep.	Pounds dressed Hogs.	Pounds of Lard and Pork.	Pounds Wool.	Bushels Wheat	Bushels Corn.	Bushels of other Grains.	Pounds Other Ag'l Prod'ts.	An'l Prod's not specified, lbs.	Flour, Barrels.
May....	..	....	....	....	......	......	3590	.....	9341	5226	.....	68713	....
June ...	..	....	240	....	......	......	25592	2964	1278	18260	.....	116046	....
July....	..	72	....	....	......	4680	26199	.....	.....	830	.....	22034	....
August .	..	....	360	....	......	......	19104	28746	1683	4387	.....	33780	190
Sept....	..	....	51	....	......	737	6093	3134	5564	1183	25954	29870	100
Oct	..	....	....	....	......	......	.....	.....	.....	.....	.....	65411	100
Total .	..	72	651	....	......	5417	80578	34844	17866	29886	25954	335854	390

W. McCREDIE, *Freight Auditor.*

RAILROAD STATISTICS.

MILWAUKEE & ST. PAUL RAILWAY.

Statement of Agricultural Products carried Eastward from the several stations on the Iowa Division of the Milwaukee & St. Paul Railway and the aggregate carried Westward for the year ending April 30th, 1869.

STATIONS.	No. of Horses.	No. of Cattle.	No. of Hogs.	No. of Sheep.	Dressed Hogs, pounds.	Lard & Pork, pounds.	Wool, pounds.	Wheat, bush.	Corn, bushels.	Other Grains, bushels.	Other Agricultural products, lbs.*	Animal products not otherwise specified, lbs.†
Lime Springs	......	93	115	....	94860	....	1570	150507	....	25070	217380	32110
Cresco	1	338	198	50	185230	....	12510	241079	6651	68928	319240	120160
Ridgeway	......	......	....	....	46290	....	250	77441	....	1820	....	4590
Conover	......	131	776	....	384360	2200	13480	145084	691	11325	129340	103270
Calmar	3	66	137	....	285790	1420	2080	141390	2366	6801	98120	79360
Ossian	......	129	688	.....	289720	460	8690	323774	21053	49049	210440	141730
Castalia	......	46	170	....	28600	....	310	41280	3207	14690	59980	6590
Postville	......	152	2137	.....	602580	15710	3790	87016	6876	9384	4585820	44080
Luana	......	419	2436	......	107950	....	....	25252	10540	9080	1540	....
Monona	......	......	....	....	24770	....	1120	61047	3646	4733	2660	2270
Total eastward	4	1374	6657	50	2050150	19790	43800	1293870	55030	200880	5624520	534160
Carried westward	6	169	9	1	25680	16272	....	613	24657	40163	12460	28310
Total	10	1543	6666	51	2075830	36062	43800	1294483	79687	241043	5636980	562470

* "Other Agricultural Products" include Flour, Potatoes and Beans.
† Animal "Products not otherwise specified" includes Eggs, Butter, Tallow and Hides.

ILLINOIS CENTRAL RAILROAD.

Statement of Agricultural Products carried eastward from the several stations on the Iowa Division of the Illinois Central Railroad for the year ending April 30th, 1869.

CEDAR FALLS AND MINNESOTA RAILROAD.

STATIONS.	No. of Horses.	No. of Cattle.	No. of Hogs.	No. of Sheep.	Dressed Hogs, pounds.	Lard & Pork, barrels.	Wool, pounds.	GRAIN. Wheat, bushels.	GRAIN. Corn, bushels.	GRAIN. Other Grain, bushels.	Flour and other Agricultural products, barrels.	Hides and animal products not otherwise specified, pounds.
Charles City	......	102	94	......	174900	......	4000	174160	......	10060	6462	41400
Nashua	......	30	228	......	182800	......	......	65950	... 350	16670	1820	10600
Plainfield	......	82	186	......	7500	......	......	19000	......	6620	......	......
Waverly	......	571	2650	75	307400	12	54000	318700	29580	86530	20160	70600
Janesville	......	......	279	......	17600	......	......	6990	1420	2380	11800	......
Total	......	785	3437	75	690200	12	58000	584800	31350	122260	40242	122600

DUBUQUE AND SIOUX CITY RAILROAD.

STATIONS.	No. of Horses.	No. of Cattle.	No. of Hogs.	No. of Sheep.	Dressed Hogs, pounds.	Lard & Pork, barrels.	Wool, pounds.	GRAIN. Wheat, bushels.	GRAIN. Corn, bushels.	GRAIN. Other Grain, bushels.	Flour and other Agricultural products, barrels.	Hides and animal products not otherwise specified, pounds.
Iowa Falls	......	180	658	......	108800	19	19300	71260	6750	14360	1005	21600
Ackley	......	675	2605	225	127500	......	12400	227790	32730	21800	2723	33200
Aplington	......	......	7	......	25800	......	......	27970	1050	1240	......	......
Parkersburg	18	45	100	......	25800	......	......	38330	......	1860	......	1000
New Hartford	......	104	164	......	16100	......	......	38960	4260	4340	......	......
Cedar Falls	......	194	850	......	87800	......	6400	133550	16400	18490	33762	75400
Waterloo	14	165	1366	......	155700	......	49300	485920	33900	19610	41202	98400
Raymond	......	......	218	......	1500	......	......	60240	1400	330	......	......
Jesup	......	230	677	75	49800	......	1000	132930	2820	16160	......	8900
Independence	6	303	3263	95	268400	......	31100	350180	37390	105350	34	58700
Winthrop	......	456	1142	208	37000	......	6200	158510	13800	67830	360	5700
Masonville	......	......	......	......	......	......	......	18980	1050	8270	......	......
Manchester	......	1109	4955	......	433600	......	30000	166740	39950	94020	8730	42600
Delaware	7	403	1614	68	69000	......	......	27290	3550	21160	3056	1200
Earlville	......	337	1226	14	61500	......	......	69930	13540	35840	69	6900
Dyersville	7	196	2119	......	2353100	129	3300	103500	34190	90800	2834	22400
Farley	4	60	278	......	76400	......	......	22990	12110	43200	......	3400
Epworth	......	30	350	......	11500	......	......	660	4580	14380	......	......
Peosta	......	51	2282	......	......	......	1800	3980	2100	4980	......	......
Total	56	4538	23874	685	3919300	148	161800	2139710	261570	584020	93775	379400

CHICAGO AND NORTHWESTERN RAILWAY.

Statement of Agricultural Products carried Eastward and Westward from the several stations on the Iowa Division of the Chicago and North-Western Railway for the year ending April 30th, 1869.

STATIONS.	No. of Horses.	No. of Cattle.	No. of Hogs.	No. of Sheep.	Dressed Hogs, pounds.	Lard & Pork, pounds.	Wool, pounds.	GRAIN. Wheat, bushels.	Corn, bushels.	Other Grains, bushels.	Other agricultural products, lbs.	Animal products not otherwise specified, lbs.	Flour, barrels
Missouri River	13	96	45	......	2100	23300	73170	1383	......	22	73425	825370	541
Council Bluffs	4	2373	6345	770	59190	52703	32960	8184	21508	1434	224606	233090	683
Missouri Valley Junction	16	1008	258	......	27830	5680	37510	5551	11	720	100840	179797	3369
Logan	4	48	......	......	73300	30670	......	1009	454	612	12040	4630	513
Woodbine	......	198	132	......	54230	5990	9650	103	6608	1485	522700	6780	8427
Dunlap	4	153	160	......	33270	470	1060	1599	914	479	155630	18290	51
Denison	21	......	......	......	5850	1440	8650	474	1066	......	42080	5210	2
Carroll	4	......	......	......	......	800	210	......	......	......	1360	12660	1
Glidden	2	16	......	......	3050	......	110	659	......	......	9080	3420	......
Jefferson	20	273	572	110	18750	2030	16190	939	2	366	5720	35560	269
Ogden	2	144	270	......	2230	800	......	......	6	......	1140	3790	......
Moingona	1	......	......	......	......	2420	2230	......	......	......	26500	4410	145
Boone	30	835	441	......	108310	80550	51740	250	7074	21	564380	164190	467
Ames	5	169	594	220	26910	2050	7220	5341	1624	31	218360	18210	1
Nevada	27	202	794	......	195630	33970	2260	26580	6157	2342	390152	51760	845
Colo	......	308	1305	......	3670	47880	4520	20716	1353	2972	130060	27880	......
State Center	26	307	2267	590	1840	7280	5420	113644	30712	4422	437470	27460	29
La Moille	......	......	......	......	......	200	......	26541	1441	668	1000	3100	......
Marshall	75	612	4729	560	229480	20420	65230	543452	105006	31358	1115468	120250	4053
Quarry	......	......	......	......	1880	......	......	11798	4262	1263	68520	820	2073
Le Grand	......	273	855	......	11620	330	4880	41360	777	......	8830	20830	130
Orford	21	98	772	......	26630	460	90	65695	894	......	27540	11760	657
Tama	......	177	2146	540	156230	28702	18340	245885	11065	3477	192508	55958	2089
Chelsea	2	394	1057	100	66050	......	......	51248	......	97	2920	6930	15
Belle Plaine	12	225	1485	110	151210	20940	17780	203068	74040	6246	65480	42320	105
Luzerne	......	18	274	85	8290	5900	......	73950	600	7847	11523	5010	......
Blairstown	5	370	2582	55	49430	9080	2800	181434	405	9679	133860	58420	1485
Norway	6	418	1373	......	10190	1750	620	110729	1463	2998	11210	3570	......
Fairfax	......	144	945	220	......	3490	......	55881	1322	1822	4360	1400	6
Cedar Rapids	99	668	3590	388	1345665	198437	26260	290048	128906	99333	654078	238530	25028
Bertram	3	102	360	1390	......	......	......	50	......	......	8350	910	......
Mount Vernon	3	135	648	299	93170	22533	6040	20662	713	11551	109775	43245	25
Lisbon	2	371	6255	......	17940	14780	1120	51163	12005	37060	40360	24850	352

Mechanicsville	3	821	5567	660	30420	17120	25500	106001	55912	89461	49690	52500	3
Clarence	56	287	3071	770	77290	75989	74670	134514	57277	75352	155294	162500	41
Louden	1	333	4995	110	64880	45853	2520	67077	24241	50524	64137	20741	17
Wheatland	98	345	4118	291	219310	20180	6718	113200	15663	71301	56340	32572	205
Calamus	30	64	557	....	14890	6470	....	25124	8271	9248	44894	17538	12
Grand Mound	4	16	48	....	28160	4860	....	38278	4510	10248	15940	3880	15
De Witt	36	1029	8787	110	110270	89611	40920	231054	58483	65942	113950	94450	117
Malone	......	....	....	....	....	700	....	15576	7774	9141	5010	....	....
Low Moor	......	96	1766	....	11950	2280	4610	18492	16630	10439	14770	....	5
Camanche	....	53	180	....	4450	3410	....	15396	16503	8074	3100	....	35
Clinton	455	996	2315	259	86310	65868	2530	44107	12639	39423	208279	99790	7809
Total	1110	14175	71658	7637	3431875	950906	573528	2968211	698486	667455	6097369	2744291	59620

CHICAGO, ROCK ISLAND AND PACIFIC RAILROAD.

Statement of Agricultural Products carried Eastward from the several Stations on the Chicago, Rock Island and Pacific Railroad, for the year ending April 30th, 1869.

STATIONS.	No. of Horses.	No. of Cattle.	No. of Hogs.	No. of Sheep.	Dressed Hogs, pounds.	Lard & Pork, pounds.	Wool, pounds.	GRAIN. Wheat, pounds.	GRAIN. Corn, pounds.	GRAIN. Other Grain, pounds.	Other Agricultural products, lbs.	Animal products not otherwise specified, pounds.	Barrels Flour.
De Soto	1	288	2405	560	800							3400	
Des Moines	10	4218	19195	2855	372725	3166050	251587	3273540	2679680	348560	197600	200825	501
Altoona		144	300					82040		12800			
Mitchelville		931	3105	936	2940			707470	140000	107600	13250	8990	
Colfax		192	2956	1080	1600	250		2692300	830840	187080	800	4905	1
Newton	2	530	3330	790	11570	1225	14888	7747470	1278040	111850	48540	69480	104
Kellogg		1120	1518	200	250			2577240	269110	82530	1890	5800	
Grinnell		1032	600	200	1350		13920	5463180	529120	191650	3880	33085	
Malcolm		290	4388	300	19200		2100	5306050	1472060	102200	5800	50650	
Brooklyn		160	1073		23720		360	3623360	349300	73900	880	36070	
Victor		404	2456	310	11950	285	125	5201850	165970	72750	500	27520	
Ladora					9640			912800	51650	2040		13543	
Marengo		240	3110	500	102266		23500	4539100	53990	327610	6418	44054	1
Homestead		228	1030	100	14510	3930	750	3376510		60950	6225	40163	
Oxford					17370			808090	62450	63930			
Clear Creek								483080		17450			
Iowa City	3	1316	16410	100	917061	60651	29059	8519758	1457103	2812561	2350	417675	5600
Downey	2	480	2817	398	550		3167	1117829	972310	615160		13373	
West Liberty		896	4050	600	25935	3245	12884	1516520	2577287	1674870		67285	500
Atalissa		128	2050	800	2616		9788	297700	1623160	621419		10331	
Moscow		112	100					20450	124430	172550			
Washington	67	3216	19850	1500	251076	48680	69415	9942180	2419345	3608620	1300	233580	378
Ainsworth		224	4282		6943			1709868	1313840	562780		48488	
Clifton	3	498	5436	1200	22332	12300	22290	1341400	480710	652150		18280	200
Fredonia	144	240	768	100				304360	1234330	388950		600	
Ononwa		960	2300		5220		1585	190930	562670	413210			
Muscatine	8	164	2869		845810	537820	44940	6103260	4583670	2485588	174080	8700	2347
Wilton	2	880	5250		69630	525	2435	5538869	2923370	1813596	240	12380	2
Durant		224	2050	200	36095	170	164	1363160	918790	1393520	422415	3080	
Fulton		80	350	200			226	20370	168730	20300	220000		
Walcott		16	157		21984		582	2280796	1000273	1258960	100700		
Davenport	59	946	7750	1000	178990	394266	69142	13805250	8541230	9149734	1919505		71743
Total	301	20157	121955	13929	2951801	4229397	572907	100866780	38783308	29406868	3126373	1372257	81377

BURLINGTON AND MISSOURI RIVER RAILROAD.

Statement of Agricultural Products carried Eastward from the several stations on the Burlington and Missouri River Railroad for the year ending April 30th, 1869.

STATIONS.	No. of Horses.	No. of Cattle.	No. of Hogs.	No. of Sheep.	Dressed Hogs, pounds.	Lard & Pork, Pounds.	Wool, pounds.	GRAIN. Wheat, bushels.	GRAIN. Corn, bushels.	GRAIN. Other Grains, bushels.	Other Agricultural products, pounds.	Animal products not otherwise specified pounds.	Barrels Flour.
*Afton	......	1548	6900	380	2720	......	17645	300	......	......	45810	51365	......
Murray	......	150	2478	960	......	......	24170	600	......	......	8385	3605	......
Osceola	......	6210	16300	3920	9300	1030	118215	14735	10290	49900	196555	48115	......
Woodburn	......	270	2100	240	......	......	920	2700	360	3525	150	3080	......
Lucas	......	......	360	......	......	......	......	3970	......	4315	......	......	......
Chariton	......	3366	10380	3120	4230	8265	99940	51740	14285	93730	190365	136685	......
Russell	......	144	480	......	......	......	......	8350	2200	7130	20000	2410	......
Melrose	......	3888	16660	2800	......	......	......	4770	4515	20280	25350	13870	......
Tyrone	......	......	720	......	......	......	......	335	1790	2320	2700	......	......
Albia	......	2412	18540	1400	76600	1200	63685	30600	4310	104070	826360	134705	......
Frederic	...	528	1560	640	......	......	......	600	......	4100	26580	110	......
Ottumwa	14	5040	31811	5200	25740	1473950	331600	116805	18415	59000	1181680	477115	......
Agency City	......	828	4920	1280	3415	......	45855	5925	2465	3470	24800	16600	......
Batavia	10	480	5680	160	2150	......	2125	8675	9695	29725	72020	10685	......
Whitfield	......	126	900	160	......	......	......	......	710	......	......	......	......
Fairfield	15	1170	11160	1780	4500	......	128981	27665	3055	77520	576605	185855	......
Glendale	......	288	2400	80	......	......	......	2300	......	7175	14200	19780	......
Rome	......	36	540	......	......	......	660	135	......	1700	440290	23520	......
Mt. Pleasant	......	1510	13340	1040	1380	110720	263925	20820	2520	29290	341695	174110	......
New London	......	342	2580	240	8200	......	......	5815	4790	19325	182145	7495	......
Danville	......	289	3840	480	3340	......	42230	......	4970	18610	304330	19170	......
†Burlington, by C., B. & Q. R. R.	52	2211	8428	1163	207145	733732	69650	31478	77641	88198	79350	330034	49349
Total	91	30836	162077	25043	348720	2328897	1209601	338318	162011	623383	4559370	1658309	49349

*Road open to Afton September, 1868.
†Does not include freight received from the B. & M. R. R. R.

DES MOINES VALLEY RAILROAD.

Classification of Freight forwarded East for six months, ending June 30th, 1869, *from the several Stations on the Des Moines Valley Railroad.*

STATIONS.	No. of Horses and Mules.	No. of Cattle.	No. of Hogs.	No. of Sheep.	No. lbs. Pork and Beef.	No. lbs. Lard and Tallow.	No. lbs. Hides	No. lbs. Wool.	No. lbs. Wheat	No. lbs. Corn.	No. lbs. Oats, Rye, and Barley.	No. lbs. Flour, Meal, etc.	No. lbs. Grass and other Seeds.
Des Moines	2	270	172	....	20693	39953	63591	24841	1050084	735354	143138	37260	10441
Woodville	......	36	....	....	....	....	....	....	601073	682970	80978	....	....
Prairie City	......	233	3132	300	11930	985	7034	493	1189171	1167050	162028	533000	....
Monroe	......	254	1221	170	....	1430	7619	714	2530863	8436377	127910	216085	1697
Otley	......	191	2227	410	....	....	151	....	753837	987904	37360	....	....
Pella	7	2438	5475	210	14335	20393	55014	6562	3685491	1749067	422160	858752	2800
Oskaloosa	1	1474	3630	1400	6710	9771	45150	19488	2459770	128556	502340	679650	1440
Leighton	......	161	614	....	....	....	160	....	355953	616391	129500	....	....
Eddyville	......	501	2204	360	520369	178099	9980	894	156695	110750	410311	356200	5490
Comstocks	......	....	....	....	....	....	237	....	60500	....	40700	....	....
Ottumwa	28	1941	1302	1170	16140	29436	18807	16105	1209373	8390	859715	80401	113053
Alpine	......	....	....	....	....	....	....	7027	....	....	....	....	....
Independent	......	88	587	....	71170	16300	2090	103088	274285	156233	332801	15850	5325
Douds	......	....	....	....	575	....	262	3000	692293	47462	79401	1818	6475
Summit	10	185	558	150	3066	4546	10045	2170	257800	16144	1143161	474	9254
Bentonsport	......	14	233	214	500	3772	7916	26185	77395	....	428710	1855	7969
Bonaparte	12	395	564	929	350	....	4397	39264	16825	53111	642854	15636	14407
Farmington	......	....	120	....	473924	116635	3428	....	82597	35410	361331	750	19041
Croton	......	....	....	....	67674	37743	831	....	....	26650	98608	1756	1800
Sand Prairie	......	....	....	....	....	....	....	....	....	....	66914	1235	1396
Total	60	8181	22039	5313	1207436	459063	236712	249831	15444005	14957819	6069920	2800822	200568

DES MOINES VALLEY RAILROAD—Continued.

Classification of freight forwarded East for six months, ending June 30th, 1869, from the several stations on the Des Moines Valley Railroad.

STATIONS.	No. Pounds of Hay.	No. Pounds of Potatoes and other roots.	No. Pounds of Green Fruit.	No. of feet Lumber and Timber.	No. M. Lath and shingles.	No. of Cords Staves, Hoop-Poles & Wood.	No. Pounds of Stone & Brick.	No. Pounds of Salt.	No. Pounds of Coal.	No. Pounds of Agricultural Imp. and Machinery.	No. Pounds of Eggs, Butter & Poultry.	No. Pounds of Furniture and Household Goods.	No. Pounds of Merchandise.
Des Moines	....	1472910	......	31000	....	....	18000	...	....	103574	1748	91207	294822
Woodville	....	110580	......	....	.....	....	......	....	....	2705	....	4420	....
Prairie City	....	480977	......	....	.....	....	....	.....	....	....	15451	4144	7361
Monroe	....	232086	......	....	.....	....	....	.....	....	7661	21783	7725	11208
Otley	....	57400	......	....	.....	....	....	....	....	40	4582	1131	23432
Pella	....	250963	......	....	...	....	2060	....	....	15176	211119	22300	36674
Oskaloosa	....	1030	......	....	.....	....	....	.....	12880000	4310	183513	29547	128903
Leighton	....	....	......	....	.....	....	....	.....	....	....	17773	18130	2535
Eddyville	973000	880	......	30	....	....	64585	2910	....	3123	812612	36456	37010
Comstocks	....	....	......	8500	.....	19¾	....	....	....	....	....	509	157
Ottumwa	....	11250	......	18500	.....	6	5385	280	....	63440	88548	51740	228664
Alpine	....	....	......	....	.....	....	....	.....	8150000	....	75916	3635	1985
Independent	....	60	......	....	.....	71	....	...	....	21875	81088	1540	2068
Douds	....	....	......	8000	30	48	60000	....	374000	2250	19113	....	5017
Summit	648000	....	1121	3360	.....	640	....	....	....	12310	205769	9726	9916
Bentonsport	....	300	....	....	.....	....	....	.....	....	2012	86629	9135	65658
Bonaparte	567900	....	......	....	.....	10	....	400	....	1580	20815	5437	403916
Farmington	18640	350	......	2840	.....	....	125	.....	36000	2450	25170	8125	37930
Croton	....	715	......	....	.....	12	....	.....	....	6663	12885	6997	6407
Sand Prairie	333165	....	......	....	.....	161	....	.....	....	65	195	1736	190748
Total	2540705	2619501	1121	72230	30	967¾	150155	3590	21440000	249234	1884709	313640	1494411

STATEMENT

Of Surplus Agricultural Products shipped from the State of Iowa by the different Railroads therein, during the year ending April 30th, 1869.

NAME OF RAILROADS.	No. of Horses.	No. of Cattle.	No. of Hogs.	No. of Sheep.	Dressed Hogs, Lbs.	Lard and Pork, Lbs.	Wool, Lbs.	GRAIN.				Other Agricultural Products, Lbs.	Flour and other Agricultural Products, Barrels.	Animal Products not otherwise specified, Lbs.	Flour, Barrels.
								Wheat, Bush.	Corn, Bush.	Other Grains, Lbs.	Other Grains, Bush.				
*Milwaukee and St. Paul Railway, Iowa Div.	10	1543	6666	51	2075830	36062	43800	1294483	79687	....	241043	5636980	....	562470	....
Cedar Falls and Minnesota Railroad	......	785	3437	75	690200	2400	58000	584800	31350	....	122260	....	40242	122600	....
Dubuque and Sioux City Railroad	56	4538	23874	685	3919300	29600	161800	2139710	261570	....	584020	....	93775	379400	....
†Chicago and Northwestern Railway	1110	14175	71658	7637	3431875	950906	573528	2968211	698486	....	667455	6097369	....	2744291	59620
Chicago, Rock Island and Pacific Railroad	301	20157	121955	13929	2951801	4229397	572907	1681113	692559	29406868	....	3126373	....	1372257	81377
Burlington and Missouri River Railroad	91	30836	162077	25043	348720	2328897	1209601	338318	162011	....	623383	4559370	....	1658309	49349
‡Des Moines Valley Railroad	60	8181	22039	5313	....	....	249831	257400	267104	6069920	....	8162717	....	3787920	....
Carried Eastward from Keokuk by the T. P. & W. and C. B. & Q. Railroads, and not received from the D. V. Raitroad, for 6 mos. ending Oct. 31, 1868	......	72	651	......	....	5417	80578	34844	17866	....	29886	25954	....	335854	390
Total	1628	80287	412357	52733	13417726	7582679	2949045	9298879	2210633	35476788	2268047	27608763	134017	10963101	190736

*"Other Agricultural Products" include Flour, Potatoes and Beans; and "Animal Products not otherwise specified," include Eggs, Butter, Tallow and Hides.

† Includes shipments both Eastward and Westward. The shipments by the other Roads are Eastward only.

‡ "Animal Products not otherwise specified," includes Pork, Beef, Lard, Tallow, Hides, Eggs, Butter and Poultry; and "Other Agricultural Products, Lbs.," include Flour, Meal, Grass-seeds, Hay, Potatoes, Roots and Green Fruits.

NOTE.—The above amounts do not include shipments Eastward from McGregor or Dubuque; an important item not reported. The shipments over the Des Moines Valley Railroad are for six months only--ending June 30, 1869.

ED WRIGHT, *Secretary of State.*

MILWAUKEE AND ST. PAUL RAILWAY.

Statement of Passengers Carried Eastward and Westward over the Milwaukee and St. Paul Railway, from the several Stations thereon, situated in the State of Iowa, for the year ending April 30, 1869, *and Revenue derived therefrom.*

STATIONS.	EASTWARD.		WESTWARD.		TOTAL.	
	No.	Revenue.	No.	Revenue.	No.	Revenue,
North McGregor	18609	$ 67415 97	12365	$ 105032 70	30974	$ 172447 67
Giard	28	8 70	44	87 85	72	97 55
Spaulding	13	5 30	21	23 35	34	28 65
Monona	1419	1014 90	1109	2097 62	2528	3112 52
Luana	696	515 20	307	480 47	1003	995 67
Postville	2420	2897 65	1219	2396 62	3639	5294 27
Castalia	542	612 10	368	480 67	910	1092 77
Ossian	1676	2749 58	1635	2720 06	3311	5469 64
Calmar	1820	3321 12	867	1740 05	2687	5061 17
Counover	2166	3844 90	1639	3567 45	3805	7412 35
Ridgeway	518	537 35	272	426 49	790	963 84
Cresco	2561	5571 22	2176	3398 76	4737	8969 98
Lime Springs	1607	2652 68	702	1197 00	2309	3849 68
Total	34075	91146 67	22724	123649 09	56799	214795 76

CHICAGO AND NORTHWESTERN RAILWAY.

Statement showing the number of Passengers carried to and from each Station on the Iowa Division for the year ending April 30th, 1869.

NAME OF STATIONS.	PASSENGERS ARRIVING AT EACH STATION.				PASSENGERS DEPARTING FROM EACH STATION.			
	1st Class.	2nd Class.	com-u't'n	exc'r sion.	1st Class.	2nd Class.	com-u't'n	exc'r sion.
Clinton	33906	74	......	3291	34529	......	......	3291
Camanche	1169	......	......	52	1145	......	......	52
Low Moor	1571	......	......	222	1897	......	......	222
Malone	374	......	......	9	268	......	......	9
DeWitt	12023	1	7	711	11352	......	7	711
Grand Mound	966	......	......	89	992	......	......	89
Calamus	1939	......	......	64	1951	......	......	64
Wheatland	4939	......	8	129	4780	......	8	129
Louden	3212	......	......	131	3160	......	......	131
Clarence	5401	2	......	287	5476	......	......	287
Stanwood	......	......	......	......	......	......	......	......
Mechanicsville	4574	......	......	150	4617	......	......	150
Lisbon	2115	......	......	97	2194	......	......	97
Mount Vernon	4114	......	......	193	3936	......	......	193
Bertram	1428	......	......	35	1571	......	......	35
Cedar Rapids	23974	569	7	665	22174	......	7	664
Fairfax	2386	......	......	39	2378	......	......	39
Norway	2386	......	8	27	2714	......	8	27
Blairstown	9815	......	......	127	10212	......	......	126
Luzerne	1516	......	......	2	1480	......	......	2
Belle Plaine	8163	2	......	49	7207	......	......	42
Chelsea	1768	......	......	3	2057	......	......	2
Tama	9670	......	......	49	8191	......	......	48
Orford	3020	......	......	11	3426	......	......	11
LeGrand	1765	......	......	7	1602	......	......	7
Quarry	906	......	......	1	842	......	......	1
Marshall	16905	50	......	98	17406	......	......	97
La Moille	672	......	......	2	3	......	......	......
State Centre	5403	......	......	9	5294	......	......	9
Colo	1486	4	......	4	1518	......	......	4
Nevada	6248	94	......	23	5938	......	......	23
Ames	4783	......	......	9	4606	......	......	9
Ontario	343	......	......	......	301	......	......	......
Boone	23545	458	......	42	23422	......	......	29
Moingona	5360	4	......	11	5704	......	......	5
Ogden	1180	......	......	2	1186	......	......	2
Beaver	99	......	......	......	23	......	......	......
Hager	78	......	......	......	5	......	......	......
New Jefferson	4311	......	......	1	4073	......	......	......
Scranton	311	......	......	......	335	......	......	......
Glidden	2004	......	......	2	1835	......	......	2
Carroll	2652	......	......	......	2548	......	......	......
East Side	3	......	......	......	3	......	......	......
Tip Top	14	......	......	......	3	......	......	......
West Side	159	......	......	......	99	......	......	......
Vail	41	......	......	......	15	......	......	......
Denison	2279	14	......	3	2114	......	......	3
Crawford	420	......	......	......	193	......	......	......
Dunlap	2544	......	......	4	2317	......	......	4
Woodbine	1523	12	......	6	1230	......	......	5
Logan	1925	......	......	51	1998	......	......	49
Missouri Valley Junction	11906	63	......	83	9811	......	......	54
Honey Creek	1228	......	......	......	1113	......	......	......
Crescent	334	......	......	......	221	......	......	......
Council Bluffs	15194	312	......	95	14971	419	......	9
Missouri River	14803	2904	......	2725	12960	2244	......	40

BURLINGTON AND MISSOURI RIVER RAILROAD.

Statement of the Number of Passengers carried, with Total and Average Mileage, during the year ending April 30, 1869.

MONTHS.	East.					West.					Total.					
	Thro. Passngrs	Way Passngrs	Total Passngrs	Thro. Pas. car-ri'd 1 m.	Way Pass car-ri'd 1 m.	Thro. Passngrs	Way Passngrs	Total Passngrs	Thro. Pas. car-ri'd 1 m.	Way Pas. car-ri'd 1 m.	Thro Passngrs	Way Passngrs	Total Passngrs	Total thro pass car'd 1 m	Total way pass car'd 1 m	Average mileage.
1868.																
May	117½	3615½	3733	18330	138671	143	4597½	4740½	22308	187646	260½	8213	8473½	40638	326317	5.1
June	181½	3966	4147½	28314	154586	126	4626	4752	19656	181889	307½	8592	8899½	47970	336475	5 2
July	7	3557	3564	1162	144470	5	4036½	4041½	830	165644	12	7593½	7605½	1992	310114	5.2
August	80½	4540½	4621	13363	193653	56½	5060½	5117	9379	216976	137	9601	9738	22742	410629	5.15
September	95	5576½	5671½	17100	256244	81	6104	6185	14580	278500	176	11680½	11856½	31680	534744	5.15
October	172½	5045½	5218	31050	235604	143	5738½	5881½	25740	266571	315½	10784	11099½	56790	502175	5.15
November	130½	4702½	4833	23490	213289	145½	5254	5399½	26190	236126	276	9956½	10232½	49680	449415	5.15
December	158	4681	4839	28440	202665	102	5035	5137	18360	217880	260	9716	9976	46800	420545	5.1
1869.																
January	92½	4436½	4529	16650	187528	94½	5026	5120½	17010	214323	187	9462½	9649½	33660	401851	5.15
February	79	4463	4542	14220	178727	125	5054	5179	22500	203468	204	9517	9721	36720	382195	5.15
March	153	5286½	5439½	27540	212935	201½	6643½	6845	36270	287204	354½	11930	12284½	63810	500139	5.2
April	164½	4871	5035½	29610	194825	236½	6267½	6504	42570	287023	401	11138½	11539½	72180	481848	5.15
Total	1431½	54741½	56173	249269	2313197	1459½	63443	64902½	255393	2743250	2891	118184½	121075½	504662	5056447	5.15

BURLINGTON AND MISSOURI RIVER RAILROAD.

Condensed Passenger Report for the year ending April 30th, 1869.

Bur-ling-ton.	844	1451½	1588½	7559	369½	430	2105½	52	244	319½	8143	......	53	59½	1037	48½	191½	132	1711	20	100	1263½	131	20	1129
631	Mid-dle-town	121	114½	218	7	7	15	1	6	5	71	......	......	1	8	......	1	......	7	3	......	11½	......	......	5
1275½	102	Dan-ville.	191½	415	7	9	23½	......	4½	10	78½	......	......	1	15½	....	2	4	22½	......	3	16	1	......	16
1443	74½	171	New Lon-don.	1200	19½	6½	83½	6½	16	8	110	......	......	2½	23	....	9½	......	27	3½	2	29½	1	......	20½
6546½	192½	331	1111½	Mt. Plea-sant.	1271½	264	1518	32	117½	102	2088½	......	6½	30½	171½	9	65	15	253½	4	14	116½	16	2	124½
331	11	3½	14½	1162½	Che-cau-qua.	81	151½	6	28	15½	124½	......	1	21½	8½	....	8	3	14½	......	2	10	....	1	9
300	6	6	9	277	52½	Glen-dale.	558½	2	32	7	117½	......	9	5	3	....	2	......	13	....	2	3	1	......	8½
1833½	14½	16	65½	1161	117½	448½	Fair-field.	223	1065½	299	2463½	......	4	26½	216	7	23½	12	156½	4	9	74½	6	2	69½
6	......	......	5	41	4	5	222	Whit-field.	85½	23	126½	......	½	5	9	....	1	......	9	......	......	8	....	......	9
209½	5	½	21	115½	34	28½	944	99	Bata-via.	257	634½	......	13	7½	38½	....	3	4	37½	1	4	21½	1	......	1
288	2	9	8	131	8	4½	231½	17	212	Agen-cy City.	1758	......	27	4½	58½	....	6½	17	45½	2	2	30½	4½	......	16
5644½	49½	58½	110	1990	100	113	2263½	110	569½	1720	Ot-tum-wa.	160½	1129	280½	2714½	80½	333½	106	1723½	29	88½	1007	84½	13	730
......	......	......	......	......	......	......	......	......	......	......	154	Mc Bride	......	......	......	......	......	......	......	......	......	......	......	......	......

56,173 TOTAL

64,902½ TOTAL

PASSENGERS WESTWARD.

27½		......	1	3½	2	5	9½	......	9	28	816	......	Chillicothe	92	125	2	10½	1	51	2	10	18	2	1	10
74	......	......	4	11	12	1	41	6½	17½	2	229	......	77½	Fred-eric.	477½	25½	38	13½	77½	5	1	75	4	......	44½
896	5	10	14½	177½	4	5	205½	11½	33	47½	2113½	......	166½	553½	Albia	270	387½	44½	870	12½	40	257½	17	4	138
30	......	......	......	9	1	......	1	......	......	......	89	......	2	17½	265½	Ty-rone	24	2	40½	......	9	17	......	1	11
168	......	3	12	59	2	......	23	2	12	17	275½	......	18	30	355	14	Mel-rose.	49½	237½	1	22	25	5	......	42½
144½	1	5	......	21	1	½	13	1	8	19½	106	......	6	11	48	3	64½	Rus-sell.	210	......	15	25½	......	......	9
1453	6½	18½	23	254½	8	9	163½	9½	25	42	1508½	......	59	82	795	44½	270½	274½	Chariton.	215	293½	1272	71½	19½	730
19	......	......	2½	4	......	......	4	......	½	2	23	......	2	7	6	......	2	......	234	Lu-cas.	20	31	2	2	14
110½	......	1	......	22½	1	......	11½	2	2	11	106	......	6	5	39	13	26	14	332	15	Wood-burn.	429½	5	4	97½
1008	5½	7	27½	103½	10	6	90½	3	35½	37	745	......	25½	65½	266½	9½	34½	30	1177	23½	470½	Osce-ola.	549	34½	1077½
167	......	5½	2	12	1	......	12	2	1	2	96½	......	1	4	15	4	6	1	47	2	3	368½	Mur-ray.	14	107
29	......	......	......	1	......	......	2	......	1	......	22	......	......	2	7	1	1	......	31	1	2	45	8	Thay-er.	164
1045	6	12	17	94½	3	4	84	6	6	16	824	......	16	42½	131½	17	51½	5	601	10	66	983	73½	128½	Af-ton.

PASSENGERS EASTWARD.

DES MOINES VALLEY RAILROAD.

Passenger report for six months, ending June 30th, 1869.

PASSENGERS

STATIONS.																									STATIONS.
	Keo-kuk.	835	107	392	540	564	302	828	57	90	162	60	1721	28	164	455	28	237	28	93	73	24	1212	...	Keokuk.
Sand Prairie	931	Sand Pra'e	24	38	27	13	97	18	....	....	6	1	23	.....	3	.....	.....	3	....	....	1	....	6	..	Sand Prairie.
Belfast.	167	35	Bel fast	27	12	13	14	2	1	1	2	1	2	1	.....	.....	1	.....	.....	.....	.....	.....	2	...	Belfast.
Croton.	405	37	22	Cro ton	83	58	3	25	...	13	4	1	19	.....	3	6	1	1	.....	.....	1	.....	11	.	Croton.
Farmington	539	35	15	113	Farm-ington	253	5	124	12	15	5	16	87	.....	2	5	....	2	....	4	1	....	22	...	Farmington.
Bonaparte	544	17	17	55	331	Bona parte	407	146	2	22	24	9	100	2	12	10	1	11	.....	.....	.....	2	13	...	Bonaparte.
Bentonsport	400	12	1	16	100	384	Be't'ns port.	148	7	28	36	8	111	.....	8	8	....	1	....	....	....	...	23	...	Bentonsport.
Summit	669	15	3	33	133	184	274	Sum-mit.	60	98	111	6	246	1	17	34	....	22	6	6	.....	2	59	..	Summit.
Kilbourne	38	3	....	3	16	2	15	121	Kilbourne	42	35	7	68	.....	3	3	....	....	...	.....	.....	....	4	...	Kilbourne.
Douds	72	5	....	10	8	15	28	110	39	Douds	109	10	149	4	11	13	1	10	1	7	1	...	13	...	Douds.
Independent	177	4	....	8	7	41	23	124	22	157	Inde-pend't.	112	364	2	11	4	3	10	...	11	1	2	20	...	Independent.
Alpine	66	1	1	1	13	13	10	12	1	20	120	Alpine	389	12	23	20	....	4	....	....	3	1	3	...	Alpine.
Ottumwa	2450	28	4	29	101	144	127	303	68	194	356	366	Ot-tumwa	293	1047	1278	52	492	60	221	151	66	1856	...	Ottumwa.

PASSENGERS

WEST. EAST.

Comstocks	83	.....	.....	1	.....	.....	.....	4	.....	4	10	14	260	Com-stocks	62	72	1	12	2	9	2	3	42	..	Comstocks.
Eddyville	211	.....	.....	3	3	9	4	9	4	17	8	17	1146	78	Eddy-ville.	518	26	96	16	45	37	3	131	...	Eddyville.
Oskaloosa	487	.....	.....	2	12	10	14	34	.....	16	.....	15	1580	73	542	Oska-loosa.	54	431	43	117	68	46	565	...	Oskaloosa.
Leighton	31	.....	.....	1	.....	2	2	2	.....	1	.....	1	65	1	37	66	Leigh-ton.	64	9	25	9	5	54	...	Leighton.
Pella	331	.....	.....	.....	4	10	7	14	.....	9	5	2	606	11	97	596	43	Pella.	324	300	159	43	448	8	Pella.
Otley	30	.....	.....	.....	.....	2	.....	6	.....	.....	.....	1	62	1	18	59	12	369	Otley	141	17	6	68	...	Otley
Monroe	89	2	.....	1	7	3	3	2	.....	6	4	.....	217	4	40	96	15	352	169	Mon-roe.	275	59	502	..	Monroe.
Prairie City	45	1	.....	.....	1	4	1	3	.....	.....	3	.....	167	2	33	65	9	151	41	237	Prairie City.	147	569	...	Prairie City.
Woodville	15	.....	.....	.....	.....	2	5	1	.....	2	3	.....	83	.....	7	66	6	39	4	39	149	Wood-ville.	405	.	Woodville.
Des Moines	1476	17	.....	8	30	18	4	83	9	26	14	3	2509	31	206	691	47	470	68	472	598	320	Des Moines.	57	Des Moines.
Dallas Centre	.....	.....	.....	.....	.....	.....	.....	.....	.....	.....	.....	.....	.....	.....	.....	.....	.....	5	.....	.....	.....	.....	41	Dallas.	Dallas Center.
Total west	9266	212	63	284	766	843	537	828	143	452	523	419	6695	201	980	1639	132	1386	282	748	747	320	41	..	
Total east	.....	835	131	457	662	901	828	1291	139	309	494	231	3279	343	1366	2426	168	1396	489	979	799	409	6028	65	
Totals	9266	1047	194	741	1428	1744	1365	2119	282	761	1017	650	9974	544	2346	4065	300	2782	771	1727	1546	729	6069	65	

Total No. Passengers, West.............. 27,507
Total No. Passengers, East........... 24,025

Total No. Passengers.............. 51,532

TABLE

Showing the number of miles in operation of the several Railroads in the State January 1st, 1869; the gross earnings for the year previous, and the amount of tax paid by each; also, the estimated number of miles constructed in 1869.

NAME OF ROAD.	No. miles of road in operat'n January 1st, 1869.	Gross earnings for the year ending January 1st 1869.	Am't of tax paid on gross earni'gs for the year ending Jan. 1st, 1869.	Estimated No. of miles road constructed since Jan. 1st, 1869.	Estimated No. of miles in operation Jan. 1st 1870
McGregor Western	84,600	$498235 03	$4982 35	....	84,600
McGregor and Missouri River	....	....	....	94,300	94,300
Cedar Falls and Minnesota	42,000	55465 67	554 65	33,110	75,110
Dubuque and Sioux City	142,885	970696 25	9706 96	....	142,885
Iowa Falls and Sioux City	....	....	....	119,500	119,500
Central Railway of Iowa	....	....	....	43,000	43,000
Dubuque Southwestern	54,760	172427 72	1724 27	....	54,760
North Western (Iowa Division)	354,000	3371682 28	33716 81	....	354,000
Chicago, Rock Island, and Pacific	277,549	1051828 84	10518 28	40,451	318,000
Burlington and Missouri River	180,333	841653 24	8416 53	98,807	279,140
St. Joseph and Council Bluffs	52,000	153854 93	1538 55	....	52,000
Sioux City and Pacific	75,500	127000 02	1270 00	4,500	80,000
Burlington, Cedar Rapids and Minnesota	....	....	....	67,000	67,000
Des Moines Valley	162,500	710240 94	7249 52	81,500	244,000
Keokuk and St Paul	25,000	71846 21	718 46	19,000	44,000
St. Louis and Cedar Rapids	....	....	....	42,250	42,250
	1451,127	8024931 13	80396 38	643,418	2094,545

NOTE.—The above Table was prepared from the best information at hand, and will not vary much from the true figures. The figures in the first column were obtained from the reports made to the State Treasurer pursuant to the provisions of sec. 1, chap. 196, Laws 1868, hence are correct. The estimates in the fourth column are made with the understanding, that the Cedar Falls and Minnesota Road will reach the State line by January 1st, 1870; the McGregor and Missouri River Railway will reach Clear Lake; the Iowa Falls and Sioux City will build twenty miles after this date (Nov. 4th); the Central Railroad of Iowa will reach Marshalltown; the Burlington and Missouri Road will be completed to the Council Bluffs and St. Jo. Crossing; the Des Moines Valley Road will reach Ft. Dodge; the Burlington, Cedar Rapids and Minnesota Road will reach he Washington Branch Junction, and be built from Cedar Rapids to Vinton; and the St. Louis and Cedar Rapids Road will reach Ottumwa.

In most of the foregoing cases, I am assured that the estimated amount of road to be built will be fully completed by the first of January, 1870. Should such be the case the total length of road built, not including side-tracks, from January 1st, 1869, to January 1st, 1870, will be 643 1-2 miles.

ED WRIGHT, *Secretary of State.*

TABLE

Showing the name of each Post-office in the several counties of the State, Nov. 1st, 1869, with the name of the township in which each Post-office is situated, and the Section, Township, and Range where located, as far as the same could be ascertained.

Offices printed in *Italics*, with a small *c h* in parenthesis, indicates County Seats.

ADAIR COUNTY.

Names of Townships.	Names of Post-Offices.	Location Post-Offices.			
		Pt. Sec.	Sec.	Tp.	Range.
Harrison	Arbor Hill	sw sw	34	76	30
....	Allamakee	....	..	...	..
Walnut	Casey	ne nw	3	77	32
Summerset	*Fontanelle, (c h)*	sw	17	75	32
....	French Creek	....	..	...	..
Greenfield	Greenfield	s hf	7	75	31
Grand River	Hebron	ne	34	75	30
Jefferson	Holladay's	nw se	27	77	31
Jackson	Jackson	sw nw	5	75	33
Greenfield	Schwearsburg	se	16	74	31

ADAMS COUNTY.

Names of Townships.	Names of Post-Offices.	Pt. Sec.	Sec.	Tp.	Range.
Carl	Carl	se se	10	73	33
Quincy	Corning	sw	35	72	34
Nodaway	East Nodaway	nw sw	17	71	35
Colony	Nevinville	....	2	73	32
Queen City	Queen City	se	25	72	34
Quincy	*Quincy (c h)*	nw	17	72	34
Jasper	Simpson	....	7	71	34

ALLAMAKEE COUNTY.

Names of Townships.	Names of Post-Offices.	Pt. Sec.	Sec.	Tp.	Range.
Union City	Clear Creek	nw	34	100	5
....	Dalby	....	..	...	..
Waterloo	Dorchester	....	24	100	6
Taylor	Harper's Ferry	....	24	97	2
Fairview	Ion	se	24	96	3
Fairview	Johnsonsporte	....	15	96	3
Lansing, town of	Lansing	ne sw	29	99	3
Ludlow	Ludlow	se	10	97	6
Makee	Lycurgus	nw se	3	98	5
Post	Myron	....	3	96	6
Post	Postville	....	32	96	6
Jefferson	Rossville	se ne	25	97	5

NOTE.—The location was obtained from the returns made by the Clerk of the District Court of each county. In most cases where the location is not given, the office is a new one, established since the returns above referred to were made.

ALLAMAKEE COUNTY—Continued.

Names of Townships.	Names of Post-Offices.	Location Post-Offices. Pt. Sec.	Sec.	Tp.	Range.
Union Prairie	Union Prairie	sw	27	98	6
Lafayette	Village Creek	nw ne	18	98	3
Franklin	Volney	se ne	13	96	5
Paint Creek	Waterville	nw	22	97	4
Makee	*Waukon (c. h.)*	sw se	30	98	5

APPANOOSE COUNTY.

Names of Townships.	Names of Post-Offices.	Pt. Sec.	Sec.	Tp.	Range.
Washington	Beetrace	ne	22	68	16
Caldwell	Caldwell	sw	33	68	17
Center	*Centerville (c. h.)*	ne	36	69	18
Pleasant	Cincinnati		4	67	18
Center	Dennis	sw	7	69	17
	Griffinsville				
Franklin	Hibbsville	ne	25	68	19
Chariton	Iconium	ne	5	70	18
Lincoln	Jerome	sw	3	68	19
Franklin	Livingston	nw	10	67	19
Independence	Milledgeville	sw	10	70	19
Taylor	Moravia		4	70	17
Washington	Moulton		14	68	16
Bellair	Numa	nw	18	68	18
Washington	Orleans	sw	35	69	16
Udell	Unionville	se	33	70	16
Walnut	Walnut City	sw	33	70	18
Wells	Wells' Mills	sw	16	69	16

AUDUBON COUNTY.

Names of Townships.	Names of Post-Offices.	Pt. Sec.	Sec.	Tp.	Range.
Exira	*Exira (c. h.)*		4	78	35
Audubon	Hamlin's Grove		25	78	34
Oakfield	Oakfield		19	78	35

BENTON COUNTY.

Names of Townships.	Names of Post-Offices.	Pt. Sec.	Sec.	Tp.	Range.
Iowa	Belle Plaine	sw sw	20	82	12
	Benton Center				
Leroy	Blairstown	se se	14	82	11
Harrison	Burke		11	86	10
Florence	Florenee	ne ne	20	82	9
Leroy	Luzerne	sw sw	18	82	11
Cedar	Mount Auburn	se se	14	86	11
Fremont	Robin	sw	27	83	9
Canton	Shellsburg	nw nw	14	84	9
Eden	Unity	nw nw	12	84	10
Polk	Urbanna	ne ne	34	86	9
Taylor	*Vinton (c. h)*	s hf sw	16	85	10

BLACK HAWK COUNTY.

Names of Townships.	Names of Post-Offices.	Pt. Sec.	Sec.	Tp.	Range.
Barclay	Barclay	nw	13	89	12
Bennington	Blakeville	ne ne	26	90	12
City of Cedar Falls	Cedar Falls	se nw	12	89	14
Cedar	Cedar Valley	nw	33	88	12
Spring Creek	Enterprise	nw nw	16	87	11
Poyner	Gilbertville	sw	23	88	12
Black Hawk	Hudson	nw sw	26	88	14

BLACK HAWK COUNTY—CONTINUED.

Names of Townships.	Names of Post-Offices.	Location Post-Offices.			
		Pt. Sec.	Sec.	Tp.	Range.
Big Creek	Laporte City	s hf	25	87	12
Lester	Lester	nw sw	16	90	11
Mt. Vernon	Nantrille	se	3	90	13
Poyner	Raymond	w hf nw	2	88	12
City of Waterloo	*Waterloo* (*c h*)	ne ne	26	89	13

BOONE COUNTY.

Names of Townships.	Names of Post-Offices.	Pt. Sec.	Sec.	Tp.	Range.
Des Moines	*Boonsboro* (*c h*)	nw	29	84	26
Pilot Mound	Casady's Corner	se nw	4	85	27
Dodge	Mineral Ridge	sw ne	18	85	26
Marcy	Moingona	ne ne	12	83	27
Des Moines	Montana	se	21	84	26
Pilot Mound	Pilot Mound	se nw	28	85	27
Cass	Prairie Hill	se sw	12	82	27
Yell	Riverside	se se	12	84	27
Douglas	Sweede Point	nw ne	36	82	26
Worth	Worth				
Yell	Yough	ne se	31	84	27

BREMER COUNTY.

Names of Townships.	Names of Post-Offices.	Pt. Sec.	Sec.	Tp.	Range.
Dayton	Buck Creek	ne ne	22	92	11
Jefferson	Denver	sw	24	91	13
Franklin	Eagle				
Frederika	Frederika	sw nw	18	93	12
Franklin	Grove Hill				
Polk	Horton	sw	26	93	14
Jackson	Janesville	nw ne	35	91	14
Leroy	Leroy				
Mayfield	Mayfield				
	Mentor				
Polk	Plainfield	ne	30	93	14
Lafayette	Spring Lake	se nw	17	92	14
Sumner	Sumner	se se	9	93	11
Frederika	Tripoli	nw se	33	93	21
Town of Waverly	*Waverly* (*c h*)	e hf nw	2	91	14

BUCHANAN COUNTY.

Names of Townships.	Names of Post-Offices.	Pt. Sec.	Sec.	Tp.	Range.
Newton	Atlanta	sw	27	87	7
Jefferson	Brandon	sw	27	87	10
Buffalo	Buffalo Grove	se	24	90	8
Perry	Chatham	se	9	89	10
Fairbank	Fairbank	ne	5	90	10
Hazelton	Hazelton	sw	11	90	9
City of Independence	*Independence* (*c h*)	se	34	89	9
Perry	Jesup	se	31	89	10
Fairbank	Kier	ne	21	90	10
Middlefield	Middlefield	nw	29	88	7
Washington	Otterville	ne	19	89	9
Liberty	Quasqueton	ne	34	88	8
Jefferson	Sunnyside	ne	19	87	10
Madison	Ward's Corners	se	14	90	7
Byron	Winthrop	se	36	89	8

BUENA VISTA COUNTY.

Names of Townships.	Names of Post-Offices.	Pt. Sec.	Sec.	Tp.	Range.
	Storm Lake				

BUTLER COUNTY.

Names of Townships.	Names of Post-Offices.	List of Post-Offices. Pt. Sec.	Sec.	Tp.	Range.
Monroe	Aplington		29	90	17
West Point	Boylan's Grove		18	92	17
Jefferson	*Butler Center* (*c. h*)	nw	18	91	16
Butler	Clarksville		18	95	15
Coldwater	Elm Springs	ne	12	93	17
Beaver	New Hartford	e hf ne	33	90	15
Albion	Parkersburg		30	90	16
Shell Rock	Shell Rock	ne ne	11	91	15
Albion	Swanton		4	90	16
Pittsford	Union Ridge	nw	20	92	18
Beaver	Willoughby		9	90	15

CALHOUN COUNTY.

Names of Townships.	Names of Post-Offices.	Pt. Sec.	Sec.	Tp.	Range.
Calhoun	*Lake City* (*c. h.*)	sw se	7	86	33
Sherman	Twin Lakes	ne	1	88	33
Lincoln	Yatesville	e hf nw	22	89	31

CARROLL COUNTY.

Names of Townships.	Names of Post-Offices.	Pt. Sec.	Sec.	Tp.	Range.
Sheridan	Browning	w hf se	12	85	34
Carroll	*Carroll City* (*c. h.*)	se	24	84	35
Newton	Carrollton	ne ne	1	82	34
Union	Coon Rapids	ne	34	82	33
Glidden	Glidden	se	30	84	33
	Macks				

CASS COUNTY.

Names of Townships.	Names of Post-Offices.	Pt. Sec.	Sec.	Tp.	Range.
Grant	Anita	ne ne	28	77	34
Pymosa	*Atlantic*, (*c. h.*)	sw sw	5	76	36
Edna	Edna	se sw	31	75	35
Turkey Grove	Grove City	ne sw	11	76	36
Cass	Lewis	se se	10	75	37
Union	Whitneyville	nw sw	8	75	34

CEDAR COUNTY.

Names of Townships.	Names of Post-Offices.	Pt. Sec.	Sec.	Tp.	Range.
Cass	Cedar Bluffs	ne ne	33	81	4
Fairfield	Cessford	se se	22	81	2
Town of Clarence	Clarence	se	22	82	2
Springdale	Downey	se	30	79	4
Town of Durant	Durant	s hf	36	79	1
Inland	Inland	se se	3	80	1
Springfield	Louden	ne nw	2	81	1
Massillon	Massillon	ne	14	82	1
Town of Mechanicsville	Mechanicsville	s hf	13	82	4
Iowa	Pedee	nw nw	9	79	3
Sugar Creek	Pleasant Hill	e hf nw	16	79	2
Red Oak	Red Oak	w hf se	2	81	3
Rochester	Rochester	se	2	79	3
Springdale	Springdale	sw	1	79	4
Fremont	Stanwood	sw	24	82	3
Town of Tipton	*Tipton* (*c. h.*)	nw	6	80	2
Springdale	West Branch	ne	7	79	4
Center	York Prairie	sw	1	80	2
Gower	Zoar	se	19	80	4

CERRO GORDO COUNTY.

Names of Townships.	Names of Post-Offices.	Location Post-Offices. Pt. Sec.	Sec.	Tp.	Range.
Lake	Clear Lake	se ne	13	96	22
Geneseo	Geneseo	se nw	10	94	20
Portland	Hackberry	ne ne	35	96	19
....	Lime Creek	....	..	..	..
Mason	*Mason City* (*c h*)	ne ne	9	96	20
Owens	Owens' Grove	se sw	32	96	19
Falls	Plymouth	ne ne	7	97	19
Lincoln	Rock	ne ne	8	97	21
Falls	Shell Rock Falls	ne ne	21	97	19

CHEROKEE COUNTY.

Names of Townships.	Names of Post-Offices.	Pt. Sec.	Sec.	Tp.	Range.
Cherokee	*Cherokee* (*c h*)	nw	26	92	40
Pilot	Pilot Rock	ne	28	91	40
Willow	Washta	sw	30	90	41

CHICKASAW COUNTY.

Names of Townships.	Names of Post-Offices.	Pt. Sec.	Sec.	Tp.	Range.
Bradford	Bradford	se sw	9	94	14
Chickasaw	*Chickasaw* (*c h*)	se ne	21	95	14
Stapleton	Crane Creek	ne sw	4	95	11
Dayton	Dayton Center	nw nw	21	95	13
Deerfield	Deerfield	se ne	4	96	14
Fredericksburg	Fredericksburg	sw sw	7	94	11
Jacksonville	Jacksonville	se	29	96	12
Utica	Little Turkey	se	14	96	11
Bradford	Nashua	se se	18	94	14
New Hampton	New Hampton	sw nw	7	95	12
Washington	North Washington	sw	17	96	13
....	Stapleton	....	..	..	..
Richland	Williamston	sw sw	12	94	13

CLARKE COUNTY.

Names of Townships.	Names of Post-Offices.	Pt. Sec.	Sec.	Tp.	Range.
Green Bay	Green Bay	se sw	30	71	25
Doyle	Hopeville	e hf se	18	71	27
Knox	Lacelle	ne ne	17	71	26
....	Laporte	....	..	..	..
Liberty	Liberty	sw sw	5	73	24
Troy	Murray	se sw	10	72	27
Osceola	*Osceola* (*c h*)	sw	17	72	25
Jackson	Ottawa	s hf sw	14	72	24
Washington	Prairie Grove	sw ne	5	73	26
Franklin	Smyrna	nw nw	22	71	24

CLAY COUNTY.

Names of Townships.	Names of Post-Offices.	Pt. Sec.	Sec.	Tp.	Range.
....	Gillett's Grove	....	..	..	..
....	*Peterson* (*c h*)	....	..	..	..
....	Spencer	....	..	..	..

CLAYTON COUNTY.

Names of Townships.	Names of Post-Offices.	Pt. Sec.	Sec.	Tp.	Range.
....	Ceres	....	..	..	..
Clayton	Clayton	....	1	93	3
Cox Creek	Cox Creek	sw	20	92	5

CLAYTON COUNTY—CONTINUED.

Names of Townships.	Names of Post-Offices.	Location Post-Offices. Pt. Sec.	Sec.	Tp.	Range.
Giard	Council Hill	sw	3	95	4
Volga	Communia	nw	18	92	4
Boardman	*Elkader (c. h.)*		22	93	5
Volga	Elkport	ne	35	92	4
Farmersburg	Farmersburg	se ne	8	94	4
Giard	Giard	nw nw	35	95	4
Garnavillo	Garnavillo	se	18	93	3
Jefferson	Guttenburg	se nw	17	92	2
Marion	Gem	se	2	94	6
Monona	Hardin	nw nw	6	95	5
Highland	Highland		..	...	..
Cox Creek	Littleport	se	25	92	5
Monona	Luana	se ne	8	95	5
Monona	Monona	se se	11	95	5
Millville	Millville	ne ne	16	91	2
Mendon	McGregor	e hf	22	95	3
Farmersburg	National	nw	23	94	4
	North McGregor		..	...	..
Read	Read	nw sw	9	93	4
Cass	Strawberry Point	e hf nw	22	91	6
Sperry	Saint Sebold	ne se	33	92	6
Sperry	Volga City	se sw	3	92	6
Wagner	Wagner	sw nw	5	94	5
Lodomillo	Yankee Settlement	se nw	35	91	5

CLINTON COUNTY.

Names of Townships.	Names of Post-Offices.	Pt. Sec.	Sec.	Tp.	Range.
Deep Creek	Boon Spring	sw	8	83	5e
Bloomfield	Brookfield	sw	6	83	3e
Olive	Buena Vista		6	80	2e
Sharon	Burgess	se	17	83	1e
Olive	Calamus	nw	17	81	2e
Camanche	Camanche	nw	34	81	6e
Waterford	Charlotte	se se	27	83	4e
Clinton City	*Clinton (c. h.)*		7	81	7e
DeWitt City	DeWitt		18	81	4e
Elk River	Elk River	ne ne	13	83	6e
Center	Elvira	se	34	81	6e
Orange	Grand Mound	se se	18	81	3e
Eden	Low Moor	se	22	81	5e
Lyons City	Lyons		31	83	7e
Eden	Malone	ne	24	81	4e
Orange	Orange	se	31	81	3e
Liberty	Toronto	Lot 9	17	82	1e
Welton	Welton	nw se	4	82	3e
Spring Rock	Wheatland	sw	10	81	1e

CRAWFORD COUNTY.

Names of Townships.	Names of Post-Offices.	Pt. Sec.	Sec.	Tp.	Range.
Union	Crawford Station		3	82	40
Denison	*Denison (c. h.)*		11	83	39
Milford	Deloit		7	84	38
	West Side		..	...	..

DALLAS COUNTY.

Names of Townships.	Names of Post-Offices.	Pt. Sec.	Sec.	Tp.	Range.
Adel	*Adel (c. h.)*		..	...	..
Spring Valley	Alton		..	...	..

DALLAS COUNTY—Continued.

Names of Townships.	Names of Post-Offices.	Location Post-Offices. Pt. Sec.	Sec.	Tp.	Range.
Boone	Boone	sw	29	78	26
	Dallas Center		..	..	..
Adel	De Soto	ne	30	78	27
Union	Dexter	ne	31	78	29
Linn	Greenvale	sw	10	79	29
Dallas	Linden	ne	3	81	29
Boone	Nordyke	se	24	78	26
Sugar Grove	Pierce's Point	sw se	7	80	27
Union	Redfield		4	78	29
Des Moines	Snyder	ne	26	81	26
	Tracy		..	..	..
Adel	Van Meter	ne	27	78	27
	Waukee Station		..	..	..
Des Moines	Xenia	se	5	81	26

DAVIS COUNTY.

Names of Townships.	Names of Post-Offices.	Pt. Sec.	Sec.	Tp.	Range.
Marion	Albany	sw	6	70	15
Bloomfield	*Bloomfield* (*c h*)	ne	25	69	14
	Brown's Mills		..	..	..
Lick Creek	Chequist	nw ne	32	70	13
Drakeville	Drakeville	sw sw	4	69	14
Lick Creek	Floris	nw nw	14	70	13
Fabius	Monterey	ne ne	33	68	15
Marion	Oak Springs	nw ne	22	70	15
Prairie	Pulaski	se	7	68	12
Wycondah	Savannah	se	3	67	14
Grove	Stilesville	nw	3	67	13
Union	Troy	ne	26	69	12
Fox River	West Grove	sw sw	35	69	15

DECATUR COUNTY.

Names of Townships.	Names of Post-Offices.	Pt. Sec.	Sec.	Tp.	Range.
	Davis City		..	..	..
Decatur	Decatur	e hf sw	27	69	26
Garden Grove	Garden Grove	nw	34	70	24
High Point	High Point		..	69	24
Center	*Leon* (*c h*)	se sw	28	69	25
New Buda	New Buda		..	67	26
Hamilton	Nine Eagles	ne	28	67	25
Franklin	Prairieville		..	70	25
Fayette	Sedgewick		..	67	27
Burrell	Terre Haute		..	68	26
Richland	Westervelt's Mills		..	70	27

DELAWARE COUNTY.

Names of Townships.	Names of Post-Offices.	Pt. Sec.	Sec.	Tp.	Range.
Oneida	Almoral	ne sw	11	89	4
Prairie	Barryville	nw	35	88	6
Richland	Campton	se sw	19	90	6
Colony	Colesburgh	nw se	4	90	3
Oneida	Delaware	ne sw	32	89	4
Delhi	*Delhi* (*c h*)	se	17	88	4
Oneida	Earlville	nw nw	36	89	4
Richland	Forestville	nw ne	22	90	6

DELAWARE COUNTY—Continued.

Names of Townships.	Names of Post-Offices.	Location Post-Offices. Pt. Sec.	Sec.	Tp.	Range.
Elk	Greeley	nw ne	29	90	4
Hazel Green	Hazel Green	ne sw	12	87	5
South Fork	Hopkinton	se	13	87	4
Delaware	Manchester	nw ne	32	89	5
Coffin's Grove	Masonville	ne	31	89	6
Milo	Milo	se	32	88	5
Richland	Mount Hope	sw nw	35	90	6
South Fork	Sand Springs	nw	27	87	3
Adams	Tower Hill	se nw	14	87	6
Union	Uniontown	ne ne	18	87	4
Honey Creek	York	sw sw	4	90	5

DES MOINES COUNTY.

Names of Townships.	Names of Post-Offices.	Pt. Sec.	Sec.	Tp.	Range.
Augusta	Augusta	sw	4	69	4
City of Burlington	*Burlington (c. h.)*	pt sec 4 5 7 8 9	9	69	2
Danville	Danville	nw	15	70	4
Franklin	Dodgeville	se	15	71	3
Franklin	Franklin Mills	se	35	71	3
Huron	Huron	se	2	72	2
Benton	Kingston	ne sw	1	71	2
Yellow Springs	Kossuth	nw	30	72	2
Washington	La Vega	ne	21	72	4
Yellow Springs	Linton	ne	3	72	3
Danville	Middletown	se	25	70	4
Yellow Springs	Northfield	se	6	72	2
Danville	Parrish	sw	33	70	4
Pleasant Grove	Pleasant Grove	ne	11	71	4
Pleasant Grove	South Flint	nw	27	71	4
Union	Vandyke	se	7	69	3

DICKINSON COUNTY.

Names of Townships.	Names of Post-Offices.	Pt. Sec.	Sec.	Tp.	Range.
Okoboji	Okoboji	se	30	99	36
Center Grove	*Spirit Lake (c. h.)*	ne	4	99	36

DUBUQUE COUNTY.

Names of Townships.	Names of Post-Offices.	Pt. Sec.	Sec.	Tp.	Range.
Liberty	Allison		22	90	2w
Table Mound	Ballyclough	sw	15	88	2e
	Bankston				
Whitewater	Cascade	sw nw	31	87	1w
Concord	Cottage Hill	ne sw	26	90	1w
City of Dubuque	*Dubuque (c. h.)*	4th ward	c.	89	3e
Jefferson	Durango	sw	36	90	1e
New Wine	Dyersville				
Taylor	Epworth		10	88	1w
Taylor	Farley		7	88	1w
	Franklin				
Mosalem	Kings	se	21	88	3e
Center	Lattner's	se	31	89	1e
Prairie Creek	New Milleray	se	11	87	1e
	New Vienna				
Prairie Creek	Ogden	se	16	87	1e
Vernon	Peosta	nw	9	88	1e
Concord	Pin Oak	ne	20	90	1w
Jefferson	Richardsville	ne	30	90	1e

DUBUQUE COUNTY—Continued.

Names of Townships.	Names of Post-Offices.	Location Post-Offices.			
		Pt. Sec.	Sec.	Tp.	Range.
Table Mound	Rockdale	nw	1	88	2e
	Sheffield				
Jefferson	Sherrill's Mount	se	13	90	1e
Iowa	Tivoli	se se	17	89	1w
Dodge	Worthington		31	88	2w
Washington	Zwingle	se se	35	87	2e

EMMET COUNTY.

Names of Townships.	Names of Post-Offices.	Pt. Sec.	Sec.	Tp.	Range.
Armstrong's Grove	Armstrong's Grove	nw	36	99	31
Emmet	Emmet	sw	26	100	34
Estherville	*Estherville* (*c. h.*)	se	10	99	34
High Lake	High Lake	se	22	98	33

FAYETTE COUNTY.

Names of Townships.	Names of Post-Offices.	Pt. Sec.	Sec.	Tp.	Range.
Fairfield	Brush Creek	se	28	92	7
Richland	Bethel	se ne	4	94	10
Clermont	Clermont	ne sw	34	95	7
Auburn	Douglas	nw ne	35	95	9
Dover	Eldorado	se sw	7	95	8
Eden	Eden	sw sw	25	95	10
Pleasant Valley	Elgin	se ne	14	94	7
Westfield	Fayette	nw	28	93	8
Windsor	Hawkeye	ne sw	20	94	9
Illyria	Illyria	nw	5	93	7
Westfield	Lima	s hf nw	13	93	8
Fremont	Mill	se	29	92	10
Jefferson	Otsego	se sw	26	91	9
Putnam	Putnam	se	28	91	7
Richland	Richfield	nw sw	2	94	10
Smithfield	Seaton	sw sw	29	92	8
Scott	Scott Center	sw	17	91	8
Fairfield	Taylorville	ne	22	92	7
Eden	Waucoma	sw se	9	95	10
Illyria	Wadena	ne sw	27	93	7
West Union	*West Union* (*c. h.*)	ne ne	17	94	8
Banks	Wilson Grove	ne nw	18	93	10

FLOYD COUNTY.

Names of Townships.	Names of Post-Offices.	Pt. Sec.	Sec.	Tp.	Range.
St. Charles	*Charles City.* (*c. h.*)	ne	12	95	16
Floyd	Floyd	se	16	96	16
Cedar	Howardville	ne	36	97	16
Union	Marble Rock	sw	9	94	17
Rock Grove	Nora Springs	se	7	96	18
Rockford	Rockford	se	10	95	18
Rock Grove	Rock Grove City	nw	21	96	18
Ulster	Ulster	sw	10	95	17

FRANKLIN COUNTY.

Names of Townships.	Names of Post-Offices.	Pt. Sec.	Sec.	Tp.	Range.
	Chapin				
	Coldwater				
	Geneva				
	Hampton (*c. h.*)				
	Ingham				
	Maysville				

FRANKLIN COUNTY—CONTINUED.

Names of Townships.	Names of Post-Offices.	Location Post-Offices Pt. Sec.	Sec.	Tp.	Range.
	Oakland Valley				
	Otisville				
	Shobe's Grove				
	Washburn				

NOTE.—No report from Franklin county. The above were taken from U. S. P. O. list

FREMONT COUNTY.

Names of Townships.	Names of Post-Offices.	Pt. Sec.	Sec.	Tp.	Range.
Scott	Bartlett	ne nw	9	70	43
Benton	Eastport			68	43
Franklin	Hamburg	se.	21	67	42
Fisher	Manti	nw sw	36	69	40
Benton	Percival			69	43
Scott	Plum Hollow	nw se	35	70	43
Sidney	*Sidney* (*c h*)	sw	26	69	42
Ross	Tabor	ne	4	70	42
	Walnut Creek				

GREENE COUNTY.

Names of Townships.	Names of Post-Offices.	Pt. Sec.	Sec.	Tp.	Range.
Jefferson	*Jefferson* (*c h*)	nw	8	83	30
Kendrick	Northville	nw nw	3	84	32
Washington	Rippey	se sw	8	82	29
Kendrick	Scranton Station	ne nw	11	83	32

GRUNDY COUNTY.

Names of Townships.	Names of Post-Offices.	Pt. Sec.	Sec.	Tp.	Range.
Palermo	*Grundy Center* (*c h*)	ne	12	87	17
Lincoln	Lincoln Center	sw	10	88	16

GUTHRIE COUNTY.

Names of Townships.	Names of Post-Offices.	Pt. Sec.	Sec.	Tp.	Range.
Bear Grove	Bear Grove	ne ne	24	79	33
Jackson	Dale City		6	78	30
Thompson	Dalmanutha				
Highland	Dodge	sw se	7	81	32
	Guthrie				
Center	Guthrie Center	sw	6	79	31
	Macksville				
Dodge	Moffit's Grove	sw sw	3	80	31
Cass	*Panora* (*c h*)	se se	32	80	30

HAMILTON COUNTY.

Names of Townships.	Names of Post-Offices.	Pt. Sec.	Sec.	Tp.	Range.
Blairsburg	Blairsburg	se	36	89	24
Webster	Homer	sw	6	87	26
Marion	Hook's Point	ne	6	86	26
Lyon	Lakin's Grove	nw	24	87	24
Scott	Randall	nw	30	86	23
Boone	*Webster City* (*c h*)	ne	1	88	26
	Williams				

HANCOCK COUNTY.

Names of Townships.	Names of Post-Offices.	Pt. Sec.	Sec.	Tp.	Range.
Ellington	*Concord* (*c h*)	se sw	31	96	23
Ellington	Ellington	sw se	29	97	23
Amsterdam	Upper Grove	sw sw	26	94	23

HARDIN COUNTY.

Names of Townships.	Names of Post-Offices.	Location Pt. Sec.	Post-Offices. Sec.	Tp.	Range.
Alden	Alden		18	89	21
Ætna	Ackley		2	89	19
Jackson	Berlin	s hf.	22	88	20
Buckeye	Cottage		25	88	21
	Delanti				
Eldora	*Eldora* (*c h*)	pt.	7 & 8	87	19
	Hardin City				
Clay	Lithopolis		28	88	19
Hardin	Iowa Falls	e hf.	13	89	21
Grant	New Providence	pt.	3 & 10	86	20
Pleasant	Point Pleasant	w hf.	18	87	20
	Tipton Grove				
Union	Union		22	86	19

HARRISON COUNTY.

Names of Townships.	Names of Post-Offices.	Pt. Sec.	Sec.	Tp.	Range.
	Bigler's Grove				
Calhoun	Calhoun	se sw	19	79	43
Harrison	Dunlap		3	81	41
Lagrange	Harris' Grove	nw sw	6	78	42
Little Sioux	Little Sioux	se.	12	81	45
Jefferson	Logan	nw nw	19	79	42
Magnolia	*Magnolia* (*c h*)	ne se	32	80	43
Saint John	Missouri Valley	ne sw	15	78	44
Taylor	Modale	se se	30	79	44
Morgan	Mondamin	ne ne	25	80	45
Jefferson	Reeder's Mills	ne ne	34	79	42
Saint John	Saint John	ne se	27	78	44
Union	Unionburg	ne se	23	78	42
	Whitesboro				
Boyer	Woodbine	sw se	14	80	42
Cincinnati	Yazoo	nw nw	13	78	45

HENRY COUNTY.

Names of Townships.	Names of Post-Offices.	Pt. Sec.	Sec.	Tp.	Range.
Jackson	Boylestown			70	6
Canaan	Cotton Grove	se.	4	72	5
Baltimore	Lowell	se.	28	70	5
Jefferson	Marshall	ne ne	9	73	7
Center	*Mt. Pleasant* (*c h*)	nw	9	71	6
New London	New London	nw	26	71	5
	Oakland Mills				
Tippecanoe	Rome	ne se	3	71	7
Salem	Salem	nw	24	70	7
Trenton	Trenton	nw nw	11	72	7
Wayne	Wayne	sw.	3	73	6
Scott	Winfield	nw	16	73	5
	Winona				

HOWARD COUNTY.

Names of Townships.	Names of Post-Offices.	Pt. Sec.	Sec.	Tp.	Range.
Howard	Busti	nw sw	31	98	13
Vernon Springs	*Cresco* (*c h*)	sw	23	99	11
Chester	Eatonville	ne ne	8	100	13
Forest City	Foreston	ne ne	15	100	12
Howard Center	Howard Center	sw sw	24	99	12

HOWARD COUNTY—Continued.

Names of Townships.	Names of Post-Offices.	Location Post-Offices.			
		Pt. Sec.	Sec.	Tp.	Range.
Forest City	Lime Springs	se	20	100	12
New Oregon	New Oregon	nw	2	98	11
Paris	Pond Valley	ne	36	98	12
Saratoga	Saratoga	sw	20	99	13

HUMBOLDT COUNTY.

Names of Townships.	Names of Post-Offices.	Pt. Sec.	Sec.	Tp.	Range.
Spring Vale	Addison	ne	26	91	29
Dakota	*Dakota (c. h.)*	sw	6	91	28
Humboldt	Lott's Creek	se	13	93	29
Rutland	Rutland	nw	29	92	29
Spring Vale	Spring Vale	e hf	1	91	29
	Sylvan Retreat				
Vernon	Viona	se	33	93	27
Wacousta	Wacousta	sw	32	93	30

IDA COUNTY.

Names of Townships.	Names of Post-Offices.	Pt. Sec.	Sec.	Tp.	Range.
Corwin	*Ida (c. h.)*		15	87	30

IOWA COUNTY.

Names of Townships.	Names of Post-Offices.	Pt. Sec.	Sec.	Tp.	Range.
Fillmore	Foote	se se	35	78	10
Sumner	Genoa Bluffs	se sw	32	80	11
Iowa	Homestead	sw sw	2	80	9
Honey Creek	Koszta	ne	14	81	12
Hartford	Ladora	ne	12	80	12
Fillmore	Lytle City	ne	1	78	10
Marengo City	*Marengo (c. h.)*	ne	25	81	11
English	Millersburg	nw sw	8	78	11
English	North English	nw sw	36	78	11
	Rest				
Troy	Stellapolis	sw sw	10	79	10
York	York Center	s hf nw	9	79	9
Hartford	Victor	nw	19	80	12

JACKSON COUNTY.

Names of Townships.	Names of Post-Offices.	Pt. Sec.	Sec.	Tp.	Range.
Perry	*Andrew (c. h.)*	se	22	85	3e
Bellevue	Bellevue			86	4e
Brandon	Canton	nw nw	19	85	1e
Richland	Cottonville	nw	27	86	3e
Farmer's Creek	Farmer's Creek	nw ne	11	85	2e
Farmer's Creek	Fulton	ne sw	24	85	2e
Butler	Garry Owen	s hf	3	86	1e
Farmer's Creek	Iron Hills	nw nw	29	85	2e
Prairie Springs	Lamotte		33	87	3e
Maquoketa	Maquoketa	e hf se	20	84	3e
Monmouth	Mill Rock	nw	27	84	1e
Monmouth	Monmouth	nw	18	84	1e
Van Buren	Mt. Alger	se ne	24	84	5e
Otter Creek	Otter Creek	sw sw	23	86	2e
Brandon	Ozark	se sw	5	85	1e
Union	Sabula	sw	20	84	7e
Tete Des Morts	Saint Donatus	center of	7	87	4e
Van Buren	Spragueville	sw nw	19	84	5e

JACKSON COUNTY—CONTINUED.

Names of Townships.	Names of Post-Offices.	Location Post-Offices.			
		Pt. Sec.	Sec.	Tp.	Range.
Jackson	Spring Brook	se	13	85	4e
Iowa	Sterling	sw	15	84	6e
Fairfield	Union Center	se	30	84	4e
Van Buren	Van Buren	sw ne	15	84	5e
Washington	Wickliffe	ne	23	85	5e

JASPER COUNTY.

Names of Townships.	Names of Post-Offices.	Pt. Sec.	Sec.	Tp.	Range.
Clear Creek	Clyde	ne sw	11	81	21
Mound Prairie	Colfax	n hf sw	1	79	21
Elk Creek	Galesburg	se ne	17	78	18
Poweshiek	Greencastle	nw	14	80	21
Malaka	Horn	sw	14	81	19
	Jasper City				
Lynn Grove	Lynnville	nw ne	11	78	17
Fairview	Monroe		36	78	20
Newton	*Newton (c h)*	nw	34	80	19
Des Moines	Prairie City	ne	2	78	21
Richland	Sugar Creek	sw ne	25	79	17
Des Moines	Vandalia	sw	20	78	21
	Warren Grove				
	Williamsville				

JEFFERSON COUNTY.

Names of Townships.	Names of Post-Offices.	Pt. Sec.	Sec.	Tp.	Range.
Polk	Abingdon	sw	33	73	11
Black Hawk	Baker	ne	23	73	10
Locust Grove	Botavia	ne	31	72	11
Locust Grove	Brookville	nw	11	72	11
Fairfield	*Fairfield (c h)*	pt 26 and	27	72	10
Walnut	Germanville	nw	27	73	8
Round Prairie	Glasgow	ne	21	71	8
Lockridge	Glendale	sw	32	72	8
Penn	Harvey's Mills	ne nw	26	73	9
Liberty	Libertyville	w hf ne	18	71	10
Lockridge	Lockridge	sw se	34	72	8
Walnut	Merrimac		36	73	8
Penn	Pleasant Plain	nw ne	11	73	9
Buchanan	Salina	ne ne ne	13	72	9
Cedar	Wooster	sw nw	13	71	9

JOHNSON COUNTY.

Names of Townships.	Names of Post-Offices.	Pt. Sec.	Sec.	Tp.	Range.
Washington	Amish		28	78	8
Sharon	Belle Air	se ne	34	78	7
	Big Springs				
Liberty	Bon Accord		18	78	6
Clear Creek	Copi	se se	30	80	7
Madison	Chase	sw	32	81	7
	Coralville				
Monroe	Danforth	sw sw	3	81	8
Washington	Frank Pierce		12	78	8
Iowa City	*Iowa City (c h)*	ne qr	10	79	6
New Port	New Port Center	se qr	18	80	5
Penn	North Liberty	se qr	12	80	7

JOHNSON COUNTY—CONTINUED.

Names of Townships.	Names of Post-Offices.	Location Post-Offices. Pt. Sec.	Sec.	Tp.	Range.
Graham	Oasis	se qr	26	80	5
Oxford	Oxford	nw qr	21	80	8
Fremont	Palestine	se se	13	77	6
Liberty	Seventy-Eight		28	78	6
Liberty	South Liberty		..	..	..
Jefferson	Shueyville		3	81	7
Big Grove	Solon	ne	24	81	6
Clear Creek	Tiffin	sw se	28	80	7
Hardin	Windham		34	79	8

JONES COUNTY.

Names of Townships.	Names of Post-Offices.	Pt. Sec.	Sec.	Tp.	Range.
Clay	*Anamosa (c h)*		..	84	4
Jackson	Bowens Prairie		..	86	3
	Castle Grove		..	..	..
	Clayford		..	85	4
Cass	Clay Mills		..	85	4
Wayne	Edinburg		25	85	3
Fairview	Fairview		..	84	4
Castle Grove	Grove Creek		..	86	4
Fairview	Highland Grove		..	84	4
Oxford	Johnson		..	85	2
Scotch Grove	Langworthy		..	85	3
Greenfield	Madison		..	84	2
Hale	Monticello		..	83	2
Madison	Oxford Mills		..	83	1
Richland	Scotch Grove		..	85	2
Monticello	Walnut Fork		..	83	3
Wayne	Wyoming		..	84	1

KEOKUK COUNTY.

Names of Townships.	Names of Post-Offices.	Pt. Sec.	Sec.	Tp.	Range.
Adams	Aurora	ne se	4	77	12
Sigourney	Baden		36	76	11
Benton	Butler	w hf se	27	74	13
Liberty	Chandler	sw ne	23	77	10
Prairie	Coal Creek	sw	29	77	13
	Creswell		..	..	..
Sigourney	Garibaldi		..	75	11
	Hayesville		..	..	..
Jackson	Ioka	se se	28	74	11
Lancaster	Lancaster	ne	30	75	11
Lancaster	Manhattan	se	3	74	11
Steady Run	Martinsburg	sw	28	74	12
Richland	Richland	sw	27	74	10
Sigourney	*Sigourney (c h)*	ne	2	75	12
English River	South English	nw nw	25	77	11
Washington	Springfield	s hf sw	28	76	13
Clear Creek	Talleyrand	ne ne	23	75	10
English River	Webster	sw se	30	77	11
Washington	What Cheer	sw sw	10	76	13
	White Pigeon		..	..	..

KOSSUTH COUNTY.

Names of Townships.	Names of Post-Offices.	Pt. Sec.	Sec.	Tp.	Range.
Algona	*Algona (c h)*	sw	2	95	29
	Buffalo Fork	se	10	97	28

KOSSUTH COUNTY—CONTINUED.

Names of Townships.	Names of Post-Offices.	Location Post-Offices. Pt. Sec.	Sec.	Tp.	Range.
....	Irvington.................	se..........	30	95	28
....	Kossuth Center............	sw..........	20	96	28
....	Seneca	ne..........	8	98	30

LOUISA COUNTY.

Names of Townships.	Names of Post-Offices.	Pt. Sec.	Sec.	Tp.	Range.
Marshall..................	Cairo.....................	nw	28	74	4
Columbus City............	Clifton...................	n hf........	23	75	5
Columbus City............	Columbus City.............	ne.	36	75	5
Concord..................	Fredonia	lot 2........	20	75	4
Grand View...............	Grand View................	sw..........	22	75	3
Grand View	Letts.....................	ne.	6	75	3
Morning Sun..............	Morning Sun...............	se....	25	73	4
Oakland..................	Port Allen................	sw..........	25	76	5
Port Louisa..............	Port Louisa...............	lot 4........	5	74	2
Jefferson	Toolsborough	nw..........	11	73	2
Morning Sun..............	Virginia Grove	nw..........	16	73	4
Wapello	*Wapello (c h)*...............	n hf........	27	74	3

LUCAS COUNTY.

Names of Townships.	Names of Post-Offices.	Pt. Sec.	Sec.	Tp.	Range.
Union	Argo......................	sw..........	3	71	23
Pleasant	Belinda...................	se..........	18	73	20
Chariton	*Chariton (c h)*..............	....	..	..	..
Warren...................	Freedom	se..	25	71	22
Warren	Henderson.................	nw........	19	71	23
Cedar	La Grange.................	se se........	25	72	20
Union	Last Chance	sw..........	7	71	23
Jackson	Lucas	ne ne.......	22	72	23
Otter Creek..............	Norwood	sw	14	73	23
....	Ola	....	..	..	..
Washington...............	Russell	ne.	6	71	20
Jackson..................	Tallahoma	se..........	1	72	23
Liberty..................	White Breast	ne ne.......	22	73	22

LEE COUNTY.

Names of Townships.	Names of Post-Offices.	Pt. Sec.	Sec.	Tp.	Range.
Van Buren	Belfast	ne sw	2	66	7
Cedar	Big Mound	sw..........	20	69	7
Charleston...............	Charleston................	e hf.........	22	67	6
Marion	Clay's Grove..............	ne se	29	69	6
Van Buren................	Croton....................	sw..........	20	67	7
Denmark	Denmark	sw..........	28	69	4
Franklin	Dover	se se........	8	68	6
Madison	*Fort Madison (c h)*..........	....	..	..	..
Franklin.................	Franklin Center	s hf se......	23	68	6
Jefferson	Jeffersonville	nw	16	67	5
Green Bay................	Jollyville	se..........	7	68	3
Jackson..................	Keokuk....................	....	..	..	..
Montrose	Montrose	se	10	66	5
Charleston...............	New Boston................	nw	36	67	6
Marion	Pilot Grove	sw	10	69	6
Harrison	Primrose..................	nw	23	68	7
Marion...................	Saint Paul................	ne nw	23	69	6
Montrose	Sandusky..................	se	10	66	5
Montrose.................	Summitville	sw	33	66	5

LEE COUNTY—CONTINUED.

Names of Townships.	Names of Post-Offices.	Location Post-Offices. Pt. Sec.	Sec.	Tp.	Range.
Des Moines	Vincennes	se	20	66	6
Van Buren	Warren	nw sw	1	67	7
West Point	West Point	e hf	5	68	5

LINN COUNTY.

Names of Townships.	Names of Post-Offices.	Pt. Sec.	Sec.	Tp.	Range.
Bertram	Bertram	sw	34	83	6
Rapids	Cedar Rapids		21 28	83	7
Maine	Central City	ne	2	85	6
Washington	Center Point	Cent'l. Point	9	85	8
Monroe	Dry Creek	ne	29	84	7
Fairfax	Fairfax	ne	16	82	8
Otter Creek	Flemingville	ne	16	85	7
Otter Creek	Lafayette	ne	16	85	7
Franklin	Lisbon	w hf	12	82	5
Marion	*Marion (c. h.)*	nw	6	83	6
Franklin	Mt. Vernon	s hf	10	82	5
Jackson	Nugent's Grove	nw	12	86	6
Fayette	Palo	se	20	84	8
Jackson	Paris	sw	19	86	6
Bowlder	Prairieburg	nw	28	86	5
Lime	Prospect Hill	se	12	83	5
Maine	Rural				
Spring Grove	Spring Grove				
Brown	Springville	sw	28	84	5
Spring Grove	Troy Mills	ne	5	86	7
Jackson	Valley Farm	sw	16	86	6
Brown	Viola	nw	14	84	5
Maine	Wapsa	sw	10	85	6
Maine	Waubeek	se	18	85	5
College	Western College				
Spring Grove	West Prairie	sw	23	86	7

MADISON COUNTY.

Names of Townships.	Names of Post-Offices.	Pt. Sec.	Sec.	Tp.	Range.
Monroe	Clanton	sw ne	10	74	28
Madison	Earlham	s hf sw	6	77	28
Crawford	Ellsworth	e hf sw	21	76	26
Monroe	Kasson	se sw	20	74	28
Webster	Middle River	nw	6	75	29
Walnut	Ohio	e hf ne	24	74	27
Walnut	Peru	n hf se	3	74	27
South	Saint Charles	n hf ne	24	75	26
Grand River	Venus		16	74	29
Center	*Winterset (c. h.)*	s e	36	76	28

MAHASKA COUNTY.

Names of Townships.	Names of Post-Offices.	Pt. Sec.	Sec.	Tp.	Range.
Pleasant Grove	Agricola	se qr	4	77	14
Scott	Auburn	w hf ne	26	75	17
Oskaloosa	Beacon	ne	27	75	16
Scott	Bellefontaine	se	19	75	17
Adams	Buck Horn	nw ne	15	76	15
Jefferson	Eveland Grove	sw ne	16	74	17
Jefferson	Ferry	ne ne	2	74	17
Madison	Farmersville	sw nw	24	76	16

MAHASKA COUNTY—CONTINUED.

Names of Townships.	Names of Post-Offices.	Location Post-Offices. Pt. Sec.	Sec.	Tp.	Range.
Prairie	Flint		..	...	..
Cedar	Fremont	e hf	14	74	14
Des Moines	Givin	w hf sw	12	74	16
Richland	Granville	se sw	1	77	17
Monroe	Hopewell	ne	34	76	14
Monroe	Indianapolis	se	11	76	14
Black Oak	Leighton	se sw	35	76	17
Prairie	New Sharon		13	77	16
Oskaloosa	*Oskaloosa* (*c. h.*)		..	75	15
Richland	Peoria	se nw	22	77	17
Union	Union Mills	se	22	77	15
White Oak	White Oak	nw sw	20	75	14

MARION COUNTY.

Names of Townships.	Names of Post-Offices.	Pt. Sec.	Sec.	Tp.	Range.
Indiana	Attica	nw	11	74	19
Perry	Bennington	n hf nw	13	77	21
Franklin	Caloma	se se	19	75	21
Washington	Columbia	nw	34	74	20
Dallas	Dallas	sw se	2	74	21
Clay	English Settlement	ne	18	75	18
Washington	Gosport	nw sw	15	74	20
Liberty	Hamilton	se	35	74	18
Clay	Iola	se	31	76	18
Knoxville	*Knoxville* (*c. h.*)	nw	7	75	19
	Mennon		..	...	..
Dallas	Newbern	se se	31	74	21
Summit	Otley	ne nw	32	77	19
Lake Prairie	Pella	s hf	3	76	18
Pleasant Grove	Pleasantville	sw nw	15	76	21
Red Rock	Red Rock	se	36	77	20
Franklin	Star	sw sw	13	75	21
Swan	Wheeling	nw ne	5	76	21

MARSHALL COUNTY.

Names of Townships.	Names of Post-Offices.	Pt. Sec.	Sec.	Tp.	Range.
Iowa	Albion	e hf nw	6	84	18
Bangor	Bangor	w hf	17	85	19
Liberty	Biven's Grove	nw	27	85	20
	Cedar Cross Roads		..	..	..
Eden	Edenville	s hf ne	9	82	20
Liberty	Illinois Grove	nw	8	85	20
Jefferson	Laurel	sw	22	82	18
	Liscomb		..	...	..
LeGrand	LeGrand	sw	12	83	17
Washington	Lamaile	nw	2	83	19
Marietta	Marietta		..	...	..
Marshall	*Marshalltown* (*c. h.*)	sw se	26	84	18
Minerva	Minerva	ne	3	84	20
	Quarry		..	...	..
State Center	State Center	sw ne	10	83	20
	Stanford		..	...	..
Jefferson	Timber Creek	ne	1	82	18
Vienna	Vienna	nw	22	85	17

MILLS COUNTY.

Names of Townships.	Names of Post-Offices.	Location Post-Offices. Pt. Sec.	Sec.	Tp.	Range.
Anderson	Benton	nw ne	25	73	41
Glenwood	*Glenwood (c h)*	nw sw	12	72	43
	Haynie				
Platteville	Pacific City	se se	9	72	43
	Wahaghbonsy				
White Cloud	White Cloud	nw nw	2	71	41

MITCHELL COUNTY.

Names of Townships.	Names of Post-Offices.	Pt. Sec.	Sec.	Tp.	Range.
Burr Oak	Brownville	ne	1	98	16
Jenkins	Doran	ne	34	99	15
Mitchell	*Mitchell (c h)*	s hf ne	9	98	17
Cedar	Merona	ne qr	17	97	17
	Merva				
	Nelson				
Newburg	Newburg	se sw	14	99	18
Osage	Osage	se se	23	98	17
Otranto	Otranto	nw sw	8	100	18
Jenkins	Riceville	se	25	99	15
Rock	Rock Creek	nw nw	22	98	18
Saint Ansgar	Saint Ansgar	nw	24	99	18
Staceyville	Staceyville	center sec	31	100	16
Cedar	Watertown	nw	13	97	17
Wayne	Wentworth	nw	36	100	15
Mitchell	West Mitchell	ne se	8	98	17

MONONA COUNTY.

Names of Townships.	Names of Post-Offices.	Pt. Sec.	Sec.	Tp.	Range.
Kennebec	Arcola	sw	28	84	44
Belvidere	Belvidere	se	11	83	44
Center	Castana	se	23	84	44
	Grant Center				
Maple	Mapleton	se	14	85	43
Franklin	*Onawa City (c h)*		4	83	45
Spring Valley	Spring Valley	nw	16	82	43
Soldier	Saint Clair	se	4	83	42
Grant	Ticonic	sw	22	85	44
West Fork	West Fork	nw	24	85	46

MONROE COUNTY.

Names of Townships.	Names of Post-Offices.	Pt. Sec.	Sec.	Tp.	Range.
Troy	*Albia (c h)*	nw	22	72	17
Cedar	Coalton	nw	24	73	19
	Cuba				
Jackson	East Melrose		4	71	19
Pleasant	Fredrick	s hf sw	26	73	16
Guilford	Georgetown		29	72	18
Bluff Creek	Half-Way Prairie				
Union	Lovilia		10	73	18
Jackson	Osprey	ne	32	71	19
Cedar	Thompsonville		2	73	19
Franklin	Tyrone		5	71	18
Urbana	Urbana City		34	71	16
Cedar	Weller		20	73	19

MONTGOMERY COUNTY.

Names of Townships.	Names of Post-Offices.	Location Post-Offices. Pt. Sec.	Sec.	Tp.	Range.
West	Carr's Point	se se	6	71	39
Red Oak	Frankfort	sw	17	72	37
Douglas	Grant	ne ne	9	73	36
Red Oak	*Red Oak Junction* (*c h*)	nw	28	72	38
Washington	Sciola	sw	16	72	36
Jackson	Valiska	ne nw	27	71	36

MUSCATINE COUNTY.

Names of Townships.	Names of Post-Offices.	Pt. Sec.	Sec.	Tp.	Range.
Goshen	Atalissa	e hf sw	11	78	3 w
Sweetland	Fairport	se cor	36	77	1 w
Pike	Lacey	se	28	77	4 w
Sweetland	Melpine	se cor	35	78	1 w
Moscow	Moscow	se	9	78	3 w
Muscatine	*Muscatine* (*c h*)	se	35	77	2 w
Orono	Orono		4	76	4 w
Pike	Pike	ne	11	77	4 w
Fulton	Pleasant Prairie	sw	29	78	1 e
Fulton	Prairie Mills	nw	4	78	1 e
Moscow	Summit	se se	36	78	2 w
Sweetland	Sweetland Center	center	4	77	1 w
West Liberty	West Liberty	sw	12	78	4 w
Wilton	Wilton Junction	nw	6	78	1 w

PAGE COUNTY.

Names of Townships.	Names of Post-Offices.	Pt. Sec.	Sec.	Tp.	Range.
	Braddyville				
Buchanan	Center	w hf	27	67	36
Nodaway	*Clarinda*, (*c h*)	nw	31	69	36
Amity	College Springs	nw	17	67	37
Pierce	Franklin Grove	se se	3	70	39
Nebraska	Hawleyville	n hf se	13	69	36
Harlan	Page City	nw	7	68	37
Tarkio	Tarkio	ne nw	28	69	38
Washington	Union Grove	ne	28	67	39

PALO ALTO COUNTY.

Names of Townships.	Names of Post-Offices.	Pt. Sec.	Sec.	Tp.	Range.
Emmetsburg	Black Walnut	ne	34	97	33
Emmetsburg	*Emmetsburg* (*c h*)	se	23	96	33
West Bend	Fern Valley	sw	28	95	31
Great Oak	Great Oak	sw	35	96	33
	Rush Lake				
Nevada	Soda Bar	sw	28	95	32
	West Bend	sw	22	94	31

PLYMOUTH COUNTY.

Names of Townships.	Names of Post-Offices.	Pt. Sec.	Sec.	Tp.	Range.
	Floyd Valley				
	Plymouth Center				
	Melbourne (*c h*)				

POCAHONTAS COUNTY.

Names of Townships.	Names of Post-Offices.	Location Post-offices. Pt. Sec.	Sec.	Tp.	Range.
Lizard	Lizard	w hf se	14	90	31
Des Moines	*Rolfe* (*c h*)	sw	26	93	31

POLK COUNTY.

Names of Townships.	Names of Post-Offices.	Pt. Sec.	Sec.	Tp.	Range.
Camp	Adelphi		30	78	22
Beaver	Altoona	sw	18	79	22
	Apple Grove				
Allen	Avon		27	78	23
	Bloomington				
Des Moines	*Des Moines* (*c h*)				
Elkhart	Elkhart	se se	27	81	23
Douglas	Greenwood	se cor	32	80	23
Jefferson	Lincoln	ne ne	15	80	25
Beaver	Mitchellville	nw	12	79	22
Washington	Peoria City		2	81	22
Madison	Polk City		1	80	25
Jefferson	Ridgedale	se sw	25	80	25
Four Mile	Rising Sun	nw	2	78	23
Saylor	Saylorville	ne nw	3	79	24

POTTAWATTAMIE COUNTY.

Names of Townships.	Names of Post-Offices.	Pt. Sec.	Sec.	Tp.	Range.
	Avoca				
James	Big Grove	se ne	10	75	40
Kane	*Council Bluffs* (*c h*)			75	43
Crescent	Crescent City			76	44
Rockford	Honey Creek		35	74	44
Rockford	Loveland	se nw	3	74	44
Macedonia	Macedonia	nw se	22	74	40
	Neola				
Grove	Wheeler's Grove	nw nw	28	74	39

POWESHIEK COUNTY.

Names of Townships.	Names of Post-Offices.	Pt. Sec.	Sec.	Tp.	Range.
Washington	Blue Point	nw ne	26	79	16
Bear Creek	Brooklyn		14	80	14
	Clearfield				
Deep River	Deep River	sw nw	10	78	13
Union	Forest Home	s hf se	20	78	15
Grinnell	Grinnell	nw	16	80	16
Malcolm	Malcolm	se	26	80	15
Sugar Creek	Mill Grove	e hf nw	26	78	16
Jackson	*Montezuma* (*c h*)	sw	6	78	14
Jackson	Sherman	se sw	35	78	15
Washington	Tyro	s hf ne	32	79	16
	West Brooklyn				

RINGGOLD COUNTY.

Names of Townships.	Names of Post-Offices.	Pt. Sec.	Sec.	Tp.	Range.
Lot's Creek	Caledonia	sw sw	11	67	29
Athens	Cross	se se	17	68	28
Mount Ayr	Estella	se	18	68	30
Sand Creek	Eugene				
Middle Fork	Ingart Grove	nw se	9	67	31
Mount Ayr	*Mount Ayr* (*c h*)	sw	6	68	29

RINGGOLD COUNTY—CONTINUED.

Names of Townships.	Names of Post-Offices.	Location Post-Offices. Pt. Sec.	Sec.	Tp.	Range.
Clinton	Redding	sw ne	12	67	31
Lot's Creek	Ringgold	se	21	67	29
....	Tingley	....	..	...	..
Sand Creek	Union Hill	se	16	70	28

SAC COUNTY.

Names of Townships.	Names of Post-Offices.	Pt. Sec.	Sec.	Tp.	Range.
Sac	Grant City	s hf	11	86	35
Jackson	*Sac City* (*c h*)	w hf	24	88	36

SCOTT COUNTY.

Names of Townships.	Names of Post-Offices.	Pt. Sec.	Sec.	Tp.	Range.
Allen's Grove	Allen's Grove	e hf se	28	80	2e
Hickory Grove	Amity	se nw	15	79	2e
Liberty	Big Rock	ne ne	4	80	1e
Blue Grass	Blue Grass	se	31	78	2e
Buffalo	Buffalo	sw	22	77	2e
Davenport	*Davenport* (*c h*)	....	26	78	3e
Liberty	Dixon	se se	12	80	1e
Davenport	Gilbert	sw	28	78	4e
Winfield	Long Grove	nw nw	35	80	3e
Le Claire	Le Claire	....	35	79	5e
Sheridan	Mt. Joy	sw sw	25	79	3e
....	New Hamburg	....	..	...	..
Liberty	New Liberty	sw sw	18	80	1e
Pleasant Valley	Pleasant Valley	se	7	78	5e
Princeton	Princeton	....	2	79	5e
Liberty	Round Grove	nw se	34	80	1e
Butler	Walnut Grove	w hf ne	18	80	4e
Blue Grass	Walcott	s hf	6	78	2e

SHELBY COUNTY.

Names of Townships.	Names of Post-Offices.	Pt. Sec.	Sec.	Tp.	Range.
Fairview	Altamont	sw ne	13	78	39
Jackson	Botany	sw ne	6	79	37
Indian Creek	Elkhorn	nw nw	14	78	37
Harlan	*Harlan* (*c h*)	ne sw	7	79	38
Galland's Grove	Manteno	ne ne	18	81	40

STORY COUNTY.

Names of Townships.	Names of Post-Offices.	Pt. Sec.	Sec.	Tp.	Range.
Washington	Ames	sw	2	83	24
Union	Cambridge	center	4	82	23
New Albany	Colo	ne	8	83	21
Indian Creek	Iowa Center	se se	10	82	22
Nevada	*Nevada* (*c h*)	ne	7	83	22
....	Ontario	....	..	...	..
La Fayette	Story City	ne	12	85	24

TAMA COUNTY.

Names of Townships.	Names of Post-Offices.	Pt. Sec.	Sec.	Tp.	Range.
Spring Creek	Badger Hill	n hf ne	7	85	16
....	Bovina	....	..	...	..
Buckingham	Buckingham	nw ne	4	84	14
Indian Village	Butlerville	ne	17	83	16
Salt Creek	Chelsea	nw nw	17	82	13

TAMA COUNTY—CONTINUED.

Names of Townships.	Names of Post-Offices.	Location Post-Offices Pt. Sec.	Sec.	Tp.	Range.
Crystal	Crystal	sw ne	14	85	15
Oneida	Dryden	se	36	84	13
	Ettie		..	..	..
Geneseo	Evergreen	nw se	21	86	13
Lincoln	Fifteen Mile Grove	nw	7	86	16
Richland	Helena	se se	4	82	14
Indian Village	Orford	se	27	83	16
Spring Creek	Spring Creek	s hf se	32	85	16
Tama	Tama City	nw	34	83	15
Toledo	*Toledo* (*c. h.*)	se	15	83	15
York	Waltham	sw ne	3	83	13
	West Irving		..	..	..
Perry	Wolf Creek	e hf nw	11	85	14

TAYLOR COUNTY.

Names of Townships.	Names of Post-Offices.	Pt. Sec.	Sec.	Tp.	Range.
Benton	*Bedford* (*c. h.*)	sw sw	26	68	34
Washington	Gravity		20	69	34
	Harmony		..	..	..
Holt	Holt		..	..	..
Polk	Jenks		..	..	..
Dallas	Memory		..	..	..
Ross	Ovid		..	..	..
Polk	Platte		..	..	..
Jefferson	Platteville		..	..	..
	Siam		..	..	..

UNION COUNTY.

Names of Townships.	Names of Post-Offices.	Pt. Sec.	Sec.	Tp.	Range.
Afton	*Afton* (*c. h.*)	se	16	72	29
	Cromwell		..	..	..
	Thayer		..	..	..
Platte	Union City	se ne	20	71	31

VAN BUREN COUNTY.

Names of Townships.	Names of Post-Offices.	Pt. Sec.	Sec.	Tp.	Range.
Washington	Bentonsport	se corner	12	69	9
Union	Birmingham		..	..	..
Bonaparte	Bonaparte	se	8	68	8
	Doud's Station		..	..	..
Farmington	Farmington	se	35	68	8
Village	Hickory	sw	7 & 8	70	11
Des Moines	Home		..	..	..
Village	Iowaville	sw	7 & 8	70	11
Van Buren	*Keosauqua* (*c. h.*)		..	..	..
Lick Creek	Kilbourne		..	..	..
Chequest	Lebanon		..	..	..
Jackson	Milton	se	19	68	11
Vernon	Mt. Sterling	nw	7	67	9
Van Buren	Mt. Zion		..	..	..
Farmington	Niles		..	..	..
Jackson	Oak Point	ne	5	68	11
Washington	Pierceville	ne corner	12	69	9
Van Buren	Pittsburg		..	..	..
Cedar	Sheridan	w hf ne	29	70	8
Des Moines	Upton		..	..	..

VAN BUREN COUNTY—CONTINUED.

Names of Townships.	Names of Post-Offices.	Location Post-Offices.			
		Pt. Sec.	Sec.	Tp.	Range.
Harrisburg	Utica	nw	6	69	8
Vernon	Vernon	ne	2	68	9
Union	Winchester				

WAPELLO COUNTY.

Names of Townships.	Names of Post-Offices.	Pt. Sec.	Sec.	Tp.	Range.
Agency	Agency City	ne sw	36	72	13
Washington	Alpine	n hf sw	18	71	12
Washington	Ashland	s hf se	9	71	12
	Bladensburg				
Adams	Blakesburg	w hf.	7	71	15
Cass	Chillicothe	ne	15	73	12
Polk	Christiansburg	nw	36	72	15
	Competine				
Richland	Comstock	nw se	30	73	14
Polk	Coopersville	nw	27	72	15
Dahlonega	Dahlonega	nw nw	9	72	13
Eddyville	Eddyville	nw	6	73	15
Richland	Kirkville	nw nw	8	73	14
Competine	Marysville	se	15	73	12
Center	*Ottumwa (c. h.)*	e hf	24	72	14
Center	Port Richmond	e hf	24	72	14
Washington	Williamsburg	n hf se	27	71	12

WARREN COUNTY.

Names of Townships.	Names of Post-Offices.	Pt. Sec.	Sec.	Tp.	Range.
Allen	Carlisle	se	3	77	23
Jefferson	Churchville	ne	18	76	25
Greenfield	Fort Plain	se se	36	77	24
Otter	Hammondsburg	s hf	11	75	23
Richland	Hartford	w hf nw	21	77	22
Washington	*Indianola (c. h.)*	n hf	25	76	24
Whitebreast	Lacona	sw	22	74	22
Liberty	Lawrenceburg	ne	7	74	23
Liberty	Liberty Center	sw	15	74	23
Jefferson	Lynn	sw	3	76	25
	Medora				
Virginia	New Virginia	w hf s w	27	74	25
Linn	Norwalk	ne	13	77	25
Palmyra	Palmyra	e hf nw	31	77	22
Belmont	Rose Mount	se	33	75	22
Union	Sandyville	nw sw	22	76	22
Squaw	Sharon	ne	2	74	24
Washington	Summerset	ne	31	77	23

WASHINGTON COUNTY.

Names of Townships.	Names of Post-Offices.	Pt. Sec.	Sec.	Tp.	Range.
Oregon	Ainsworth	sw ne	21	75	6
Brighton	Brighton	nw ne	31	74	8
Clay	Clay	e hf ne	31	74	9
Crawford	Crawfordsville	sw ne	15	74	6
	Dairy				
Dutch Creek	Dutch Creek	ne ne	22	75	9
	Lexington				
English River	Richmond	se ne	30	77	7
Dutch Creek	Valley	sw se	30	75	9

WASHINGTON COUNTY—Continued.

Names of Townships.	Names of Post-Offices.	Location Post-Offices. Pt. Sec.	Sec.	Tp.	Range.
Washington	*Washington (c h)*	sw	17	75	7
Lime Creek	Wassonville	sw sw	19	77	8
Iona	Yatton	nw nw	20	77	6

WAYNE COUNTY.

Names of Townships.	Names of Post-Offices.	Pt. Sec.	Sec.	Tp.	Range.
Bethlehem	Bethlehem	se se	24	70	21
Cambria	Cambria	se cor	21	70	22
Grand River	Clio	nw	1	67	23
Confidence	Confidence	center	14	70	20
Corydon	*Corydon (c h)*	e hf sw	19	69	21
Genoa	Genoa	sw nw	13	67	20
	Grand River				
Walnut	Kniffin	w pt	18	68	20
Lewisburg	Lewisburg	center	20	69	23
Grand River	Linnville	se	20	67	23
New York	New York	sw ne	22	70	21
Promise City	Promise City	center	26	69	20
	Selma				
Warsaw	Warsaw	nw nw	8	67	21

WEBSTER COUNTY.

Names of Townships.	Names of Post-Offices.	Pt. Sec.	Sec.	Tp.	Range.
Washington	Border Plains	s hf	30	88	27
Wahkonsa	*Fort Dodge (c h)*	se	19	89	28
	Greenside				
Sumner	Hesperian	se	16	87	28
Otho	Otho	nw se	28	88	28
Dayton	West Dayton	se ne	14	86	28

WINNEBAGO COUNTY.

Names of Townships.	Names of Post-Offices.	Pt. Sec.	Sec.	Tp.	Range.
Center	Benson Grove	se se	36	99	24
Forest	*Forest City (c h)*	e hf ne	35	98	24
Pleasant	Lake Mills	nw se	2	99	23

WINNESHIEK COUNTY.

Names of Townships.	Names of Post-Offices.	Pt. Sec.	Sec.	Tp.	Range.
Bluffton	Bluffton	se	9	99	9
Burr Oak	Burr Oak				
Madison	Burr Oak Springs				
Calmar	Calmar				
Canoe	Canoe	ne	18	99	8
Bloomfield	Castalia				
Calmar	Conover				
Decorah	*Decorah (c h)*		16	98	8
Washington	Festina	se	23	96	9
Washington	Fort Atkinson	se	7	96	9
Frankville	Frankville				
Decorah	Freeport				
Hesper	Hesper				
Highland	Highlandville	nw	34	100	7
Pleasant	Locust Lane	nw	6	99	7
Jackson	New Alba				
Washington	Old Mission	nw	34	96	9
Military	Ossian	se	10	96	8

WINNESHIEK COUNTY—CONTINUED.

Names of Townships.	Names of Post-Offices.	Location Post-Offices.			
		Pt. Sec.	Sec.	Tp.	Range.
Fremont	Plymouth Rock				
Lincoln	Ridgeway				
Calmar	Spillville				
Canoe	Spring Water	se	24	99	8
	Twin Springs				
Glenwood	Woodville	nw	36	98	7

WOODBURY COUNTY.

Names of Townships.	Names of Post-Offices.	Pt. Sec.	Sec.	Tp.	Range.
	Correctionville				
	Hamlin				
	Oto				
	Sioux City (*c h*)				
	Smithland				
	Woodbury				
	Wolfdate				

NOTE.—No reports from Woodbury county. Post-offices taken from U. S. P. O. list.

WORTH COUNTY.

Names of Townships.	Names of Post-Offices.	Pt. Sec.	Sec.	Tp.	Range.
Bristol	Bristol	ne nw	8	99	22
Hartland	Hartland	e hf nw	7	100	21
Northwood	*Northwood* (*c h*)	se se	29	100	20
Silver Lake	Silver Lake	nw	26	100	22
	Wales				

WRIGHT COUNTY.

Names of Townships.	Names of Post-Offices.	Pt. Sec.	Sec.	Tp.	Range.
Troy	Bach Grove	nw	15	90	26
Belmond	Belmond	ne	25	93	24
Clarion	Clarion	sw	31	91	24
Eagle Grove	Eagle Grove	nw nw	21	91	26
Wall Lake	Empire	sw	26	91	24
Iona	Fryeburg	nw se	33	92	23
Liberty	*Goldfield* (*c h*)	se	33	92	26
Boone	Luni	nw	20	93	26
Woolstock	Woolstock	sw	20	90	25

ALPHABETICAL

List of Post-Offices in the State, Nov. 1st, 1869.

Offices printed in italics with a small *c h* in parenthesis, indicate county seats. Offices having a * prefixed, denote a Money Order Office.

Names of Post-Offices.	Counties.	Names of Post-Offices.	Counties.
Abingdon	Jefferson	Bach Grove	Wright
Ackley	Hardin	Baden	Keokuk
**Adel* (c h)*	Dallas	Badger Hill	Tama
Adelphi	Polk	Baker	Jefferson
Addison	Humboldt	Ballyclough	Dubuque
**Afton* (c h)*	Union	Bangor	Marshall
Agency City	Wapello	Bankston	Dubuque
Agricola	Mahaska	Barclay	Black Hawk
Ainsworth	Washington	Barryville	Delaware
Albany	Davis	Bartlett	Fremont
**Albia* (c h)*	Monroe	Beacon	Mahaska
Albion	Marshall	Bear Grove	Guthrie
Alden	Hardin	**Bedford* (c h)*	Taylor
**Algona* (c h)*	Kossuth	Beetrace	Appanoose
Alpine	Wapello	Belfast	Lee
Altoona	Polk	Belinda	Lucas
Allamakee	Allamakee	Belle Air	Johnson
Allen's Grove	Scott	Bellefontaine	Mahaska
Allison	Dubuque	*Belle Plaine	Benton
Almoral	Delaware	Bellevue	Jackson
Altamont	Shelby	Belmond	Wright
Alton	Dallas	Belvidere	Monona
Ames	Story	Bennington	Marion
Amish	Johnson	Benson Grove	Winnebago
Amity	Scott	Benton	Mills
**Anamosa* (c h)*	Jones	Benton Center	Benton
Andrew (c h)	Jackson	Bentonsport	Van Buren
Anita	Cass	Berlin	Hardin
Aplington	Butler	Bertram	Linn
Apple Grove	Polk	Bethel	Fayette
Arbor Hill	Adair	Bethlehem	Wayne
Arcola	Monona	Big Grove	Pottaw'ttamie
Argo	Lucas	Bigler's Grove	Harrison
Armstrong's Grove	Emmet	Big Mound	Lee
Ashland	Wapello	Big Rock	Scott
Atalissa	Muscatine	Big Springs	Johnson
Atlanta	Buchanan	Birmingham	Van Buren
†*Atlantic (c h)*	Cass	Biven's Grove	Marshall
Attica	Marion	Black Walnut	Palo Alto
Auburn	Mahaska	Blairsburg	Hamilton
Augusta	Des Moines	Blairstown	Benton
Aurora	Keokuk	Bladensburg	Wapello
Avoca	Pottaw'ttamie	Blakesburg	Wapello
Avon	Polk	Blakeville	Black Hawk

†Removed from Lewis by vote of the people, Oct. 12, 1869.

ALPHABETICAL LIST OF POST-OFFICES—CONTINUED.

Names of Post-Offices.	Counties.	Names of Post-Offices.	Counties.
**Bloomfield* (c. h.)	Davis	Campton	Delaware
Bloomington	Polk	Canoe	Winneshiek
Blue Grass	Scott	Canton	Jackson
Blue Point	Poweshiek	Carl	Adams
Bluffton	Winneshiek	Carlisle	Warren
Bon Accord	Johnson	*Carroll City* (c. h.)	Carroll
Bonaparte	Van Buren	Carrollton	Carroll
Boone	Dallas	Carr's Point	Montgomery
Boon Spring	Clinton	Cascade	Dubuque
**Boonsboro* (c. h.)	Boone	Casey	Adair
Border Plains	Webster	Casaday'sCorner	Boone
Botany	Shelby	Castalia	Winneshiek
Botavia	Jefferson	Castana	Monona
Bovina	Tama	Castle Grove	Jones
Bowen's Prairie	Jones	Cedar Blnffs	Cedar
Boylestown	Henry	*Cedar Falls	Black Hawk
Boylan's Grove	Butler	*Cedar Rapids	Linn
Braddyville	Page	Cedar Cross Roads	Marshall
Bradford	Chickasaw	Cedar Valley	Black Hawk
Brandon	Buchanan	Center	Page
Brighton	Washington	Center Point	Linn
Bristol	Worth	**Centerville* (c. h.)	Appanoose
Brookfield	Clinton	Central City	Linn
*Brooklyn	Poweshiek	Ceres	Clayton
Brookville	Jefferson	Cessford	Cedar
Browning	Carroll	Chandler	Keokuk
Brown's Mill	Davis	Chapin	Frankliu
Brownville	Mitchell	**Chariton* (c. h.)	Lucas
Brush Creek	Fayette	**Charles City* (c. .h)	Floyd
Buck Creek	Bremer	Charleston	Lee
Buck Horn	Mahaska	Charlotte	Clinton
Buckingham	Tama	Chase	Johnson
Buena Vista	Clinton	Chatham	Buchanan
Buffalo	Scott	Chelsea	Tama
Buffalo Fork	Kossuth	Chequist	Davis
Buffalo Grove	Buchanan	*Cherokee* (c. h.)	Cherokee
Burgess	Clinton	*Chickasaw* (c. h.)	Chickasaw
Burke	Benton	Chillicothe	Wapello
**Burlington* (c. h.)	Des Moines	Christiansburg	Wapello
Burr Oak	Winneshiek	Churchville	Warren
Burr Oak Springs	Winneshiek	Cincinnati	Appanoose
Busti	Howard	Clanton	Madison
Butler	Keokuk	Clarence	Cedar
Butler Center (c. h.)	Butler	**Clarinda* (c. h.)	Page
Butlerville	Tama	Clarion	Wright
		Clarksville	Butler
Cairo	Louisa	Clay	Washington
Calamus	Clinton	Clayford	Jones
Caldwell	Appanoose	Clay Mills	Jones
Caledonia	Ringgold	Clay's Grove	Lee
Calhoun	Harrison	Clayton	Clayton
Calmar	Winneshiek	Clear Creek	Allamakee
Caloma	Marion	Clearfield	Poweshiek
Camanche	Clinton	Clear Lake	Cerro Gordo
Cambria	Wayne	*Clermont	Fayette
Cambridge	Story	Clifton	Louisa

ALPHABETICAL LIST OF POST OFFICES—Continued.

Names of Post-Offices.	Counties.
*† *Clinton (c h)*	Clinton
Clio	Wayne
Clyde	Jasper
Coal Creek	Keokuk
Coalton	Monroe
Coldwater	Franklin
Colesburg	Delaware
Colfax	Jasper
College Springs	Page
Colo	Story
Columbia	Marion
Columbus City	Louisa
Communia	Clayton
Competine	Wapello
Comstock	Wapello
Concord (c h)	Hancock
Confidence	Wayne
Conover	Winneshiek
Coon Rapids	Carroll
Coopersville	Wapello
Copi	Johnson
Coralville	Johnson
Corning	Adams
Corectionville	Woodbury
**Corydon (c h)*	Wayne
Cottage	Hardin
Cottage Hill	Dubuque
Cotton Grove	Henry
Cottonville	Jackson
**Council Bluffs (c h)*	Po'tawat'amie
Council Hill	Clayton
Cox Creek	Clayton
Crane Creek	Chickasaw
Crawford	Crawford
Crawfordsville	Washington
Crawford Station	Crawford
Crescent City	Pot'awat'amie
**Cresco (c h)*	Howard
Creswell	Keokuk
Cromwell	Union
Cross	Ringgold
Croton	Lee
Crystal	Tama
Cuba	Monroe
Dahlonega	Wapello
Dairy	Washington
Dakota (c h)	Humboldt
Dalby	Allamakee
Dale City	Guthrie
Dallas	Marion
Dallas Center	Dallas
Dalmanutha	Guthrie
Danforth	Johnson
Danville	Des Moines
**Davenport (c h)*	Scott
Davis City	Decatur
Dayton Center	Chickasaw
Decatur	Decatur
**Decorah (c h)*	Winneshiek
Deerfield	Chickasaw
Delanti	Hardin
Delaware	Delaware
Delhi (c h)	Delaware
Deloit	Crawford
Denison (c h)	Crawford
Denmark	Lee
Dennis	Appanoose
Denver	Bremer
Deep River	Poweshiek
De Soto	Dallas
**Des Moines (c h)*	Polk
*DeWitt	Clinton
Dexter	Dallas
Dixon	Scott
Dodge	Guthrie
Dodgeville	Des Moines
Doran	Mitchell
Dorchester	Allamakee
Doud's Station	Van Buren
Douglas	Fayette
Dover	Lee
Downey	Cedar
Drakeville	Davis
Dryden	Tama
Dry Creek	Linn
**Dubuque (c h)*	Dubuque
Dunlap	Harrison
Durango	Dubuque
Durant	Cedar
Dutch Creek	Washington
*Dyersville	Dubuque
Eagle	Bremer
Eagle Grove	Wright
Earlham	Madison
Earlville	Delaware
East Melrose	Monroe
East Nodaway	Adams
Eastport	Fremont
Eatonville	Howard
*Eddyville	Wapello
Eden	Fayette
Edenville	Marshall
Edinburg	Jones
Edna	Cass
**Eldora (c h)*	Hardin
Eldorado	Fayette
Elgin	Fayette

†Removed from DeWitt by vote of the people, October 12, 1869.

ALPHABETICAL LIST OF POST-OFFICES—CONTINUED.

Names of Post-Offices.	Counties.	Names of Post-Offices.	Counties.
**Elkader* (c h)	Clayton	Franklin Grove	Page
Elkhart	Polk	Franklin Mills	Des Moines
Elkhorn	Shelby	Frank Pierce	Johnson
Elkport	Clayton	Frankville	Winneshiek
Elk River	Clinton	Frederika	Bremer
Ellingtou	Hancock	Frederick	Monroe
Ellsworth	Madison	Fredericksburg	Chickasaw
Elm Springs	Butler	Fredonia	Louisa
Elvira	Clinton	Freedom	Lucas
Emmet	Emmet	Freeport	Winneshiek
Emmetsburg (c h)	Palo Alto	Fremont	Mahaska
Empire	Wright	French Creek	Allamakee
English Settlement	Marion	Fryeburg	Wright
Enterprise	Black Hawk	Fulton	Jackson
Epworth	Dubuque		
Estella	Ringgold	Galesburg	Jasper
Estherville (c h)	Emmet	Garden Grove	Decatur
Ettie	Tama	Garibaldi	Keokuk
Eugene	Ringgold	Garnavillo	Clayton
Eveland Grove	Mahaska	Garry Owen	Jackson
Evergreen	Tama	Gem	Clayton
Exira (c h)	Audubon	Geneseo	Cerro Gordo
		Geneva	Franklin
Fairbank	Buchanan	Genoa	Wayne
Fairfax	Linn	Genoa Bluffs	Iowa
**Fairfield* (c h)	Jefferson	Georgetown	Monroe
Fairport	Muscatine	Germanville	Jefferson
Fairview	Jones	Giard	Clayton
Farley	Dubuque	Gilbert	Scott
Farmersburg	Clayton	Gilbertsville	Black Hawk
Farmer's Creek	Jackson	Gillet's Grove	Clay
Farmersville	Mahaska	Givin	Mahaska
*Farmington	Van Buren	Glasgow	Jefferson
Fayette	Fayette	Glendale	Jefferson
Fern Valley	Palo Alto	**Glenwood* (c h)	Mills
Ferry	Mahaska	Glidden	Carroll
Festina	Winneshiek	*Goldfield* (c. h.)	Wright
Fifteen Mile Grove	Tama	Gosport	Marion
Flemiogville	Linn	Grand Mound	Clinton
Flint	Mahaska	Grand River	Wayne
Florence	Benton	Grandview	Louisa
Floris	Davis	Grant	Montgomery
Floyd	Floyd	Grant Center	Monona
Floyd Valley	Plymouth	Grant City	Sac
**Fontanelle* (c h)	Adair	Granville	Mahaska
Foote	Iowa	Gravity	Taylor
Forest City (c h)	Winnebago	Great Oak	Palo Alto
Forest Home	Poweshiek	Greeley	Delaware
Foreston	Howard	Green Bay	Clarke
Forestville	Delaware	Greencastle	Jasper
Fort Atkinson	Winneshiek	Greenfield	Adair
**Fort Dodge* (c h)	Webster	Greenside	Webster
**Fort Madison* (c h)	Lee	Greenvale	Dallas
Fort Plain	Warren	Greenwood	Polk
Frankfort	Montgomery	Griffinsville	Appanoose
Franklin	Dubuque	*Grinnell	Poweshiek
Franklin Center	Lee	Grove City	Cass

ALPHABETICAL LIST OF POST-OFFICES—CONTINUED.

Names of Post-Offices.	Counties.	Names of Post-Offices.	Counties.
Grove Creek	Jones	Iconium	Appanoose
Grove Hill	Bremer	*Ida* (*c h*)	Ida
Grundy Center (*c h*)	Grundy	Illinois Grove	Marshall
Guthrie	Guthrie	Illyria	Fayette
Guthrie Center	Guthrie	**Independence* (*c h*)	Buchanan
*Guttenburg	Clayton	Indianapolis	Mahaska
		**Indianola* (*c h*)	Warren
Hackberry	Cerro Gordo	Ingart Grove	Ringgold
Half-Way Prairie	Monroe	Ingham	Franklin
Hamburg	Fremont	Inland	Cedar
Hamilton	Marion	Ioka	Keokuk
Hamlin	Woodbury	Iola	Marion
Hamlin's Grove	Audubon	Ion	Allamakee
Hammondsburg	Warren	Iowa Center	Story
**Hampton* (*c h*)	Franklin	**Iowa City* (*c h*)	Johnson
Hardin	Clayton	*Iowa Falls	Hardin
Hardin City	Hardin	Iowaville	Van Buren
Harlan (*c h*)	Shelby	Iron Hills	Johnson
Harmony	Taylor	Irvington	Kossuth
Harper's Ferry	Allamakee		
Harris' Grove	Harrison	Jackson	Adair
Hartford	Warren	Jacksonville	Chickasaw
Hartland	Worth	Janesville	Bremer
Harvey's Mills	Jefferson	Jasper City	Jasper
Hawkeye	Fayette	**Jefferson* (*c h*)	Greene
Hawleyville	Page	Jeffersonville	Lee
Haynie	Mills	Jenks	Taylor
Hayesville	Keokuk	Jerome	Appanoose
Hazel Green	Delaware	Jesup	Buchanan
Hazleton	Buchanan	Johnson	Jones
Hebron	Adair	Johnsonporte	Allamakee
Helena	Tama	Jollyville	Lee
Henderson	Lucas		
Hesper	Winneshiek	Kasson	Madison
Hesperian	Webster	*Keokuk	Lee
Hibbsville	Appanoose	**Keosauqua* (*c h*)	Van Buren
Hickory	Van Buren	Kier	Buchanan
High Lake	Emmet	Kilbourne	Van Buren
Highland	Clayton	King's	Dubuque
Highland Grove	Jones	Kingston	Des Moines
Highlandville	Winneshiek	Kirkville	Wapello
Holladay's	Adair	Kniffin	Wayne
Holt	Taylor	**Knoxville* (*c h*)	Marion
Home	Van Buren	Kossuth	Des Moines
Homer	Hamilton	Kossuth Center	Kossuth
Homestead	Iowa	Koszta	Iowa
Honey Creek	Pot'awat'amie		
Hook's Point	Hamilton	Lacelle	Clarke
Hopeville	Clarke	Lacey	Muscatine
Hopewell	Mahaska	Lacona	Warren
Hopkinton	Delaware	Ladora	Iowa
Horn	Jasper	Lafayette	Linn
Horton	Bremer	Lagrange	Lucas
Howard Center	Howard	*Lake City* (*c h*)	Calhoun
Howardville	Taylor	Lake Mills	Winnebago
Hudson	Black Hawk	Lakin's Grove	Hamilton
Humboldt	Humboldt	Lamaille	Marshall
Huron	Des Moines	Lamotte	Jackson

ALPHABETICAL LIST OF POST-OFFIDES—CONTINUED.

Names of Post-Offices.	Counties.	Names of Post-Offices.	Counties.
Lancaster	Keokuk	*Lyons	Clinton
Langworthy	Jones	Lytle City	Iowa
*Lansing	Allamakee		
Laporte	Clarke	Macedonia	Pot'awat'amie
La Porte City	Black Hawk	McGregor	Clayton
Last Chance	Lucas	Macks	Carroll
Lattner's	Dubuque	Macksville	Guthrie
Laurel	Marshall	Madison	Jones
La Vega	Des Moines	**Magnolia* (c. h.)	Harrison
Lawrenceburg	Warren	Malcolm	Poweshiek
Lebanon	Van Buren	Malone	Clinton
Le Claire	Scott	*Manchester	Delaware
Legrand	Marshall	Manhattan	Keokuk
Leighton	Mahaska	Manteno	Shelby
**Leon* (c. h.)	Decatur	Manti	Fremont
Leroy	Bremer	Mapleton	Monona
Lester	Black Hawk	*Maquoketa	Jackson
Lotts	Louisa	Marble Rock	Floyd
*Lewis	Cass	**Marengo* (c. h.)	Iowa
Lewisburg	Wayne	Marietta	Marshall
Lexington	Washington	**Marion* (c. h)	Linn
Liberty	Clarke	Marshall	Henry
Liberty Center	Warren	**Marshaltown* (c. h.)	Marshall
Libertyville	Jefferson	Martinsburg	Keokuk
Lima	Fayette	Marysville	Wapello
Lime Creek	Cerro Gordo	Maysville	Franklin
Lime Springs	Howard	*Mason City* (c. h.)	Cerro Gordo
Lincoln	Polk	Masonville	Delaware
Lincoln Center	Grundy	Massillon	Cedar
Linden	Dallas	Maxfield	Bremer
Linnville	Wayne	Mechanicsville	Cedar
Linton	Des Moines	Medora	Warren
Lisbon	Linn	*Melbourne* (c. h.)	Plymouth
Liscomb	Marshall	Melpine	Muscatine
Lithopolis	Hardin	Memory	Taylor
Littleport	Clayton	Mennon	Marion
Little Sioux	Harrison	Mentor	Bremer
Little Turkey	Chickasaw	Merrimac	Jefferson
Livingston	Appanoose	Merona	Mitchell
Lizard	Pocahontas	Merva	Mitchell
Lockridge	Jefferson	Middlefield	Buchanan
Locust Lane	Winneshiek	Middle River	Madison
Logan	Harrison	Middletown	Des Moines
Long Grove	Scott	Mill	Fayette
Lott's Creek	Humboldt	Milledgeville	Appanoose
Louden	Cedar	Millersburg	Iowa
Loveland	Pot'awat'amie	Mill Grove	Poweshiek
Lovilia	Monroe	Mill Rock	Jackson
Lowell	Henry	Millville	Clayton
Low Moor	Clinton	Milo	Delaware
Luana	Clayton	Milton	Van Buren
Lucas	Lucas	Mineral Bidge	Boone
Ludlow	Allamakee	Minerva	Marshall
Luni	Wright	Missouri Valley	Harrison
Luzerne	Benton	**Mitchell* (c. h.)	Mitchell
Lycurgus	Allamakee	Mitchellville	Polk
Lynn	Warren	Modale	Harrison
Lynnville	Jasper	Moffit's Grove	Guthrie

ALPHABETICAL LIST OF POST-OFFICES—Continued.

Names of Post-Offices.	Counties.	Names of Post-Offices.	Counties.
Moingona	Boone	North English	Iowa
Mondamin	Harrison	North Liberty	Johnson
Monmouth	Jackson	North McGregor	Clayton
Monona	Clayton	Northville	Greeue
Monroe	Jasper	North Washington	Chickasaw
Montana	Boone	*Northwood* (*c h*)	Worth
Monterey	Davis	Norwalk	Warren
**Montezuma* (*c h*)	Poweshiek	Norwood	Lucas
*Monticello	Jones	Nugent's Grove	Linn
Montrose	Lee	Numa	Appanoose
Moravia	Appanoose		
Morning Sun	Louisa	Oakfield	Audubon
Moscow	Muscatine	Oakland Valley	Franklin
Moulton	Appanoose	Oakland Mills	Henry
Mt. Alger	Jackson	Oak Point	Van Buren
Mt. Auburn	Benton	Oak Springs	Davis
**Mt. Ayr* (*c h*)	Ringgold	Oasis	Johnson
Mt. Hope	Delaware	Ogden	Dubuque
Mt. Joy	Scott	Ohio	Madison
**Mt. Pleasant* (*c h*)	Henry	Okoboji	Dickinson
Mt. Sterling	Van Buren	Ola	Lucas
*Mt. Vernon	Linn	Old Mission	Winneshiek
Mt. Zion	Van Buren	*Onawa C.ty* (*c h*)	Monona
Murray	Clarke	Ontario	Story
**Muscatine* (*c h*)	Muscatine	Oran	Fayette
Myron	Allamakee	Orange	Clinton
		Orford	Tama
Nantrille	Black Hawk	Oria	Taylor
Nashua	Chickasaw	Orleans	Appanoose
National	Clayton	Orono	Muscatine
Nelson	Mitchell	Osage	Mitchell
Neola	Pot'awat'amie	**Osceola* (*c h*)	Clarke
**Nevada* (*c h*)	Story	**Oskaloosa* (*c h*)	Mahaska
Nevinville	Adams	Osprey	Monroe
New Alba	Winneshiek	Ossian	Winneshiek
Newbern	Marion	Otho	Webster
New Buda	Decatur	Otisville	Franklin
Newburg	Mitchell	Otley	Marion
New Boston	Lee	Oto	Woodbury
New Hamburg	Scott	Otranto	Mitchell
New Hampton	Chickasaw	Ottawa	Clarke
New Hartford	Butler	Otter Creek	Jackson
New Liberty	Scott	Otterville	Buchanan
New London	Henry	**Ottumwa* (*c h*)	Wapello
New Milleray	Dubuque	Owen's Grove	Cerro Gordo
*New Oregon	Howard	Oxford	Johnson
Newport Center	Johnson	Oxford Mills	Jones
New Providence	Hardin	Ozark	Jackson
New Sharon	Mahaska		
**Newton* (*c h*)	Jasper	Pacific City	Mills
New Vienna	Dubuque	Page City	Page
New Virginia	Warren	Palestine	Johnson
New York	Wayne	Palmyra	Warren
Niles	Van Buren	Palo	Linn
Nine Eagles	Decatur	*Panora* (*c h*)	Guthrie
Nora Springs	Floyd	Paris	Linn
Nordyke	Dallas	Parkersburg	Butler
Northfield	Des Moines	Parrish	Des Moines

ALPHABETICAL LIST OF POST-OFFICES—Continued.

Names of Post-Offices.	Counties.
Pedee	Cedar
*Pella	Marion
Peoria	Mahaska
Peoria City	Polk
Peosta	Dubuque
Percival	Fremont
Peru	Madison
Peterson (c. h.)	Clay
Pierceville	Van Buren
Pierce's Point	Dallas
Pike	Muscatine
Pilot Grove	Lee
Pilot Mound	Boone
Pilot Rock	Cherokee
Pin Oak	Dubuque
Pittsburg	Van Buren
Plainfield	Bremer
Platte	Taylor
Platteville	Taylor
Pleasant Grove	Des Moines
Pleasant Hill	Cedar
Pleasant Plain	Jefferson
Pleasant Prairie	Muscatine
Pleasant Valley	Scott
Pleasantville	Marion
Plum Hollow	Fremont
Plymouth	Cerro Gordo
Plymouth Center	Plymouth
Plymouth Rock	Winneshiek
Point Pleasant	Hardin
Polk City	Polk
Pond Valley	Howard
Port Allen	Louisa
Port Louisa	Louisa
Port Richmond	Wapello
Postville	Allamakee
Prairieburg	Linn
Prairie City	Jasper
Prairie Grove	Clarke
Prairie Hill	Boone
Prairie Mills	Muscatine
Prairieville	Decatur
Primrose	Lee
Princeton	Scott
Promise City	Wayne
Prospect Hill	Linn
Pulaski	Davis
Putnam	Fayette
Quarry	Marshall
Quasqueton	Buchanan
Queen City	Adams
**Quincy (c. h.)*	Adams
Randall	Hamilton
Raymond	Black Hawk
Rapids	Boone
Read	Clayton
Redding	Ringgold
Redfield	Dallas
Red Oak	Cedar
Red Oak Junction (c. h.)	Montgomery
Red Rock	Marion
Reeder's Mills	Harrison
Rest	Iowa
Riceville	Mitchell
Richardsville	Dubuque
Richfield	Fayette
Richland	Keokuk
Richmond	Washington
Ridgedale	Polk
Ridgeway	Winneshiek
Riley	Clarke
Ringgold	Ringgold
Ripley	Greene
Rising Sun	Polk
Riverside	Boone
Robin	Benton
Rochester	Cedar
Rock	Cerro Gordo
Rock Creek	Mitchell
Rockdale	Dubuque
Rockford	Floyd
Rock Grove City	Floyd
Rolfe (c. h.)	Pocahontas
Rome	Henry
Rose Mount	Warren
Rossville	Allamakee
Round Grove	Scott
Rural	Linn
Russell	Lucas
Rush Lake	Palo Alto
Sabula	Jackson
Sac City (c. h.)	Sac
Saint Ansgar	Mitchell
Saint Charles	Madison
Saint Clair	Monona
Saint Donatus	Jackson
Saint John	Harrison
Saint Paul	Lee
Saint Sebold	Clayton
*Salem	Henry
Salina	Jefferson
Sand Springs	Delaware
Sandusky	Lee
Sandyville	Warren
Saratoga	Howard
Savannah	Davis
Saylorville	Polk
Schwearsburg	Adair
Sciola	Montgomery
Scotch Grove	Jones
Scott Center	Fayette
Scranton Station	Greene
Seaton	Fayette

ALPHABETICAL LIST OF POST-OFFICES—CONTINUED.

Names of Post-Offices.	Counties.	Names of Post-Offices.	Counties.
Sedgewick	Decatur	Swanton	Butler
Selma	Wayne	Swede Point	Boone
Seneca	Kossuth	Sweetland Center	Muscatine
Seventy-Eight	Johnson	Sylvan Retreat	Humboldt
Sharon	Warren		
Sheffield	Dubuque	Tabor	Fremont
Shellrock	Butler	Tallahoma	Lucas
Shellrock Falls	Cerro Gordo	Talleyrand	Keokuk
Shellsburg	Benton	Tama City	Tama
Sheridan	Van Buren	Tarkio	Page
Sherman	Poweshiek	Taylorville	Fayette
Shobe's Grove	Franklin	Terre Haute	Decatur
Shueyville	Johnson	Thayer	Union
Siam	Taylor	Thompsonville	Monroe
**Sidney* (c h)	Fremont	Ticonic	Monona
**Sigourney* (c h)	Keokuk	Timber Creek	Marshall
Silver Lake	Worth	Tiffin	Johnson
Simpson	Adams	Tingley	Ringgold
**Sioux City* (c h)	Woodbury	**Tipton* (c h)	Cedar
Smithland	Woodbury	Tipton Grove	Hardin
Smyrna	Clarke	Tivoli	Dubuque
Snyder	Dallas	**Toledo* (c h)	Tama
Soda Bar	Palo Alto	Toolsborough	Louisa
Solon	Johnson	Toronto	Clinton
South English	Keokuk	Tower Hill	Delaware
South Flint	Des Moines	Tracy	Dallas
South Liberty	Johnson	Trenton	Henry
Spencer	Clay	Tripoli	Bremer
Spillville	Winneshiek	Troy	Davis
Spirit Lake (c h)	Dickinson	Troy Mills	Linn
Sprague ville	Jackson	Twin Lakes	Calhoun
Spring Brook	Jackson	Twin Spring	Winneshiek
Spring Creek	Tama	Tyro	Poweshiek
Springdale	Cedar	Tyrone	Monroe
Springfield	Keokuk		
Spring Grove	Linn	Ulster	Floyd
Spring Lake	Bremer	Union	Hardin
Springvale	Humboldt	Unionburg	Harrison
Spring Valley	Monona	Union Center	Jackson
Springville	Linn	Union City	Union
Springwater	Winneshiek	Union Grove	Page
Staceyville	Mitchell	Union Hill	Ringgold
Stanford	Marshall	Union Mills	Mahaska
Stanwood	Cedar	Union Prairie	Allamakee
Stapleton	Chickasaw	Union Ridge	Butler
Star	Marion	Uniontown	Delaware
State Center	Marshall	Unionville	Appanoose
Stellapolis	Iowa	Unity	Benton
Sterling	Jackson	Upper Grove	Hancock
Stilesville	Davis	Upton	Van Buren
Storm Lake	Buena Vista	Urbanna	Benton
Story City	Story	Urbanna City	Monroe
Strawberry Point	Clayton	Utica	Van Buren
Sugar Creek	Jasper		
Summerset	Warren	Valiska	Montgomery
Summit	Muscatine	Valley	Washington
Summitville	Lee	Valley Farm	Linn
Sumner	Bremer	Van Buren	Jackson
Sunnyside	Buchanan	Vandalia	Jasper

ALPHABETICAL LIST OF POST-OFFICES—CONTINUED.

Names of Post-Offices.	Counties.
Vandyke	Des Moines
Van Meter	Dallas
Venus	Madison
Vernon	Van Buren
Victor	Iowa
Vienna	Marshall
Village Creek	Allamakee
Vincennes	Lee
* *Vinton* (*c h*)	Benton
Viola	Linn
Viona	Humboldt
Virginia Grove	Louisa
Volga City	Clayton
Volney	Allamakee
Wacousta	Humboldt
Wadena	Fayette
Wagner	Clayton
Wahaghbonsy	Mills
Walcott	Scott
Wales	Worth
Walnut City	Appanoose
Walnut Creek	Fremont
Walnut Fork	Jones
Walnut Grove	Scott
Waltham	Tama
* *Wapello* (*c h*)	Louisa
Wapsa	Linn
Ward's Corners	Buchanan
Warren	Lee
Warren Grove	Jasper
Warsaw	Wayne
Washburn	Franklin
* *Washington* (*c h*)	Washington
Wassonville	Washington
* *Waterloo* (*c h*)	Black Hawk
Watertown	Mitchell
Waterville	Allamakee
Waubeck	Linn
Waucoma	Fayette
Waukee Station	Dallas
Waukon (*c h*)	Allamakee
Waverly (*c h*)	Bremer
Wayne	Henry
Webster	Keokuk
* *Webster City* (*c h*)	Hamilton
Weller	Monroe
Wells' Mills	Appanoose
Welton	Clinton
Wentworth	Mitchell
West Bend	Palo Alto
West Branch	Cedar
West Brooklyn	Powesheik
West Dayton	Webster
Western College	Linn
Westervelt's Mills	Decatur
West Fork	Monona
West Grove	Davis
West Irving	Tama
West Liberty	Muscatine
West Mitchell	Mitchell
West Point	Lee
West Prairie	Linn
West Side	Crawford
* *West Union* (*c h*)	Fayette
What Cheer	Keokuk
*Wheatland	Clinton
Wheeler's Grove	Pottaw'ttamie
Wheeling	Marion
White Breast	Lucas
White Cloud	Mills
White Oak	Mahaska
White Pigeon	Keokuk
Whitesboro	Harrison
Whitneyville	Cass
Wickliffe	Jackson
Williamsburg	Wapello
Williamston	Chickasaw
Williams	Hamilton
Williamsville	Jasper
Willoughby	Butler
Wilson Grove	Fayette
Wilton Junction	Muscatine
Winchester	Van Buren
Windham	Johnson
Winfield	Henry
Winona	Henry
* *Winterset* (*c h*)	Madison
Winthrop	Buchanan
Wolf Creek	Tama
Wolfdate	Woodbury
Woodbine	Harrison
Woodbury	Woodbury
Woodville	Winnesheik
Woolstock	Wright
Wooster	Jefferson
Worth	Boone
Worthington	Dubuque
Wyoming	Jones
Xenia	Dallas
Yankee Settlement	Clayton
Yatesville	Calhoun
Yatton	Washington
Yazoo	Harrison
York	Delaware
York Center	Iowa
York Prairie	Cedar
Yough	Boone
Zoar	Cedar
Zwingle	Dubuque

OFFICIAL REGISTER FOR THE YEAR 1870.

STATE GOVERNMENT.

Samuel Merrill, Clayton county, Governor.
 Wm. H. Fleming, Clinton county, Private Secretary to the Governor.
Madison M. Walden, Appanoose county, Lieutenant-Governor.
Ed Wright, Cedar county, Secretary of State.
 F. A. Warner, Polk county, Deputy.
John A. Elliott, Mitchell county, Auditor of State.
 Samuel A. Ayres, Polk county, Deputy.
Samuel E. Rankin, Washington county, Treasurer of State.
 Isaac Brandt, Polk county, Deputy.
Cyrus C. Carpenter, Webster county, Register of State Land Office.
 John M. Davis, Johnson county, Deputy.
Abraham S. Kissell, Scott county, Superintendent of Public Instruction.
 Lewis J. Coulter, Linn county, Deputy.
John C. Merrill, Clayton county, State Librarian.
F. M. Mills, State Printer.
James S. Carter, State Binder.
Prof. A. N. Currier, Johnson county, Superintendent of Weights and Measures.

THE JUDICIARY.

SUPREME COURT.

Chester C. Cole, Polk county, Chief Justice.
George G. Wright, Van Buren county, Judge.
Joseph M. Beck, Lee county, Judge.
John F. Dillon, Scott county, Judge.
Charles Linderman, Page county, Clerk.
Henry O'Connor, Muscatine county, Attorney-General.
Edward H. Stiles, Wapello county, Reporter of the Decisions.

TIMES AND PLACES OF HOLDING COURT.

REGULAR TERMS.

At Des Moines, on the first Mondays of June and December in each year.

ARGUMENT TERMS.

At Davenport on the first Mondays of April and October in each year, to which place all causes from the counties of Scott, Clinton, Jackson, Johnson, Iowa, Cedar, Muscatine, Louisa and Washington must be taken.

At Dubuque on the third Mondays of April and October in each year, to which all causes from the counties of Dubuque, Clayton, Allamakee, Winneshiek, Hancock, Mitchell, Chickasaw, Floyd, Worth, Cerro Gordo, Tama, Hardin, Bremer, Butler Black Hawk, Grundy, Buchanan, Delaware, Fayette, Jones, Linn, Benton and Howard must be taken.

Causes from all counties not specified in the above lists will be taken to Des Moines.

DISTRICT COURTS.

JUDGES.

Joshua Tracy, Des Moines county, 1st judicial district.
Harvey Tannehill, Appanoose county, 2d judicial district.
James G. Day, Fremont county, 3d judicial district.
Henry Ford, Harrison county, 4th judicial district.
Hugh W. Maxwell, Warren county, 5th judicial district.
Ezekiel S. Sampson, Keokuk county, 6th judicial district.
J. Scott Richman, Muscatine county, 7th judicial district.
James H. Rothrock, Cedar county, 8th judicial district.
James Burt, Dubuque county, 9th judicial district.
Milo McGlathery, Fayette county, 10th judicial district.
Daniel D. Chase, Hamilton county, 11th judicial district.
William B. Fairfield, Floyd county, 12th judicial district.

DISTRICT ATTORNEYS.

George B. Corkhill, Henry county, 1st judicial district.
James B. Weaver, Davis county, 2d judicial district.
Charles E. Millard, Mills county, 3d judicial district.
Orson Rice Dickinson county, 4th judicial district.
Samuel D. Nichols, Guthrie county, 5th judicial district.
Moses A. McCoid, Jefferson county, 6th judicial district.
Lyman Ellis, Clinton county, 7th judicial district.
William G. Thompson, Linn county, 8th judicial district.
J. B. Powers, Black Hawk county, 9th judicial district.
C. T. Granger, Allamakee county, 10th judicial district.
John H. Bradley, Marshall county, 11th judicial district.
John E. Burke, Bremer county, 12th judicial district.

The terms of the officers of the Twelfth judicial district will expire on the 31st day of December 1872; those of the others on the 31st day of December, 1870.

CIRCUIT JUDGES.

John B. Drayer, Henry county, 1st circuit, 1st judicial district.
John C. Power, Des Moines county, 2d circuit, 1st judicial district.
Robert Sloan, Van Buren county, 1st circuit. 2d judicial district.
Henry L. Dashiell, Monroe county, 2d circuit, 2d judicial district.
R. L. Douglass, Pottawattamie county, 1st circuit, 3d judicial district.
James W. McDill, Union county, 2d circuit, 3d judicial district.
Addison Oliver, Monona county, 1st circuit, 4th judicial district.
J. M. Snyder, Humboldt county, 2d circuit, 4th judicial district.
John Mitchell, Polk county, 1st circuit, 5th judicial district.
Frederick Mott, Madison county, 2d circuit, 5th judicial district.
Lucian C. Blanchard, Poweshiek county, 1st circuit, 6th judicial district.
..............................2d circuit, 6th judicial district.
Henry H. Benson, Muscatine county, 1st circuit, 7th judicial district.
George B. Young, Clinton county, 2d circuit, 7th judicial district.
William E. Miller, Johnson county, 1st circuit, 8th judicial district.
Sylvanus Yates, Cedar county. 2d circuit, 8th judicial district.
Winslow T. Barker, Dubuque county, 1st circuit, 9th judicial district.
Sylvester Bagg, Black Hawk county. 2d circuit, 9th judicial district.
Martin V. Burdick, Winneshiek county, 1st circuit, 10th judicial district.
Benjamin T. Hunt, Clayton county. 2d circuit, 10th judicial district.
Henry Hudson, Boone county. 1st circuit, 11th judicial district,.
S. L. Rose, Hamilton county, 2d circuit, 11th judicial district.
George W. Ruddick, Bremer county, 1st circuit, 12th judicial district.
Harvey N. Brockaway, Hancock county, 2d circuit, 12th judicial district.

The terms of all the Circuit Judges expire December 31st. 1873.

THE MILITIA.

The Governor, Commander-in-Chief.

Brigadier-General, Nathaniel B. Baker, Clinton county, Adjutant and Inspector General, Acting Quartermaster-General, and acting as Paymaster-General.

SPECIAL AIDS.

Lt.-Col. Joseph C. Stone, Burlington, Des Moines county.
Lt.-Col. Wm. B. Leach, Cedar Rapids, Linn county.
Lt.-Col. Alexander Voorhees, Manchester, Delaware county.
Lt.-Col. Samuel D. Pryce, Iowa City, Johnson county.

Capt. Wm. H. Fleming, Military Secretary, Des Moines, Polk county.

THIRTEENTH GENERAL ASSEMBLY

Of the State of Iowa, to convene at the Capitol, in Des Moines, Monday, Jan. 10. 1870.

SENATE.

Dists.	COUNTIES.	SENATORS.	POST-OFFICE.
1	Lee	E. S. McCulloch	Primrose
2	Van Buren	Jacob G. Vale	Bonaparte
3	Davis	*Henry C. Traverse	Bloomfield
4	Appanoose	†W. F. Vermillion	Centerville
5	Monroe and Wayne	*Edward M. Bill	Albia
6	Clarke, Lucas, and Union	*James D. Wright	Chariton
7	Decatur, Ringgold, and Taylor	*Isaac W. Keller	Mount Ayr
8	Adams, Fremont, and Page	*Napoleon B. Moore	Clarinda
9	Montgomery, Cass, Mills, and Pottawattamie	*Jefferson P. Casady	Council Bluffs.
10	Des Moines	Charles Beardsley	Burlington
11	Henry	John P. West	Mt. Pleasant
12	Jefferson	*Abial R. Pierce	Fairfield
13	Wapello	‖Augustus H. Hamilton	Ottumwa
14	Louisa	James S. Hurley	Wapello
15	Washington	*Granville G. Bennett	Washington
16	Muscatine	Samuel McNutt	Muscatine
17	Keokuk	J. W. Havens	Sigourney
18	Mahaska	‡John. N. Dixon	Oskaloosa
19	Marion	†John M. Cathcart	Attica
20	Warren	*George E. Griffith	Indianola
21	Madison, Adair, Dallas, and Guthrie	Benjamin F. Murray	Winterset
22	Scott	Robert Lowry	Davenport
	"	H. R. Claussen	Davenport
23	Clinton	Alexander B. Ireland	Camanche
24	Cedar	*William P. Wolf	Tipton
25	Johnson	*Samuel H Fairall	Iowa City
26	Iowa	*Matthew Long	Stellapolis
27	Poweshiek and Tama	Joseph Dysart	Vinton
28	Jasper	Frank T. Campbell	Newton
29	Polk	B. F. Allen	Des Moines
30	Jackson	*Lewis B. Dunham	Maquoketa
31	Jones	John McKean	Anamosa
32	Linn	*Robert Smyth	Mount Vernon
33	Benton	*James Chapin	Vinton
34	Marshall and Hardin	*Wells S. Rice	Marshalltown
35	Dubuque	*F. M. Knoll	Dubuque
	"	M. B. Mulkern	Dubuque
36	Delaware	*Joseph Grimes	Colesburg
37	Buchanan	*William G. Donnan	Independence
38	Black Hawk	George W. Couch	Waterloo
39	Clayton	*Homer E. Newell	McGregor
40	Fayette	*William Larrabee	Clermont
41	Allamakee	*L. E. Fellows	Lansing
42	Winneshiek	‖H. C. Bulis	Decorah
43	Chickasaw, Floyd, and Howard	*John G. Patterson	Charles City
44	Bremer, Butler, and Grundy	R. B. Clarke	Janesville
45	Hamilton, Story, and Boone	*Isaac J. Mitchell	Boonsboro

SENATE—CONTINUED.

Dists.	COUNTIES.	SENATORS.	POST-OFFICE.
46	Mitchell, Worth, Cerro Gordo, Franklin, Wright, Hancock, Winnebago, and Kossuth....................	*Marcus Tuttle........	Clear Lake....
47	Webster, Greene, Carroll, Calhoun, Sac, Humboldt, Pocahontas, Buena Vista, Palo Alto, Clay, Emmet, and Dickinson......................	*Theodore Hawley....	Fort Dodge...
48	Audubon, Shelby, Harrison, Monona, Crawford, Ida, Woodbury, Plymouth, Cherokee, O'Brien, Sioux, and the unorganized counties of Lyon and Osceola.........................	Charles Atkins.........	Onawa City...

* Elected in 1867 for full term. † Elected in 1869 to fill vacancy.
‡ Elected in 1868 to fill vacancy. ‖ Re-elected.

NOTE.—Mr. McCulloch was a member of the House in the Fourth and Fifth Legislative Assemblies; also of the House in the Third and Eighth, and of the Senate in the Fifth and Sixth General Assemblies. Mr. McNutt was a member of the House in the Tenth, Eleventh, and Twelfth General Assemblies; Mr. McKean in the Eleventh and Twelfth; Mr. Fellows, Mr. Griffith, Mr. Traverse, and Mr. Bennett in the Eleventh; Mr. Murray in the Twelfth; Mr. Wolf in the Tenth; Mr Grimes in the Seventh; Mr. West in the Ninth and Eleventh, and Mr. Smyth in the First, also of the House in the Sixth Legislative Assembly. Mr. Hurley was a member of the Senate in the Ninth and Tenth General Assemblies; Mr. Dysart in the Ninth; Mr. Patterson in the Tenth and Eleventh; Mr. Knoll in the Tenth and Eleventh, also of the House in the Ninth.

HOUSE OF REPRESENTATIVES.

Dists.	COUNTIES.	REPRESENTATIVES.	POST-OFFICE.
1	Lee	Christian Hirschler....	Fr'nklin Cent'r
	Lee	David S. Bell..........	Big Mound....
	Lee	Patrick Gibbons......	Keokuk ......
2	Des Moines......................	William Harper.......	Kossuth.......
	"	Thomas J. Sater.......	Danville......
3	Henry...........................	Joshua G. Newbold....	Hillsboro......
	"	JoshuaW. Satterthwaite	Mt. Pleasant...
4	Jefferson	Joseph Ball...........	Fairfield......
	"	William Hopkirk.	Lockridge ....
5	Van Buren......................	*Joel Brown..........	Birmingham..
	"	George N. Rosser......	Troy, Davis Co
6	Wapello	*Charles Dudley......	Agency City..
	"	John H. Carver.......	Kirkville......
7	Davis..........................	Timothy O. Norris....	Troy..........
8	Monroe	Benjamin F. Elbert.. ..	Albia.........
9	Appanoose......................	Claudius B. Miller.....	Moravia.......
10	Lucas..........................	A. H. Stutsman........	Chariton......
11	Wayne..........................	Lewis Miles, Jr........	Corydon......
12	Decatur........................	Frederick Teale........	Decatur ......
13	Clarke.........................	John L. Millard.......	Osceola.......

*Members in the House of the Twelfth General Assembly.

HOUSE OF REPRESENTATIVES—CONTINUED.

Dists.	COUNTIES.	SENATORS.	POST-OFFICE.
14	Union and Adams	*Neal W. Rowell	Afton
15	Ringgold and Taylor	*Leonard T. McCoun	Bedford
16	Page	William Butler	Clarinda
17	Mills	*John Y. Stone	Glenwood
18	Fremont	James M. Hood	Hamburg
19	Pottawattamie	John Beresheim	Council Bluffs
20	Cass, Adair, and Montgomery	W. W. Merritt	Red Oak J'c'tn
21	Madison	John H. Hartenbower	Winterset
22	Warren	Alexander H. Swan	Indianola
23	Marion	D. T. Durham	Iola
	“	B. F. Keables	Pella
24	Mahaska	M. E. Cutts	Oskaloosa
	“	John F. Lacey	Oskaloosa
25	Keokuk	*John Morrison, Jr.	Butler
	“	B. A. Haycock	Richland
26	Washington	*Joseph D. Miles	Crawfordsville.
	“	A. Conner	Washington
27	Louisa	George D. Harrison	Columbus City
28	Muscatine	John Mahin	Muscatine
	“	William C. Evans	West Liberty
39	Cedar	James W. Beaty	Clarence
	“	J. Q. Tufts	Durant
30	Scott	*Matthias J. Rohlfs	Davenport
	“	Carlos C. Applegate	Le Claire
	“	John W. Green	Davenport
31	Clinton	*Aylett R. Cotton	Lyons
	“	Samuel H. Rogers	Wheatland
	“	Benjamin Spencer	Maquoketa
32	Jackson	James Dunne	Otter Creek
	“	Emory De Groat	Van Buren
33	Johnson	*John P. Irish	Iowa City
	“	A. B. Cornell	Iowa City
34	Iowa	James P. Ketcham	Marengo
35	Poweshiek	Erastus Snow	Grinnell
36	Polk	*John A. Kasson	Des Moines
	“	George W. Jones	Des Moines
37	Jasper	Caleb Bundy	Prairie City
	“	John H. Tait	Newton
38	Dallas	Cole Noel	Adel
39	Greene, Calhoun, Pocahontas, and Humboldt	Gillum S. Tolliver	Jefferson
40	Shelby, Audubon, and Guthrie	Wm. H. Campbell	Panora
41	Harrison	George H. McGavren	Missouri Vall'y
42	Boone	John F. Hopkins	Swede Point
43	Story	William K. Wood	Iowa Center
44	Tama	*James Wilson	Buckingham
45	Benton	*John W. Traer	Vinton
46	Marshall	Delos Arnold	Marshaltown
47	Linn	Oliver O. Stanchfield	Cedar Rapids.
	“	E. A. Warner	Waubeek
48	Jones	* John Russell	Clay Mills
	“	P. G. Bonewitz	Langworthy
49	Dubuque	Theophilus Crawford	Peosta
	“	John Christoph	Dyersville
	“	William Mills	Dubuque
	“	Fred O'Donnell	“

27

Dists.	COUNTIES.	REPRESENTATIVES.	POST-OFFICE.
50	Delaware	* Cummings Sanborn	Earlville
51	Clayton	Samuel Murdock	Garnavillo
	"	H. B. Taylor	Strawberry Pt.
52	Allamakee	* Pierce G. Wright	Waukon
	"	D. Dickerson	Hardin
53	Buchanan	Daniel S. Lee	Independence
54	Fayette	* Aaron Brown	Fayette
	"	Joseph Hobson	West Union
55	Winneshiek	* Horace B. Williams	Hesper
	"	A. O. Loman	Decorah
56	Mitchell and Howard	Amos S. Faville	Mitchell
57	Chickasaw	George W. Butterfield	Nashua
58	Floyd	H. O. Pratt	Charles City
59	Bremer	O. C. Harrington	Waverley
60	Black Hawk	T. B. Carpenter	Cedar Falls
	"	Jesse Wasson	La Porte City
61	Butler and Grundy	S. B. Dumont	Union Ridge
62	Hardin	Henry L. Huff	Eldora
63	Wright, Hamilton and Franklin	* John D. Hunter	Webster City
64	Webster	Galusha Parsons	Fort Dodge
65	Winnebago, Worth, Hancock and Cerro Gordo	B. F. Hartshorn	Mason City
66	Kossuth, Palo Alto, Emmet and Dickinson	Harwood G. Day	Estherville
67	Woodbury, Plymouth, Sioux, O'Brien, Lyon and Osceola	Constant R. Marks	Sioux City
68	Sac, Buena Vista, Cherokee and Clay	George H. Wright	Grant City
69	Monona, Crawford, Carroll and Ida	J. D. Miracle	Denison

* Members in the House of the Twelfth General Assembly.

NOTE.—Mr. Russell was a member of the House in the Ninth, Tenth and Eleventh General Assemblies, and Speaker in the Twelfth. Mr. Brown, of Van Buren, Mr. Dudley, Mr. Rohlfs, Mr. Wright, of Allamakee, and Mr. Williams, were members of the House in the Eleventh and Twelfth General Assemblies. Mr. Rosser in the Fifth; Mr. Harper in the Third; Mr. Arnold in the Sixth; Mr. Millard in the Eighth; Mr. Christoph in the Tenth; and Mr. Cotton in the Twelfth, and of the Constitutional Convention of 1857. Mr. Murdock was a member of the House in the Seventh and Eighth Legislative Assemblies. Mr. Crawford was a member of the Constitutional Convention of 1844, a member of the Senate in the First and Second General Assemblies, and of the House in the Third and Seventh. Mr. Cutts was a member of the Senate in the Tenth and Eleventh General Assemblies, and Mr. Brown, of Fayette, in the Sixth and Seventh.

PUBLIC INSTITUTIONS.

STATE UNIVERSITY OF IOWA,

IOWA CITY, JOHNSON COUNTY.

Established 1847.

BOARD OF TRUSTEES.

The Governor, *ex-officio* President.
Lewis W. Ross, Pottawattamie county; term expires 1872.
Charles W. Hobart, Johnson county; term expires 1872.
R. M. Burnett, Muscatine county; term expires 1870.
H. C. Bulis, Winneshiek county; term expires 1870.
Coker F. Clarkson, Grundy county; term expires 1870.
Christian W. Slagle, Jefferson county; term expires 1870.
John P. Irish, Johnson county; term expires 1872.
Rev. James Black, D. D., President of the Faculty; *ex.officio* Trustee.
William J. Haddock, Secretary of the Board.
Ezekiel Clark, Treasurer of the Board.

The Trustees of the State University are elected by the General Assembly for four years. The Treasurer and Secretary are chosen by the Board of Trustees, and hold office during the pleasure of that body. The Board also elects a President and the requisite number of professors and tutors.

ASYLUM OF THE BLIND,

VINTON, BENTON COUNTY.

Established at Iowa City in 1853. *Removed to Vinton, August*, 1862.

BOARD OF TRUSTEES.

James McQuinn, Benton county, President of the Board; term expires 1870:
John Hodgdon. Dubuque county; term expires 1872.

James Chapin, Benton county, Treasurer of the Board; term expires 1872.

Joseph Dysart, Tama county; term expires 1870.

Charles H. Conklin, Benton county; term expires 1870.

William G. Donnan, Buchanan county; appointed by the Board to fill vacancy.

S. A. Knapp, Principal of the Institution; *ex-officio* Trustee.

—

The Trustees of the Asylum of the Blind are chosen by the General Assembly for the term of four years. The Board elects its own officers, and chooses the Principal, Matron, Teachers, etc., of the Asylum, and from the employes selects a Steward.

INSTITUTION OF THE DEAF AND DUMB.

Established at Iowa City, Johnson County, January 31*st*, 1855. *Permanently located at Council Bluffs, Pottawattamie County, July* 4*th*, 1866.*

—

BOARD OF TRUSTEES.

The Governor.

N. H. Brainerd, Johnson county; term expires 1871.

John C. Shrader, Johnson county; term expires 1870.

J. T. Turner, Johnson county; term expires 1872.

Ed Wright, Cedar county, Secretary of State.

Abraham S. Kissell, Scott county, Superintendent of Public Instruction.

Benjamin Talbott, Principal of the Institution.

—

The Trustees of the above Institution are appointed by the Governor and Senate for four years. Vacancies occurring during the recess of the General Assembly are filled by the Governor till the next session of that body. The Board elects one of its own members Treasurer; it also chooses the Principal, Matron, and other officers, etc., of the Institution, and from the employes chooses a Steward.

—

COMMISSIONERS *under the act of April* 3*d*, 1866, *to locate the Institution at Council Bluffs.*

Thomas Officer, Pottawattamie county.

Caleb Baldwin. " "

Grenville M. Dodge, " "

---

* The Institution remains at Iowa City, awaiting the erection of the buildings at Council Bluffs.

IOWA HOSPITAL FOR THE INSANE.

MOUNT PLEASANT, HENRY COUNTY.

Established in 1855.

BOARD OF TRUSTEES.

Maturin L. Fisher, Clayton county; term expires 1872.
Martin L. Edwards, Henry county; term expires 1874.
George Acheson, Jefferson county; term expires 1874.
Micajah T. Williams, Mahaska county; term expires 1874.
Andrew W. McClure, Henry county; term expires 1870.
Benjamin Crabb, Washington county; term expires 1872.
Luke Palmer, Des Moines county; term expires 1870.

Mark Ranney, M. D., Superintendent.
Martin L. Edwards, Treasurer.

The Trustees of the "Iowa Hospital for the Insane," are elected by the General Assembly for the term of six years. The Board holds an annual meeting on the first Wednesday of December, at which time the President and Secretary of the Board are elected. The Board also appoints the Medical Superintendent, the Matron, and one or more Assistant Physicians.

ADDITIONAL INSTITUTION FOR THE INSANE,

LOCATED AT INDEPENDENCE, BUCHANAN COUNTY.

Commissioners to superintend the selection of the location, and erection of suitable buildings for use of said Institution.

E. T. Morgan, Webster county.
Maturin L. Fisher, Clayton county.
G. W. Bemis, Buchanan county.

STATE AGRICULTURAL COLLEGE AND MODEL FARM,

STORY COUNTY.

Established March 31, 1868.

BOARD OF TRUSTEES.

A. S. Welch. President of the College and *ex-officio* President of the Board.
The Governor.
Peter Melendy, Black Hawk county; term expires 1872.
James D. Wright, Lucas county; term expires 1872.
O. H. P. Buchanan, Henry county; term expires 1872.
Charles E. Leffingwell, Clinton county; term expires 1872.
John Russell, Jones county; term expires 1870.
Benjamin F. Gue, Webster county; term expires 1870.
James Woodbury, Decatur county; term expires 1872.
J. C. Cusey, Humboldt county; term expires 1870.
Oliver Mills, Cass County; term expires 1872.
Theron A. Morgan, Keokuk county; term expires 1870.
R. W. Humphrey, Floyd county; term expires 1870.
R. A. Richardson, Fayette county; term expires 1872.

C. A. Dunham, Des Moines County, Superintendent of College Building.

P. S. Brown, Fayette county, Superintendent of Agricultural College Farm, and *ex-officio* Secretary of the Board of Trustees.

S. E. Rankin, Washington county, Treasurer.

The Trustees are elected by the General Assembly for the term of four years. The Board of Trustees meet annually on the second Monday of January, at which time the Treasurer is elected. The Board appoints the Superintendent of Agricultural College Farm during its pleasure, and has power to elect a President, &c.

IOWA SOLDIERS ORPHANS HOME.

HOMES AT DAVENPORT, SCOTT COUNTY, CEDAR FALLS, BLACK HAWK COUNTY AND GLENWOOD, MILLS COUNTY.

Established as a State Institution in 1866.

BOARD OF TRUSTEES.

John L. Davis, Scott county; term expires 1870.
William Slatter, Des Moines county; term expires 1870.

John Bell, Scott county; term expires 1870.
P. G. Wright, Allamakee county; term expires 1870.
John Meyer, Jasper county; term expires 1870.
E. C. Bosbyshell, Mills county; term expires 1870.
J. B. Powers, Black Hawk county; term expires 1870.

The Trustees of the "Iowa Soldiers Orphans Home" are elected by the General Assembly for the term of two years.

IOWA REFORM SCHOOL.

SITUATED IN THE NORTHWESTERN PART OF LEE COUNTY.

Organized in the year 1868.

BOARD OF TRUSTEES.

Isaac T. Gibson, 1st Congressional District, Treasurer of the Board; term expires 1872.
J. A. Parvin, 2d Congressional District, President of the Board; term expires 1874.
E. O. Clemens, 3d Congressional District; term expires 1872.
James D. Ladd, 4th Congressional District; term expires 1870.
M. A. Dashiell, 5th Congressional District, Secretary; term expires 1870.
William J. Moir, 6th Congressional District; term expires 1874.
Joseph McCarty, Superintendent.

The Trustees of the "Iowa Reform School" are elected by the General Assembly for the term of six years, the terms of office being so arranged that two shall expire biennially.

PENITENTIARY OF THE STATE.

FORT MADISON, LEE COUNTY.

Established February 25, 1839.

Martin Heisey, Des Moines county, Warden.
Charles A. Manning, Van Buren county, Deputy Warden.
Charles Hilles, Lee County, Clerk.
Joseph McDowell, Chaplain.
Augustus W. Hoffmeister, Physician.

The Warden is elected by joint ballot of the General Assembly at each regular session. He appoints the Clerk, Deputy Warden, Chaplain, and Guards; and with the concurrence of the Governor appoints the Physician, and on the nomination of the latter, appoints the Steward.

COMMISSIONERS OF LEGAL INQUIRY.

William H. Seevers, Mahaska county; term expires 1872.
Samuel H. Fairall, Johnson county; term expires 1872.
Elijah Odell, Clayton county; term expires 1872.

The Commissioners of Legal Inquiry are appointed by the Governor and Senate every sixth year.

COUNTY GOVERNMENT.

Table showing the names of the County Auditors, Clerks of the District Court, Treasurers and Recorders, with the County-Seats of the several counties, for the year 1870.

COUNTIES.	COUNTY-SEATS.	COUNTY AUDITORS.	CLERKS OF THE DISTRICT COURT.	TREASURERS.	RECORDERS.
Adair	Fontanelle	John H. Bailey	James Rany	James C. Gibbs	Wesley Taylor
Adams	Quincy	Jhilson P. Cummins	James Widner	Walter E. McDuffee	Arthur L Wells
Allamakee	Waukon	M. B. Hendrick	John W. Pratt	James Duffy	David W. Reed
Appanoose	Centerville	Barton A. Ogle	Kelita P. Morrison	Charles W. Bowen	Eugene C. Haynes
Audubon	Exira	Albert I. Brainard	John N. Scott	Charles Vangorder	[N.] Frank Stotts
Benton	Vinton	E. Marion Evans	Buren R. Sherman	Stephen A. Marine	Philip M. Coder
Black Hawk	Waterloo	Daniel W. Foote	Gustavus A. Eberhart	Romaine A. Whitaker	James W. McClure
Boone	Boonsboro	W. C. Harrah	Henry R. Wilson	A. Downing	Alonzo J. Barkley
Bremer	Waverly	Louis Case	Marquis F. Gillett	Wm. V. Lucas	Edward C. Dougherty
Buchanan.*	Independence	....	David L. Smith	....	John Hollett
Buena Vista	Prairieville	O. C. Johnson	Olans H. Dahl	Almond Eldred	Ole H. Storla
Butler	Butler Center	A. J. Tompkins	James W. Davis	J. F. Wright	George M. Craig
Calhoun	Lake City	H. W. Sprague	*William H. Fitch*	S. T. Hutchison	*J. W. Hollenbeck*
Carroll.*	Carroll	....	John K. Deal	....	William A. Young
Cass	Atlantic	Luther L. Alexander	James K. Powers	Wilkins Warwick	Henry Temple
Cedar	Tipton	E. M. Brink	William Elliott	E. H. Pound	Jesse James
Cerro Gordo	Mason City	Charles B. Senior	Frank M. Rogers	Henry I. Smith	Henry Keerl
Cherokee	Cherokee	I. Armstrong	Joel H. Davenport	D. F. Gearhart	Elisha Kingsbury
Chickasaw	New Hampton	George A. Hamilton	Zelotes Bailey	William W. Birdsall	Benjamin E. Morton

* No report of officers elect for 1869 has been received by this office.—SECRETARY OF STATE.

NOTE.—The County Auditors and Treasurers were chosen at the general election in 1869. Their term of office will commence on the first Monday of January, 1870, and expire on the first Monday of January, 1872. The Clerks of the District Courts and Recorders were chosen in 1868, and their terms of office expire on the first Monday of January, 1871.

LIST OF COUNTY OFFICERS—CONTINUED.

COUNTIES.	COUNTY-SEATS.	COUNTY AUDITORS.	CLERKS OF THE DISTRICT COURT.	TREASURERS.	RECORDERS.
Clarke*	Osceola		Allen H. Burrows		Harvey H. Hess
Clay	Peterson	Samuel Gonser	Samuel W. Dubois	Samuel W. Dubois	John J. Bicknell
Clayton	Elkader	M. E. Duff	Henry S. Granger	Henry Kellner	William D. Crooke
Clinton	Clinton	Kirke W. Wheeler	Noel B. Howard	Edwin R. Lucas	Joseph D. Fegan
Crawford	Denison	Andrew D. Molony	Andrew D. Malony	Morris McHenry	Thomas Dobson
Dallas	Adel	J. Perkins	Newton G. Long	S. J. Garontto	John W. Coons
Davis	Bloomfield	Wm. Van Benthusen	Ambrose H. Hill	Henry Nulton	H. Marion York
Decatur	Leon	George Burton	Edward K. Pitman	S. C. Thompson	William J. Sullivan
Delaware	Delhi	Jeremiah B. Boggs	Andrew J. Brown	Joseph M. Holbrook	Henry Harger
Des Moines	Burlington	Emory S Huston	William Garrett	William Horner	Samuel Pollock
Dickinson	Spirit Lake	Samuel L. Pillsbury	Walter B. Brown	Milton J. Smith	Milton J. Smith
Dubuque	Dubuque	Stephen Hempstead	H. A. Rooney	Wm. G. Stewart	Warner Lewis
Emmet	Estherville	Howard Graves	Henry Jenkins	D. M. L. Bemis	Howard Graves
Fayette	West Union	Hiram Hoagland	William B. Lakin	James Stewart	Edwin H. Kinyon
Floyd	Charles City	J. P. Knight	Ebenezer A. Teeling	J. S. Childs	Gustavus B. Eastman
Franklin	Hampton	R. S. Benson	R. S. Benson	Arthur T. Reeve	Henry Meyer, Sr
Fremont*	Sidney		John C. Shockley		D. G. Bodenhamer
Greene	Jefferson	Marshall B. McDuffie	I. D. Howard	James Standford	John H. Clark
Grundy	Grundy Center	W. C. Williams	James M. Comstock	E. H. Beckman	E. H. Beckman
Guthrie	Panora	E. C. Mount	Charles Hill	Joseph Kenworthy	Godfrey Jerne
Hamilton*	Webster City		Albert A. Wicks		Samuel Baxter
Hancock	Concord	John Christie, Jr	Lambert B. Bailey	John Maben †	John Maben
Hardin	Eldora	E. A. Arnold	Samuel A. Reed	Solon F. Benson	Samuel S. Waldo
Harrison	Magnolia	William H. Eaton	John W. Stocker	George S. Bacon	J. Cutler Milliman
Henry	Mt. Pleasant	Oc. H. Snyder	Thomas A. Bereman	Reason Banks	A. R. Warren
Howard	Cresco	Charles S. Thurber	S. A. Stone	Manley M. Moon	William H. Patterson
Humboldt	Dakota City	Andrew W. McFarland	Andrew W. McFarland	Charles Bergk	William H. Locke

Ida	Ida	Obed Waterman	Obed Waterman	J. H. Moorehead	William J. Wagoner
Iowa	Marengo	Joseph G. Berstler	John Hughes, Jr.	Charles Baumer	M. W. Stover
Jackson	Andrew	Thomas E. Blanchard	E. J. Holmes	James A. Bryan	John Donnelley
Jasper	Newton	George R. Ledyard	Wm. R. McCully	E. H. Bartow	G. W. Chinn
Jefferson	Fairfield	David B. Miller	George H. Case	Lewis P. Vance	Henry C. Rock
Johnson	Iowa City	Garret D. Palmer	Benjamin King	Aaron J. Hershire	Joseph S. Lodge
Jones	Anamosa	Charles Cline	Jacob C. Dietz	Laurence Schoonover	Richard McDaniel
Keokuk	Sigourney	Louis Hollingsworth	John M. Brunt	John Q. Howard	James E. Woods
Kossuth	Algona	A. E. Wheelock	James L. Paine	John E. Blackford	Harvey M. Taft
Lee	Fort Madison	Edmund Jaeger	Charles Doerr	A. C. Roberts	Noble Warwick
Linn	Marion	J. P. Coulter	Andrew J. McKean	Richard T. Wilson	John J. Daniels
Louisa	Wapello	Wm. G. Allen	John Hale	Whitney S. Kremer	N. W. McKay
Lucas	Chariton	Robert McCormick	Nelson B. Gardner	James B. Custer	Jonathan B. Smith
Lyon	Not organized				
Madison	Winterset	Samuel L. Holliday	Daniel E. Cooper	John A. Pitzer	Oziah A. Moser
Mahaska	Oskaloosa	James Ruan	Charles P. Searle	James A. Young	John Larmer
Marion	Knoxville	Joseph Brobst	Henry L. Bousquet	Edward Baker	Allen Hamrick
Marshall	Marshalltown	Jabez Banbury	Heman P. Williams	Henry A. Gerhart	Francis M. Thomas
Mills	Glenwood	David M. Mitchell	Thomas P. Ballard	Caleb B. Atkins	Jason M. Powell
Mitchell	Mitchell	Arthur W. Clyde	Calvin S. Prime	Charles Sweney	Gerrit S. Needham
Monona	Onawa City	John K. McCaskey	John K. McCaskey	James Armstrong	John E. Selleck
Monroe	Albia	Samuel T. Craig	Josiah T. Young	John R. May	Calvin Barnard
Montgomery	Red Oak Junction	Reuben M. Roberts	Reuben M. Roberts	Wayne Stennett	William P. Wiley
Muscatine	Muscatine	R. H. McCampbell	John D. Walker	Robert T. Thompson	Milford M. Kennedy
O'Brien	O'Brien	Archibald Murray	H. T. Parker	R. B. Crego	Archibald W. Murray
Osceola	Not organized				
Page	Clarinda	Wm. M. Alexander	Wm. W. Russell	Henry Dorsey	Dan J. De Long
Palo Alto	Emmetsburg	Wm. E. Cullen	Robert Shea	James P. White	William D. Powers
Plymouth	Melbourne	Arthur E. Rea	A. C. Sheetz	John H. Morf	John H. Morf
Pocahontas	Rolfe	Wm. D. McEwen	Wm. D. McEwen	James J. Bruce	Thomas S. Macvey
Polk	Des Moines	John B. Miller	Harry H. Griffiths	Charles G. Lewis	Irving W. Thomas
Pottawattamie	Council Bluffs	E. B. Bowman	Wm. G. Crawford	John W. Chapman	George A. Haynes

LIST OF COUNTY OFFICERS—Continued.

COUNTIES.	COUNTY-SEATS.	COUNTY AUDITORS.	CLERKS OF THE DISTRICT COURT.	TREASURERS.	RECORDERS.
Poweshiek	Montezuma	Josephus F. Head	John W. Cheshire	George W. Kierulff	John Hall
Ringgold	Mount Ayr	John McFarland	Thomas Ross	C. W. Dake	Warren R. Turk
Sac	Sac City	Wm. H. Hobbs	Wm. H. Hobbs	Ed. R. Duffie	Nathan W. Condron
Scott	Davenport	R. G. Leonard	Mahlon D. Snyder	Henry Egbert	Frank M. Suiter
Shelby	Harlan	Harmon C. Holcomb	Harmon C. Holcomb	Milo H. Adams	Benjamin I. Kinsey
Sioux	Calliope	G. H. Root	Carlos Boone	Rufus Stone	Rufus Stone
Story	Nevada	Commodore P. MCord	Joseph A. Fitzpatrick	Eldred G. Day	Samuel Bates
Tama	Toledo	Thomas S. Free	Leonard B. Blinn	Theodore Shaeffer	Jacob Yeiser, Jr.
Taylor	Bedford	Russell B. Kinsell	Elisha T. Smith	John M. Cobb	James P. Flick
Union*	Afton	....	Alonzo F. Ickis	....	J. Calvin Lucas
Van Buren	Keosauqua	Alex. Brown	James W. Latham	Joshua S. Sloan	Russell Johnston
Wapello	Ottumwa	George D. Hackworth	Leonidas M. Godley	Alfred Lotspiech	Daniel W. Tower
Warren	Indianola	John D. Ingalls	*Charles McKay*	Paris P. Henderson	*Miles W Judkins*
Washington	Washington	Ralph Dewey	Christopher T. Jones	Robert Glasgow	Thomas Rowan
Wayne	Corydon	B. S. Jones	Martin Read	George W. Dean	A. R. Meredith
Webster	Fort Dodge	Wilson Lumpkin	Wilson Lumpkin	Jonathan Hutchison	David H. Taylor
Winnebago	Forest City	Hiram K. Landrue	Eugene Secor	Robert Clark	Nelson K. Landrue
Winneshiek*	Decorah	....	Marvin P. Hathaway	....	Cyrus McKay
Woodbury	Sioux City	George W. Wakefield	F. J. Lambert	B. F. Smith	P. J. B. Marion
Worth	Northwood	B. K. Walker	Horace V. Dwelle	D. McKercher	D. McKercher
Wright	Clarion	John L. Morse	Lemuel P. Davis	William W. Gates	O. K. Eastman

* No report of officers elect for 1869 has been received by this office.—[Secretary of State.

TABLE

Showing the Sheriffs, Surveyors, Superintendents of Common Schools, and Coroners of the several counties of the State for the year 1870.

COUNTIES.	SHERIFFS.	SURVEYORS.	SUPERINTENDENTS OF COMMON SCHOOLS.	CORONERS.
Adair	George Salisbury	J. M. Joseph	J. W. Peet	J. S. Waggoner
Adams	William Bixler	Able A. Nolan	Benjamin Widner	John W. Morris
Allamakee	Robert Bathan	John G. Ratcliff	Lenthel Eells	A. G. Collins
Appanoose	Henry H. Wright	J. J. Wall	Thomas Wentworth	E. O. Smith
Audubon	Samuel R. Thomas	P. I. Whitteel	David B. Beers	H. R. Smith
Benton	Henry M. Wilson	James A. Brown	H. M. Hoon	Moses Denman
Black Hawk	Worcester F. Brown	John Ball	Edward G. Miller	Walter O. Richards
Boone	George W. Crooks	Lawrence Regan	L. W. Fisk	W. D Templin
Bremer	Charles M. Kingsley	S. H. Wallis	Childs S. Harwood	C. O. Paquin
Buchanan*				
Buena Vista	Llewellyn A. Jones	Daniel Smith	Fletcher A. Blake	Joseph H. M. Delong
Butler	Lyman L. Smith	O. W. McIntosh	W. A. Lathrop	T. G. Copeland
Calhoun	A. T. Bowers	Seldon H. Richardson	E. L. Hobbs	E. V. Blackley
Carroll*				
Cass	James Barnes	William Waddell	E. D. Hawes	John W. Montgomery
Cedar	John D. Shearer	Martin G. Miller	A. B. Oakley	Austin Parsons
Cerro Gordo	William B. Stillson	Charles T. Vincent	Asa S. Allen	George B. Rockwell
Cherokee	George Filer	A. L. Porter	Oscar Chase	Levi Rogers
Chickasaw	Earl W. Beach	Henry H. Potter	W. P. Bennett	Amos Babcock
Clarke*				
Clay	Thomas Dodd	Peter M. Moore	Charles Carver	J. W. Brockshink
Clayton	James Davis	Sanford L. Peck	John Everall	Horace D. Brownsen
Clinton	Thomas G. Ferreby	Benjamin B. Hart	Roswell B. Millard	Charles H. Lothrop

* No report of officers elect for 1869 has been received at this office.—SECRETARY OF STATE.

LIST OF COUNTY OFFICERS—CONTINUED.

COUNTIES.	SHERIFFS.	SURVEYORS.	SUPERINTENDENTS OF COMMON SCHOOLS.	CORONERS.
Crawford	Samuel P. Blankinship	Morris M. Henry	N. Jay Wheeler	William Iseminger
Dallas	John M. Rogers	E. T. Abbott	Amos Dilley	Macklin E. Coons
Davis	Daniel Bradbury	Thomas Duffield	Moses Downing	Cyrus D. Chapman
Decatur	Ezekiel J. Sankey	William F. Craig	W. C. Jackson	John Sylvester
Delaware	Cyrus H. Smith	Hezekiah G. Doolittle	John Kenneday	Albert Boomer
Des Moines	James H. Latty	William H. Gillespie	Thomas J. Trulock	William A. Haw
Dickinson	Daniel Bennett	Walter B. Brown	Joshua H. Pratt	W. S. Beers
Dubuque	William D. Bucknam	Otto H. Cruseirs	John J. E. Norman	J. O'Hea Cantillon
Emmet	Giles W. Robbins	D. W. Perry	S. W. Brown	William Peterson
Fayette	Jacob Swank	J. H. McAlvin	Marshall M. House	Lewis Armstrong
Floyd	David M Ferguson	Horace Stearns	Harvey Wilbur	W. H. Palmer
Franklin	Amos B. Henderson	Obadiah Smith	J. Cheston Whitney	Charles M. Walton
Fremont*				
Greene	Clinton Dewitt	Jacob M. Toliver	Isaac L. Kephart	D. J. Bowman
Grundy	J. A. Vennum	E. A. Crary	Lorenzo D. Tracy	J. S. B. Thompson
Guthrie	Thomas Turner	James W. Nation	James Grandstaff	T. W. Harl
Hamilton*				
Hancock	J. H. Beadle	E. Marshall	A. R. Barnes	S. Whitcombe
Hardin	Nelson Gibbs	J. J. Shrieber	Enos P. Stubbs	S. P. Smith
Harrison	J. J. Peck	George Madison	Horace H. McKenney	Asher Servis
Henry	William T. Spearman	Thomas A. Mann	George W. Thompson	J. Jones
Howard	Jerry F. Powell	Peter N. Glathart	Charles F. Breckenridge	Jacob J. Clemmer
Humboldt	Charles Simmons	W. Thomson	E. C. Miles	A. Harvey
Ida	Alonzo J. Teall	William J. Wagoner	Mathew G. Aldrich	John A. Logan
Iowa	John M. Richardson	John L. Williams	Constant S. Lake	Frank M. Jeffers
Jackson	Morris S. Allen	Alexander C. Simpson	J. W. Fleming	James W. Eckles

Jasper	William C. Hawk	Charles C. Turner	Sanford J. Moyer	
Jefferson	Jacob S. Gantz	Isaac H. Crumley	John N. Edwards	Richard J. Mohr
Johnson	Samuel P. McCaddon	Christian Hess	Richard L. Garter	R. W. Pryce
Jones	Orrin B. Crane	Daniel L. Blakeslee	Alexander Hughes	V. C. Williston
Keokuk	Andrew Stranahan	John A. Benson	J. A. Lowe	H. F. B. Passig
Kossuth	John M. Pinkerton	John B. Jones	Albert W. Osborne	L. A. Sheetz
Lee	John A. Bishop	I. A. Davis	William G. Kent	Rufus Goodnough
Linn	John G. Hayzlett	George A. Gray	William Langham	A. Laurence
Louisa	John L. Grubb	Thomas W. Bailey	Lewis A. Riley	George Presbury
Lucas	Gaylord Lyman	Joseph Chenoworth	John W. Perry	W. H. Huyck
Lyon	Not organized			
Madison	John S. Tullis	A. W. Wilkinson	Henry W. Hardy	Alfred Hood
Mahaska	James W. Hinesley	Nathaniel Caven	George T. Carpenter	David Needham
Marion	J. P. Kelly	O. H. S. Kennedy	Aaron Yetter	Michael Wikle
Marshall	J. L. Herbert	William Bremner	Cyrus C. Shaw	B. F. Kierulff
Mills	James W. Turner	Charles W. Spalding	John B. Mallett	Mathew H. McCluskey
Mitchell	William Ramsdell	Warren H. Knowlton	Miss Julia C. Addington	D. O. Sayles
Monona	Edwin R. Pierce	Joseph Dungan	Winslow A. Green	Richard Stebbins
Monroe	Alexander McDonald	James M. Porter	William A. Nichol	Casper Dull
Montgomery	Hiram G. McMillin	Ephraim P. Milner	Benjamin E. A. Simons	Elias H. Burris
Muscatine	Abraham E. Keith	JohnA. Mathewson	Charles Hamilton	John Beard
O'Brien	S. B. Hulbert	J. H. Schofield	J. F. Schofield	Frank Vaughn
Osceola	Not organized			
Page	Joshua J. Round	William R. Callicotte	Elijah Miller	Frank E. Norton
Palo Alto	John M. Hefley	Martin Coonvin	Jeremiah L. Martin	Gilbreath Franklin
Plymouth	Thomas S. McElhaney	Austin C. Sheetz	William Hunter	Andrew Black
Pocahontas	Oscar Slosson	George W. Strong	David Miller	Joseph Clason
Polk	Peter H. Van Slyck	P. B. Reed	J. A. Nash	A. G. Fields
Pottawattamie	Perry Reel	E. W. Davenport	G. L. Jacobs	Henry Osborne
Poweshiek	Anderson M. Harden	William R. Cowley	Leonard F. Parker	William S. Green
Ringgold	D. B. Marshall	Henry H. Ross	William J. Buck	William Cavin

*No report of officers elect for 1869 has been received at this office.—[SECRETARY OF STATE.

LIST OF COUNTY OFFICERS—CONTINUED.

COUNTIES.	SHERIFFS.	SURVEYORS.	SUPERINTENDENTS OF COMMON SCHOOLS.	CORONERS.
Sac	William Impson	Charles Wilson	Rasselas Ellis	R. G. Platt
Scott	Gustavus Schnitzer	Thomas Murray	Roderick Rose	J. J. Tomson
Shelby	Christian Goodyear	Charles W. Dey	P. C. Truman	Theron W. Winters
Sioux	Thomas H. Dunham	William West	Eli Johnson	O. J. Dunham
Story	Alf. Goodin	Madison C. Allen	John R. Hays	Charles P. Robinson
Tama	Knight Dexter	C. W. Hyatt	John R. Stewart	Nathan Fisher
Taylor	Jesse Laird	Josiah Litteer	John S. Boyd	Mahlon C. Connett
Union*				
Van Buren	George W. Summerville	E. B. Kirkindall	George B. Walker	Silas Tolman
Wapello	Samuel A. Swiggett		Henry C. Cox	J. C. Hinsey
Warren	Elbert J. Kuhn	John S. Hoyt	Alonzo L. Kimball	D. S. Montgomery
Washington	Abraham Bunker	D. C. Kyle	Isaac G. Moore	Jackson Roberts
Wayne	John N. Wright	Burris Moore	Enos Rushton	E. W. Fullerton
Webster	Jacob Waltz	George Killam	J. M. Philips	
Winnebago	Peter Lewis	J. H. T. Ambrose	Martin Cooper	D. C. Hayes
Winneshiek*				
Woodbury	George W. Kingsworth	F. W. Davis	A. M. Hunt	George W. Vanderhale
Worth	T. K. Hundely	H. V. Dwelle	Franklin Parker	Simon Rustad
Wright	Wm. D. Hulse	George A. McKay	John D Sands	Christopher Crounse

LIST OF COUNTIES

Composing the Several Judicial Districts and Circuits in the State of Iowa.

FIRST JUDICIAL DISTRICT.

First Circuit—Lee and Henry.
Second Circuit—Des Moines and Louisa.

SECOND JUDICIAL DISTRICT.

First Circuit—Van Buren, Wapello, and Davis.
Second Circuit—Appanoose, Monroe, Lucas, and Wayne.

THIRD JUDICIAL DISTRICT.

First Circuit—Page, Montgomery, Fremont, Mills and Pottawattamie.
Second Circuit—Clarke, Decatur, Union, Ringgold, Adams, and Taylor.

FOURTH JUDICIAL DISTRICT.

First Circuit—Harrison, Shelby, Crawford, Monona, Woodbury, Ida, Cherokee, Plymouth, Sioux, O'Brien, Osceola, and Lyon.
Second Circuit—Sac, Calhoun, Humboldt, Pocahontas, Buena Vista, Clay, Palo Alto, Kossuth, Emmet, and Dickinson.

FIFTH JUDICIAL DISTRICT.

First Circuit—Warren, Polk, and Dallas.
Second Circuit—Madison, Adair, Cass, Audubon, Carroll, Greene, and Guthrie.

SIXTH JUDICIAL DISTRICT.

First Circuit—Washington, Jefferson, Keokuk, and Poweshiek.
Second Circuit—Mahaska, Marion, and Jasper.

SEVENTH JUDICIAL DISTRICT.

FIRST CIRCUIT—Scott, and Muscatine.
SECOND CIRCUIT—Clinton and Jackson.

EIGHTH JUDICIAL DISTRICT.

FIRST CIRCUIT—Benton, Tama, Iowa, and Johnson.
SECOND CIRCUIT—Cedar, Linn, and Jones.

NINTH JUDICIAL DISTRICT.

FIRST CIRCUIT—Dubuque, and Delaware.
SECOND CIRCUIT—Buchanan, Black Hawk, and Grundy.

TENTH JUDICIAL DISTRICT.

FIRST CIRCUIT—Allamakee, Winneshiek, and Howard.
SECOND CIRCUIT—Clayton, Fayette, and Chickasaw.

ELEVENTH JUDICIAL DISTRICT.

FIRST CIRCUIT—Marshall, Story, and Boone.
SECOND CIRCUIT—Hardin, Franklin, Hamilton, Wright, and Webster.

TWELFTH JUDICIAL DISTRICT.

FIRST CIRCUIT—Bremer, Floyd, and Butler.
SECOND CIRCUIT—Mitchell, Worth, Winnebago, Hancock, and Cerro Gordo.

TIMES AND PLACES OF HOLDING THE DISTRICT COURTS OF IOWA.

ADAIR—*Fontanelle*—First Monday in February and first Monday in September.

ADAMS—*Quincy*—Fifteenth Monday after the fourth Monday in January and July.

ALLAMAKEE—*Waukon*—Fourth Monday after the third Monday in May and on the third Monday of December.

APPANOOSE—*Centerville*—First Monday in March and October.

AUDUBON—*Exira*—Second Monday in September.

BENTON—*Vinton*—First Mondays of March and October.

BLACK HAWK—*Waterloo*—Fifth Monday after the third Monday in April, and third Monday in September, and first Monday of January.

BOONE—*Boonsboro*—Fourth Mondays in April and September.

BREMER—*Waverly*—Fourth Monday in January and second Mondays in May and September.

BUCHANAN—*Independence*—Second Thursday aftert he third Monday in April, and on the third Monday in October.

BUENA VISTA—*Prairieville*—Attached to the county of Clay.

BUTLER—*Butler Center*—Seventh Monday after the second Monday in May and September.

CALHOUN—*Lake City*—First Thursday after the fourth Monday in April.

CARROLL—*Carroll*—Thursday after the Second Monday in September.

*CASS—*Atlantic*—Thursday after the first Monday in February and the Thursday after the first Monday in September.

CEDAR—*Tipton*—First Mondays in June and December.

CERRO GORDO—*Mason City*—Sixth Monday after the second Monday in May and September.

CHEROKEE—*Cherokee*—First Thursday after the Monday fixed for holding court in Clay county.

CHICKASAW—*New Hampton*—Third Monday after the third Monday in January and the third Monday after the second Monday in September.

CLARKE—*Osceola*—Twelfth Monday after the fourth Monday in January and July.

CLAY—*Peterson*—Eighth Monday after the second Monday in April.

CLAYTON—*Elkader*—Third Mondays of January and May and second Monday in September.

*CLINTON—*Clinton*—First Mondays of March and September, and fourth Monday of November.

CRAWFORD—*Denison*—Third Monday in April.

DALLAS—*Adel*—Third Monday in February and first Monday in October.

DAVIS—*Bloomfield*—Fourth Monday in May and sixth Monday after the third Monday of October.

DECATUR—*Leon*—Tenth Monday after the fourth Monday in January and July.

DELAWARE—*Delhi*—Third Monday in April and fourth Monday in October.

DES MOINES—*Burlington*—First Monday in January, first Monday in October, and third Monday in April.

DICKINSON—*Spirit Lake*—First Thursday after the Monday fixed for holding court in Emmet county.

DUBUQUE—*Dubuque*—First Mondays in February and June, and second Monday in November.

EMMET—*Estherville*—Seventh Monday after the second Monday in April.

FAYETTE—*West Union*—Second Monday after the third Monday in May, and first Monday in December.

---

* County seat of Cass county removed from Lewis to Atlantic, and that of Clinton county from De Witt to Clinton by vote of the electors at the general election of 1869.

FLOYD—*Charles City*—Last Monday of April and first Monday in September.

FRANKLIN—*Hampton*—Fifth Monday after the fourth Monday in April and September.

FREMONT—*Sidney*—Fifth Monday after the fourth Monday in January and July.

GREENE—*Jefferson*—First Monday in April and third Monday in September.

GRUNDY—*Grundy Center*—Fourth Monday in September.

GUTHRIE—*Panora*—Second Monday in February and fourth Monday in September.

HAMILTON—*Webster City*—Third Monday after the fourth Monday in April and September.

HANCOCK—*Concord*—Fifth Monday after the second Monday in May and September.

HARDIN—*Eldora*—Fourth Mondays in March and August.

HARRISON—*Magnolia*—Eleventh Monday after the second Monday in April, and third Monday in December.

HENRY—*Mt. Pleasant*—Second Mondays in March, June and November.

HOWARD—*Cresco*—Second Monday after the third Monday in January, and second Monday after the second Monday of September.

HUMBOLDT—*Dakota City*—Fourth Monday after the second Monday in April.

IDA—*Ida*—Attached to the county of Sac.

IOWA—*Marengo*—First Mondays in February and September.

JACKSON—*Andrew*—First Tuesdays after the fourth Mondays of March and September, and the first Tuesday after the second Monday in December.

JASPER—*Newton*—Fourth Mondays in March and November.

JEFFERSON—*Fairfield*—First Mondays in January and September.

JOHNSON—*Iowa City*—First Monday in January, second Monday in May, and third Monday in October.

JONES—*Anamosa*—Third Mondays in June and December.

KEOKUK—*Sigourney*—First Mondays in February and October.

KOSSUTH—*Algona*—Fifth Monday after the second Monday in April.

LEE—*Fort Madison*—Third Monday in May and first Monday in December.

LEE—*Keokuk*—First Monday in February and second Monday in September.

LINN—*Marion*—Fourth Monday in March, and second Mondays of July and November.

LOUISA—*Wapello*—First Monday in April and fourth Monday in October.

LUCAS—*Chariton*—Second Monday after the third Monday of March and October.

MADISON—*Winterset*—Third Monday in January and Fourth Monday in August.

MAHASKA—*Oskaloosa*—Third Mondays in February and October.

MARION—*Knoxville*—Second Mondays in March and November.

MARSHALL—*Marshalltown*—First Mondays in April and September.

MILLS—*Glenwood*—Third Monday after the Fourth Monday in January and and July.

MITCHELL—*Mitchell*—Second Monday after the second Monday in May and September.

MONONA—*Onawa City*—Tenth Monday after the Second Monday in April and second Monday in December.

MONROE—*Albia*—Fourth Monday after the third Monday of March and October.

MONTGOMERY—*Red Oak Junction*—Sixteenth Monday after the fourth Monday in January and July.

MUSCATINE—*Muscatine*—First Mondays of January and June and third Monday of October.

O'BRIEN—*O'Brien*—Attached to the county of Cherokee.

PAGE-*Clarinda*-Seventh Monday after the fourth Monday in January and July.

PALO ALTO—*Soda Bar*—First Thursday after the Monday fixed for holding court in Pocahontas county.

PLYMOUTH—*Melbourne*—Attached to the county of Woodbury.

POCAHONTAS—*Milton*—Sixth Monday after the second Monday in April.

POLK—*Des Moines*—Fourth Monday in February and fourth Monday in October.

POTTAWATTAMIE—*Council Bluffs*—Fourth Monday in January and July.

POWESHIEK—*Montezuma*—Second Mondays in April and December.

RINGGOLD—*Mt. Ayr*—Ninth Monday after the fourth Monday in January and July.

SAC—*Sac City*—Fourth Monday in April.

SCOTT—*Davenport*—First Mondays of February, May and November.

SHELBY—*Harlan*—Second Monday in April.

SIOUX—*Calliope*—Attached to the county of Woodbury.

STORY—*Nevada*—Third Mondays in April and September.

TAMA—*Toledo*—Third Mondays in February and September.

TAYLOR—*Bedford*—Eighth Monday after the fourth Monday in January and July.

UNION—*Afton*—Fourteenth Monday after the fourth Monday in January and July.

VAN BUREN—*Keosauqua*—Second Monday in January and third Monday in August.

WAPELLO—*Ottumwa*—Second Monday after the second Monday in January, and second Monday after the third Monday in August.

WARREN—*Indianola*—First Monday in January and second Monday in August.

WASHINGTON—*Washington*—Third Mondays in January and September.

WAYNE—*Corydon*—Third Mondays in March and October.

WEBSTER—*Fort Dodge*—Second Monday after the fourth Monday in April and September.

WINNEBAGO—*Forest City*—Fourth Monday after the second Monday in May and September.

WINNESHIEK—*Decorah*—Third Monday after the third Monday in May, and the fourth Monday after the second Monday in September, and the fourth after the third Monday in January.

WOODBURY—*Sioux City*—Ninth Monday after the second Monday in April and first Monday in December.

WORTH—*Northwood*—Third Monday after the second Monday in May and September.

WRIGHT—*Clarion*—Fourth Monday after the fourth Monday in April and September.

TIMES OF HOLDING CIRCUIT COURTS IN THE STATE OF IOWA FOR 1870 *AND* 1871.

FIRST JUDICIAL DISTRICT.

FIRST CIRCUIT.—Henry county, fourth Monday in January; third Monday in May; first Monday in September, and first Monday in December for 1870 and 1871.

—Lee county, at Fort Madison; first Tuesday in January; second Tuesday in April; second Tuesday in August.

—Keokuk, fourth Monday in February; second Tuesday in June and first Tuesday in November, for 1870 and 1871.

SECOND CIRCUIT.—Des Moines county, first Monday in February; third Monday in May; fourth Monday in August; second Monday in November.

—Louisa county, first Monday in January; third Monday in March; third Monday in June; third Monday in September; second Monday in December for 1870, and on the second Monday in March; third Monday in June; third Monday in September, and second Monday in December for 1871.

SECOND JUDICIAL DISTRICT.

FIRST CIRCUIT.—Van Buren county.—Fourth Monday of February; fourth Monday of May; fourth Monday of September, and fourth Monday of November.

—Wapello County.—Second Monday of March; second Monday of June; first Monday of October, and second Monday of December.

—Davis county.—Second Monday of February; third Monday of April; the Friday before the second Monday of August; and the first Monday after the fourth Monday of October.

SECOND CIRCUIT.—Appanoose county.—First Monday of January; second Monday of May; first Monday of August and first Monday of November.

—Monroe county.—First Monday of February; second Monday of June; first Monday of September; and the first Monday of December.

—Lucas county.—Fourth Monday of January; fifth Monday of May; fourth Monday of August; and fourth Monday of November.

—Wayne county.—Third Monday of January; fourth Monday of May; third Monday of August; and third Monday of November; for the years 1870 and 1871.

Times of holding the terms in the third Judicial District, not yet fixed.

FOURTH JUDICIAL DISTRICT.

FIRST CIRCUIT—Woodbury county.—First Mondays in February, May, August, and November.

—Sioux county.—Second Mondays in February, May, August, and November.

—Plymouth county.—First Thursday following the second Mondays in February, May, August, and November.

—Cherokee county.—Third Mondays in February, May, August, and November.

—O'Brien county.—First Thursday following the third Mondays in February, May, August, and November.

—Monona county.-Fourth Mondays in February, May, August and November.

—Ida county.—Second Thursday following the fourth Monday in February, May, August, and November.

—Harrison county.—Second Mondays in March, June, September, and December.

—Shelby county—Third Mondays in March, June, September, and December.

—Crawford county—First Thursday following third Monday in March, June, September, and December for 1870 and 1871.

SECOND CIRCUIT—Pocahontas county—First Mondays in February, May, August and November.

—Palo Alto county—First Thursday following first Monday in February, May, August and November.

—Emmet county—Second Mondays in February, May, August and November.

—Dickinson county—First Thursday following the second Monday in February, May, August and November.

—Clay county—Third Mondays in February, May, August and November.

—Buena Vista county—First Thursday following third Monday in February, May, August and November.

—Sac county—Fourth Mondays in February, May, August and November.

—Calhoun county—First Thursday following the fourth Monday in February, May, August and November.

—Humboldt county—First Monday after the fourth Monday in February, May, August, and November.

—Kossuth county—Second Monday after the fourth Monday in February, May, August and November, for the years of 1870 and 1871.

FIFTH JUDICIAL DISTRICT.

FIRST CIRCUIT—Polk County, first Monday in January; first Monday in April; first Monday in July; third Monday in September.

—Warren county, first Monday in February; second Monday in May; first Monday in August; first Monday in November.

—Dallas county, first Monday in March; first Monday in June; first Monday in September; first Monday in December.

SECOND CIRCUIT—Adair county, fourth Wednesday in February; second Wednesday in May; first Wednesday in August; first Wednesday in November.

—Madison county, fourth Monday in March; second Monday in June; fourth Monday in September; first Monday in December.

—Carroll county, second Thursday in March; fourth Thursday in May; Third Thursday in August; third Thursday in November.

—Cass county, fourth Monday in February; third Monday in May; Second Monday in August; first Monday in November.

—Greene county, second Monday in March; fifth Monday in May; fourth Monday in August; third Monday in November.

—Guthrie county, Third Monday in March; first Monday in June; fifth Monday in August; fourth Monday in November.

—Audubon county—First Monday in March, fourth Monday in May, third Monday in August, second Monday in November.

SIXTH JUDICIAL DISTRICT.

FIRST CIRCUIT—Poweshiek county—First Monday of February, third Monday of May, first Monday of August, and the fourth Monday of October.

—Jefferson county—Second Monday of February, Fifth Monday of May, third Monday of August, and fourth Monday of November.

—Keokuk county—Fourth Monday of February, first Monday of June, fourth Monday of August, and first Monday of December.

—Washington county—Return not received.

SECOND CIRCUIT—Mahaska county—First Mondays in January, April and July, and third Monday of September.

—Marion county—Second Mondays of January, April, and July, and fourth Monday of September.

—Jasper county—Third Mondays of January, April and July, and first Monday of October, for the years 1870 and 1871.

SEVENTH JUDICIAL DISTRICT.

FIRST CIRCUIT—Scott county for the year 1870—Second Monday of January, third Monday of March, second Monday of June, fourth Monday of September, and second Monday of December. For 1871—Third Monday of March, second Monday of June, fourth Monday of September, and second Monday of December.

—Muscatine county for the years 1870 and 1871—Third Monday of February, third Monday of May, first Monday of September, and second Monday of November.

SECOND CIRCUIT—Clinton county for the years 1870 and 1871—Second Monday of January, fourth Monday of April, second Monday of June, and fourth Monday of October.

—Jackson county for the years 1870 and 1871—First Monday of February, second Monday of May, first Monday of September, and second Monday of November.

EIGHTH JUDICIAL DISTRICT.

FIRST CIRCUIT—Benton county—First Monday in January, first Monday in May, Third Monday in August, and first Monday in November.

—Tama county—Third Monday in January, third Monday in April, first Monday in August, and third Monday in October.

—Johnson county—Second Monday in February, first Monday in April, second Monday in July, and third Monday in November.

—Iowa county—First Monday in March, third Monday in May, fourth Monday in July, and first Monday in October.

SECOND CIRCUIT—Linn county—Fourth Monday in January, second Monday in May, second Monday in September, and second Monday in December.

—Cedar county—Second Monday in February, second Monday in April, fourth Monday in August, and fourth Monday in October.

—Jones county—Third Monday in February, third Monday in April, first Monday in September, and first Monday in November for 1870 and 1871.

Times of holding the terms in the Ninth Judicial District not yet fixed.

TENTH JUDICIAL DISTRICT.

FIRST CIRCUIT—Howard County—for the year 1870—February 28th; May 2d; July 6th; October 31st. For 1871—February 27th; May 1st; July 5th, and October 30th.

—Allamakee County—for the year 1870—January 3d; April 11th; July 11th; November 7th. For 1871—January 2d; April 10th; July 10th, and November 6th.

—Winneshiek County—for the year 1870—January 10th; April 18th; July 18th; November 14th. For 1871—January 9th; April 17th; July 17th, and November 13th.

SECOND CIRCUIT—Clayton County—for the year 1870—January 3d; March 21st; June 20th; October 24th. For 1871—January 2d; March 20th; June 19th, and October 23d.

—Fayette County—for the year 1870—February 21st; April 25th; June 27th; October 17th. For 1871—February 20th; April 24th; June 26th, and October 16th.

—Chickasaw County—for the year 1870—January 11th; March 29th; June 13th; September 26th. For 1871—January 10th; March 28th; June 12th, and September 25th.

Times of holding the terms in the Eleventh and Twelfth Judicial Districts not yet fixed.

IOWA IN THE XLI CONGRESS.

SENATORS FROM IOWA.

James Harlan, Mount Pleasant; term expires March 4th, 1873.

.... ; term expires March 4th, 1871.

REPRESENTATIVES FROM IOWA.

George W. McCreary, Keokuk, 1st District.
William Smyth, Marion, 2d District.
William B. Allison, Dubuque, 3d District.
William Loughridge, Oskaloosa, 4th District.
Francis W. Palmer, Des Moines, 5th District.
Charles Pomeroy, Fort Dodge, 6th District.

FEDERAL OFFICERS IN IOWA.

JUDICIAL.

Samuel F. Miller, Keokuk, Associate Justice of the Supreme Court of the United States and presiding Judge of the Eighth Circuit of the United States.

James M. Love, Ottumwa, Judge of the United States District Court, District of Iowa.

George B. Corkhill, Mt. Pleasant, Clerk of the United States Circuit Court.
John C. Burns, Dubuque, Clerk of the United States District Court.
George W. Clark, Indianola, United States Marshal.
James S. Clark, Indianola, Deputy.
Harry H. Fulton, Keokuk, Deputy.
P. M. Crawford, Dubuque, Deputy.
Fitzroy Sessions, Cedar Falls, Deputy.

REGISTERS IN BANKRUPTCY.

John Bruce, Keokuk, 1st Congressional District.
John N. Crawford, Davenport, 2d Congressional District.
B. W. Poor, Dubuque, 3d Congressional District.
Daniel Anderson, Albia, 4th Congressional District.
John Mitchell, Des Moines, 5th Congressional District.
Charles W. Lowrie, Boonsboro, 6th Congressional District.

UNITED STATES COMMISSIONERS APPOINTED BY THE CIRCUIT COURT OF THE UNITED STATES FOR THE DISTRICT OF IOWA.

Wm. G. Woodward—Muscatine—Muscatine.
Stephen Sibley—Des Moines—Polk.
H. B. Ten Eyck—Keokuk—Lee.
J. N. Rogers—Davenport—Scott.
D. C. Bloomer—Council Bluffs—Pottawattamie.
M. T. Williams—Oskaloosa—Mahaska.
R. Ambler—Mt. Pleasant—Henry.
Geo. Frazee—Burlington—Des Moines.
H. B. Hendershott—Ottumwa—Wapello.
C. W. Simmons—Boonsboro—Boone.
W. G. Hammond—Iowa City—Johnson.
Henry Hospers—Pella—Marion.
J. B. Powers—Cedar Falls—Black Hawk.
W. I. Hayes—Clinton—Clinton.
Thos. Sargent—Fort Dodge—Webster.
D. M. Harris—Panora—Guthrie.
W. T. Smith—Oskaloosa—Mahaska.
H. J. Skiff—Montezuma—Poweshiek.
D. F. Ellsworth—Eldora—Hardin.
John Currier—Sioux City—Sioux.
John S. Stacy—Anamosa—Jones.
Geo. Woodbury—Leon—Decatur.
John A. Hull—Boonsboro—Boone.
Rush Clark—Iowa City—Johnson.
James H. Shields—Dubuque—Dubuque.
B. W. Poor—Dubuque—Dubuque.
F. Wilcox—Burlington—Des Moines.
John Rogers—Sigourney—Keokuk.
J. N. W. Rumple—Marengo—Iowa.
S. Harned—Sigourney—Keokuk.
R. G. Reineger—Charles City—Floyd.
J. W. Wilson—Newton—Jasper.
S. W. Matteson—Decorah—Winneshiek.
Geo. C. Wright—Waverly—Bremer.
D. D. Miracle—Webster City—Hamilton.
S. S. Etheridge—Des Moines—Polk.
A. J. Jordan—McGregor—Clayton.
S. G. Vananda—Manchester—Delaware.
H. J. B. Cummings—Winterset—Madison.
D. D. Gregory—Afton—Union.
W. S. Hamilton—Bloomfield—Davis.

John Williams—Iowa City—Johnson.
W. M. Lellan—Dubuque—Dubuque.
Thomas S. Free—Toledo—Tama.
C. W. Dunbar—Maquoketa—Jackson.
William L. Redman—Bellevue—Jackson.
Joseph Lyman—Council Bluffs—Pottawattamie.
L. W. Ross—Council Bluffs—Pottawattamie.
E. R. Page—Council Bluffs—Pottawattamie.
James S. George—Waterloo—Black Hawk.
James Ballou—Dubuque—Dubuque.
I. W. Card—Mason City—Cerro Gordo.
A. M. Bryson—Osage—Mitchell.
M. M. Moulton—Monticello—Jones.
George B. Corkhill—Mt. Pleasant—Henry.
W. F. Brannan—Muscatine—Muscatine.
D. W. Gage—Ames—Story.
A. H. Kagy---Muscatine---Muscatine.
Samuel Holmes—Hamburg—Fremont.
Delos Arnold—Marshalltown—Marshall.
Jed Lake—Independence—Buchanan.
E. C. Rice—Marshalltown—Marshall.
James Thorington—Davenport—Scott.
Frank Springer, Jr—Burlington—Des Moines.
Thomas S. Wilson—Dubuque—Dubuque.
William Cook—West Union—Fayette.
A. W. Eastman—Cedar Rapids—Linn.

INTERNAL REVENUE.

Willis Drummond—McGregor—Supervisor of Internal Revenue for the District of Iowa, Minnesota, Nebraska and Dakota.

ASSESSORS.

James B. Weaver—1st Collection District—office at Bloomfield.
S. S. Farwell—2d Collection District—office at Monticello.
Lucius L. Huntley—3d Collection District—office at Dubuque.
John Connell—4th Collection District—office at Toledo.
A. R. Anderson—5th Collection District—office at Sidney.
John Scott—6th Collection District—office at Nevada.

COLLECTORS.

Francis Springer—1st Collection District—office at Burlington.
N. Boardman—2d Collection District—office at Lyons.
M. M. Trumbull—3d Collection District—office at Dubuque.
Alonzo J. Pope—4th Collection District—office at Sigourney.
Lampson P. Sherman, 5th Collection District—office at Des Moines.
Thomas E. McCracken—6th Collection District—office at Marshalltown.

LIST OF NEWSPAPERS AND PERIODICALS PUBLISHED IN THE STATE DECEMBER 1, 1869.

NAME OF PAPER.	ON WHAT DAY PUBLISHED.	WHERE PUBLISHED	COUNTY.	BY WHOM PUBLISHED.	CHARACTER.
Annals of Iowa	Quarterly	Iowa City	Johnson	State Historical Society	Historical
Atlas, Grundy County	Friday	Grundy Center	Grundy	A. C. Peckham	Republican
Advertiser, Tipton	Thursday	Tipton	Cedar	Mulford & Longley	Republican
Advertiser, Eddyville	Saturday	Eddyville	Wapello	W. J. Palmer & Co.	Republican
Advance, Marshall County	Wednesday	Marshalltown	Marshall	F. H. Barnhart	Democratic
Ægis, Story County	Wednesday	Nevada	Story	V. A. Ballou	Republican
Advocate, Lyons City	Wednesday	Lyons	Clinton	A. P. Durlin	Democratic
Advocate, Boone County	Thursday	Boonsboro	Boone	O. A. Chesney	Republican
Advocate, Floyd County	Tuesday and Friday	Charles City	Floyd	Valentine Baltuff	Republican
Anzeiger, Iowa Staats	Saturday	Des Moines	Polk	Voigt & Co.	Neutral
Age, Iowa	Weekly	Clinton	Clinton	....	....
Bugle, Council Bluffs	Daily	Council Bluffs	Pottawattamie	C. H. Babbitt	Democratic
Bugle, Council Bluffs	Weekly	Council Bluffs	Pottawattamie	C. H. Babbitt	Democratic
Bulletin, Buchanan County	Friday	Independence	Buchanan	William Toman	Republican
Bulletin, Des Moines	Daily	Des Moines	Polk	Orwig & Co	Republican
Bulletin, Des Moines	Saturday	Des Moines	Polk	Orwig & Co	Republican
Blade, Pella	Wednesday	Pella	Marion	Curtis & Betzer	Republican
Citizen, Central Iowa	Saturday	Oskaloosa	Mahaska	Hunter Brothers	Republican
Chronicle, Lansing	Monday	Lansing	Allamakee	J. I. Taylor	Neutral
Citizen, Tama	Thursday	Tama City	Tama	Wm. G. Cambridge	Republican
Chronicle, Wilton	Thursday	Wilton	Muscatine	H. C. Ashbaugh	Republican
Courier, Waterloo	Thursday	Waterloo	Black Hawk	Hartman & Logan	Republican
Citizen, Loyal	Saturday	Centerville	Appanoose	Madison M. Walden	Republican
Constitution	Daily	Keokuk	Lee	Thomas W. Claggett	Democratic
Constitution	Wednesday	Keokuk	Lee	Thomas W. Claggett	Democratic
Conservator, Progressive	Tuesday	Oskaloosa	Mahaska	P. C. Welch	Democratic
Courier, Ottumwa	Daily	Ottumwa	Wapello	J. M. Hedrick & Co	Republican
Courier, Ottumwa	Thursday	Ottumwa	Wapello	J. M. Hedrick & Co.	Republican
Courier, Muscatine	Daily	Muscatine	Muscatine	Barnhart Brothers & Witmer	Democratic
Courier, Muscatine	Weekly	Muscatine	Muscatine	Barnhart Brothers & Witmer	Democratic

LIST OF NEWSPAPERS AND PERIODICALS—Continued.

NAME OF PAPERS.	ON WHAT DAY PUBLISHED.	WHERE PUBLISHED	COUNTY.	BY WHOM PUBLISHED.	CHARACTER.
Citizen, American	Wednesday	Steamboat Rock	Hardin	Delos S. Ring	Democratic
Copperhead	Thursday	Ottumwa	Wapello	McCully & Evans	Democratic
Collegian, Griswold	Monthly	Davenport	Scott	Griswold College	Educational
Democrat, Chariton	Tuesday	Chariton	Lucas	Faith & Beatty	Democratic
Democrat, Humboldt Co., True	Friday	Springvale	Humboldt	S. H. Taft	Republican
Democrat, Bloomfield	Thursday	Bloomfield	Davis	T. O. Walker	Democratic
Democrat, Davenport	Daily	Davenport	Scott	Richardson Bros	Democratic
Democrat, Davenport	Thursday	Davenport	Scott	Richardson Bros	Democratic
Democrat, Fort Madison	Wednesday	Fort Madison	Lee	C. L. Morehous	Democratic
Democrat, Iowa	Saturday	Fairfield	Jefferson	M. M. Bleakmore	Democratic
Democrat, Page County	Saturday	Clarinda	Page	Ridenour & Loy	Democratic
Democrat, Boone County	Wednesday	Montana	Boone	L. Raguet	Democratic
Democrat, Marion County	Tuesday	Knoxville	Marion	J. L. McCormack	Democratic
Des Moines, Upper	Wednesday	Algona	Kossuth	J. H. Warren	Republican
Democrat, Decorah	Thursday	Decorah	Winneshiek	R. V. Shurley & Co.	Democratic
Demokrat, National	Thursday	Dubuque	Dubuque	F. A. Gniffke	Democratic
Excelsior, Maquokcta	Thursday	Maquoketa	Jackson	W. S. Belden	Republican
Express, Monticello	Thursday	Monticello	Jones	G. W. Hunt	Republican
Enterprise, West Liberty	Friday	West Liberty	Muscatine	C. D. Eaton	Republican
Era, Jefferson	Friday	Jefferson	Greene	M. H. & M. L. Money	Republican
Express, Montgomery	Saturday	Red Oak Junction	Montgomery	W. Eaton	Republican
Eagle, Vinton	Wednesday	Vinton	Benton	Hanford & Holt	Republican
Evangelist	Monthly	Adel	Dallas	Allen Hickey	Religious
Eureka, Anamosa	Thursday	Anamosa	Jones	E. Booth & Son	Republican
Enterprise, Birmingham	Saturday	Birmingham	Van Buren	W. S. Moore	Independent.
Evergreen	Monthly	Dubuque	Dubuque	E. A. Guilbert	Masonic
Enterprise, Garden Grove	Weekly	Garden Grove	Decatur	H. M. Belvel	....
Freeman, Hamilton	Wednesday	Webster City	Hamilton	J. D. Hunter	Republican
Fra Fjaernt og Naer	Monday	Decorah	Winneshiek	B. Anundsen	*Norwegian*

Gazette, Adams County	Thursday	Corning	Adams	A. L. Wells	Republican
Gazette and Argus	Daily	Burlington	Des Moines	C. I. Barker & Co.	Democratic
Gazette and Argus	Weekly	Burlington	Des Moines	C. I. Barker & Co.	Democratic
Gazette, Cedar Falls	Friday	Cedar Falls	Black Hawk	C. W. & E. A. Snyder	Republican
Gazette, Davenport	Daily	Davenport	Scott	Gazette Company	Republican
Gazette, Davenport	Thursday	Davenport	Scott	Gazette Company	Republican
Gazette, Des Moines Valley	Thursday	Eddyville	Wapello	John Wilcox	Republican
Gazette, Monona County	Thursday	Onawa	Monona	W. A. Greene	Republican
Gazette, Dallas	Thursday	Adel	Dallas	G. A. Atwood	Republican
Gazette, Clarence	Friday	Clarence	Cedar	McLaughlin & McMillan	Republican
Gazette, West Union	Saturday	West Union	Fayette	Charles H. Talmadge	Republican
Gazette, Western	Thursday	Western	Linn	D. D. Weimer	Republican
Gazette, Washington	Friday	Washington	Washington	Gazette Printing Co	Democratic
Guide, Ackley	Weekly	Ackley	Hardin		
Gate City	Daily	Keokuk	Lee	J. B. Howell	Republican
Gate City	Wednesday	Keokuk	Lee	J. B. Howell	Republican
Gleaner and Herald	Thursday	Prairie City	Jasper	Jacob Sanders	Republican
Hawkeye, Burlington	Daily	Burlington	Des Moines	Edwards & Beardsley	Republican
Hawkeye, Burlington	Tuesday & Thursday	Burlington	Des Moines	Edwards & Beardsley	Republican
Hawkeye, Burlington	Thursday	Burlington	Des Moines	Edwards & Beardsley	Republican
Herald, Clinton	Tues., Thurs. & Sat.	Clinton	Clinton	Herald Printing Co.	Republican
Herald, Clinton	Saturday	Clinton	Clinton	Herald Printing Co.	Republican
Herald, Dubuque	Daily	Dubuque	Dubuque	Ham & Carver	Democratic
Herald, Dubuque	Wednesday	Dubuque	Dubuque	Ham & Carver	Democratic
Hawkeye, Mount Vernon	Friday	Mount Vernon	Linn	S. H. Bauman	Republican
Herald, Oskaloosa	Thursday	Oskaloosa	Mahaska	Hunter & Leighton	Republican
Herald, Poweshiek County	Wednesday	Grinnell	Poweshiek	Hillyer & Evans	Republican
Herald, Western	Saturday	Carroll	Carroll	J. F. H. Sugg	Republican
Herald, New Hampton	Friday	New Hampton	Chickasaw	G. M. Reynolds	Republican
Harrisonian	Friday	Missouri Valley	Harrison	D. M. Harris	Democratic
Herald, Page County	Saturday	Clarinda	Page	George H. Powers	Republican
Homestead, Iowa	Friday	Des Moines	Polk	Wm. Duane Wilson	Agricultural
Intelligencer, Ames	Tuesday	Ames	Story	A. McFadden	Republican
Intelligencer, Charles City	Thursday	Charles City	Floyd	A. B. F. Hildreth	Republican
Iowan, Eastern	Saturday	Sabula	Jackson	J. F. H. Sugg	Neutral
Independent, Humboldt County	Thursday	Dakota	Humboldt	Wood & Jackson	Republican

LIST OF NEWSPAPERS, PERIODICALS, ETC.—CONTINUED.

NAME OF PAPER.	ON WHAT DAY PUBLISHED.	WHERE PUBLISHED	COUNTY.	BY WHOM PUBLISHED.	CHARACTER.
Independent, Moulton	Friday	Moulton	Appanoose	King & Hill	Neutral.
Journal, Sioux City	Thursday	Sioux City	Woodbury	George D. Perkins	Republican
Journal, Bellevue	Thursday	Bellevue	Jackson	W. Pollock	Republican
Journal, Clayton County	Wednesday	Elkader	Clayton	Joseph Eiboeck	Republican
Journal, Muscatine	Daily	Muscatine	Muscatine	Mahin Brothers	Republican
Journal, Muscatine	Tues., Thurs. and Sat.	Muscatine	Muscatine	Mahin Brothers	Republican
Journal, Muscatine	Friday	Muscatine	Muscatine	Mahin Brothers	Republican
Journal, Mt. Pleasant	Friday	Mt. Pleasant	Henry	Frank Hatton	Republican
Journal, Indianola	Thursday	Indianola	Warren	E. W. Brady	Republican
Journal, People's	Thursday	Vinton	Benton	A. H. Brown	Republican
Journal, Decatur County	Thursday	Leon	Decatur	James & Stockton	Republican
Journal, Davenport	Daily	Davenport	Scott	Journal Printing Company	Republican
Journal, Davenport	Weekly	Davenport	Scott	Journal Printing Company	Republican
Jurist, Western	Bi-monthly	Des Moines	Polk	Mills & Company	Legal
Journal, Iowa Stock	Monthly	Sigourney	Keokuk	J. H. Sanders & Company	Agricultural.
Journal, Iowa School	Monthly	Des Moines	Polk	Mills & Company	Educational.
Leader, Queen City	Tuesday	Queen City	Adams	Sherman & Dodge	Neutral
Ledger, Eldora	Friday	Eldora	Hardin	R. H. McBride	Republican
Ledger, Fairfield	Thursday	Fairfield	Jefferson	Junkin & Robinson	Republican
Leader, Tama County	Tuesday and Friday	Easton	Tama	W. W. Yarham	Republican
Mirror, Lansing	Tuesday	Lansing	Allamakee	T. C. Medary	Republican
Monitor, Corydon	Saturday	Corydon	Wayne	Monitor Company	Republican
Mirror, Lyons	Saturday	Lyons	Clinton	Beers & Eaton	Republican
Monitor, Wright County	Wednesday	Clarion	Wright	Will F. Smith	Republican
Messenger, Cass County	Saturday	Atlantic	Cass	H. Clay Johnson	Republican
Madisonian, Winterset	Wednesday	Winterset	Madison	H. J. B Cummings	Republican
News, McGregor	Saturday	McGregor	Clayton	McGregor News Printing Co	Republican
Nonpareil, Council Bluffs	Daily	Council Bluffs	Pottawattamie	Nonpareil Printing Company	Republican
Nonpareil, Council Bluffs	Weekly	Council Bluffs	Pottawattamie	Nonpareil Printing Company	Republican

News, Sigourney	Wednesday	Sigourney	Keokuk	J. W. Havens	Republican
News, Waverly Democratic	Thursday	Waverly	Bremer	Waverly News Company	Democratic
Northwest, Iowa	Thursday	Fort Dodge	Webster	B. F. Gue	Republican
News, Mitchell	Thursday	Mitchell	Mitchell	Cravath & Day	Republican
Observer, De Witt	Wednesday	De Witt	Clinton	S. H. Shoemaker	Republican
Opinion, Glenwood	Saturday	Glenwood	Mills	Morgan & Lunt	Republican
Observer, North Iowa	Weekly	Fayette	Fayette	....	....
Post, die Keokuk	Tues., Thurs. and Sat.	Keokuk	Lee	Emil Bischof	*German*
Post, die Keokuk	Thursday	Keokuk	Lee	Emil Bischof	*German*
Press, Winnebago	Thursday	Forest City	Winnebago	Linn & Howard	Republican
Pioneer, Brighton	Friday	Brighton	Washington	Robert H. Moore	Republican
Pokrok (Progress)	Wednesday	Cedar Rapids	Linn	....	*Bohemian*
Patriot, Chariton	Wednesday	Chariton	Lucas	Ragsdale Brothers	Republican
Press, Hampton Free	Friday	Hampton	Franklin	L. B. Raymond	Republican
Press, State	Wednesday and Sat	Decorah	Winneshiek	Howland & Huntington	Republican
Press, Mechanicsville	Saturday	Mechanicsville	Cedar	H. Leslie	Republican
Press, Strawberry Point	Thursday	Strawberry Point	Clayton	Teed & Vines	Neutral
Press, Mitchell County	Thursday	Osage	Mitchell	T. M. Atherton	Republican
Press, Newton Free	Thursday	Newton	Jasper	W. S. Benham	Republican
Post, Nashua	Friday	Nashua	Chickasaw	Andy Felt	Republican
Press, Atlantic Free	Daily	Atlantic	Cass	E. O. Upham	Democratic
Press, Democratic Free	Wednesday	Atlantic	Cass	Upham & Sibley	Democratic
Pioneer, Leon	Friday	Leon	Decatur	Frazier & Co	Democratic
Press, State	Wednesday	Iowa City	Johnson	John P. Irish	Democratic
Press, Washington	Wednesday	Washington	Washington	H. A. Burrell	Republican
Press, Henry County	Wednesday	Mt. Pleasant	Henry	Snyder Brothers	Republican
Plaindealer, Ft. Madison	Thursday	Ft. Madison	Lee	J. G. Wilson	Republican
Post, Council Bluffs	Thursday	Council Bluffs	Pottawattamie	L. Mader	*German*
Plaindealer, Cresco	Weekly	Cresco	Howard	....	....
Recorder, Jesup	Thursday	Jesup	Buchanan	J. A. Cole	Republican
Republic, Iowa	Thursday	Bellevue	Jackson	Fanning Brothers	Republican
Republican, Montezuma	Wednesday	Montezuma	Poweshiek	O. H. P. Grove & Bro	Republican
Republican, Decorah	Friday	Decorah	Winneshiek	A. K. Bailey & Bro	Republican
Register, Adair County	Thursday	Fontanelle	Adair	Kilburn & Rutt	Republican
Review, Denison	Saturday	Denison	Crawford	James D Ainsworth	Republican

LIST OF NEWSPAPERS AND PERIODICALS—Continued.

NAME OF PAPER.	ON WHAT DAY PUBLISHED.	WHERE PUBLISHED	COUNTY.	BY WHOM PUBLISHED.	CHARACTER.
Register, Marion	Wednesday	Marion	Linn	S. W. Rathbun	Republican
Register, Iowa State	Daily	Des Moines	Polk	Register Printing Company	Republican
Register, Iowa State	Wednesday	Des Moines	Polk	Register Printing Company	Republican
Republican, Iowa City	Wednesday	Iowa City	Johnson	N. H. Brainerd	Republican
Reporter, Iowa State	Wednesday	Waterloo	Black Hawk	Smart & Parrott	Republican
Record, Ringgold	Thursday	Mt. Ayr	Ringgold	George B. Roby	Republicon
Republican, Keosauqua	Thursday	Keosauqua	Van Buren	Henry & Lea	Republican
Republican, Progressive	Wednesday	Marengo	Iowa	Spering & Crenshaw	Republican
Register, Sioux City	Saturday	Sioux City	Woodbury	Wm. Freney & Co	Democratic
Republican, Cerro Gordo	Thursday	Mason City	Cerro Gordo	Noys & Sirrine	Republican
Republican, Davis County	Thursday	Bloomfield	Davis	E. T. White	Republican
Republican, Tama County	Thursday	Toledo	Tama	M. B. C. True	Republican
Republican, Wapello	Saturday	Wapello	Louisa	L. W. Myers	Republican
Republican, Waverly	Thursday	Waverly	Bremer	Butler & Mallahan	Republican
Republican, Jasper	Thursday	Newton	Jasper	Besack, Allum & Rodgers	Republican
Reporter, Franklin	Wednesday	Hampton	Franklin	J. C. Whitney	Republican
Recorder, Monroe	Weekly	Monroe	Jasper		
Standard, Montana	Saturday	Montana	Boone	Brainard Brothers	Republican
Standard, Waukon	Thursday	Waukon	Allamakee	A. M. May	Republican
Sentinel, Iowa Falls	Wednesday	Iowa Falls	Hardin	Woodruff & Mathews	Republican
Sun, Winterset	Wednesday and Sat.	Winterset	Madison	C. S. Wilson & Company	Republican
Sentinel, Democratic	Wednesday	Newton	Jasper	H. A. Hanson	Democratic
Statesman, Des Moines	Daily	Des Moines	Polk	Jos. W. Snow	Democratic
Statesman, Des Moines	Wednesday	Des Moines	Polk	Jos. W. Snow	Democratic
Southwest, Iowa	Saturday	Bedford	Taylor	Lucas & Patrick	Republican
Signal, Linn County	Friday	Cedar Rapids	Linn	Thomas G. Newman	Democratic
Star of the West	Thursday	Clarksville	Butler	Frank Case	Republican
Star, Western	Thursday	Magnolia	Harrison	J. H. Waterman	Republican
Sentinel, Clarke County	Friday	Osceola	Clarke	Dague & Thompson	Republican
Staatszeitung, Iowa Staats	Weekly	Dubuque	Dubuque		*German*

Times, North Iowa	Wednesday	McGregor	Clayton	Richardson & Audrick	Democratic
Times, Cresco	Thursday	Cresco	Howard	I. A. Hoxie	Republican
Tribune, Iowa	Saturday	Iowa City	Johnson	Ballard & Huff	Republican
Times, Dubuque	Daily	Dubuque	Dubuque	Barnes & Ryan	Republican
Times, Dubuque	Wednesday	Dubuque	Dubuque	Barnes & Ryan	Republican
Times, Marshall County	Thursday	Marshalltown	Marshall	Chapin & Sower	Republican
Tribune, Afton	Thursday	Afton	Union	W. R. Roberts	Republican
Times, Cedar Rapids	Thursday	Cedar Rapids	Linn	Ayers Bros	Republican
Times, Sioux City	Daily	Sioux City	Woodbury	Charles Collins	Neutral
Times, Sioux City	Saturday	Sioux City	Woodbury	Charles Collins	Neutral
Times, Fremont	Saturday	Hamburg	Fremont	W. A. Putney	Republican
Tribune die Iowa	Tues., Thurs. & Sat.	Burlington	Des Moines	John A. Dalldorf	*German*
Tribune die Iowa	Weekly	Burlington	Des Moines	John A. Dalldorf	*German*
Times, Fort Dodge	Friday	Fort Dodge	Webster	C. B. Ingham	Democratic
Times, Volga Valley	Saturday	Fayette	Fayette	Vines & Cole	Republican
Union, Fayette County	Wednesday	West Union	Fayette	McClintock & Wood	Democratic
Union, Delaware County	Wednesday	Manchester	Delaware	Lyman L. Ayers	Republican
Union, Belle Plain	Thursday	Belle Plain	Benton	D. H. Frost	Republican
Union, Albia	Thursday	Albia	Monroe	Val Mendel	Republican
Union, American	Weekly	Sidney	Fremont		
Voter, Iowa	Thursday	Knoxville	Marion	Sperry & Barker	Republican
Vindicator, Northern	Thursday	Estherville	Emmet	Northrop & Bates	Republican
Vedette, Guthrie	Thursday	Panora	Guthrie	Lew. Apple	Republican
Volkszeiting Iowa	Thursday	Clinton	Clinton	F. G. Pfeiffer	*German*
Weekblad, Pella (Holland)	Tuesday	Pella	Marion	Henry Hospers	Republican
Wage Die (*Scales*)	Bi-monthly	New Buda	Decatur	H. Kompe	*German*

NOTE.—In all cases where the day of publication could not be ascertained, the word "Weekly" is inserted.

The *Worth County Pioneer*, published on Friday, at Northwood, Worth County, by P. D. Swick, has been received since the above was in type.

TABLE

Showing the number of persons between the ages of five and twenty-one years; the number and average attendance in Public Schools; the number of Teachers, male and female; the amount paid Teachers; the amounts of the different school funds received for the year ending October 4th, 1869; also, the number of School-houses and their value; the number of volumes in District Libraries; and the value of school apparatus, in the several Counties of the State.

Name of County.	No. of males between 5 and 21 years.	No. of females between 5 and 21 years.	Total No. males and females bt. 5 and 21 yrs	No. attending school during the year.	Average No. attending school during the year	No. of male teachers.	No. of female teachers.	Aggregate amount paid teachers during the year.	Amount teacher's fund rec'd from semi-annual apportionment.	Amount teacher's fund received from district tax.	No. of school-houses.	Value of school-houses.	Amount of school-house fund raised by district tax.	Amount of contingent fund raised by district tax.	No. of volumes in district libraries.	Value of apparatus belonging to the public schools.
Adair	546	469	1015	323	252	25	29	4064.75	1186.97	4523.90	33	24069.75	2911.67	3024.13	291	450.00
Adams	763	654	1417	1103	654	33	31	6969.10	3531.32	5187.69	31	14775.00	6922.38	1498.96	4	480.00
Allamakee	3594	3446	7040	5416	3427	55	141	23969.16	6984.18	16303.43	113	49622.12	7305.19	5655.12	6	1697.85
Appanoose	3373	3056	6429	5053	2886	95	85	17106.89	6682.28	13287.65	106	60735.00	22359.74	3023.46	....	160.00
Audubon	184	173	357	317	165	7	10	2675.00	626.31	2375.00	10	2300.00	44.70	575.95	....	125.00
Benton	4114	3791	7905	6086	3882	91	162	29462.72	8311.58	24128.02	143	113725.50	18097.13	12263.34	438	906.00
Black Hawk	3636	3411	7047	5516	3346	56	178	4191.86	8478.77	28735.13	113	82560.00	18567.58	11952.94	64	1273.75
Boone	2793	2487	5280	3582	2294	70	56	19758.40	4580.93	14906.31	67	66279.00	18896.46	3916.97	....	510.00
Bremer	2265	2055	4310	2929	1720	42	97	16238.05	1105.44	12153.73	80	42035.00	14108.23	5761.14	5	1666.00
Buchanan	3043	2885	5928	4255	2552	59	147	25198.93	10932.65	12698.49	112	75157.86	10351.30	5790.07	48	1850.00
Buena Vista	77	75	152	111	23	3	3	678.78	1170.86	678.75	3	1550.00	738.76	186.60	....	25.00
Butler	1733	1587	3320	2551	1460	42	116	14403.00	4954.88	11957.97	73	34680.00	6757.51	4092.86	....	1216.00
Calhoun	291	227	518	324	42	8	15	3028.50	2365.72	2015.17	10	4680.00	4689.09	1397.78	124	75.00
Carroll	321	319	640	430	187	7	12	3800.50	....	2667.00	22	19060.00	1999.99	10855.88	....	....
Cass	698	749	1447	977	540	22	43	5355.15	2690.68	6084.01	42	33710.00	2975.96	1905.63	....	373.00
Cedar	3834	3540	7374	3475	3152	90	158	30008.11	8887.32	25188.72	134	89105.00	14174.40	10395.67	....	221.89

Cerro Gordo	644	617	1261	905	526	15	55	7303.75	3215.10	6518.46	41	28500.00	3159.81	2694.34	490	1385.00
Cherokee	180	162	342	130	55	6	9	1506.80	....	595.31	8	3677.77	1616.03	369.92	....	130.00
Chickasaw	1783	1733	3516	2813	1626	54	96	13429.50	2758.80	7570.17	67	30830.00	4261.74	4158.60	20	1355.00
Clarke	1681	1616	3297	2157	1317	43	60	9108.48	3385.11	7266.36	58	42670.00	2946.20	2790.02	....	155.00
Clay	133	106	239	102	44	3	6	915.00	612.25	915.00	5	3070.00	126.89	388.12	....	75.00
Clayton	5142	4872	10014	7703	3795	94	162	32268.09	16765.48	23816.03	146	107523.00	14266.16	13797.92	24	4063.50
Clinton	6021	6010	12031	7614	5049	88	196	37408.35	13468.00	27042.50	141	205025.43	15119.83	11258.94	5	2524.75
Crawford	391	345	736	482	358	7	27	6608.00	1564.05	5885.98	22	19100.00	4166.10	1831.09	2	775.00
Dallas	2157	1955	4112	2994	1766	66	82	15440.55	4571.61	11329.79	78	46960.00	9841.69	2723.59	....	620.00
Davis	3302	3107	6409	4903	2927	74	86	13007.97	6527.75	9326.04	84	33415.75	4736.79	1762.65	....	86.75
Decatur	2464	2186	4650	3770	2008	74	50	11317.77	6706.11	10606.13	74	34630.00	4357.99	3050.50	....	975.00
Delaware	3193	3054	6247	5304	2914	73	150	23843.81	7018.31	18874.27	112	76668.38	11504.53	6797.00	5	1931.00
Des Moines	5272	4997	10269	6164	3659	57	127	26909.12	11903.62	7402.11	80	100315.00	6828.90	11850.78	8	10.00
Dickinson	217	207	424	171	84	3	9	579.26	86.60	602.32	5	983.00	413.18	277.60	....	....
Dubuque	7314	7320	14634	8089	5289	68	149	49652.91	17975.45	30004.41	110	215376.80	1641.17	18093.42	154	1632.00
Emmet	207	158	365	194	123	....	11	816.00	193.91	751.72	5	1880.00	188.70	172.45	....	....
Fayette	3282	3218	6500	4872	3479	81	201	20310.53	10110.35	21579.29	127	77497.00	17647.16	5605.06	5	1050.50
Floyd	1598	1599	3197	2260	1292	38	87	9909.50	3948.01	7864.48	59	48925.00	7147.86	4400.20	....	774.00
Franklin	798	766	1564	1209	742	18	57	9793.14	2009.73	10147.73	42	43700.00	7896.85	5464.66	252	868.00
Fremont	2061	1898	3959	2716	1382	51	56	13911.25	4375.50	11703.15	50	36662.00	8413.44	4536.49	50	1950.94
Greene	731	609	1340	823	452	18	36	8254.33	6947.47	6426.80	29	19725.00	3692.97	1517.47	....	175.00
Grundy	955	794	1749	1252	716	23	64	9134.98	2922.27	9707.77	47	24769.00	5113.64	2943.25	2	633.75
Guthrie	1082	1034	2116	1235	762	49	55	9418.93	20397.45	6408.48	56	27838.00	4444.73	3329.03	174	747.00
Hamilton	1026	865	1891	1376	802	23	33	8201.02	1962.05	6983.91	34	24561.00	6264.75	2972.14	34	217.00
Hancock	147	135	282	198	114	6	14	3085.30	863.02	2742.45	13	9400.00	3236.54	1599.71	346	460.00
Hardin	2536	2364	4900	3284	2469	46	103	18755.31	7287.33	13778.79	73	62585.00	12388.98	5128.99	....	....
Harrison	1594	1508	3057	2722	1329	55	65	14148.91	4839.08	8694.19	61	32297.00	7417.92	3899.35	341	632.87
Henry	4002	3814	7816	6136	3524	71	146	28191.48	....	25308.15	96	112140.00	24149.02	6862.97	220	730.00
Howard	1185	983	2168	1680	1015	33	70	10973.08	10335.37	13930.73	57	37176.00	5374.33	3652.75	2	1890.00
Humboldt	373	299	672	497	333	11	34	4332.67	970.38	2491.87	18	9100.00	3093.09	1390.61	....	283.00
Ida	46	30	76	76	56	1	3	633.00	1540.67	1482.00	4	3500.00	....	472.50	....	18.00
Iowa	2831	2572	5403	4630	2573	92	102	20292.80	7187.43	13923.35	98	102641.02	6102.14	9499.81	814	931.00

STATISTICAL TABLE—Coutinued.

Name of County.	No. males between 5 and 21 years.	No. females between 5 and 21 years.	Total No. males and females bt. 5 and 21 yrs	No. attending school during the year.	Average No. attending school during the year	No. of male teachers.	No. of female teachers.	Aggregate amount paid teachers during the year.	Amount teacher's fund received from semi-annual app'rtionment	Amount teacher's fund received from district tax.	No. of school-houses.	Value of school-houses.	Amount of school-house fund raised by district tax.	Amount of contingent fund raised by district tax.	No. of volumes in district libraries.	Value of apparatus belonging to the public schools.
Jackson	4396	4167	8563	5657	3476	69	202	26969.91	10567.11	13756.10	142	82620.00	13201.88	7806.88	42	2539.63
Jasper	4214	3623	7837	5566	3221	65	90	25603.81	9131.97	21500.83	127	96625.00	18011.90	9089.61	196	1324.00
Jefferson	3565	2174	6739	5196	3026	69	87	18188.47	7755.40	14288.86	83	82045.00	18895.93	4531.46	640	......
Johnson	4584	4253	8837	6843	4058	68	183	28739.84	17273.71	20614.36	129	112478.00	11062.48	13027.88	4	1150.00
Jones	4091	3837	7928	6208	4058	71	167	25319.97	8211.65	18199.07	126	79630.00	10411.16	6330.17	82	2334.90
Keokuk	3819	3485	7304	5424	3198	88	125	23451.50	9349.12	15695.59	117	77758.00	18916.18	7846.24	49	923.50
Kossuth	410	400	810	745	490	16	27	4830.00	1442.45	2618.91	12	11400.00	3411.10	1315.80	378	......
Lee	6677	6554	13231	7666	5133	76	156	41886.64	19540.39	17383.81	117	169960.00	25554.94	6058.47	....	793.00
Linn	5629	5326	10955	8189	4987	118	207	35495.97	12752.58	28162.74	156	167679.00	22198.23	11314.42	50	1045.60
Louisa	2554	2407	4961	3935	2508	59	64	15328.35	4744.46	14865.93	69	40260.50	7366.86	5717.05	....	765.00
Lucas	2022	1779	3801	3232	1777	61	56	13161.50	4856.23	6976.84	66	46571.00	5380.48	4403.58	11	232.40
Lyon	Not	orga	nized	....	....	....	....	....	....	....	....	....	....	....	....	......
Madison	2563	2303	4866	3696	2233	66	67	19574.23	4981.76	11689.75	81	79580.28	12940.72	7150.73	212	1230.00
Mahaska	4352	4297	8649	6309	3777	86	142	28096.53	7516.85	24065.27	120	118568.00	33416.25	8517.30	245	1971.00
Marion	4977	4597	9574	6026	3397	91	94	19853.67	10419.46	13935.48	104	76866.00	13560.50	4428.33	7	......
Marshall	3079	2789	5868	4159	2224	67	116	22998.80	6115.61	19701.85	95	78425.00	15437.43	9691.02	15	1423.10
Mills	1414	1410	2824	2008	1113	32	47	10719.25	3398.62	8649.74	43	39190.00	4186.04	3359.49	82	1268.40
Mitchell	1542	1487	3029	2231	1297	28	94	10500.60	3848.91	6342.26	61	41570.00	6539.62	3921.28	....	330.00
Monona	533	527	1060	789	514	24	30	7322.54	2117.62	4391.00	37	21678.50	2732.70	1665.65	179	1554.60
Monroe	2550	2405	4955	4190	2224	57	86	12302.50	7541.06	8664.52	75	43090.00	4751.14	3381.17	24	281.00
Montgomery	647	578	1225	779	471	19	24	4196.00	2662.53	1984.33	27	13195.56	1681.89	1098.78	2	140.00
Muscatine	4010	3849	7859	4648	2950	58	130	16547.34	10474.50	26145.58	94	95151.00	9689.19	11157.04	300	1290.50

O'Brien	No	re-	port	....	....	....	....	....	....	....	....	....	....	....	....	....	....
Osceola	Not	orga	nized	....	....	....	....	....	....	....	....	....	....	....	....	....	....
Page	1786	1656	3442	2708	1568	58	52	12346.45	5552.58	9291.70	51	35085.00	7838.94	4295.11	....	976.00
Palo Alto	153	121	274	141	87	6	7	982.00	130.00	185.00	8	3725.00	1969.25	358.40	1	156.00
Plymouth	181	143	324	131	91	8	1	921.50	244.71	579.14	7	2263.00	1075.89	729.65	....	172.30
Pocahontas	169	155	324	174	107	9	7	2050.00	1491.52	1615.18	11	15240.00	3584.00	529.00	....	686.00
Polk	4803	4679	9482	6314	4089	81	116	34021.43	13075.58	17959.69	103	181229.50	73648.13	16029.06	534	143.00
Pottawattamie	2168	2225	4393	1959	1193	52	42	19036.79	7817.25	14190.52	61	110565.00	23275.31	8084.02	680	1482.00
Poweshiek	2591	2265	4856	3661	2204	56	97	22267.25	9829.14	16023.52	89	73967.40	12445.99	6446.90	63	951.00
Ringgold	1063	1023	2086	1619	896	45	60	9337.75	5129.96	8360.04	58	20288.00	8374.10	1319.90	43	1640.00
Sac	212	230	442	351	209	13	15	3518.64	174.47	3518.64	14	8200.00	800.50	1925.69	501	540.00
Scott	6415	6352	12767	7694	4740	95	125	61462.33	23462.74	50035 83	104	192350.00	26936.17	17430.80	192	2854.00
Shelby	406	349	755	577	388	17	17	4432.00	3075.09	4179.73	21	13545.00	2632.38	2992.99	27	665.00
Sioux	No	re-	port	....	....	....	....	....	....	....	....	....	....	....	....	....
Story	2069	1904	3973	2909	1814	63	80	16756.78	5273.39	12789.15	75	48806.83	11873.38	5906.38	27	1520.00
Tama	2816	2563	5379	4151	2489	77	123	24276.91	7952.63	19784.02	111	70464.50	13671.91	10137.33	7	1508.55
Taylor	1284	1178	2462	1594	890	35	41	7619.54	3086.93	8851.74	40	25957.00	3686.79	2315.88	....	100.00
Union	1026	944	1970	1277	741	28	57	8692.51	6194.85	7167.34	48	21835.00	6926.52	3110.27	....	1434.00
Van Buren	3546	3241	6787	5111	3098	89	123	20322.00	7861.74	14097.29	103	84142.00	13897.58	4650.59	14	530.00
Wapello	4359	4032	8391	5912	4260	76	101	23897.46	33774.86	18305.69	92	112894.00	15194.59	6930.48	....	1162.00
Warren	3381	3216	6597	5462	3235	58	117	21613.30	7821.55	18966.64	101	60568.00	4303.24	3090.84	....	760.00
Washington	4060	3760	7820	6602	4124	89	152	25349.50	11474.38	20402.51	117	85454.00	13958.34	8316.35	5	287.50
Wayne	2125	1902	4027	3193	1743	62	46	13419.96	6397.88	9173.65	74	28182.50	7841.08	3517.70	....	495.00
Webster	1729	1630	3359	2530	1457	37	69	11674.50	3540.55	9041.14	53	35427.50	14307.46	5043.28	13	532.12
Winnebago	249	228	477	296	165	4	9	2068.75	275.00	2274.45	10	10225.00	3270.32	1374.89	....	......
Winneshiek	4365	3906	8271	5748	2857	59	126	20155.06	7938.99	15391.73	119	73436.00	16974.19	7536.21	....	659.00
Woodbury	761	704	1465	570	431	5	17	5521.47	5019.22	3034.90	13	39757.00	7386.40	3029.21	....	75.00
Worth	494	467	961	426	210	12	27	3122.60	1641.90	1924.10	20	10933.00	2579.10	1025.07	386	229.00
Wright	405	379	784	623	175	16	30	6639.65	1179.49	4793.44	31	17298.00	3009.15	2948.51	....	915.40
Totals	215812	202356	418168	296138	178329	4479	7515	1438964.04	599053.02	1106040.21	6407	5295364.45	919366.53	483475.29	8932	79178 05

NOTE.--The above table was compiled from information furnished by the Superintendent of Public Instruction.—SECRETARY OF STATE.

ABSTRACT

Of Votes cast in the several Counties of the State of Iowa for the office of Judge of the Supreme Court, for Superintendent of Public Instruction, full term, and for Superintendent of Public Instruction to fill vacancy, of said State, at the General Election held on the 12*th day of October, A. D.* 1869.

COUNTIES.	Judge of the Supreme Court.		Superintendent of Public Instruction (Full Term.)			Sup't of Pub. Ins to fill unexpired term of Hon. D. Franklin Wells—deceased.		
	John F. Dillon.	W. F. Brannan.	Abraham S. Kissell	H. O. Dayton.	Edmund Jaeger.	Abraham S. Kissell	H. O. Dayton.	Edmund Jaeger.
Adair	472	220	472	218	....	472	218	....
Adams	524	205	523	205	....	523	205	....
Allamakee	1482	1436	1448	1461	....	840	1443	....
Appanoose	1373	1089	1372	......	1089	1372	......	1089
Audubon	114	118	114	118	....	114	118	....
Benton	1789	804	1790	814	....	1790	804	....
Black Hawk	1518	205	1518	204	....	1516	205	....
Boone	1137	742	1136	744	....	906	577	....
Bremer	971	325	948	175	....	885	218	....
Buchanan	1278	519	1147	414	....	1278	422	7
Buena Vista	165	31	165	8	....	165	6	....
Butler	689	244	688	246	....	582	4	....
Calhoun	104	64	104	64	....	104	64	....
Carroll	247	114	247	......	104	247	......	83
Cass	563	337	599	351	....	137	71	....
Cedar	1513	701	1471	661	....	1510	105	....
Cerro Gordo	496	108	496	80	....	496	......	....
Cherokee	187	22	187	......	....	187	......	....
Chickasaw	860	415	860	218	194	860	218	190
Clarke	943	333	943	30	303	943	7	55
Clay	111	5	111	......	....	111	......	....
Clayton	1877	1398	1875	1400	....	1540	......	....
Clinton	3370	2494	3373	637	1717	3367	123	338
Crawford	225	145	215	......	....	218	......	....
Dallas	1030	377	1030	378	....	1030	378	....
Davis	1320	1196	1319	1196	....	1319	1196	....
Decatur	1041	687	1041	987	....	935	......	....
Delaware	1819	......	1819	952	....	1819	952	....
Des Moines	2011	1506	2011	1482	....	1912	1465	....

OFFICIAL CANVASS, 1869—CONTINUED.

COUNTIES.	Judge of the Supreme Court.		Superintendent of Public Instruction (Full Term.)			Supt. of Pub. Ins. to fill unexpired term of Hon. D. Franklin Wells—deceased.		
	John F. Dillon.	W. F. Brannan	Abraham S. Kissell	H. O. Dayton.	Edmund Jæger.	Abraham S. Kissell	H. O. Dayton.	Edmund Jæger.
Dickinson	143	9	139	......	9	134	......	9
Dubuque	1923	3272	1907	3272	....	1920	1392	....
Emmet	165	14	165	......	9	165	......	9
Fayette	1334	687	1334	658	....	1334	231	....
Floyd	908	272	908	272	....	708	272	....
Franklin	627	82	627	52	....	627	52	....
Fremont	867	907	873	404	502	745	......	....
Greene	472	219	472	197	22	472	219	....
Grundy	355	26	358	22	....	357	22	....
Guthrie	611	398	611	215	184	611	215	184
Hamilton	660	109	661	108	1	661	49	3
Hancock	136	34	136	......	14	136	22	....
Hardin	1117	335	1135	337	....	1135	337	....
Harrison	843	705	840	127	....	786	......	....
Henry	1987	649	1986	649	....	1986	649	....
Howard	530	307	532	......	....	531	1	....
Humboldt	335	111	335	111	....	322	108	....
Ida	42	1	42	......	....	42	......	....
Iowa	1249	867	1248	......	869	1221	......	774
Jackson	1576	1677	1569	1322	74	1570	1322	74
Jasper	2162	716	2164	594	....	1598	......	....
Jefferson	1564	1056	1563	1056	....	1563	1056	....
Johnson	1857	1796	1788	1730	....	1781	1732	....
Jones	1618	725	1617	724	....	1552	625	....
Keokuk	1551	1213	1560	1212	....	1561	1212	....
Kossuth	352	1	353	......	....	353	......	....
Lee	2650	2814	2649	2835	....	2648	2836	....
Linn	2299	1063	2440	1065	....	2442	941	....
Louisa	1277	698	1276	607	89	1276	607	89
Lucas	903	597	903	600	....	903	600	....
Lyon	Not organized		......	......	....	......	......	....
Madison	1366	785	1366	......	785	1360	......	785
Mahaska	1949	967	1947	707	....	1851	641	....
Marion	2071	1995	2117	1995	....	1534	591	....
Marshall	1736	456	1997	40	6	1701	3	3
Mills	684	440	675	440	....	510	......	....
Mitchell	1119	221	1119	163	44	1118	87	18
Monona	364	153	364	......	140	364	......	111

OFFICIAL CANVASS, 1869—CONTINUED.

COUNTIES.	Judge of the Supreme Court.		Superintendent of Public Instruction (Full Term).			Supt. of Pub. Ins. to fill unexpired Term of Hon. D. Franklin Wells—deceased.		
	John F. Dillon.	W. F. Brannan.	Abraham S. Kissell	H. O. Dayton.	Edmund Jæger.	Abraham S. Kissell	H. O. Dayton.	Edmund Jæger.
Monroe	1076	705	1076	705	....	1076	705	....
Montgomery	395	293	395	293	....	350	255	....
Muscatine	1545	517	1564	469	16	1564	182	22
O'Brien	56	......	57	......	....	32	......	....
Osceola	Not o	rganiz	ed.	......	....	......	......	....
Page	721	331	721	331	....	721	329	....
Palo Alto	50	64	50	......	64	50	......	64
Plymouth	96	......	95	......	....	95	......	....
Pocahontas	109	23	109	23	....	109	23	....
Polk	2323	960	2324	959	....	2071	959	....
Pottawattamie	1132	1008	1133	1007	....	1096	968	....
Poweshiek	1293	609	1343	......	....	1240	......	....
Ringgold	504	222	504	215	....	504	215	....
Sac	185	51	185	28	....	185	28	....
Scott	2428	1391	2383	1349	72	2385	1349	72
Shelby	166	90	171	18	....	167	......	....
Sioux	16	7	16	......	....	16	......	....
Story	992	374	992	375	....	989	374	....
Tama	1150	394	1198	......	....	1084	......	....
Taylor	706	250	706	250	....	705	239	....
Union	498	276	496	276	....	496	200	....
Van Buren	1682	1217	1632	1217	....	1639	1074	....
Wapello	1927	1642	1920	1645	....	1582	1492	....
Warren	1462	574	1460	573	....	1420	541	....
Washington	1498	716	1500	716	....	1447	661	....
Wayne	996	677	395	448	...	995	677	....
Webster	670	503	670	504	....	670	504	....
Winnebago	183	......	183	......	....	183	......	....
Winneshiek	1253	579	1250	579	....	683	......	....
Woodbury	477	312	489	217	....	489	216	....
Worth	204	5	204	5	....	204	5	....
Wright	269	78	269	19	59	......	......	....
Total	96693	56385	96888	46768	6366	91209	35607	3979

SCATTERING VOTES.

For Judge of the Supreme Court..

Geo. Gillaspy, Delaware....................953
C. Watson, Worth....................7

Superintendent of Public Instruction—Full Term..

D. S. Glidden, Tama....................30
H. O. Howard, Wayne....................29
E. D. Jaegar, Cerro Gordo....................25
Abraham F. Kissell, Mills....................12
H. S. Dayton, Franklin....................4
M. D. Bulton, Shelby....................2
C. Watson, Worth....................1
M. O. Dayton, Fayette....................10
"Scattering," Mitchell....................4
"Scattering," Buchanan....................2

For Superintendent of Public Instruction, to fill Vacancy..

W. F. Brannan, Cerro Gordo....................80
D. S. Glidden, Tama....................30
E. D. Jaeger, Cerro Gordo....................25
H. S. Dayton, Franklin....................10
A. Peck, Union....................2
H. C. Laub, Crawford....................1
C. Watson, Worth,....................1
"Scattering," Mitchell....................4

MAJORITIES.

Dillon's majority over Brannan....................40,308
Kissell's majority over Dayton (full term)....................50,120
Kissell's majority over Dayton (vacancy)....................55,602

The vote for Governor and Lieutenant-Governor was not canvassed, and remains as the work of the incoming Legislature. The majorities of Merrill and Walden will be about the same as that of Judge Dillon. Merrill's majority at his first election—in 1867—was 26,799.

Total vote for Judge of the Supreme Court, 154,014. John F. Dillon over Wm. F. Brannan, 40,308; Dillon's majority over all others, 39,372.

Total vote for Superintendent of Public Instruction, 150,14. Abraham S. Kissell over H. O. Dayton, 50,120; Kissell, (including 12 votes for Abraham F. Kissell), over all others, 43,659. To fill vacancy—Kissell over Dayton, 55,602; Kissell's majority, 51,470.

Total vote, in 1868, was 194,439; diminution this year, 40,407, or 20.78 per cent; Republican falling off, 23,706, or 19.69 per cent; Democratic falling off, 16,702, or 22.56 per cent. The vote for Governor, when canvassed, will show a still larger Democratic loss.

TABLE

Showing the votes cast in the several counties of the State of Iowa for and against the several propositions to strike the word "white" from the Constitution of said State, at the General Election held on the 3d day of November, A. D. 1868, *the votes cast at the same election for Secretary of State; and the vote cast for Governor in* 1867.

COUNTIES.	FOR GOVERNOR.		SECRETARY OF STATE.		AMENDMENTS TO THE CONSTITUTION.									
					First Amendment		*Second Amendment.*		*Third Amendment.*		*Fourth Amendment.*		*Fifth Amendment.*	
	Samuel Merrill.	Charles Mason.	Ed Wright.	David Hammer.	For.	Against.	For.	Against.	For.	Against.	For.	Against.	For.	Against.
Adair	235	108	312	139	276	158	276	158	276	158	276	158	276	158
Adams	310	132	427	166	382	186	383	186	383	187	383	186	383	187
Allamakee	1216	1307	1549	1413	1467	1433	1468	1433	1468	1433	1468	1433	1468	1433
Appanoose	1347	1151	1516	1248	1310	1350	1308	1351	1308	1351	1308	1351	1308	1351
Audubon	80	92	101	101	82	107	84	107	84	107	84	107	82	108
Benton	1510	738	2583	1179	2282	1351	2283	1356	2283	1356	2283	1351	2282	1351
Black Hawk	1410	610	2587	844	2306	939	2308	937	2308	937	2308	937	2309	936
Boone	1079	870	1363	998	1216	1088	1218	1088	1218	1088	1210	1089	1217	1088
Bremer	1000	480	1468	540	1318	583	1322	590	1323	590	1322	591	1322	591
Buchanan	1394	825	1869	930	1787	971	1788	971	1788	971	1788	971	1788	971
Buena Vista	26	2	57	4	49	11	49	11	49	11	49	11	49	11
Butler	678	306	1117	412	976	499	984	499	985	499	985	499	985	499
Calhoun	83	51	105	68	95	75	95	75	95	75	95	75	95	75
Carroll	113	46	173	82	69	114	69	114	69	114	69	114	69	114
Cass	303	190	419	248	341	294	342	293	342	293	338	293	342	293
Cedar	1838	1032	2464	1395	2187	1563	2191	1563	2188	1563	2187	1563	2187	1566
Cerro Gordo	345	51	441	73	386	102	386	102	386	102	386	102	386	102
Cherokee	40	14	64	16	58	21	58	21	58	21	58	21	58	21

Chickasaw	758	333	1023	492	873	551	873	551	871	551	871	551	871	551
Clarke	741	324	1061	427	868	515	867	512	870	512	870	514	871	511
Clay	61	6	76	......	70	4	70	4	70	4	70	4	70	4
Clayton	2555	1744	2789	1937	2214	2141	2512	2143	2514	2141	2514	2141	2514	2141
Clinton	2140	1763	3259	2317	2852	2377	2854	2377	2854	2377	2854	2377	2854	2377
Crawford	136	117	188	138	159	150	159	150	159	150	159	150	159	150
Dallas	819	448	1249	597	1129	639	1131	638	1131	639	1131	638	1131	638
Davis	1327	1219	1520	1410	1277	1543	1278	1542	1278	1542	1278	1542	1278	1542
Decatur	863	872	1023	1024	825	1097	829	1094	829	1094	829	1094	829	1094
Delaware	1506	902	2026	1031	1883	1090	1884	1090	1884	1090	1884	1090	1884	1090
Des Moines	2158	1898	2573	1971	2094	2260	2098	2253	2099	2253	2098	2253	2099	2253
Dickinson	102	4	125	9	108	20	108	20	108	20	108	20	108	20
Dubuque	1915	3335	2635	4096	2292	4341	2292	4341	2291	4341	2291	4341	2292	4391
Emmet	113	19	138	28	119	31	119	31	119	31	119	31	119	31
Fayette	2124	967	2119	1039	1886	1089	1894	1083	1893	1089	1889	1089	1889	1089
Floyd	766	299	1230	403	1140	456	1140	456	1140	456	1140	456	1140	456
Franklin	397	55	516	79	468	109	474	71	474	71	474	71	474	70
Fremont	800	860	979	1081	794	1128	799	1128	799	1128	799	1128	799	1128
Greene	301	215	421	233	320	307	332	298	332	298	332	301	332	301
Grundy	276	8	530	74	466	112	466	111	466	111	466	111	466	111
Guthrie	455	398	547	414	502	418	502	418	502	418	502	418	502	416
Hamilton	464	121	638	167	546	211	548	211	548	211	548	211	548	211
Hancock	64	24	89	24	75	29	75	29	75	29	75	29	75	29
Hardin	1076	419	1584	535	1415	622	1416	622	1417	622	1416	622	1416	622
Harrison	694	603	928	739	711	862	711	862	711	862	711	862	711	862
Henry	2332	866	2800	1052	2229	1330	2234	1324	2235	1323	2234	1322	2234	1323
Howard	613	339	673	381	618	413	619	412	619	413	619	413	619	412
Humboldt	249	71	271	80	217	116	217	116	217	116	217	116	217	116
Ida	15	1	21	7	13	9	13	9	13	9	13	9	13	9
Iowa	1170	968	1491	1172	1306	1249	1307	1249	1306	1249	1307	1250	1307	1249
Jackson	1724	1855	2033	2131	1788	2259	1786	2262	1786	2260	1786	2261	1788	2259

TABLE OF VOTES—Continued.

COUNTIES.	For Governor.		Secretary of State.		Amendments to the Constitution.									
					First Amendment.		*Second Amendment.*		*Third Amendment.*		*Fourth Amendment.*		*Fifth Amendment.*	
	Samuel Merrill.	Charles Mason.	Ed Wright.	David Hammer.	For.	Against.	For.	Against.	For.	Against.	For.	Against.	For.	Against.
Jasper	1816	678	2780	1237	2538	1347	2539	1347	2541	1346	2541	1347	2541	1347
Jefferson	1785	1315	1887	1320	1694	1386	1698	1383	1698	1383	1699	1383	1699	1383
Johnson	1945	2023	2213	2062	1876	2207	1876	2200	1876	2199	1877	2198	1877	2197
Jones	1741	1204	2402	1289	2238	1351	2242	1350	2241	1350	2240	1350	2241	1350
Keokuk	1494	1298	1940	1510	1738	1632	1740	1632	1740	1632	1740	1632	1740	1632
Kossuth	217	13	333	30	347	30	348	29	348	29	348	29	348	29
Lee	2576	3057	3062	3189	2441	3523	2441	3523	2441	3523	2441	3523	2441	3523
Linn	2627	1171	3624	1649	3403	1721	3388	1738	3411	1717	3411	1716	3412	1712
Louisa	1343	693	1597	766	1343	878	1350	872	1350	874	1349	875	1350	875
Lucas	789	670	988	688	782	793	783	793	783	793	783	793	783	793
Lyon (unorganized)	......	......	......	......	......	......	......	......	......	......	......	......	......	......
Madison	1183	744	1504	944	1312	1061	1313	1061	1312	1061	1313	1061	1314	1061
Mahaska	2064	1338	2644	1518	2267	1627	2267	1629	2267	1627	2267	1626	2267	1626
Marion	2064	1969	2270	2184	1978	2261	1979	2261	1979	2261	1979	2256	1979	2256
Marshall	1384	450	2334	618	2175	700	2172	700	2172	700	2166	700	2166	700
Mills	629	516	841	552	683	609	683	609	683	609	683	609	683	609
Mitchell	721	153	1176	296	1043	356	1043	356	1042	356	1043	356	1043	356
Monona	266	137	369	167	300	222	300	222	300	222	300	222	300	222
Monroe	1096	754	1290	916	1196	942	1197	942	1196	943	1198	941	1198	941
Montgomery	261	188	356	228	305	251	306	251	306	251	306	251	306	251
Muscatine	2068	1461	2539	1584	2204	1760	2206	1759	2206	1759	2206	1759	2206	1758
O'Brien	6	3	10	1	6	4	6	4	6	4	6	4	6	4

Osceola (unorganized)	......	......	......	......	......	......	......	......	......	......	......	......	......	......
Page	673	399	931	475	770	572	780	571	778	572	780	568	772	565
Palo Alto	39	56	41	64	22	73	22	73	22	73	22	73	22	73
Plymouth	50	5	95	24	67	49	67	49	67	49	67	49	67	49
Pocahontas	80	20	93	19	92	19	92	19	92	19	92	19	92	19
Polk	2157	1659	2916	1694	2653	1817	2654	1814	2654	1818	2654	1814	2655	1814
Pottawattamie	834	976	1117	1050	852	1149	856	1149	856	1149	856	1149	855	1150
Poweshiek	1050	562	1687	793	1478	846	1481	846	1481	846	1483	846	1483	846
Ringgold	433	205	515	255	451	291	451	289	453	289	454	191	459	284
Sac	111	34	132	45	112	59	112	59	112	59	112	59	112	59
Scott	1846	1736	3556	1777	3255	1745	3251	1746	3257	1746	3251	1747	3250	1746
Shelby	107	109	152	130	117	147	118	147	118	147	118	147	118	147
Sioux	8	......	6	5	6	5	6	5	6	5	6	5	6	5
Story	767	406	1059	425	926	523	929	523	929	523	929	523	929	523
Tama	936	448	1864	805	1673	942	1672	940	1670	941	1673	941	1673	941
Taylor	540	228	714	325	622	372	621	372	621	372	621	372	621	372
Union	363	298	488	353	423	383	423	383	423	383	423	383	423	383
Van Buren	1881	1509	2029	1607	1686	1714	1687	1713	1687	1713	1687	1713	1687	1713
Wapello	1835	1785	2118	1830	1830	1878	1834	1877	1834	1877	1834	1877	1832	1877
Warren	1318	670	1947	939	1659	1038	1663	1038	1662	1038	1660	1042	1662	1035
Washington[3]	1824	1024	2325	1328	2092	1409	2095	1412	2097	1410	2097	1410	2097	1410
Wayne	868	607	1026	748	887	828	889	826	888	827	888	827	889	827
Webster	599	476	739	549	690	582	691	582	691	582	691	582	691	582
Winnebago	147	1	159	16	69	17	69	17	69	17	69	17	69	17
Winneshiek	1318	525	2300	1092	2202	1122	2202	1122	2202	1122	2202	1122	2202	1122
Woodbury	253	237	429	323	340	289	340	389	340	389	339	389	339	389
Worth	180	36	259	41	207	68	207	68	206	69	207	68	204	68
Wright	191	62	239	57	190	98	190	98	190	98	190	98	190	98
Total	90204	62966	120265	74461	105384	81119	105498	81050	105524	81038	105502	80929	105515	81050

NOTE—The proposition to amend the Constitution of the State of Iowa was submitted to the people pursuant to the provisions of Chapter 68, Laws of the Twelfth General Assembly, and voted on at the General Election held November 3d, A. D. 1868, the result of which is shown by the foregoing table, was:

First—To strike the word "white" from Section one of Article two, which Section defines the right of suffrage.

Second—To strike the word "white" from Section thirty-three of Article three, which Section provides for taking the census.

Third—To strike the word "white" from Section thirty-four, of Article three, which Section provides for the apportionment of Senators in the General Assembly.

Fourth—To strike the word "white" from Section thirty-five, of Article three, which Section provides for the apportionment of Members of the House of Representatives in the General Assembly.

Fifth—To strike the word "white" from Section one, of Article six, which Section defines the militia of the state.—[SECRETARY OF STATE.

TABLE

Showing the vote of the State of Iowa by counties, for Presidential Candidates at each Presidential election from 1852 to 1868; also, the popular vote and majorities.

COUNTIES.	1852.			1856.			1860.				1864.		1868.	
	Scott.	Pierce.	Hale.	Fremont.	Buchanan.	Fillmore.	Lincoln.	Douglas.	Bell.	Breckenridge.	Lincoln.	McClellan.	Grant.	Seymour.
Adair	....	....	....	72	27	4	42	44	1	1	119	47	313	139
Adams	....	....	....	113	73	3	161	92	....	....	180	76	427	166
Allamakee	142	123	....	630	560	28	1185	1151	9	5	1145	1330	1543	1403
Appanoose	247	335	25	191	853	487	853	1223	18	43	874	920	1519	1236
Audubon	....	....	....	28	31	4	48	59	....	....	28	52	101	101
Benton	80	89	....	558	426	123	1028	722	5	2	1119	560	2587	1172
Black Hawk	....	....	....	566	292	33	1122	551	4	17	1489	433	2580	841
Boone	40	84	....	203	359	66	365	447	1	....	405	460	1362	995
Bremer	....	....	....	327	172	43	544	452	....	18	737	257	1470	538
Buchanan	123	148	....	709	343	21	962	621	1	10	1054	601	1872	926
Buena Vista	....	....	....	....	....	....	6	6	....	....	6	9	57	4
Butler	....	....	....	223	142	29	483	246	1	....	559	241	1118	424
Calhoun		....	....	9	14	....	19	20	....	....	12	24	104	67
Carroll	....	....	....	....	....	....	25	26	....	....	33	32	156	82
Cass	....	....	....	132	84	....	167	136	4	1	180	128	420	248
Cedar	338	354	102	1116	701	176	1548	963	29	5	1518	832	2470	1381
Cerro Gordo	....	....	....	101	40	1	157	58	2	7	228	11	441	73
Cherokee	....	....	....	....	....	....	10	3	....	....	8	1	64	15
Chickasaw	....	....	....	351	102	32	550	306	....	1	576	292	996	526
Clarke	20	32	37	346	338	77	592	444	....	....	611	207	1062	426
Clay	....	....	....	....	....	....	8	13	....	....	24	11	76	4

PRESIDENTIAL CANVASS—CONTINUED.

COUNTIES.	1852.			1856.			1860.				1864.		1868.	
	Scott.	Pierce.	Hale.	Fremont.	Buchanan.	Fillmore.	Lincoln.	Douglas.	Bell.	Breckinridge.	Lincoln.	McClellan.	Grant.	Seymour.
Clayton	471	461	.....	1420	754	67	2089	1571	5	14	2110	1642	2783	1952
Clinton	278	336	.....	1245	839	142	1974	1450	51	60	1896	1410	3283	2292
Crawford	.....	.....	.....	36	8	.....	47	31	....	....	49	17	188	38
Dallas	79	89	.....	487	319	20	612	434	6	5	632	327	1254	590
Davis	592	614	12	201	1019	752	843	1424	226	25	1021	968	1520	1410
Decatur	55	133	2	243	583	183	680	898	11	....	689	577	1024	1018
Delaware	233	204	18	801	500	149	1268	785	20	3	1300	630	2034	1021
Des Moines	984	1154	80	1338	1413	522	1994	1678	156	10	2050	1514	2572	1958
Dickinson	..	.....	.....	.....	.....	.....	46	7	....	....	.....	.....	121	10
Dubuque	600	1150	6	1322	2427	256	2092	3058	63	56	1742	3318	2633	4091
Emmet	.....	.....	.....	.....	.....	.....	36	.....	....	....	41	.....	136	28
Fayette	167	117	21	1043	452	117	1529	835	....	5	1413	799	2124	1051
Floyd	.....	.....	.....	324	124	14	560	201	1	21	587	185	1233	400
Franklin	.....	.....	.....	110	32	.....	228	69	....	....	236	56	516	78
Fremont	95	67	.....	156	203	108	402	516	66	....	511	448	977	1082
Greene	.....	.....	.....	73	117	.....	121	146	....	....	153	103	423	231
Grundy	.....	.....	.....	65	2	.....	141	19	....	....	202	18	530	75
Guthrie	7	39	.....	196	205	12	326	302	....	....	280	273	547	412
Hamilton	.....	.....	.....	.....	.....	.....	224	100	2	13	260	80	638	167
Hancock	.....	.....	.....	.....	.....	.....	29	4	....	....	35	17	89	24
Hardin	.....	.....	.....	580	195	18	713	382	2	3	815	305	1586	535
Harrison	.....	.....	.....	170	124	9	385	357	1	5	341	291	932	732
Henry	832	513	223	1767	767	308	2149	1065	66	....	2069	669	2802	1044

Howard				207	63		386	272					674	380
Humboldt							55	8		10	74	31	271	80
Ida							4	6			10		23	5
Iowa	112	101	1	492	326	79	782	681	11		792	662	1490	1164
Jackson	554	739	12	1163	1332	276	1575	1504	40	15	1598	1609	2040	2117
Jasper	160	113	3	878	455	38	1208	649	13	50	1349	638	2799	1232
Jefferson	757	796	97	1188	1023	206	1462	1245	38	4	1389	962	1895	1309
Johnson	415	531	38	1215	961	282	1804	1448	111	26	1546	1397	2221	2050
Jones	266	338	22	964	663	10	1453	1095	4	24	1531	941	2410	1277
Keokuk	326	403	42	895	830	107	1330	1193	2	14	1149	938	1938	1503
Kossuth				85	12		64	20			74	14	332	30
Lee	1379	1708	201	1780	2158	650	2618	2635	136	20	2506	2223	3060	3191
Linn	522	592	80	1632	971	273	2226	1290	80	24	2253	1087	3630	1642
Louisa	468	368	105	993	642	200	1310	738	26	14	1305	559	1599	761
Lucas	80	85	3	288	355	176	586	483	8		565	382	992	683
Lyon	Not or	gan	ized.											
Madison	103	150		580	519	61	737	1332	8	10	808	586	1506	944
Mahaska	599	541	39	1224	940	268	1639	1331	18	1	1836	954	2646	1511
Marion	411	489	13	1069	1322	225	1508	1607	4	21	1458	1452	2268	2182
Marshall	31	52		531	199	104	854	403	16		1096	367	2339	611
Mills	42	91		287	153	102	441	327	14	16	485	237	842	551
Mitchell				334	135	1	585	172	1	6	579	106	1177	293
Monona				41	56	13	109	89		2	122	88	372	
Monroe	204	295	36	622	603	98	879	749	5	18	848	592	1290	913
Montgomery				63	58	17	152	81	2	10	144	91	357	225
Muscatine	562	605	30	1094	895	328	1838	1283	109	85	1767	1242	2539	1576
O'Brien							8	10	3		2	5	10	1
Osceola	Not or	gan	ized.											
Page	29	40		100	171	169	469	287	10	22	521	168	936	474
Palo Alto							4	29					42	62
Plymouth							32	6			19		95	23

PRESIDENTIAL CANVASS—Continued.

COUNTIES.	1852.			1856.			1860.				1864.		1868.	
	Scott.	Pierce.	Hale.	Fremont	Buchanan.	Fillmore.	Lincoln.	Douglas.	Bell.	Breck'nridge	Lincoln.	McClellan.	Grant.	Seymour.
Pocahontas	.....	.....	.....	.....	.....	.....	21	10	....	....	32	8	93	19
Polk	401	439	13	1065	888	91	1302	1075	37	22	1509	1092	2913	1694
Pottawattamie	111	182	.....	259	353	84	413	412	28	31	502	303	1121	1042
Poweshiek	61	45	2	459	255	87	721	484	2	....	753	454	1686	791
Ringgold	.....	.....	.....	92	52	64	348	181	3	....	319	76	519	257
Sac	.....	.....	.....	25	35	.....	15	40	....	....	44	22	132	45
Scott	517	641	81	1675	1119	329	2737	1379	115	79	2674	1402	3612	1763
Shelby	.....	.....	.....	62	19	.....	100	64	....	....	61	78	153	129
Sioux	.....	.....	.....	.....	.....	.....	3	10	2	....	1	3	6	5
Story	.....	.....	.....	232	272	79	418	332	....	....	549	342	1058	423
Tama	.....	.....	.....	470	206	90	775	413	5	....	873	388	1862	805
Taylor	.....	9	.....	119	183	31	353	248	7	....	434	135	717	321
Union	.....	.....	.....	102	121	17	198	208	....	....	196	167	488	352
Van Buren	981	1028	48	1092	1396	324	1667	1548	19	57	1577	1015	2026	1606
Wapello	683	762	20	1093	1175	252	1398	1685	22	38	1398	1268	2119	1821
Warren	95	82	13	855	519	112	1152	795	40	2	1170	622	1946	933
Washington	473	369	181	1188	629	403	1723	1055	60	20	1663	937	2314	1323
Wayne	•63	59	.....	183	363	170	579	648	7	3	520	430	1031	739
Webster	.....	.....	.....	389	269	31	253	213	1	53	318	319	736	549
Winnebago	.....	.....	.....	.....	.....	.....	24	25	....	....	39	13	161	16

Winneshiek	68	68	......	770	209	13	1382	780	....	....	1495	850	2300	1092
Woodbury	......	.....	......	......	......	......	129	117	5	8	157	93	430	323
Worth	......	......	......	......	......	......	109	30	....	....	123	31	259	41
Wright	......	......	......	51	24	......	......	......	....	....	86	42	241	61
Army Vote, 1864	......	......	......	......	......	......	......	......	....	....	16844	1883	......	......
Totals	15856	17762	1606	45196	37663	9669	70302	55069	1763	1034	88966	49586	120399	74040
Majority	......	1906	......	7533	......	......	15233	......	....	...	39380	......	46359	......
Aggregate	......	......	35224	......	......	92528	......	......		128168	......	138552	......	194439

TABLE

Showing the names of the Stations on the several Railroads in the State of Iowa, Dec. 1st, 1869, the distance of each Station from Des Moines, and from other points therein named.

EXPLANATIONS.

The data used in most cases in making up the following tables, was furnished by the several Railroad Companies of the State, and the distances from Des Moines to the various stations are computed as follows, to-wit:

To all points on the Burlington and Missouri River Railroad, west of, and including Corning, *via* Council Bluffs and Pacific City; to all other points *via* Ottumwa; to all points on the Sioux City and Pacific and western end of the Iowa Falls and Sioux City Railways, *via* Grand Junction and Missouri Valley; to all points on the Chicago and Northwestern Railway *via* Grand Junction: to all points on the Iowa Falls and Sioux City, and Dubuque and Sioux City Railways, west of Farley, *via* Grand Junction and Fort Dodge, and to all points east of and including Farley, and on the Dubuque Southwestern, *via* Grand Junction and Cedar Rapids; to all points on the Central Railroad of Iowa, *via* Grand Junction and Marshalltown; to all points on the Cedar Falls and Minnesota Railway, *via* Grand Junction, Fort Dodge, and Cedar Falls; to all points on the McGregor and Missouri River Railway, *via* Grand Junction, Fort Dodge, Cedar Falls, and Charles City; to all points on the Milwaukee and St. Paul Railway, (Iowa Division), *via* Grand Junction, Fort Dodge, Cedar Falls, Charles City, and Calmar; and to all points on the Keokuk and St. Paul, and the Burlington, Cedar Rapids and Minnesota Railway, *via* Ottumwa and Burlington.

Names of stations printed in Italics or small caps with a (c h) in parenthesis, are county seats, and those printed in small caps are Railroad Junctions.

McGregor and Missouri River Railway.

Distance from Station to Station.	NAMES OF STATIONS.	Distance from Des Moines.	Distance from Calmar.	Distance from Mason City.
	CALMAR	265.24	......	75
6	Fort Atkinson	259.24	6	69
12	Lawler	247.24	18	57
9	*New Hampton* (c h)	238.24	27	48
8	Chickasaw	230.24	35	40
12	CHARLES CITY (c h)	218.24	47	28
12	Flood Creek	230.24	59	16
6	Nora Springs	236.24	65	10
10	*Mason City* (c h)	246.24	75	......

Milwaukee and St. Paul Railway—(Iowa Division.)

Distance from Station to Station.	NAMES OF STATIONS.	Distance from Des Moines.	Distance from McGregor.	Distance from Le Roy.
	McGREGOR	308.24	......	85
6	Giard	302.24	6	79
9	Monona	293.24	15	70
4	Luana	289.24	19	66
7	Postville	282.24	26	59
6	Castalia	276.24	32	53
5	Ossian	271.24	37	48
6	CALMAR	265.24	43	42
3	CONOVER	268.24	46	39
7	Ridgeway	275.24	53	32
9	*Cresco* (c h)	284.24	62	23
11	Lime Springs	295.24	73	12
6	Chester	301.24	79	6
6	Le Roy	307.24	85	......
	Decorah (c h)	278.24	56	49

Cedar Falls and Minnesota Railroad.

Distance from Station to Station.	NAMES OF STATIONS.	Distance from Des Moines.	Distance from Cedar Falls.	Distance from State Line.
	Cedar Falls	175.50	....	76.11
1	CEDAR FALLS JUNC.	176.50	1	75.11
7.48	Janesville	183.98	8.48	67.63
6.23	*Waverly* (c h)	190.21	14.71	61 40
8.54	Plainfield	198.75	23.25	52.86
7.88	Nashua	206.63	31.13	44.98
11.61	CHARLES CITY (c h)	218.24	42.74	33.37
5.61	Floyd	223.85	48.35	27.76
6.38	Orchard	230 23	54.73	21.38
4.79	Osage	235.02	59.52	16.59
3.58	*Mitchell* (c h)	238.60	63.10	13.01
4.57	St. Ansgar	243.17	67.67	8.44
7.56	Mond	250.73	75.23	.88
.88	State Line	251.61	76.11	......

TABLE OF DISTANCES—Continued.

Dubuque and Sioux City Railroad.

Distance from station to station.	NAMES OF STATIONS.	Distance from Des Moines.	Distance from Fort Dodge.	Distance from Dubuque.
	DUBUQUE (C. H.)	272.4	191.5	......
10	Julien	262.4	181 5	10
5	Peosta	257.4	176 5	15
4	Epworth	253.4	172 5	19
4	FARLEY	249.4	168.5	23
6	Dyersville	245.5	162.5	29
8	Earlville	237.5	154.5	37
4	Delaware	233.5	150.5	41
6	Manchester	227.5	144.5	47
7	Masonville	220 5	137.5	54
7	Winthrop	213.5	130 5	61
8	*Independence* (c. h.)	205.5	122.5	69
9	Jesup	196.5	113.5	78
9	Raymond	187 5	104.5	87
6	*Waterloo* (c. h.)	181.5	98.5	93
5	C. F. & MINN. JUNC.	176 5	93.5	98
1	Cedar Falls	175.5	92.5	99
10	New Hartford	165.5	82.5	109
8	Parkersburg	157.5	74.5	117
6	Aplington	151.5	68.5	123
9	ACKLEY	142.5	59.5	132
10.5	Iowa Falls	132.0	49 0	142.5
6.9	Alden	125.1	42.1	149.4
8.1	Williams	117.0	34 0	157.5
5.2	Blairsburg	111.8	28.8	162.7
9	*Webster City* (c. h.)	102 8	19.8	171 7
8.9	Duncombe	93.9	10 9	181.6
10.9	FORT DODGE (C H.)	83.0	....	191.5

Sioux City and Pacific Railroad.

Distance from station to station.	NAMES OF STATIONS.	Distance from Des Moines.	Distance from Mo. Valley.	Distance from Sioux City.
	Missouri Valley	154.3	......	76
6	CALIFORNIA JUNC.	160.3	6	70
5	*Ferry*	165.3	11	75
5	Modale	165.3	11	65
6	Mondamin	171.3	17	59
7	River Sioux	178.3	24	52
8	Blencoe	186.3	32	44
6	*Onawa* (c. h.)	192.3	38	38
17	Sloan	209.3	55	21
14	Sargent's Bluffs	223.3	69	7
7	SIOUX CITY (C. H.)	230.3	76	....
26.5	Le Mars .... L. F. & S. C. R. R.	256.8	102.5	26.5
8.5	Remsen	265.3	111.0	35.0
8.5	....	273 8	119.5	43.5

*Computed via Grand Junction and Fort Dodge, the distance from Des Moines to Ackley is 142.5 miles; to Steamboat Rock, 154.5 miles.

Dubuque Southwestern Railroad.

Distance from station to station.	NAMES OF STATIONS.	Distance from Des Moines.	Distance from Cedar Rapids	Distance from Farley.
	CEDAR RAPIDS	193.4	....	56
4	*Marion* (c. h.)	197.4	4	52
10	Springville	207.4	14	42
4	Viola	211.4	18	38
7	*Anamosa* (c. h.)	218.4	25	31
7	Langworthy	225.4	32	24
4	Monticello	229.4	36	20
6	Sand Springs	235.4	42	14
7	Worthington	242.4	49	7
7	FARLEY	249.4	56	....

Central Railroad of Iowa.

Distance from station to station.	NAMES OF STATIONS.	Distance from Des Moines.	Distance from Marshalltown	Distance from Ackley.
*	ACKLEY	167.1	43	....
12*	Steamboat Rock	155.1	31	12
4	*Eldora* (c. h.)	151.1	27	16
10	Union	141.1	17	26
5	Liscomb	136.1	12	31
5	Albion	131.1	7	36
7	MARSHALLTOWN (C. H.)	124.1	....	43

St. Joseph and Council Bluffs Railroad.

Distance from station to station.	NAMES OF STATIONS.	Distance from Des Moines.	Distance from St. Joseph.	Distance from Council Bluffs
....	St. Joseph, Mo.	273	....	132
79	Hamburg	194	79.0	53
11	East Nebraska City	183	90.0	42
5	Percival	178	95.0	37
9	Bartlett	169	104 0	28
12	PACIFIC CITY	157	116.0	16
8	Trader's Point	149	124.0	8
8	COUNCIL BLUFFS (C. H.)	141	132.0	....

St Louis and Cedar Rapids Railroad.

Distance from station to station.	NAMES OF STATIONS.	Distance from Des Moines.	Distance from Ottumwa.	Distance from Coatesville.
....	Coatesville	128.25	42.25	......
7.50	Moulton	120.75	34.75	7.50
7	West Grove	113.75	27.75	14.50
7.25	*Bloomfield* (c. h.)	106.50	20.50	21.75
9.50	Saponica	97.00	11.00	31 25
11	OTTUMWA (C. H.)	86.00	....	42.25

TABLE OF DISTANCES—Continued.

Chicago, Rock Island and Pacific Railroad.

Distance from station to station.	Names of Stations.	Distance from Des Moines.	Distance from Davenport.	Distance from Council Bluffs.
....	DAVENPORT (C. H.)	175	....	316
12½	Walcott	162½	12½	303½
4½	Fulton	158	17	299
2¾	Durant	155¼	19¾	296¼
5¾	WILTON	149½	25½	290½
	Oskaloosa Division.			
12½	*Muscatine* (*c. h.*)	162	38	303
13	Onawa	175	51	316
7	Fredonia	182	58	323
2½	Clifton	184½	60½	325½
8	Ainsworth	192½	68½	333½
7½	*Washington* (*c. h.*)	200	76	341
3¼	Moscow	146¼	28¾	287¼
5	Atalissa	141¼	33¾	282¼
5¼	West Liberty	136	39	277
5½	Downey	130½	44½	271½
10	*Iowa City* (*c. h.*)	120½	54½	261½
7½	Tiffin	113	62	254
7½	Oxford	105½	69½	246½
5	Homestead	100½	74½	241½
5¼	South Amana	95¼	79¾	236¼
5¼	*Marengo* (*c, h.*)	90	85	231
6	Ladora	84	91	225
6½	Victor	77½	97½	218½
7½	Brooklyn	70	105	211
6	Malcolm	64	111	205
9	Grinnell	55	120	196
11	Kellog	44	131	185
9	*Newton* (*c h.*)	35	140	176
5¾	Vowels	29¼	145¾	170¼
6¼	Colfax	23	152	164
6	Mitchellville	17	158	158
7	Altoona	10	165	151
10	DES MOINES (C. H.)	....	175	141
10	Nordyke	10	185	131
5	Boone	15	190	126
4	Van Meter	19	194	122
3	De Soto	22	197	119
7½	Earlham	29½	204½	111½
5½	Dexter	35	210	106
5	Stuart	40	215	101
5	Guthrie	45	220	96
7	Casey	52	227	89
8	Adair	60	235	81
8	Anita	68	243	73
7	Wiota	75	250	66
7	*Atlantic* (*c. h.*)	82	257	59
19	Avoca	101	276	40
8	Shelby	109	284	32
11	Neola	120	295	21
13	Lima	133	308	8
8	COUNCIL BLUFFS (C. H.)	141	316	....

Chicago and Northwestern Railway, (Iowa Division.)

Distance from station to station.	Names of Stations.	Distance from Des Moines.	Distance from Clinton	Distance from Council Bluffs.
2.0	Lyons	276.7	2.0	352.4
.....	CLINTON (C. H.)	274.7	....	350.4
4.5	Camanche	270.2	4.5	345.9
5.0	Low Moor	265.2	9.5	340.9
4.5	Malone	260.7	14.0	336.4
5 0	De Witt	255.7	19.0	331.4
5.8	Grand Mound	249.9	24.8	325.6
5.8	Calamus	244 1	30.6	319.8
4.1	Wheatland	240.0	34.7	315.7
5.0	Louden	235.0	39.7	310.7
7.0	Clarence	228.0	46.7	303.7
5.0	Stanwood	223.0	51.7	298.7
5.2	Mechanicsville	217.8	56.9	293.5
6.9	Lisbon	210.9	63.8	286 6
1.4	Mt. Vernon	209 5	65.2	285 2
6.8	Bertram	202.7	72.0	278.4
9.3	CEDAR RAPIDS	193.4	81.3	269.1
8 3	Fairfax	185.1	89.6	260.8
6.7	Norway	178.4	96.3	254.1
9.4	Blairstown	169.0	105.7	244.7
5 1	Luzerne	163.9	110.8	239.6
5.1	Belle Plaine	158.8	115.9	234.5
6.4	Chelsea	152.4	122.3	228.1
9.9	Tama City	142.5	132.2	218.2
7 2	Orford	135.3	139.4	211.0
2 8	Le Grand	132.5	142 2	208 2
2.8	Quarry	129.7	145.0	205.4
5.6	MARSHALTOWN (C. H,)	124.1	150.6	199.8
7.3	Lamoille	116 8	157.9	192.5
7.0	State Center	109.8	164.9	185.5
7.8	Colo	102.0	172.7	177.7
7.0	*Nevada* (*c. h.*)	95.0	179.7	170.7
8.4	Ames	86.6	188.1	162.3
4.0	Ontario	82.6	192.1	158.3
5.1	Side Track	77.5	197.2	153 2
5.1	*Boonsboro* (*c. h.*)	72.4	202.3	148.1
5.5	Moingona	66.9	207.8	142.6
5 8	Ogden	61.1	213 6	136.8
5.4	Beaver	55.7	219.0	131.4
5.7	GRAND JUNCTION	50.0	224.7	125.7
6.8	*Jefferson* (*c. h.*)	56 8	231.5	118.9
9.0	Scranton	65.8	240.5	109.9
9.9	Glidden	75.7	250.4	100.0
7.2	*Carrroll City* (*c. h.*)	82.9	257.6	92.8
6.1	East Side	89.0	263.7	86 7
4.0	Tip Top	93.0	267.7	82 7
3.2	West Side	96 2	270.9	79.5
6.0	Vail	102.2	276.9	73.5
8 7	*Denison* (*c. h.*)	110 9	285 6	64.8
9.4	Crawford	120.3	295.0	55.4
7.9	Dnnlap	128.2	302.9	47.5
9.7	Woodbine	137.9	312.6	37.8
8.0	Logan	145 9	320.6	29.8
8.4	Mo. VALLEY JUNCTION	154.3	329.0	21.4
9 2	*Honey Creek	163.5	338.2	12.2
5.3	*Crescent	168.8	343.5	6.9
6.9	COUNCIL BLUFFS (C. H.)	141.0	350.4	....

*Computed *via* Council Bluffs, the distance from Des Moines to Honey Creek is 153.2 miles; to Crescent, 147.9 miles.

TABLE OF DISTANCES—Continued.

Burlington & Missouri River Railroad.

Distance from station to station.	Names of Stations.	Dist. from Des Moines	Dist. from Burlington	Dist. from B. & M. and C. B. & St. Joe crossing
	BURLINGTON (C H)......	160.72	....	275.11
9.20	Middletown............	151.52	9.20	265.91
3.60	Danville	147.92	12.80	262.31
6.25	New London	141.67	19.05	256.06
8.45	*Mt. Pleasant* (*c h*).. ...	133.22	27 50	247.61
7.10	Rome	126.12	34.60	240.51
7.20	Glendale.....	118.92	41.80	233.31
8.58	*Fairfield* (*c h*)	110.34	50.38	224.73
4.74	Whitfield.......... ..	105.60	55.12	219.99
6.61	Batavia	98.99	61.73	213.38
7.17	Agency City	91.82	68.90	206.21
5 82	*Ottumwa* (*c h*)..........	86.00	74.72	200.39
8.51	Chillicothe	94.51	83.23	191.88
7.01	Frederick	102.42	91 14	183.97
8.30	*Albia* (*c h*)...	110.72	99 44	175.67
8.95	Tyrone.......	119.67	108.39	166.72
5.94	Melrose................	125.61	114.33	160.78
8.11	Russell	133.72	122.44	152.67
7.50	*Chariton* (*c h*)	141.22	129.94	145.17
8.42	Lucas	149.64	138 36	136.75
7.54	Woodburn	157.18	145.90	129.21
10.34	*Osceola* (*c h*)..........	167.52	156.24	118.87
9.97	Murray	177.49	166.21	108.90
5.92	Thayer................	184 41	172.13	102.98
8.08	*Afton* (*c h*)	192 49	180.21	94.90
9 39	Highland..............	201.88	189.60	85.51
5,72	Cromwell...............	207.60	195.32	79.79
8 39	Prescott	215.99	203.71	71.40
7.31	Corning	221.09	211.02	64.09
3.98	Brookville	217.11	215.00	60.11
5.00	Nodaway	212.11	220.00	55.11
4.89	Vallisca................	207.22	224 89	50.22
8.11	Halnestead............	199 11	233.00	42 11
7.63	*Red Oak* (*c h*)............	191.48	240.63	34.48
5.53	....	185.95	246.16	28.95
3.96	Emerson	181.99	250.12	24.99
5.28	Hastings	176.71	255.40	19.71
5.13	Milton	171.58	260.53	14.58
5.41	....	166.17	265 94	9 17
5.36	*Glenwood* (*c h*)............	160.81	271.30	3.81
3.81	B. & M. and C. B. & St. Joe crossing............	157,00	275.11	....

Keokuk and St. Paul Railroad.

Dist. from station to stati'n	Names of Stations.	Distance from Des Moines.	Distance from Burlington.	Distance from Keokuk.
	BURLINGTON (C H)......	160.72	....	44.00
8.3	Wever	169.02	8.30	35.70
10.7	*Fort Madison* (*c h*).......	179.72	19.00	25.00
8	* Junction.................	187.72	27.00	17.00
5	* Montrose	192.72	32.00	12.00
6	*Sandusky	198.72	38.00	6.00
6	KEOKUK	161.00	44.00	....

Des Moines Valley Railroad.

Distance from station to station.	Names of Stations.	Dist. from Des Moines	Dist. from Keokuk.	Dist. from Fort Dodge
	KEOKUK	161	.... ..	244
14	Sand Prairie.	147	14	230
6	Belfast.	141	20	224
5	Croton	136	25	219
5	Farmington....	131	30	214
5	Bonaparte..................	126	35	209
4	Bentonsport..	122	39	205
6	Summit	116	45	199
9	Douds	107	54	190
4	Independent	103	58	186
9	Alpine	94	67	177
8	OTTUMWA (C H)	86	75	169
8	Comstocks	78	83	161
8	Eddyville............	70	91	153
9	*Oskaloosa* (*c h*)	61	100	144
6	Leighton	55	106	138
8	Pella	47	114	130
9	Otley	38	123	121
5	Monroe	33	128	116
9	Prairie City............	24	137	107
6	Woodville	18	143	101
8	Altoona.....................	10	151	93
10	DES MOINES (C H)	.... ..	161	83
5	Valley Junction......	5	166	78
10	Waukee	15	176	68
6	Dallas Center	21	182	62
6	Minburn	27	188	56
7	Perry	34	195	49
9	Rippey	43	204	40
7	Grand Junction.........	50	211	33
8	Peyton......................	58	219	25
8	Gowrie..........	66	227	17
8	Rothsay	74	235	9
9	FORT DODGE (C H).....	83	244	.....

Burlington, Cedar Rapids and Minnenesota Railway.

Dist. from station to stati'n	Names of Stations.	Distance from Des Moines.	Distance from Burlington.	Dist. from Washington Branch Junct'n
	BURLINGTON (C H).....	160.72	....	42
9	Latty	169.72	9	33
3	Sperry	172 72	12	30
3	Kossuth	175.72	15	27
5	Linton	180.72	20	22
3	Morning Sun	183.72	23	19
7	*Wapello* (*c h*)..............	190.72	30	12
12	WASHINGTON B'NCH JUNCTION	202.72	42	......

* Computed *via* Keokuk, the distance from Des Moines to Sandusky is 167 miles; to Montrose 173 miles; and to Junction 178 miles.

www.ingramcontent.com/pod-product-compliance
Lightning Source LLC
LaVergne TN
LVHW010232110826
845151LV00004B/1270

* 9 7 8 1 4 2 5 5 2 6 2 3 8 *